Global Health in the 21st Century

Mark A. Boyer and Shareen Hertel, Series Editors

International Studies Intensives (ISI) is a book series that springs from the desire to keep students engaged in the world around them. Books in the series address a wide array of topics in the international studies field, all devoted to getting students involved in the ways in which international events affect their daily lives. ISI books focus on innovative topics and approaches to study that cover popular and scholarly debates and employ new methods for presenting theories and concepts to students and scholars alike. ISI books pack a lot of information into a small space—they are meant to offer an intensive introduction to subjects often left out of the curriculum. ISI books are relatively short, visually attractive, and affordably priced.

Titles in the Series

The Rules of the Game: A Primer on International Relations
Mark R. Amstutz
Development Redefined: How the Market Met Its Match
Robin Broad and John Cavanagh
Protecting the Global Environment
Gary C. Bryner
A Tale of Two Quagmires: Iraq, Vietnam, and the Hard Lessons of War
Kenneth J. Campbell
Celebrity Diplomacy
Andrew F. Cooper
Global Health in the 21ˢᵗ Century: The Globalization of Disease and Wellness
Debra L. DeLaet and David E. DeLaet
Terminate Terrorism: Framing, Gaming, and Negotiating Conflicts
Karen A. Feste
The Global Classroom: An Essential Guide to Study Abroad
Jeffrey S. Lantis and Jessica DuPlaga
Sixteen Million One: Understanding Civil War
Patrick M. Regan
People Count! Networked Individuals in Global Politics
James N. Rosenau
Paradoxes of Power: U.S. Foreign Policy in a Changing World
David Skidmore
Global Democracy and the World Social Forums
Jackie Smith and Marina Karides, et al.

Forthcoming in the Series

Watching Human Rights
Mark Gibney
Democratic Uprisings in the Middle East and North Africa: Youth, Technology, and Modernization
Mahmood Monshipouri
The Stealth Pandemic: Violence Against Women, A Global Assessment and Analysis
David L. Richards and Jillienne Haglund
The Global Political Economy of Food
Kimberly Weir
Spirits Talking: Conversations on Right and Wrong in the Affairs of States
Stephen D. Wrage

Global Health in the 21st Century

The Globalization of Disease and Wellness

Debra L. DeLaet, Ph.D.
David E. DeLaet, M.D.

Routledge
Taylor & Francis Group

LONDON AND NEW YORK

First published 2012 by Paradigm Publishers

Published 2016 by Routledge
2 Park Square, Milton Park, Abingdon, Oxon OX14 4RN
711 Third Avenue, New York, NY 10017, USA

Routledge is an imprint of the Taylor & Francis Group, an informa business

Library of Congress Cataloging-in-Publication Data
    DeLaet, Debra L., 1968–
    Global health in the 21st century : the globalization
of disease and wellness / Debra L. DeLaet and David E.
DeLaet.
    p.   cm. — (International studies intensives)
    Global health in the twenty first century
    Includes bibliographical references and index.
    ISBN 978-1-59451-732-7 (hardcover : alk. paper) —
ISBN 978-1-59451-733-4 (pbk. : alk. paper)
    I. DeLaet, David E. II. Title. III. Title: Global
health in the twenty first century. IV. Series:
International studies intensives.
    [DNLM: 1. World Health. 2. Communicable Disease
Control. 3. Health Promotion. 4. International
Cooperation. 5. Internationality. 6. Socioeconomic
Factors. WA 530.1]
    362.1—dc23   2011042233

ISBN 13: 978-1-59451-732-7 (hbk)
ISBN 13: 978-1-59451-733-4 (pbk)

Contents

List of Tables, Figures, and Boxes

Tables

Figures

Boxes

Preface

Global Health in the 21st Century: The Globalization of Disease and Wellness is a comprehensive introduction to the subject of global health. Global health issues pose some of the most significant economic, political, social, and ethical challenges of the 21st century. Perhaps no other public policy issue has greater potential to affect the longevity and quality of human life across the globe. Countless lives were saved during the 20th century due to public health interventions such as vaccination programs (to fight smallpox, polio, and measles) and the creation of public water systems and other public sanitation measures that led to a significant reduction in deadly communicable illnesses. Despite these advances, millions of people do not live in a social or political environment conducive to the promotion of the highest attainable standard of human health. Expanding access to public health interventions like routine childhood vaccination and public health infrastructure (clean water, clean air, and safe workplaces and roads) has the potential to raise standards of living, health outcomes, and the average lifespan across the globe.

Because public health interventions have such great potential to improve the quality and longevity of human life, the international community has embraced global health as a policy priority. Two of the eight United Nations Millennium Development Goals—promoting child health and maternal health—are directed at public health goals and interventions. Transnational non-governmental organizations (NGOs) working on public health programs have proliferated and have raised public awareness about important global health challenges. The Global Fund to Fight AIDS, Tuberculosis, and Malaria is just one prominent example of NGO efforts to promote public health. This book is premised on the belief that such efforts have great potential to improve the lives of human beings across the globe and, accordingly, should be a top policy priority for countries, international organizations, NGOs, and engaged citizens everywhere.

Three basic themes provide the organizational framework for this introduction to global health. First, global health is characterized by interconnectedness among human beings. Human health is not solely the product of individual genetics or behavior. Instead, the health of individual human beings is fundamentally shaped by economic, political, and social factors, such as education and income levels, governmental policies regulating the provision of health care, and transnational economic and political relations. The health of a wealthy individual can be affected by poverty and environmental degradation in developing countries, just as the health of a person in a relatively poor country can be shaped by the consumption patterns of average people in a developed country. The health of the animal and plant worlds also affects human health. Human health is a phenomenon that crosses borders of all kinds—territorial, national, class-based, political, and ecological. In this way, public health is, by definition, a global phenomenon that cannot be fully understood without considering international economic, political, and social structures and processes.

A second and related theme woven throughout the book is the importance of the globalization of disease and wellness. If individual health is shaped by communal factors (national income, public health infrastructure, civil society, and the health of the natural environment), then at a global level, health is shaped by these social, political, and ecological determinants of health writ large. The health of a population in one country is inextricably intertwined with the health of people in other countries. Countries, as well as people, are increasingly interdependent in the globalizing world of the 21st century. Transnational public health challenges have causes and consequences that transcend national borders, and countries cannot effectively promote public health in isolation. Health care itself is being globalized, and "medical tourism" is on the rise as people travel to other countries to seek care that is either more affordable or more accessible abroad. For example, the relative cost of specific treatments in developing countries may be sufficiently low to more than offset the cost of international travel. Another example involves individuals traveling to undergo procedures or receive treatments that are not licensed in their countries of origin. In this age of globalization, consumers may cross international borders to purchase medications more affordably or because specific drugs are not approved in their home country, or they might even order regulated medications via the Internet.

Finally, this book develops the theme that global health should be of concern to all engaged citizens—not just medical practitioners, health care experts, or policy makers. In order to succeed, global health interventions need to be informed by the expertise of a wide-ranging field of individuals, from doctors, to engineers, to educators, to social workers. Thus, any responsible and effective approach to global health needs to be multidisciplinary. Global health needs to be based on knowledge from a variety of disciplines, and, thus, we need to draw on research and insight from professionals working in a range of fields outside medicine and public policy. Take, for example, the goal of expanding access to clean water in the developing world. We need doctors and scientists to help identify and treat waterborne outbreaks of deadly illnesses. But we also need economists and engineers to help us understand what type of public water system is affordable, physically sound, and economically and environmentally stable over time in a given location. We need anthropologists and social scientists to help us identify cultural, social, or political obstacles to implementing specific public water schemes in particular communities. The flip side of this coin is that individuals working in various professions—doctors, social workers, educators, and engineers—need to be educated about the importance of global health so that they develop the necessary commitment that will motivate them to support and contribute to public health endeavors.

This commitment to multidisciplinary perspectives distinguishes this book from existing global health texts. It intentionally weaves together concerns and perspectives from the social sciences, humanities, science, and medicine. The few existing texts on global health have been written primarily by doctors and practitioners in the field of public health. Although such perspectives are obviously important, they do not always capture underlying political and social themes that are essential to understanding global health. Thus, this book brings in social science and humanistic perspectives to complement the natural science and medical perspectives that are part of any book on global health. We have consciously sought to write a comprehensive and synthetic overview of global health that will appeal not only to students who intend to specialize in public health but also to students in the social sciences and the humanities who may be interested in global health issues but do not plan to pursue careers in this area.

Organization of the Book

This book is organized into four parts, with a total of eleven chapters. Each chapter includes discussion questions and a list of Web resources pertinent to the topic under consideration.

"Part I: Foundations of Global Health" introduces key concepts and frameworks that undergird the study and practice of global health. Chapter 1 provides a definition of global health and explores the reasons that it should be a global policy priority in the 21st century. The chapter also explains the ways in which public health approaches differ from the practice of medicine and from health care policy. It also introduces the concept of global governance and considers potential global solutions to critical transnational health challenges. Chapter 2 introduces key concepts in global health. It provides an overview of the determinants of health and looks at the primary measures and indicators of health. Chapter 3 places the discussion of global health in an ecological context. In doing so, the chapter explores the concept of ecological balance, in which humans and microbes coexist in specific ecologies (local, regional, and global). With the concept of ecological balance as a frame, the chapter aims to examine the interconnections among globalization, ensuing changes to the environment, and the related challenges to global health that result.

"Part II: Medical Aspects of Global Health" looks closely at the causes of disease, the mechanisms for disease transmission, the global burden of disease, and possible solutions to major disease threats in a globalized world. Chapter 4 provides an overview of communicable diseases currently threatening global health. This chapter examines HIV/AIDS, tuberculosis, and influenza as significant transnational health challenges. It also discusses the benefits and risks of the use of vaccinations and antibiotics for the promotion of public health. Chapter 5 provides an overview of noncommunicable diseases currently threatening global health, including obesity, cardiovascular disease, and diseases associated with tobacco abuse. Such illnesses, often referred to as the diseases of globalization, are endemic in developed countries and are on the rise in developing countries still suffering from a high burden of communicable illness.

"Part III: The International Relations of Global Health" focuses on health-related topics of concern to scholars and practitioners of international relations. Chapter 6 provides an overview of critical inequities in global health. To this end, it examines territorially based inequities that distinguish population health outcomes in different countries. It also explores poverty-based inequities, racial and ethnic inequities, and gender-based disparities in global health. Chapter 7 explores the nexus between transnational health challenges and security. This chapter considers the ways in which global health problems can destabilize states and contribute to violence and, conversely, how warfare undermines human health and human security. The chapter includes a discussion of biowarfare and bioterrorism. It also considers the arguments for and against "securitizing" global health challenges. Chapter 8 looks at the relationship between global health and human rights. It explores the tension between the fact that there is an articulated right to health in international human rights law and the reality that so many human beings do not have access to clean water, sanitation, adequate food, or basic health care that would ensure a right to health in practice. It also looks at international humanitarian law and professional codes of ethics pertaining to a human right to health.

"Part IV: Promoting Global Health" examines a wide range of public health programs and interventions intended to promote the attainment of the highest possible standards of health among populations across the globe. Chapter 9 examines top-down approaches to promoting global health through international organizations. In particular, the chapter analyzes the work of the World Health Organization and considers the progress that the international community has made toward reaching the health-related Millennium Development Goals. It includes a discussion of the global eradication of smallpox, a major public health success story. Chapter 10 looks at top-down approaches to promoting global health through states. It examines in greater detail the comparative approaches to health systems and health care policy in different countries and provides case studies of Rwanda, South Africa, Cuba, South Korea, the United Kingdom, and the United States. Chapter 11 discusses bottom-up approaches to promoting global health by non-state actors. It examines the activities of prominent NGOs working on global health—for example, Doctors Without Borders and Save the Children—and considers the role of large funding organizations like the Gates Foundation. It also examines the ways in which non-state actors work with states and international organizations to promote global health. The chapter concludes by looking at the role of citizens and consumers in promoting global health. The Conclusion reviews the book's core themes and encourages readers to consider the role that they might play as engaged citizens in taking on the global health challenges of the 21st century.

Features of This Innovative Text

Global Health in the 21st Century is the first comprehensive, interdisciplinary global health text appropriate for both undergraduate- and graduate-level courses. It offers a variety of pedagogical attractions to facilitate teaching and learning:

- An international relations scholar teams up with a medical doctor to provide practical and theoretical perspectives into this growing subject area.
- The structure of the chapters is consistent throughout, with each chapter having an introduction, conclusion, discussion questions, and a list of Web resources.
- Key terms and concepts are highlighted in text boxes and strategically distributed throughout the chapters as the content is developed.
- "Under the Microscope" special-feature boxes include "The Inequitable Effects of Natural Disasters," "Disease and Death in the Shadow of War," and "Women's Health Initiatives in the UN System."
- Helpful tables and figures graphically illustrate important data and trends including those related to the demographic transition, impacts on and of the burden of disease, and links between health expenditures and outcomes.

Global Health in the 21st Century offers an up-to-date picture of global health worldwide, covering specific topics such as race, ethnicity, and gender as well as providing a more general overview of the medical and political dimensions of this most important issue area.

Acknowledgments

Most of this book was written during my sabbatical leave, and so I owe a debt of gratitude to my colleagues and the administration at Drake University for helping to make this sabbatical possible. I want to thank my students at Drake University, especially those who have taken my global health course. These students raised provocative questions and shared thoughtful insights that have informed my thinking on the subject. Drake students continually remind me why I love to teach, and for that I am grateful. In particular, I want to thank Nate Baggett for his careful reading of an earlier draft of this book. He provided thoughtful suggestions for revisions, both substantive and editorial, that significantly improved the quality of this book.

I want to thank the staff at Paradigm Publishers for all of their efforts. I especially want to thank Jennifer Knerr. It has been a real pleasure to work with her throughout all stages of the project, and I have appreciated her enthusiasm, thoughtful feedback, and constructive suggestions for improvements. I also want to thank Laura Janik, who provided a very thoughtful review of the book, as did another anonymous reviewer.

I need to thank my friends and family for helping to make my sabbatical fun as well as productive. I thank Kristen Rummelhart for the almost daily coffee sessions that cleared my mind and helped me to be productive. Above all, I want to thank my family. I especially want to thank my brother Dave for agreeing to this cockamamie scheme to coauthor a book together. His contributions have been invaluable, and it has been fun to work with him. My parents, Jack and Sandy DeLaet, have been a constant source of love and support through the years. Todd Knoop, as always, is a faithful and supportive partner who helps me find balance in work, family, and life in general. My daughters Edie and Daphne are just great. They tipped the life/work balance in favor of the life side of the scale, and for that I'm grateful. They're worth it.

Debra DeLaet
Drake University

I want to first thank my sister Deb for her invitation to collaborate on this book. It has been a great experience working with her and a nice departure from the routine of my clinical work. I want to thank my parents, Jack and Sandy DeLaet, for their guidance and support over the years. I also want to thank my wife, Rebecca, for her support throughout my career, particularly during the writing of this text. I want to thank my children, Jack and Ali, for their patience during this project. To their repeated question, "When are you going to be done with that book?," I can finally answer, "Now."

David DeLaet
Mount Sinai School of Medicine

PART I

Foundations of Global Health

CHAPTER 1

Introduction to Global Health

Introduction

Because a public health model is at the foundation of global health, this chapter examines the evolution of the discipline of public health and explains how public health differs from a medical approach to health. The chapter also provides an overview of major challenges to global health in the contemporary world and discusses why the study of global health is important not only for medical practitioners but also for policy makers and engaged citizens everywhere. The chapter introduces the concept of global governance and considers potential governing solutions available to address the challenges at stake in global health.

What Is Global Health?

Global health is grounded in the concept of **public health**, a broad, multidisciplinary approach to health that emphasizes the health of communities and populations, preventive care, and the socioeconomic determinants of illness. Global health also has roots in the practice of **international health**, a term that traditionally has been used to describe health work abroad, especially on poverty-related illnesses in developing countries. A key distinction in the usage of the terms *public health* and *international health* is that *public health* tends to be applied in the context of specific communities or countries, whereas *international health*

is used to describe health work in countries, especially developing countries, outside the home country of the particular practitioner or scholar. In addition, *international health* tends to be used to describe health work that encompasses medical care for individuals as well as health programs for specific communities or populations, in contrast to public health, which primarily focuses on population health programs.[1]

Global health represents an evolution and integration of these concepts. Rather than focusing on population health in single countries (public health) or on the health of both individuals and populations in countries other than one's own country (international health), **global health** is concerned with health issues that transcend national boundaries and emphasizes both individualized medical care and public health programs for populations in developed as well as developing countries.[2] In this way, global health represents the broadest conception of health that spans from individual health care to public programming both within and across countries. The following definition has been offered by a group of scholars and practitioners in the field: "Global health is an area for study, research, and practice that places a priority on improving health and achieving equity in health for all people worldwide. Global health emphasizes transnational health issues, determinants, and solutions; involves many disciplines within and beyond the health

---

APPROACHES TO HEALTH

Global Health: a multidisciplinary approach to health that focuses on transnational health challenges, is concerned with the broad socioeconomic determinants of health across the globe, and incorporates both individual health care and preventive, public health programming.

International Health: a term used to describe health work abroad with a particular focus on poverty-related illnesses in developing countries.

Public Health: a multidisciplinary approach to health that is concerned with the health of specific communities and populations, emphasizes the socioeconomic determinants of illness, and prioritizes preventive care.

---

sciences and promotes interdisciplinary collaboration; and is a synthesis of population based prevention with individual level clinical care."[3] In short, global health is a truly *global* conception of health.

Because the discipline of public health has played a critical role in shaping the concept of global health, it will be useful to explore the evolution of public health in greater depth. In 1920, Charles-Edward Amory Winslow, a leading figure in the development of the concept of public health, put forth the following definition:

> Public health is the science and art of preventing disease, prolonging life and promoting physical health and efficacy through organized community efforts for the sanitation of the environment, the control of communicable infections, the education of the individual in personal hygiene, the organization of medical and nursing services for the early diagnosis and preventive treatment of disease, and the development of social machinery which will ensure every individual in the community a standard of living adequate for the maintenance of health, so organizing these benefits in such a fashion as to enable every citizen to realize his birthright and longevity.[4]

The core of this definition has stood the test of time. In the United States, numerous public health agencies at the state and local levels have adopted this definition, and scholars of public health still cite it as a useful definition.[5] The **World Health Organization (WHO)**, a permanent international health organization created within the United Nations (UN) system that serves as a primary global authority for coordinating health programs and activities, has adopted a similarly broad definition of health as a "state of complete physical, mental, and social well-being and not merely the absence of disease or infirmity."[6]

The study and practice of public health are grounded in several core assumptions. First, public health is just that—a *public* rather than an individualized conception of health. It deals with the health of whole communities rather than simply considering the health of particular individuals in isolation. In this way, *public health* is a much broader concept than *medicine*. The practice of medicine involves medical practitioners working in one-on-one relationships with patients to treat injuries or disease, to monitor the health of individual patients, and to promote healthy practices that contribute to wellness. In contrast, *public health* involves the health of entire communities.

Second, the concept of public health tends to stress the importance of preventive rather than curative approaches to health. Of course, medical practitioners recognize the importance of prevention, and routine "wellness checks" for healthy patients are an example of a preventive approach within the practice of medicine. Nevertheless, the medical model is still heavily reliant on a curative approach to health—doctors must spend a great deal of their time treating sick patients. In contrast, public health practitioners, on balance, spend a relatively much greater amount of time investigating, promoting, and implementing preventive solutions to health challenges.

Third, public health approaches recognize poverty as a major factor undermining the attainment of the highest possible standards of health. Therefore, the concept of public health engages more directly with socioeconomic determinants of health than a medical model, which, in general, is more likely to focus on genetic and behavioral determinants of health.[7]

Finally, public health approaches are concerned with almost any issue or factor that has the potential to significantly affect the health of a community. In this way, the concept of public health differs not only from the concept of medicine but also from the concept of health care. Health care involves "the financing, provision, or governance of health services," and health care policy describes governmental actions (or inactions) in this area.[8] Although health care policy is necessarily an important piece of the public health puzzle, public health still encompasses a broader range of issues and policy arenas. Any policy area with potentially significant health implications, including economic policy, education, employment, housing, or public infrastructure, falls under the umbrella of public health.

As these assumptions indicate, public health is a broad and complicated topic. Public health does not focus primarily on individual traits and behaviors that contribute to, or undermine, a person's health but on the economic, political, and social determinants of health—such as education, income, and **public goods** (like roads, clean air, and clean water)—that contribute to the health and well-being of individuals living in a community. It considers environmental factors that contribute to the health of whole populations. Public health is an incredibly broad conception of health that covers a wide range of potential topics: chronic disease as well as communicable illness; food, road, and workplace safety; nutrition; access to adequate health care; and clean air and drinking water.

Conceptualizing health in this way suggests that public health is not—and *cannot be*—a subject that is of concern only to medical practitioners or public officials responsible for health care policy. The practice of medicine and health care policy are pieces of the public health puzzle, but they do not complete it. To be sure, medical professionals play an essential role in the promotion of public health. However, public health does not fall solely under the purview of doctors and nurses. Similarly, health care policy is a necessary but insufficient tool for promoting public health. Because public health is fundamentally shaped by governmental policy, public officials can play an instrumental role in helping to determine the health of the communities that they govern. Bureaucrats play a critical role in monitoring food, water, and workplace safety.

Yet, public health goes further still, beyond medical practitioners and public officials, in requiring contributions from people from many walks of life. Engineers are an essential part of the process of creating safe roads, public buildings, and workplaces. Educators are key in helping to teach about nutrition and hygiene and to promote the levels of education that contribute to good health. Social workers can have an impact on public health through their contacts with populations who are vulnerable to poverty-related health problems. Agricultural practices can fundamentally shape the health of communities, and, in this way, people working in agriculture—from small-scale farmers to executives in agribusinesses—have an influence on the quality of health in their communities. In short, individuals working in a vast array of professions have the potential to shape public health, for better or worse, in the communities where they live and work, whether or not they explicitly consider themselves to be involved in public health work. Thus, efforts to promote and improve public health require knowledge among professionals in many fields and commitment among the citizenry at large.

To talk about *global health* is simply to apply this broad conception of health on an even larger scale. In fact, the Association of Schools of Public Health has taken the position that the concepts of public health and global health are essentially indistinguishable.[9] If public health is the health of communities, then global health is public health on the grandest possible scale—it is the health of the human community. The *global* dimension of public health underscores the importance of the globalization of disease and wellness. If individual health is shaped by communal factors (national income, public health infrastructure, civil society, and the health of the natural environment), then at a global level, health is shaped by these socioeconomic determinants of health writ large. The health of particular individuals is significantly shaped by transnational economic, political, social, and ecological processes and structures. Health is a phenomenon that reflects the **interdependence** of countries and the interconnectedness of human beings across borders. The health of a wealthy individual can be affected by poverty and environmental degradation in developing countries, just as the health of a person in a relatively poor country can be shaped by the consumption patterns of average people in a developed country or the policies of governments in these countries. Transnational public health challenges have causes and consequences that transcend national borders, and countries cannot effectively promote public health in isolation.

In fact, perhaps the idea that global health is the health of the human community is too limiting in that the logic of public health suggests that human health is inextricably linked to the health of the environment in which humans live. In this way, human health is inevitably connected to the health of the plant and animal worlds as well. Economic and social changes alter the ecological environments in which people live and can lead to new microbial threats to human health. The destruction of natural plant and animal habitats can undermine public health when it reduces the quality of air, soil, and water. Thus, at the broadest global level, interconnectedness—both among humans across the globe and among human beings and animals and plants—fundamentally shapes human health.

KEY CONCEPTS IN GLOBAL HEALTH

Economic Liberalization: the reduction of governmental regulations on private market forces in the economic realm.

Globalization: the increasing interconnectedness of populations across the globe in the economic, social, and political spheres.

Interdependence: mutual vulnerability and mutual sensitivity to transnational phenomena among the states and peoples of the world.

Public Good: a good or service available to everyone in a society in which the total benefits to society are greater than the benefits to actors who produce the good.

As this discussion illustrates, global health is an incredibly broad subject. Understanding global health requires knowledge from a wide variety of disciplines. The attainment of the highest possible level of health for humans across the globe—the promotion of which is the core mandate of the WHO—cannot be achieved through only small advances in narrow areas of specialization. To date, the most significant advances in human health have come in many forms: vaccination programs that have led to the eradication of (or a reduction in) deadly diseases, improved sanitation and expanded access to clean water, access to improved nutrition and safer foods, workplace safety regulations, and improvements in road safety.

Thus, this broad conceptualization of global health indicates that any meaningful global efforts to tackle global health challenges will require extensive financial resources, commitment among citizenries across the globe, and significant cooperation among countries and global agencies working on public health. When conceived in this manner, the promotion of global health seems like an overwhelming challenge, perhaps one that is not worth the effort and resources required. For readers daunted by this challenge, there is an essential question that must be addressed: Why should we care about global health?

Why Should We Care About Global Health?

This book is based on the premise that global health should be a priority on the public policy agendas of countries across the globe. It should be a subject of study in university curricula for students, regardless of their major areas of study or professional aspirations. Informed and engaged citizens, from the local to the global levels, should understand the fundamentals of global health. But why? Why should students learn about global health if they do not plan to work in this field? Why should citizens care about global health? Answering this question requires, first, addressing a more basic question: Why should we care about public health in general?

The answers to this question are manifold. It is probably obvious why medical practitioners should care about public health. Doctors, nurses, and other medical practitioners who focus on the health of individual patients must understand the social determinants of health if they are to treat individual patients effectively. Their efforts to promote wellness in patients and to treat illness will be more likely to succeed if they are operating in an environment where *public* health is taken seriously.

It is perhaps less obvious why the average person should care about global health or public health in general. Nevertheless, there are compelling reasons why all of us should care about global health and why we need to understand the ways in which our own health is connected to the health of other human beings within our own countries and across the globe.

Self-interest is one important reason to care about public health in general. Students raised in advanced industrialized countries may take the public dimension of their own health for granted. For example, when a person has been raised with access to clean water, safe food, and well-designed buildings and roads, it might be easy to forget that one's health depends on these public goods. The invisibility of the public dimensions of individual health might be particularly pronounced for students who grew up with the advantages of relative wealth and social privilege. Many college students have had the advantage of middle-class upbringings, in which the social determinants of health are stacked in their favor. In this context, it is easy to think of health as a product of a combination of factors inherent to particular individuals—individual behavior (for instance, nutrition and exercise) and genetic determinants (a family risk of high blood pressure or heart disease, for example).

However, health is not exclusively a product of individual and familial traits. Rather, socioeconomic factors play a major role in shaping the relative health of individuals. Whether a particular community has access to clean water, clean air, nutritious food, and safe roads and workplaces is determined, in large part, by social, economic, and political factors beyond the control of particular individuals. Therefore, self-interest is a reason that students and engaged citizens everywhere should care about the public dimensions of health.

Indeed, major advances in quality of life and life span in the 20th century have resulted from the building up of public health infrastructure as well as policy advances and governmental regulations that contribute to public health. Firm estimates of the number of human lives saved during the 20th century due to public health advancements do not exist. But the number is certainly considerable. Countless lives have been saved due to vaccinations that have virtually eradicated deadly diseases like smallpox and have reduced deaths and disabling complications from serious childhood illnesses such as measles and polio. Innumerable lives have been saved through the creation of

public water systems that have cut down on deadly waterborne illnesses like cholera. The building of public sewers, garbage collection, and other sanitation measures are examples of public health interventions that have dramatically reduced deaths from communicable illnesses and improved the quality of human health. In short, advances in the average life span correlate with the development of public health infrastructure that has accompanied the growth of the modern state.[10] To the extent that individuals embrace the advances that have contributed to a social environment that produces better health outcomes for individuals, they should care about public health.

While it is significant that human life expectancy increased dramatically in the 20th century, it should not be surprising that life expectancy among the poor has not advanced in the same way. As shown in Figure 1.1, although life expectancy in low-income countries has been steadily increasing in recent

FIGURE 1.1 Improvements in Life Expectancy, 1960–2010

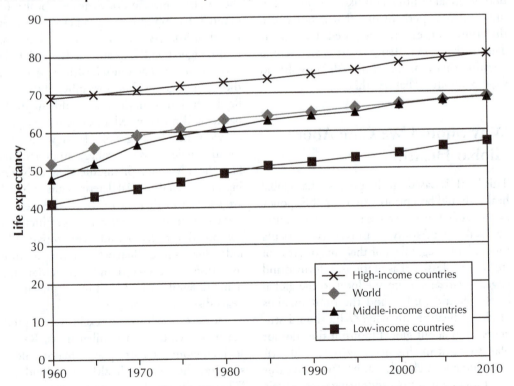

Source: World Bank, *World Databank: Health Nutrition and Population Statistics.* Available online at: http://databank.worldbank.org/ddp/home.do?Step=3&id=4.

decades, it still remains well below life expectancy indicators in high-income countries. Indeed, at an estimated fifty-seven years, life expectancy in low-income countries is still below mid-20th-century life expectancy measures in high-income countries. In some cases, the poor can be expected to live shorter lives at the beginning of the 21st century than would have been the case one hundred years ago. Although industrialization and economic development have been accompanied by many advances in public health infrastructure, they also have created new public health challenges, ranging from environmental health hazards resulting from industrialization to the spread of the diseases associated with economic growth and development (obesity, diabetes, and heart disease).

Individuals with socioeconomic advantages might argue that the health challenges faced by the poor do not concern them, at least not on the grounds of self-interest. Responding to this point is complicated. It must be acknowledged that many problems that practitioners identify as major public health challenges involve illnesses that primarily threaten the poor—cholera outbreaks are most likely to strike vulnerable populations in zones of conflict and abject poverty; tuberculosis and malaria are more prevalent among the poor than the wealthy; even obesity and diabetes (diseases that tend to rise along with the level of economic development in a country) often are of highest prevalence in poor populations within both developed and less developed countries.

Nevertheless, individuals who are relatively well off and, thus, believe themselves to be immune to public health threats should still care about public health out of self-interest. Low-income populations can serve as a sort of looking glass through which one can see the vulnerabilities of any given society. When the poor are threatened by a public health challenge, it may only be a matter of time before the health of the society at large is threatened. Even if it is true that poor populations are especially vulnerable to particular communicable illnesses, it is worth remembering that communicable illnesses are just that—communicable.

Viruses, bacteria, and parasites do not recognize or respect the distinctions of social class, and if poor populations in a society are decimated by a communicable disease, the entire population could ultimately be at risk.

The global dimension of this problem is also evident. Germs do not respect national boundaries, and thus diseases prevalent among the poor in any part of the world have the potential to threaten the health of individuals—regardless of their social status—anywhere in the world. For example, when poor people contract tuberculosis and cannot afford to follow through with complete courses of antibiotics, they often receive only intermittent and improper treatment that has led to the development of antibiotic-resistant strains of the bacteria. It has been estimated that one-third of the world's population has been infected with tuberculosis—a disease that the WHO declared a global health emergency in 1993. Poor populations are the most likely to suffer from tuberculosis. Nevertheless, tuberculosis does not discriminate. If this problem is not addressed effectively, the risk of the development and spread of antibiotic-resistant strains of tuberculosis could potentially threaten the health of much larger segments of human society across the globe.

In addition to pragmatic concerns, there are moral reasons to care about global health. Perhaps readers are not convinced that they should be particularly concerned about public health out of self-interest. Nevertheless, considerations of justice and human rights suggest that engaged citizens should care about public health. Students of international relations often focus on war, terrorism, and state-sponsored violence as the major threats to humanity in international affairs. These issues are undeniably important. Yet, in terms of sheer numbers of deaths and obstacles to quality of life, global health challenges arguably constitute a much greater threat to humanity. Approximately 7.7 million children alone die annually across the globe from preventable diseases and inadequate nutrition.[11] The number of avoidable deaths from preventable diseases and inadequate nutrition rises significantly when adult deaths are included in the equation. For example, over 500,000 women die each year due to complications from pregnancy and childbirth; most of these deaths would be preventable with adequate public health interventions.[12]

Of course, many people would argue that, because global health problems are not *caused* by governments and tend to result from inaction rather than governmental action, they are a different sort of problem. Conservatives might argue that governments have no obligation to try to prevent the deaths of people who cannot afford better health care or to aid countries that do not have the resources to improve public infrastructure. Indeed, they might argue that any governmental efforts to promote public health, however well-intentioned, might have unintended consequences and might waste public resources without actually improving the health status of poor populations. They might also argue that, because public health likely involves the growth of government through regulations designed to promote a social safety net and an increase in taxes to pay for the development of public infrastructure, the enforcement of regulations, and public health interventions, there is an unacceptable trade-off with individual liberty and the free market. Some environmentalists concerned with overpopulation on the global level might argue that public health advancements, by increasing the life span of human populations across the globe, might place undue pressure on the earth's ability to sustain human life in the long term.[13] These ideological and moral disagreements need to be acknowledged and are explored at various places throughout the book.

While acknowledging that there is not global consensus on this matter, this book is grounded in the premise that engaged citizens should care about global health for moral as well as pragmatic reasons. To the extent that governments have any responsibility for protecting and contributing to the quality of life of their citizens, it is important to remember that global health challenges have as much potential to affect the longevity and quality of human life across the globe as war, terrorism, human rights, or other prominent issues that have captured the attention of scholars, policy makers, and citizens. For this reason, we believe that it is essential for engaged citizens everywhere to have a basic understanding of global health, even if they ultimately disagree that it should be a priority on policy agendas at the local, national, and global levels. We look forward to introducing this subject and welcome ongoing debate and dialogue over its importance.

Major Global Health Challenges in the 21st Century

Globalization can be defined as the "widening, intensifying, speeding up, and growing impact of world-wide interconnectedness."[14] Globalization takes place in the economic, political, and social spheres and reduces the extent to which geographic distance serves as a barrier to the movement of people, goods, ideas, and other things across territorial borders. For our purposes, the most pertinent effect of globalization is that it reduces the barriers to the transnational transmission of germs, medicines, medical technology, and other social and cultural variables (for example, food and dietary practices) that shape human health. As a result, globalization has produced dramatic effects (both positive and negative) on human health, and the increasing globalization of disease and wellness in the 21st century underscores the importance of paying attention to significant global health challenges. Transnational public health challenges have causes and consequences that transcend national borders. Thus, solutions for many global health challenges need to be transnational as well, and countries cannot effectively promote public health in isolation.

This book explores a variety of global health challenges that are especially pressing in the increasingly globalized world of the 21st century. These challenges include communicable diseases that readily cross borders, such as acquired immune deficiency syndrome (AIDS), malaria, tuberculosis, and various forms of influenza (a common but sometimes deadly virus). Millions of people across the globe die from preventable communicable illnesses each year. Over 5 million deaths annually can be attributed to HIV/AIDS, tuberculosis, and malaria alone. Communicable illnesses not only have obvious implications for global health but also are of interest because they have the capacity to disrupt social, political, and economic structures at the local, national, and global levels. For instance, the AIDS crisis in Africa has fundamentally altered the demographic makeup of countries in which it is particularly acute. In southern Africa, for example, numerous countries are burdened by staggering HIV-prevalence rates: 26.1 percent in Swaziland, 23.9 percent in Botswana, 23.2 percent in Lesotho, 18.1 percent in South Africa, and just over 15 percent in Namibia, Zambia, and Zimbabwe.[15] The magnitude of the AIDS crisis in southern Africa has led to the emergence of AIDS orphans throughout the region, and governments and civil societies in countries hit hard by the disease are faced with the challenge of responding to the needs of these vulnerable children. Moreover, because AIDS-related deaths have been so high in age cohorts of individuals who would otherwise be in the key years of their labor productivity and who typically play a major caregiving role within families and communities, the AIDS crisis has created a demographic vacuum in which middle-aged persons are outnumbered by the elderly and the very young. This demographic imbalance threatens to undermine both economic development and social stability in countries hit hard by AIDS.

Public health threats in a globalizing world also include noncommunicable illnesses with causes and consequences that transcend national boundaries. Obesity, diabetes, and heart disease are prominent examples of globalized diseases that will present major public health challenges across the globe in the 21st century. These diseases are often thought of as diseases of prosperity and, in fact, are endemic in countries with highly advanced economies. However, obesity, diabetes, and heart disease are becoming more and more prevalent throughout the developing world as well. This development is due in no small part to the globalization of the Western diet and changing consumption and eating patterns in developing countries.

In this regard, these noncommunicable illnesses can be thought of as diseases of industrialization, urbanization, and economic development. With economic development and its many benefits come fast-food restaurants as well as fundamental shifts in work patterns, with wage labor in a market economy displacing unpaid labor in the home or in small, traditional villages. Thomas Friedman famously claimed that no two countries with a McDonald's restaurant had engaged in war against each other (a claim that has been debunked), and economic liberals often highlight the positive effects that **economic liberalization** has on peace. Fewer scholars and pundits have explored the ways in which economic liberalization and globalization have transformed health in the developing world.

To point out this relationship is not to suggest that economic liberalization has only negative effects on public health. To the contrary, economic liberalization has led to higher national income in developing countries, and higher national income has the potential to improve public health in myriad ways. Economic development can contribute to advancements in public health by increasing the financial resources of human communities that can be used to improve public infrastructure, like safe roads and public water systems that enhance human health. Increasing national resources might be directed to the enforcement of new workplace safety or environmental regulations that can advance health standards in a country. An expanding economy also may increase the financial resources of individuals and families and, in doing so, contribute to the socioeconomic improvements, including higher levels of education and income, that correlate with better health outcomes. Nevertheless, globalization also has the potential to affect public

UNDER THE MICROSCOPE

Millions of Lives at Stake in Global Health

Millions of lives are at stake in the practice and study of global health. According to the Joint United Nations Programme on HIV/AIDS, more than 25 million people have died from AIDS-related causes since 1981. AIDS killed an estimated 2 million people in 2007 alone.[a] The WHO estimates that approximately 781,000 people, mostly children, die from malaria each year.[b] In 2007, tuberculosis killed approximately 1.7 million people. Thousands of people die each year from complications related to influenza; in the United States alone, roughly 36,000 people die from flu-related complications, according to the Centers for Disease Control and Prevention.[c] Influenza deaths rise dramatically in global pandemics, and it has been estimated that the global influenza pandemic of 1918 killed upward of 100 million people across the globe.[d] This staggering figure has contributed to heightened public alert about the deadliness of novel strains of influenza and has raised awareness of, and concern about, the so-called swine flu (H1N1) and avian flu (H5N1). Avian flu is an incredibly deadly influenza strain that has been passed from birds to humans but has not yet proved to have high rates of human-to-human transmission.

The number of people who die each year from preventable public health problems far outpaces the number of people who die from war, terrorism, or state-sponsored violence.

[a]UNAIDS (Joint United Nations Programme on HIV/AIDS), *2008 Report on the Global AIDS Epidemic* (July 2008). Available online at: http://data.unaids.org/pub/GlobalReport/2008/JC1510_2008GlobalReport_en.zip.

[b]World Health Organization, *Malaria*, Fact Sheet 94 (October 2011). Available online at: http://www.who.int/mediacentre/factsheets/fs094/en/.

[c]William W. Thompson, David K. Shay, Eric Weintraub, Lynette Brammer, Nancy Cox, Larry Anderson, and Keiji Fukuda, "Mortality Associated with Influenza and Respiratory Syncytial Virus in the United States," *Journal of the American Medical Association* 289: 2 (2003): 179–186.

[d]John M. Barry, *The Great Influenza: The Story of the Deadliest Pandemic in History* (New York: Penguin Books, 2005).

health in negative ways, and the globalization of the Western diet, with the concomitant rise in obesity, diabetes, and heart disease, is one such negative effect. In the end, the relationship among public health, environmental health, and economic development can be a paradoxical one in which human social and economic practices cut both ways, advancing public health in some ways and undermining it in others.

In short, major global health challenges of the 21st century include both communicable and noncommunicable illnesses. In each case, the core themes of this book are central. In our increasingly globalized world, the determinants of health are shaped by transnational factors that cannot be controlled by particular countries in isolation or by individuals seeking to maximize their own health. Human health is interconnected. It has causes and consequences

For example, extrapolating from R.J. Rummel's estimate of 169 million murders by states during the 20th century, one might estimate that, on average, 1.69 million state murders occur each year.[e] This figure is staggering; yet, it does not come close to the 7.7 million children, on average, who die each year from preventable illness. If war, terrorism, and state-sponsored violence are serious public threats that require appropriate governmental responses, then surely global health problems warrant equal, if not greater, attention.

Despite the sobering nature of these figures, grounds for optimism exist. Notably, global health initiatives helped reduce the number of childhood deaths resulting from preventable illness from 11 million annually through the first decade of the 21st century to 7.7 million in 2010.[f] It has been estimated that 4 million lives in sub-Saharan Africa could be saved if available, cost-effective maternal, neonatal, and child health interventions were expanded to reach 90 percent of the populations in targeted countries.[g] Simple, cost-effective solutions for many of the most serious global health challenges exist. Global vaccination campaigns, which have been instrumental in the eradication of smallpox and the virtual elimination of polio as a threat in the vast majority of countries, are a prominent case in point. Millions of lives have been saved due to large-scale public health interventions.[h] For example, the creation of public water systems, water treatment mechanisms, and public sewers has cut down on deadly waterborne illnesses and saved countless lives. The challenges are significant but not insurmountable. Success in global health is possible.

---

[e]R.J. Rummel, *Death by Government* (New Brunswick, NJ: Transaction, 1994): 1–28.

[f]World Health Organization, *Reducing Mortality from Major Killers of Children*, Fact Sheet 178, available online at: http://www.who.int/inf-fs/en/fact178.html; Denise Grady, "Global Death Rates Drop for Children 5 or Younger," *New York Times*, May 23, 2010, available online at: http://www.nytimes.com/2010/05/24/health/24child.html?emc=eta1.

[g]Ingrid K. Friberg, Mary V. Kinney, Joy E. Lawn, Kate J. Kerber, M. Oladdoyin Odubanjo, Anne-Marie Bergh, Neff Walker, Eva Weissman, Micky Chopra, and Robert E. Black, "Sub-Saharan Africa's Mothers, Newborns, and Children: How Many Lives Could Be Saved with Targeted Health Interventions?" *PLoS Medicine* 7: 6 (2010). Available online at: http://www.plosmedicine.org/article/info%3Adoi%2F10.1371%2Fjournal.pmed.1000295.

[h]Ruth Levine, *Case Studies in Global Health: Millions Saved* (Sudbury, MA: Jones and Bartlett Publishers, 2007).

---

that transcend national borders. The globalization of health care has contributed to the blurring of national borders as patients increasingly travel internationally for treatment or purchase medications from abroad. Human health—at the local, national, and global levels—is, in a fundamental way, a *public* good. As a result, any effort to respond to the global health challenges of the 21st century must be, in large part, public in nature.

Global Governance and Health

Governance involves "the actions and means adopted by a society to promote collective action and deliver collective solutions in pursuit of common goals."[16] Although they are related, governance and government are not the same thing. Governmental institutions typically play a prominent role in governance. Nevertheless, a society can achieve governance, as defined above, without having adopted formal laws backed by governmental enforcement mechanisms. Applied to the area of health, this definition of governance suggests that health governance involves efforts to identify and implement collective solutions to health challenges.[17] **Global governance**, then, involves the approaches adopted at the global level to promote and deliver collective solutions to challenges that are transnational in nature and that derive from informal norms as well as formal laws. **Global health governance** simply refers to collective efforts to promote and protect population health on a global scale and encompasses the following actions: international trade in health care services, cross-national regulatory mechanisms (such as the Framework Convention on Tobacco Control), intergovernmental collaboration on disease surveillance and monitoring, and the provision of global health aid.[18]

Global governance involves actions and inputs by multiple actors at many levels, including international organizations, states, and non-state actors. At the international level, a wide range of organizations are involved in global health governance. These organizations include UN organs and specialized agencies, such as the WHO, the United Nations Children's Fund (UNICEF), the United Nations Development Programme (UNDP), and the Joint United Nations Programme on HIV/AIDS (UNAIDS). Multilateral development banks, most notably the World Bank, influence global health governance through their work on economic development and poverty reduction. In fact, the World Bank is the primary source of health care funding for developing countries.[19] Finally, regional organizations, such as the European Union (EU), the Organization of American States (OAS), and the African Union (AU), play a role in promoting health within their respective systems of regional governance. Because of their reach, international organizations can play a critical role in coordinating and raising awareness about global health programs and initiatives. At the same time, international organizations have generally limited functions and powers

and are not in a position to enforce collective solutions to global health challenges.

States play a critical role in global health governance. National governments influence population health at home and abroad through the adoption of policies that determine the nature of the national health system, the creation of public health infrastructure, the development of programs designed to address specific health challenges, and international development and health aid. Although their influence and power may be declining in an era of globalization, states remain the most powerful actors in the international system. Particularly in developed countries, health-related spending and policy actions by states easily dominates health governance activities by international organizations and non-state actors. Thus, states remain key players in global health governance.

Non-state actors contribute in important ways to global health governance. Thousands of non-state actors, ranging from health advocacy organizations to corporations, contribute to global governance in health. Prominent examples include Pfizer, the world's largest pharmaceutical company; the Gates Foundation; and Doctors Without Borders (Médecins sans Frontières). The dynamics of globalization have contributed to the increasing importance of non-state actors in the area of health. In a globalizing world, non-state actors can play a significant role by filling policy gaps created by globalizing dynamics that limit states' ability to meet critical needs. In short, non-state actors, in response to the forces of globalization and conditions of interdependence, play an increasingly important role in mobilizing global norms, resources, and policies around the issue of global health.[20]

Notably, global health governance blurs the distinction among states, international organizations, and non-state actors (both nonprofit and for-profit), as these actors often collaborate in seeking collective solutions to common problems. **Public-private partnerships (PPPs)**, which involve formal partnerships between governments and the private sector designed to achieve common or overlapping objectives, play an especially critical role in global health governance.[21] The label "public-private

> ## KEY TERMS AND ACTORS IN GLOBAL HEALTH GOVERNANCE
>
> **Global Governance:** approaches adopted at the global level to promote and deliver collective solutions to challenges that are transnational in nature.
>
> **Global Health Governance:** approaches adopted at the global level to promote and deliver collective solutions to transnational health challenges.
>
> **Public-private Partnerships (PPPs):** formal partnerships between governments and the private sector involving collaboration, normally involving government funding to private actors to implement specific programs or services, intended to provide public goods.
>
> **World Health Organization (WHO):** a permanent international health organization created within the United Nations system that serves as a primary global authority for coordinating health programs and activities.

partnerships" typically is reserved for collaborative initiatives that involve at least one private, for-profit actor and one nonprofit or public organization.[22] Prominent examples of PPPs for health include the Global Alliance for Vaccines and Immunisation (GAVI), the Global Polio Eradication Initiative, and the Roll Back Malaria campaign. Such partnerships reflect the growing reality that neither state nor non-state actors have the resources, capacity, or resolve to solve pressing global health problems independently.

Conclusion

Global health issues pose some of the most significant economic, political, social, and ethical challenges of the 21st century. Perhaps no other public policy issue has greater potential to affect the longevity and quality of human life across the globe. Significant increases in life expectancy across the globe can be attributed in large part to the development of public health infrastructure and expanded access to simple, cost-effective preventive measures like vaccinations. Despite dramatic improvements in human health over the course of the last century, it is a sad fact that millions of people across the globe live without the benefits of a strong public health infrastructure or access to

basic public health interventions. Many people across the globe—in developed as well as developing countries—do not have access to clean water, clean air, nutritious food, or health care. Moreover, low-income populations across the globe are often affected by the costs of globalization without having access to the benefits of public health infrastructure. Not surprisingly, the lower life expectancy among poor people across the globe correlates with their lack of access to public health infrastructure and interventions. This relationship among poverty, relatively poorer health outcomes, and the absence of public health interventions is not coincidental.

Although this book emphasizes the relationship between poverty and public challenges, it does not focus exclusively on these challenges. It is worth repeating that diseases, both communicable and noncommunicable, do not discriminate on the basis of economic class, nationality, or political borders. The health of human beings is truly interconnected—the health of individuals is shaped by the health of other people and communities across the globe. It is affected by the health of the animal and plant worlds. Human health has causes, consequences, and solutions that cross many borders—first and foremost territorial borders, but national, class-based, political, and ecological borders as well.

Because global health is such a broad and complicated field, it requires knowledge from professionals working in a broad array of fields and commitment among engaged citizens everywhere. By introducing students to this topic, we hope to engage their interest, concern, and passion. It is our view that global health should be a top policy priority for countries across the globe in the 21st century. Promoting global health will require transnational cooperation not only among governments but also among networks of professionals working in areas that have the possibility to shape global health outcomes and among engaged global citizens across the globe. We hope that this book helps students understand the subject of global health and encourages them to become active in promoting solutions to global health problems in their own communities, their own countries, and beyond.

Discussion Questions

1. Is the definition of global health provided in this chapter too broad? Why or why not?

2. How does public health differ from medicine and health care?

3. What does it mean to say that human health is interconnected?

4. What is the relationship between poverty and global health?

5. Do you agree with the assertion that engaged citizens should care about global health? Why or why not?

6. Should global health be a public policy priority in your country in the 21st century? Why or why not?

Web Resources

American Public Health Association: http://www.apha.org/

Centers for Disease Control and Prevention: http://www.cdc.gov/

The Educated Citizen and Public Health (an initiative of the Association of American Colleges and Universities): http://www.aacu.org/public_health/index.cfm

World Health Organization: http://www.who.int/en/

World Health Report (annual publication of the World Health Organization): http://www.who.int/whr/en/index.html

CHAPTER 2

Key Concepts in Global Health

Introduction

This chapter introduces key concepts in global health. It provides an introduction to the determinants of health, including biological and behavioral factors as well as economic, social, and cultural determinants. It introduces the key indicators of health and provides an overview of commonly used measures of burden of disease. The chapter describes the relative burden of various diseases among different populations and in different geographic regions. Lastly, the chapter covers the concepts of demographic transition and epidemiological transition as they relate to the economic development of a population and the associated variations in the health status and age composition of that population.

Determinants of Health

In studying global and comparative population health, it is critical for students to first understand the key variables that contribute to the well-being of any individual, regardless of geographic location. As this chapter shows, the overall health status of an individual is determined by a complex interaction of both individual variables and social, cultural, and environmental factors.

Historically, the health sciences have focused on a **biomedical model of health**, which emphasizes individual-level determinants of

health, including genetics, individual behaviors, and direct exposure to harmful particles and organisms.[1] However, marked population differences in health status between countries—for example, 2007 data reveal the average life expectancy at birth is 83 years in Japan versus 42 years in Afghanistan—clearly suggest that individual factors alone cannot explain health outcomes, thus dictating the need for a more complex model.[2] **Social epidemiology** emerged as a field in which scholars and practitioners attempt to explain factors external to the individual that contribute to health outcomes.[3] These factors include, but are not limited to, socioeconomic status, education, culture, the physical environment, and access to health care services. The purpose of this section is to review the major determinants of health. In doing so, the chapter demonstrates that a complex interplay of both individual and external variables provides the best explanation for most health outcomes.

Biological Determinants of Health

Genetic makeup is one innate factor that determines the health of an individual. Certain diseases occur only among individuals who inherit specific gene variants. For example, sickle cell anemia, a condition characterized by abnormally functioning red blood cells, manifests only when an individual inherits an abnormal gene from both parents. Though the severity

KEY CONCEPTS IN THE DETERMINANTS OF HEALTH

Biomedical Model of Health: a model of health that emphasizes individual-level determinants of health, including genetics, individual behaviors, and direct exposure to harmful particles and organisms.

Demographic Transition: the shift of a population from one of high levels of both fertility and mortality and a low rate of population growth to one of low levels of both fertility and mortality and a low rate of population growth.

Epidemiological Transition: a change in mortality and disease patterns whereby a society experiences a shift from a period of high and fluctuating mortality rates largely attributable to communicable diseases to a period of lower and more stable mortality rates primarily due to chronic, noncommunicable diseases.

Gender: social roles and categories associated with men and women that are based on culturally prevailing constructs of presumed "normal," "appropriate," or "ideal" behavior and identities of men (masculinity) and women (femininity).

Social Capital: a broad range of economic, cultural, and personal resources attained through the social relationships of individuals living and interacting together in communities.

Social Epidemiology: a field in which scholars and practitioners attempt to explain factors external to the individual, including socioeconomic status, levels of education, culture, and access to health care, that contribute to health outcomes.

of the disease may vary from one person to another, all individuals inheriting two abnormal gene variants will exhibit some features of the condition, while those with one or no abnormal gene variant will not develop the disease. More commonly, however, diseases with a genetic predisposition do not present in such an all-or-none fashion. Rather, the inheritance of gene variants places an individual at increased risk for a specific condition, but whether a susceptible person develops the disease depends on other factors. For example, although Type II diabetes mellitus has a substantial genetic component, whether a genetically susceptible individual develops the disease is also strongly influenced by factors such as obesity. Similarly, an individual's risk for cardiovascular disease is significantly increased if there is a family history of the disease, but other factors—such as

smoking, age, biological sex, and the presence or absence of other medical conditions such as diabetes mellitus, hypercholesterolemia (high cholesterol), hypertension (high blood pressure), and obesity—contribute to the development of disease.[4]

Another innate determinant of health is biological sex. Social and cultural determinants of health often impact men and women differently. However, biological sex also contributes to the development of specific diseases. Certain cancers are possible in only one gender—ovarian and cervical cancer in women and prostate cancer in men. A perhaps less obvious example is the sex-specific risk of cardiovascular disease. Among individuals less than 60 years of age, men have a twofold risk of cardiovascular disease as compared with women, a disparity that decreases with age until the disease rate is equivalent between genders, by the eighth decade of life.[5]

Age is another biological variable that determines individual health. For example, children are much more likely to succumb to diarrheal illnesses, particularly in lesser developed countries where access to appropriate rehydration therapy may be limited.[6] Conversely, chronic illnesses such as osteoarthritis, hypertension, and Type II diabetes mellitus by their very nature cause increasing morbidity and mortality with the increasing age of an individual. As previously referenced, advancing age is also a risk factor for cardiovascular disease, with risk increasing after 45 years of age for men and 55 years of age for women.[7]

Behavioral Determinants of Health

The health of an individual is also determined by personal behaviors. Individual choices about whether to use seat belts, child restraints, or motorcycle helmets have obvious health implications. Sexual behaviors affect the likelihood of acquiring sexually transmitted diseases such as human immunodeficiency virus (HIV), viral hepatitis, syphilis, gonorrhea, and Chlamydia. Chronic alcohol abuse increases one's risk for developing liver disease. As a final example, physical inactivity and smoking can greatly increase an individual's risk of developing cardiovascular disease.[8]

Although personal behaviors have clear effects on health outcomes, it is important to note that political, social, and, in some instances, genetic variables shape individual behaviors with health consequences. In the case of motor vehicle safety, governmental policies and educational outreach can fundamentally shape individual behavior, leading to much-improved health outcomes. Similarly, education regarding safe sexual practices is critical in preventing sexually transmitted diseases. In the case of health risks associated with alcohol abuse, research suggests a strong genetic predisposition to alcoholism. Social factors can greatly influence one's physical activity level. Smoking behavior is influenced by socioeconomic status as well as by the behavior of others. Individuals of lower income and educational attainment are more likely to smoke, and it has also been demonstrated that children of smokers are more likely to smoke.[9] As these examples indicate, personal behaviors are not entirely "individualized." Rather, behavioral determinants of health are rooted in a social and political context.

In a similar vein, it is important to consider the manner in which individual behavior influences not only individual health outcomes but also population health outcomes. By adhering to safe motor vehicle practices, an individual impacts his or her own well-being as well as that of others. As another example, secondhand smoke exposure among children has been shown to increase the risk of sudden infant death syndrome, respiratory and middle ear infections, and more frequent and severe asthma attacks. The most intimately shared environment is that of the pregnant mother and the developing fetus, and thus the health status and behavioral choices of the mother obviously have a profound impact on the immediate and future health of the fetus. Smoking during pregnancy has been shown to increase the risk of a child being born prematurely and of small birth weight. Such birth outcomes not only affect early child health and development but may also increase the risk of adverse health outcomes as an adult, including an increased risk of cardiovascular disease.[10]

Economic, Social, and Political Determinants of Health

Social factors, including socioeconomic status, employment, and education, have a significant impact on health. Poverty greatly influences one's risk of developing specific diseases. As an example, transmission of HIV is much greater among individuals living in developing countries.[11] It has been shown that even in more developed countries, poverty is the single most important risk factor associated with HIV infection among heterosexuals living in urban settings.[12] Individuals of lower-income status are more likely to smoke, thus increasing their risk of conditions such as cancer and cardiovascular disease while posing a risk of secondhand smoke exposure to close contacts.

Another social factor that shapes health outcomes is the employment status of an individual. Employment obviously contributes directly to one's financial well-being, which itself has effects on health. Employment status often determines health insurance coverage in specific countries. Variables related to employment, occupation, and unpaid labor can have negative consequences on one's health, and certain occupations increase the risk of exposure to potential physical health hazards.

Work-related health risks are often unequally distributed according to **gender**. For example, in developing countries, women are often responsible for unpaid tasks of maintaining the home, such as providing water and fuel. These responsibilities have been shown to increase the risk of exposure to waterborne illnesses such as schistosomiasis as well as mosquito-borne illnesses such as malaria.[13] Cooking on open stoves in such settings also increases women's risk of burns and illnesses due to smoke pollution.[14] In more developed countries, women often constitute a higher percentage of the labor force in industries such as textiles and clothing manufacturing, and thus they also suffer higher rates of asthma and allergies due to exposure to dust in the workplace.[15] Conversely, men are more likely to suffer accidents in the workplace.[16] Further, men in developed countries report greater occupational exposure than women to noise, vibrations, extreme temperatures, chemicals, and physical stress and are thus more likely to suffer illnesses associated with such exposures.[17]

Employment can influence health outcomes in more subtle ways. For example, the Whitehall study in Britain demonstrated that, among British civil servants, employment grade was associated with adverse cardiovascular outcomes in a continuous and downward-sloping gradient.[18] In other words, individuals with a lower job rank were more likely to have cardiovascular disease; when comparing groups of workers across job rank categories, workers in the lower job rank category consistently had higher rates of heart disease than workers in the next highest ranking group. As the study was conducted among civil servants, all of whom earned above living wage and had access to health care services, the implication is that psychosocial pathways contributed to this increased cardiovascular risk.

One's educational attainment also determines health outcomes in both direct and indirect ways. Directly, appropriate educational interventions can lead to the adoption of healthy lifestyle practices. As previously referenced, education regarding safe sexual practices has been shown to reduce the transmission of sexually transmitted diseases such as HIV/AIDS. Educational interventions also have been associated with decreased tobacco use among adolescents. Indirectly, higher educational attainment typically leads to better employment with associated higher income and social status. This, in turn, impacts health in ways previously described in this section.

One's physical environment also has clear implications for health. As an example, individuals living in developing countries have less consistent access to clean water supplies, with the resultant increased risk of waterborne illnesses. These populations also are at increased risk for respiratory illnesses associated with higher rates of indoor air pollution. Highlighting the fact that individual health determinants do not operate in isolation, young children in these populations are particularly vulnerable to these adverse health outcomes.[19] Studies have suggested that one's environment has an important effect on health outcomes in developed countries as well. As an example, one's risk of developing respiratory conditions such as asthma increases if there is early postnatal exposure to common allergens such as dust mites and cockroaches,[20] and asthma severity is often impacted by outdoor air pollution.[21]

UNDER THE MICROSCOPE

Determinants of Cardiovascular Disease

The likelihood that an individual will develop a specific disease state and the severity with which that disease will manifest in an individual are determined by many interdependent risk factors, risks often unevenly distributed by gender, race, and socioeconomic status. A review of the determinants of the development of cardiovascular disease illustrates the complex interplay among individual, behavioral, social, and political determinants of health.

An individual's likelihood of developing cardiovascular disease is influenced by biological factors such as genetic susceptibility and gender. Risk increases with advancing age. Interestingly, gender discrepancies noted among younger individuals are not seen when comparing elderly males and females. It has been suggested that individual biological risk of cardiovascular disease may be increased by prematurity and low birth weight, the risk of which is, in turn, impacted by maternal health status, behavior, and access to appropriate health care.

The development of cardiovascular disease is further influenced by individual behaviors such as level of physical activity and smoking, behaviors that are not only influenced by educational interventions but also often shaped by the behavior patterns of the members of one's family and community. Further, the community-level behavior patterns can be influenced by availability of green space, access to healthy foods, and perceived safety of the neighborhood—factors that are themselves shaped by complex economic and political determinants. As was shown in the previously discussed Whitehall study, even the employment grade of an individual can increase his or her risk of cardiovascular disease.

Additionally, whether one has access to affordable and appropriate health care can contribute not only to the development of disease but also to the severity of disease expression. As there are many underlying medical conditions that serve as risk factors for the development of cardiovascular disease (for example, hypertension, Type II diabetes mellitus, and hypercholesterolemia), consistent access to health care for individuals with these conditions is critical in the prevention of cardiovascular disease. Social and political factors also play an important role in shaping the risk of cardiovascular disease. For example, access to appropriate care for cardiovascular disease may be limited for both women and minority groups. Historically, even research studies of interventions for cardiovascular management have been biased against women and minority groups.

The example of cardiovascular disease clearly demonstrates the complicated interplay among individual, social, and political variables that determine the health of an individual in regard to a specific health condition.

One's local environment and community can affect health outcomes in other ways as well. In the past several decades, considerable research has been done on the concept of **social capital**. Social capital suggests that individuals gain access to a broader range of economic and cultural resources through the social relationships they create.[22] Studies have suggested that higher levels of individual-level social capital are associated with better self-rated health.[23] Conversely, it has been suggested that social mistrust is closely associated with higher rates of mortality and violent crime.[24] Other studies have highlighted the effect that neighborhoods have on disease states such as obesity, Type II diabetes mellitus, hypertension, and mental health disorders.[25] As one specific example, it has been shown that obesity is associated with poor access to healthy foods and neighborhood green space for exercise.[26]

Finally, governmental policies shape individual and population health outcomes in significant ways. National health policy may lead to more efficient and effective spending of health care dollars, resulting in a greater number of individuals having access to affordable health care services. Further, economic and taxation policies may contribute to more uniform distribution of national wealth, and educational policy may ensure better access to appropriate educational and vocational opportunities for individuals. In this way, public policy can result in better living conditions for a greater number of individuals in a given population. National and local legislation can also directly shape individual behaviors in a manner that results in better health outcomes. As previously mentioned, adoption of safe motor vehicle practices can be influenced by legislation. As an additional example, smoke-free air laws have been shown to reduce secondhand smoke exposure among nonsmoking youth.

Population Health Assessment

Whereas the prior section addressed the determinants of individual health, this section introduces concepts pertinent to **population health**. In order to evaluate the health status of populations, one must have an understanding of the key indicators of population health as well as measures commonly used to assess the burden that specific diseases place on a population. Additionally, knowledge of these concepts is critical to inform national, state, and local policy-setting in ways likely to improve the health of a specific population. To this end, this section provides definitions for commonly used indicators of population health and measures of disease burden. Additionally, the section provides an overview of global trends of comparative population health.

Key Indicators of Population Health

When assessing population health, it is imperative to have available a set of key indicators of health that can be consistently applied such that reliable comparisons might be made between various populations. These indicators should also be able to provide insight into variants of health by gender and age within and across populations.

The **mortality rate** is one of the most basic indicators used in studies of population health. Simply stated, a mortality rate is an estimate of the proportion of a population that dies during a specified period. A mortality rate can be determined for any population or subpopulation (for example, **adult mortality rate**) for any defined period of time, based on the specific health outcomes one wishes to assess. Another commonly employed health indicator is **life expectancy at birth**, defined as the average number of years that a newborn is expected to live if mortality patterns at the time of its birth were to prevail throughout the child's life. A similar health indicator is the **health-adjusted life expectancy (HALE)**, defined as the average number of years that a person can expect to live in full health by taking into account the years the person is in less than full health due to disease and/or injury.

Current estimates of these population health indicators for the six World Health

KEY INDICATORS OF HEALTH

Adult Mortality Rate: the probability of dying between the ages of 15 and 60 years (per 1,000 population) per year among a hypothetical cohort of 100,000 people who would experience the age-specific mortality rate of the reporting year.

Health-adjusted Life Expectancy (HALE): the average number of years that a person can expect to live in full health by taking into account the years the person is in less than full health due to disease and/or injury.

Infant Mortality Rate: the probability of a child born in a specific year or period dying before reaching the age of one, if subject to age-specific mortality rates of that period.

Life Expectancy at Birth: the average number of years that a newborn is expected to live if mortality patterns at the time of its birth were to prevail throughout the child's life.

Maternal Mortality Ratio: the annual number of female deaths from any cause related to or aggravated by pregnancy or its management (excluding accidental or incidental causes) during pregnancy and childbirth or within 42 days of termination of pregnancy, irrespective of the duration or site of the pregnancy, per 100,000 live births, for a specified year.

Mortality Rate: an estimate of the proportion of a population that dies during a specified period. The numerator is the number of persons dying during the period; the denominator is the total number of people in the population, usually estimated as the midyear population.

Neonatal Mortality Rate: the number of registered deaths in the neonatal period (the first 28 completed days of life) per 1,000 live births in a given year or period of time.

Under-five Mortality Rate: the probability (expressed as a rate per 1,000 live births) of a child born in a specific year or period dying before reaching the age of five, if subject to age-specific mortality rates of that period.

Organization (WHO) global regions are presented in Table 2.1, along with the gross national income per capita of those regions. As the data demonstrate, poverty is associated with poorer health outcomes for each of these key health indicators. Also, it appears that these poorer health outcomes are particularly noteworthy for women and young children living in poverty, as evidenced by the somewhat greater disparity between higher- and lower-income regions for **maternal mortality ratio** and **neonatal, infant, and under-five mortality rates** as compared with the other key health indicators. The reasons for these contrasting health outcomes are likely multifactorial. An introduction to the factors that lead to disparate health outcomes was provided in the previous section on the determinants of health, and Chapter 6 explores this topic in greater depth.

TABLE 2.1 Key Indicators of Population Health, by WHO Region, 2008

	Africa	Americas	Southeast Asia	Europe	Eastern Mediterranean	Western Pacific
Neonatal mortality rate (per 1,000 live births)	40	9	34	7	35	11
Infant mortality rate (per 1,000 live births)	85	15	48	12	57	18
Under-five mortality rate (per 1,000 live births)	142	18	63	14	78	21
Maternal mortality ratio[a] (per 100,000 live births)	900	99	450	27	420	82
Adult mortality rate (per 1,000 population)	392	126	218	149	203	113
Life expectancy at birth (years)	52	73	63	71	63	72
Health-adjusted life expectancy (HALE) at birth[b] (years)	45	67	57	67	56	67
Gross national income per capita (PPP int. $)	2,279	24,005	3,043	22,849	3,805	8,958

[a]2005 data
[b]2007 data

Source: World Health Organization, "Part II: Global Health Indicators," *World Health Statistics 2010.* Available online at: http://www.who.int/whosis/whostat/EN_WHS10_Part2.pdf.

Common Measures of Disease Burden

In evaluating population health, it is important to assess not only the health status of that population but also the diseases that most significantly contribute to mortality, morbidity, and disability for that population. To do so, one must be familiar with commonly used measures of **burden of disease**. This section introduces these measures and provides a brief overview of the categories of diseases. Additionally, this section highlights data on the global burden of disease.

Individual **mortality**, **morbidity**, and **disability** may occur due to injury or the presence of disease. Typically, diseases are broadly categorized as either communicable or noncommunicable. **Communicable diseases** are transmitted directly or indirectly from one individual to another via a microbial agent such as a virus, bacteria, parasite, or fungus. Key examples of

a communicable disease include tuberculosis, malaria, and HIV. Conversely, **noncommunicable diseases**, such as Type II diabetes mellitus, occur in the absence of such infectious agents and are not transmissible between individuals. Communicable diseases and noncommunicable diseases are explored in much greater detail in Chapters 4 and 5, respectively.

Measures commonly used to describe disease burden include prevalence, incidence, and cause-specific mortality rates. **Prevalence** is defined as "the number of affected persons present in the population at a specific time divided by the number of persons in the population at that time."[27] Typically, this measure is applied as *point prevalence*, with the assessment made at one specific point in time rather than over a period of time. **Incidence** is "the number of new cases of a disease that occur during a specified period of time in a population at risk for developing the disease."[28] Whereas prevalence measures the current burden of disease in

---

KEY HEALTH TERMS

Communicable Diseases: diseases that are transmitted directly or indirectly from one individual to another via a microbial agent such as a virus, bacteria, parasite, or fungus.

Disability: an impairment, activity limitation, or participation restriction.

Morbidity: the state of having a disease.

Mortality: a fatal outcome; death.

Noncommunicable Diseases: diseases that occur in the absence of infectious agents and are not transmissible between individuals.

Population Health: the health outcomes of a group of individuals, including the distribution of such outcomes within the group.

---

a population, incidence reflects the current risk of developing the disease in those not currently affected by the disease. These two measures are related in that, as disease incidence increases, so too does disease prevalence. Prevalence also increases with improvements in disease management that allow an individual to survive a specific illness for a greater duration of time. Conversely, prevalence decreases if individuals are cured of the illness or die. Population disease burden can also be assessed using **cause-specific mortality rates**, an estimate of the proportion of a population that dies during a specified period as a result of a specific disease or injury. For example, the WHO routinely includes cause-specific mortality rates for tuberculosis, malaria, and HIV/AIDS in its updated global health reports.

These measures are useful in demonstrating how commonly a specific disease or injury occurs within a population as well as the contribution of that disease or injury to the overall mortality rate of a population. However, these are imperfect measures of disease burden in that they fail to capture the contribution of a specific disease or injury to morbidity and disability within a population.[29] Therefore, measures of population health have been developed that allow for the combined impact of death, disability, and morbidity to be considered simultaneously.[30] The most commonly used of these measures is the **disability-adjusted life year (DALY)**. The DALY is defined as the sum of years of potential life lost due to premature mortality and the years of productive life lost due to disability; in essence, it "measures the difference between a current situation and an ideal situation where everyone lives up to the age of standard life expectancy, and in perfect health."[31]

Applying this measure, the WHO periodically determines the leading causes of disease burden to global populations. The most recently published estimates for the ten leading causes of disease burden, stratified by country income, are presented in Table 2.2. As can be seen, communicable diseases contribute the majority of disease burden in low-income countries, whereas high-income countries are much more likely to suffer morbidity, disability, and mortality as a result of noncommunicable diseases. Disease burden in middle-income countries appears to more closely parallel that of high-income countries than low-income countries, with the exception that communicable diseases such as lower respiratory infections and HIV/AIDS are significant contributors to morbidity, disability, and

TABLE 2.2 Leading Causes of Burden of Disease (DALYs), Countries Grouped by Income, 2004

Disease or injury	DALYs (millions)	Percentage of total DALYs	Disease or injury	DALYs (millions)	Percentage of total DALYs
World			**Low-income countries**		
Lower respiratory infections	94.5	6.2	Lower respiratory infections	76.9	9.3
Diarrheal diseases	72.8	4.8	Diarrheal diseases	59.2	7.2
Unipolar depressive disorders	65.5	4.3	HIV/AIDS	42.9	5.2
Ischemic heart disease	62.6	4.1	Malaria	32.8	4.0
HIV/AIDS	58.5	3.8	Prematurity and low birth weight	32.1	3.9
Cerebrovascular disease	46.6	3.1	Neonatal infections	31.4	3.8
Prematurity and low birth weight	44.3	2.9	Birth asphyxia and birth trauma	29.8	3.6
Birth asphyxia and birth trauma	41.7	2.7	Unipolar depressive disorders	26.5	3.2
Road traffic accidents	41.2	2.7	Ischemic heart disease	26.0	3.1
Neonatal infections	40.4	2.7	Tuberculosis	22.4	2.7
Middle-income countries			**High-income countries**		
Unipolar depressive disorders	29.0	5.1	Unipolar depressive disorders	10.0	8.2
Ischemic heart disease	28.9	5.0	Ischemic heart disease	7.7	6.3
Cerebrovascular disease	27.5	4.8	Cerebrovascular disease	4.8	3.9
Road traffic accidents	21.4	3.7	Alzheimer's and other dementias	4.4	3.6
Lower respiratory infections	16.3	2.8	Alcohol use disorders	4.2	3.4
Chronic obstructive lung disease	16.1	2.8	Hearing loss, adult onset	4.2	3.4
HIV/AIDS	15.0	2.6	Chronic obstructive lung disease	3.7	3.0
Alcohol use disorders	14.9	2.6	Diabetes mellitus	3.6	3.0
Refractive errors	13.7	2.4	Trachea, bronchus, lung cancers	3.6	3.0
Diarrheal diseases	13.1	2.3	Road traffic accidents	3.1	2.6

Source: Reproduced from the World Health Organization, *The Global Burden of Disease: 2004 Update.* Available online at: http://www.who.int/healthinfo/global_burden_disease/GBD_report_2004update_full.pdf.

mortality in middle-income countries. Careful inspection of the data in Table 2.2 provides further insights. For one, it can be seen that in low-income regions, considerable disease burden results from pregnancy- and birth-related disease and injury, again highlighting that women and young children living in poverty are particularly vulnerable to poor health outcomes. Additionally, the data demonstrate that with socioeconomic advances, populations are faced with increasing morbidity and mortality associated with advancing age, such as dementia and chronic illnesses such as ischemic heart disease, chronic obstructive lung disease, and cancers.

COMMON MEASURES OF DISEASE BURDEN

Burden of Disease: the impact of a health problem in a particular area (for example, at the country, region, or global level) or for a specific group (such as men and women or different ethnic groups), typically measured by morbidity, mortality, or a combination of both.

Cause-specific Mortality Rate: an estimate of the proportion of a population that dies during a specified period as a result of a specific disease or injury.

Disability-adjusted Life Years (DALYs): the sum of years of potential life lost due to premature mortality and the years of productive life lost due to disability.

Incidence: the number of new cases of a disease that occur during a specified period of time in a population at risk for developing the disease.

Prevalence: the number of affected persons present in the population at a specific time, divided by the number of persons in the population at that time.

Demographic and Epidemiological Transitions

This chapter would be incomplete without a discussion of the two distinct yet closely related concepts of epidemiological transition and demographic transition. As described earlier in this chapter, individual health is determined by the interplay among individual, social, and political variables. Further, population health is closely linked with economic, social, and political determinants. The concepts of epidemiological transition and demographic transition serve as examples of how these variables interact to shape not only the health of populations but also population growth, as well as the relative burden of specific diseases within populations. This section provides a brief review of these two concepts and discusses the implications of these transitions for specific populations.

Epidemiological Transition

The concept of **epidemiological transition** was first described in 1971 by Abdel Omran as a transition of a population in which "a long shift occurs in mortality and disease patterns whereby pandemics of infection are gradually displaced by degenerative and man-made diseases as the chief form of morbidity and primary cause of death."[32] In essence, a population moves from a period when mortality rates are high and fluctuating, with death largely attributable to famine and infectious diseases, to a state of lower and more stable mortality rates, with morbidity and mortality largely due to chronic, noncommunicable diseases.

The determinants that influence this transition are complex. However, most research has suggested that cultural and socioeconomic factors leading to improvements in living conditions, nutrition, and hygiene have contributed most significantly to this transition, particularly for most Western populations that began this transition in the 19th century. Advances in public health and medicine, including improved public sanitation, immunizations, and development of therapies such as antibiotics, have played an additional role in populations undergoing this transition more recently.[33]

Most developed countries have undergone such a transition, with relatively low and more stable mortality rates and disease burden attributable most significantly to noncommunicable diseases. Conversely, many developing countries exhibit higher mortality rates with significant disease burden due to infectious diseases, suggesting the epidemiological transition has not yet been completed.

Demographic Transition

The **demographic transition** represents the shift of a population from one of high levels of fertility and mortality and a low rate of population growth to one of low levels of fertility and mortality and a low rate of population growth.[34] Socioeconomic, public health, and medical advances within a population result in decreased mortality rates for that population, particularly improving health outcomes for infants and young children. As depicted in Figure 2.1, the decline in mortality leads to a resultant increase in the population growth rate, particularly among younger members of the population. After some time, there is a subsequent decline in the fertility rate of the population, with a resultant slowing of population growth until there is again a zero, or sometimes negative, population growth rate.

The reasons for the decline in population fertility rates are unclear yet likely multifactorial. In part, this decline is presumably attributable to the fact that, with the realization of a greater likelihood of child survival to adulthood, there is an associated parental desire for fewer births with a greater financial investment in the health and education for each child.[35] Also, it is likely that, in addition to reducing infant and child mortality rates, the socioeconomic advances of a population also allow for greater educational and employment opportunities for women and, in turn, a desire for fewer children.[36] As many populations began the demographic transition in the late 18th and 19th centuries, the role of such medical advances as contraception in the decline in fertility rates is likely minimal, though access to contraceptives may play a

FIGURE 2.1 The Demographic Transition

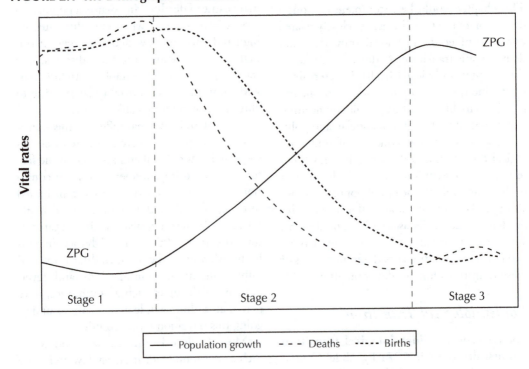

ZPG = zero population growth

Source: Adapted from the Australian Department of Families, Housing, Community Services and Indigenous Affairs, *Policy Research Paper No. 13.* Available online at: http://www.facs.gov.au/about/publicationsarticles/research/socialpolicy/Documents/prp13/sec1.htm.

greater role in populations more recently entering this transition period.[37]

As represented in Figure 2.2, the most notable result of this transition is ultimately a shift in the age composition of the involved population, represented by a greater ratio of older to younger members. In stage 1 of the demographic transition, populations experience high levels of fertility and mortality and a relatively low rate of population growth. In stage 2, high levels

FIGURE 2.2 Population Pyramids Representing the Stages of Demographic Transition

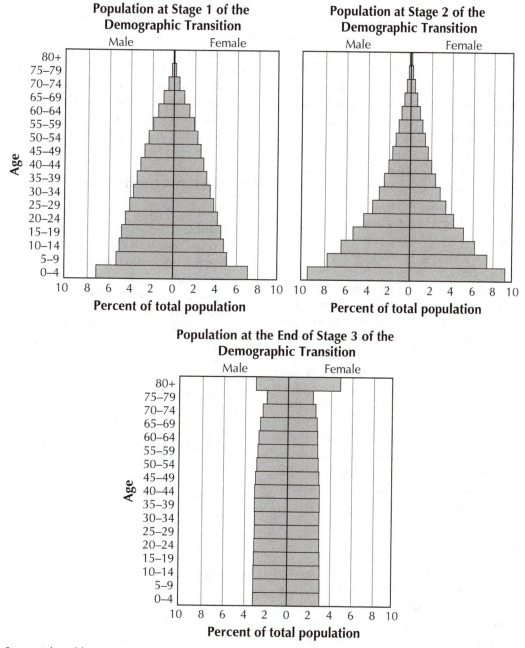

Source: Adapted from U.S. Census Bureau, "International Population Reports WP/02," *Global Population Profile: 2002* (Washington, DC: U.S. Government Printing Office, 2004). Available online at: http://www.census.gov/prod/2004pubs/wp-02.pdf.

of fertility coupled with decreasing mortality rates lead to relatively high rates of population growth. Finally, in stage 3, populations experience low rates of population growth as fertility rates decline to match lower mortality rates.

Implications of the Demographic and Epidemiological Transitions

The demographic and epidemiological transitions have several key implications for population health. The socioeconomic gains of a society have considerable positive influence on population health, typically more so than advances in medicine. Investments made in improving living conditions, sanitation, nutrition, and hygiene lead to a decrease in infectious disease burden and, thus, reduced mortality of members of the population typically most vulnerable to infectious diseases, namely, infants and young children. As infant and child mortality falls, and prior to the anticipated subsequent decline in fertility rates, population growth, particularly among the young, necessitates further investments in resources to support the care and education of these younger members of the population. When fertility rates decline, population shifts ultimately lead to an aging population that will be faced with the morbidity associated with chronic, noncommunicable diseases. This shift tends to occur at the same time that fewer young adults are entering the workforce. Thus, governments facing these implications of the demographic transition are faced with the challenges of taking care of larger aging populations—for example, by funding pension plans and expanding health care—at the same time that their tax base may be decreasing due to a smaller workforce.

Conclusion

A wide variety of individual, social, and political variables shape human health across the globe. Notably, these variables do not operate in isolation. Rather, a complex interplay among personal behaviors, social environment, and public policy is responsible for variations in individual and population health outcomes. Poverty and levels of national economic development also are

critical in determining the distribution of disease within particular countries and the overall health of a given population, as Chapter 6 will discuss in greater detail. The epidemiological transition and the demographic transition demonstrate the ways in which improvements in the socioeconomic status of a population as well as advances in medicine affect not only the distribution of disease within particular countries but also the demographic composition of specific populations. In turn, the demography of a given population has important consequences for national health policies and health outcomes in specific countries. Thus, it is critical for students of global and comparative health to have a solid understanding of the determinants of health as well as the interrelated effects among them.

Discussion Questions

1. What are the major determinants of health?
2. Do you agree with the assertion that health is largely determined by individual-level variables? Why or why not?
3. What populations appear to be disproportionately burdened by disease? What indicators of population health and measures of disease burden support your conclusions?
4. How does the DALY differ from other measures of disease burden?
5. How is the age composition of a population altered by the demographic transition? What would be the expected impact of the epidemiological transition on the burden of disease within a population? How might this shape economic and health care policy for the impacted population?

Web Resources

WHO The Determinants of Health: http://www.who.int/hia/evidence/doh/en/

WHO Global Burden of Disease: http://www.who.int/healthinfo/global_burden_disease/en/

WHO Statistical Information System: http://www.who.int/whosis/whostat/en/

CHAPTER 3

The Ecological Foundations of Global Health

Introduction

This chapter explores the connections among the environment, ecology, and human health. It places the discussion of global health in an ecological context. In doing so, it explores the concept of ecological balance, in which humans, other animals, plants, and microbes coexist in specific ecosystems (local, regional, and global). When economic and social changes upset an ecological balance, new threats to human health can emerge. With the concept of ecological balance as a frame, the chapter examines the interconnections among globalization, ensuing changes to the environment, and the related challenges to global health that result. The chapter concludes with a discussion of two issues that illustrate the ecological foundations of human health: (1) water, the environment, and global health, and (2) climate change as one of the most significant contemporary challenges to human health at a global level.

Environmental Health

Explorations of the connections between the environment and human health focus on causes of disease located outside individual human beings. One of the challenges in exploring environmental health, then, is to define the **environment**. What is the line of demarcation between individuals and the environments in which they live? At first glance, it might

appear that answering this question would be easy. However, the task of defining the concept of the environment for the purposes of understanding environmental causes of health problems is more complicated than it might appear to be on its face.

One approach is to identify environmental risk factors as everything that is not genetic.[1] In this approach, any cause of a disease that cannot be traced to genetics should be considered an environmental risk factor. Thus, environmental risk factors include causes of disease originating from the physical spaces in which people live *as well as* the cultural, economic, and social conditions and influences that affect human health and well-being. This approach defines the environment very broadly and even includes individual behavior or lifestyle choices as environmental risk factors.

An alternative approach is to include behavioral or lifestyle factors within the realm of the individual rather than that of the environment. In this case, the environment refers to the physical spaces and conditions in which human beings live. Under this approach, the environment encompasses both the "natural" world in which particular individuals and groups live, including the animal and plant life that is native to a particular area, and the physical spaces of human communities that have been shaped by human constructions, including domesticated animals, agricultural crops, buildings, and roads. However, this approach does not include other psychosocial determinants of human health as environmental risk factors. For instance, cultural influences are not considered environmental under this approach to defining the environment.

One of the difficulties in reaching consensus on a precise and appropriate definition of the environment as it relates to human health is determining whether it is useful to draw distinctions between natural and social causes of disease. On the one hand, it might be helpful to distinguish between the natural environment and the social world in which people live. For one thing, natural and social risk factors affect health in different ways and, thus, might require different types of solutions. In addition, questions about individual responsibility become relevant. Individuals cannot control genetic risk factors, and they also appear to have little control over the natural environment of the spaces where they live. They might appear to have more control over the social conditions in which they live, especially in the area of lifestyle and individual behavior. Thus, proponents of individual responsibility in health matters might stress the importance of distinguishing between natural and social environmental risk factors.

However, the distinction between natural and social risk factors can be somewhat arbitrary. The physical and social aspects of human communities are inextricably intertwined. The physical spaces in which people live not only include natural elements but are also fundamentally shaped by human activities and design. Furthermore, there are interactive effects between the natural environment and the social environment. Human productive and social activities alter the natural world in important ways. For instance, agricultural and industrial activity significantly changes natural landscapes, making it hard to disentangle natural and social factors. Even genetics are not absolutely isolated from human influence: "Mutation, natural selection, and other mechanisms of evolution have changed the genetic composition of humanity according to environmental conditions existing in the past. In this context, . . . all diseases are entirely environmental."[2] Because it is so difficult to isolate natural conditions from social ones, the conceptualization of the environment used in this chapter will be a broad one that encompasses both the natural and social dimensions of the spaces and communities in which people live.

If the environment refers to the broad range of natural and social conditions of the spaces and communities where human beings live, then **environmental health** also encompasses a wide range of factors. Accordingly, the World Health Organization (WHO) defines environmental health as "all the physical, chemical, and biological factors external to a person, and all related factors impacting behaviours" that have the potential to affect health.[3] Thus, environmental health is concerned not only with the physical, chemical, and biological agents that affect human health but also with a broad range of factors external to the individual that can shape human health.[4] At the most basic level, environmental health deals with issues such as sanitation, housing conditions, public infrastructure, air and water quality, exposure to natural toxins or pollutants resulting from human activity, resource management, and occupational injury. More broadly, environmental health considers the ways in which economic status, public policy, culture, ethnicity, or gender might influence the health consequences of other environmental factors.

Environmental health is an incredibly important piece of the global health puzzle. Estimates suggest that up to one-third of the global burden of disease can be attributed to environmental risk factors.[5] Notably, these estimates were generated from a model that did *not* include genetic or behavioral risk factors (including smoking or dietary practices). Additionally, these estimates focus on actual *disease* caused by environmental risk factors and not merely ill health.[6] Thus, estimates that are based on the broadest definition of the environment and that consider poor health rather than just disease would generate even higher estimates of the negative health consequences stemming from environmental risk factors.

Five environmental risk factors—unsafe water, sanitation, and hygiene; urban outdoor air pollution; indoor smoke from solid fuels; global climate change; and lead exposure—are responsible for an estimated 10 percent of deaths and disease burden globally.[7] These risk factors contribute to a number of serious illnesses. Acute respiratory infections (ARIs), diarrhea, perinatal conditions, and cancer are among the major illnesses that constitute a significant percentage of the global burden of disease that can be largely attributed to environmental risk factors.[8] Indoor air pollution and urban air pollution are major contributors to ARIs, and lack of access to clean water is one of the primary causes of diarrhea, especially in low-income countries where diarrhea often has fatal consequences. Other environmental risk factors include food preservatives, chemical exposures, and radioactive agents, which have carcinogenic effects. Traffic accidents are another serious health problem across the globe for which environmental risk factors—in this case, engineering and planning issues—play a major role.[9]

As shown in Table 3.1, environmental risk factors are especially likely to affect health outcomes in less developed countries. Children under the age of five years are the most likely to be at risk to suffer from environmental health problems; an estimated 43 percent of the global burden of disease attributed to environmental risk factors falls on children under five years old.[10] Approximately 20 percent of deaths and disease burden in children across the globe can be attributed to environmental risk factors.[11]

Additionally, there is commonly a gender dimension to environmental health problems in the developing world. Consider the negative health consequences of indoor air pollution. The health problems stemming from indoor air pollution often disproportionately affect women. In part, this gender divide in environmental health risk is due to cultural environmental factors. In many developing countries,

TABLE 3.1 Deaths and DALYs Attributable to Five Environmental Risks, and to All Five Risks Combined by Region, 2004

Risk	World	Low and middle income	High income
Percentage of deaths			
Indoor smoke from solid fuels	3.3	3.9	0.0
Unsafe water, sanitation, hygiene	3.2	3.8	0.1
Urban outdoor air pollution	2.0	1.9	2.5
Global climate change	0.2	0.3	0.0
Lead exposure	0.2	0.3	0.0
All five risks	**8.9**	**10.2**	**2.6**
Percentage of DALYs			
Indoor smoke from solid fuels	2.7	2.9	0.0
Unsafe water, sanitation, hygiene	4.2	4.6	0.3
Urban outdoor air pollution	0.6	0.6	0.8
Global climate change	0.4	0.4	0.0
Lead exposure	0.6	0.6	0.1
All five risks	**8.5**	**9.1**	**1.2**

Source: Reproduced from the World Health Organization, *Global Health Risks: Mortality and Burden of Disease Attributable to Selected Major Risks* (2009): 24. Available online at: http://www.who.int/healthinfo/global_burden_disease/GlobalHealthRisks_report_full.pdf.

women are responsible for cooking for their families. Poor women commonly live in small, substandard housing that does not have adequate ventilation. They typically rely on solid fuels, including wood, charcoal, dung, and crop residues, to cook. Because their homes do not have adequate ventilation, cooking with these solid fuels causes indoor air pollution, and women and children are more likely than adult men to suffer the health effects, especially a higher incidence of ARIs, of this environmental problem.[12] Tentative evidence also exists that indoor air pollution resulting from cooking with solid fuels increases the risk of cancer and exacerbates the health problems associated with other diseases, including tuberculosis and AIDS.[13]

Although developing countries carry a higher percentage of the global burden of disease stemming from environmental risk factors, environmental health remains a serious problem in high-income countries as well. Environmental risk factors contribute to the prevalence of communicable illnesses in both the developed and the developing world. However, because high-income countries have gone through the *epidemiological transition* (introduced in Chapter 2), noncommunicable illnesses constitute the highest percentage of the burden of disease in high-income countries. In high-income countries, roughly 87 percent of deaths is attributable to noncommunicable illnesses.[14] Notably, environmental risk factors, including chemicals and carcinogens prevalent in industrialized societies, and dietary patterns that prevail in the developed world are major contributors to these diseases. Occupational exposures to hazardous toxins in highly industrialized countries lead to increased risks of specific diseases among workers in certain industries—for example, an increased risk of blood cancer among workers in the oil, rubber, and gas industries (due to benzene exposure), an increased risk of lung cancer among workers in shipbuilding, insulation, or various sectors of the automobile industry (due to asbestos exposure), and an increased risk of lung disease among workers in mining industries (due to exposure to a variety of air pollutants). Another

example of an environmental risk factor is air pollution as a trigger for asthma, a condition that has a higher prevalence in densely populated areas, where air quality tends to be poor.

In short, environmental determinants play a critical role in shaping the health of human societies. For this reason, one cannot understand global health without paying attention to environmental health. Yet, environmental health alone does not provide a complete picture of the complicated interconnections among humans, the environments in which they live, and human health. To complete this picture, we need to place this discussion of environmental health into a broader ecological context.

Ecological Balance and Global Health

Key Terms and Definitions

Ecology is essential in explaining the complicated relationship between the environment and human health. Ecology is concerned with the interactive effects that occur among human beings, other living organisms, and nonliving objects in particular physical spaces. Stated more simply, ecology is the study of the interactions of human beings and the environments in which they live.[15] An ecological approach stresses that humans coexist with other living organisms (plant, animal, and microbial) as well as nonliving objects. Ecology examines interactions within **ecosystems**, which can be defined as all of the living organisms and nonliving objects—including humans, other animals, plants, microbes, soil, water, and air—in a particular environment or physical area. Humans live in many ecosystems simultaneously, and we can talk about ecology at multiple levels. There are local ecosystems, regional ecosystems, and global ecosystems.

The concept of **ecological balance** is central to understanding the connections between the environment and human health. Ecological balance refers to a state of equilibrium in which there are relatively stable relationships among

---

KEY ENVIRONMENTAL HEALTH DEFINITIONS

Ecological Balance: a state of equilibrium in which there are relatively stable relationships between the various living and nonliving organisms in a particular environment.

Ecology: the study of the interactions of human beings and the environments in which they live.

Ecosystem: all of the living organisms and nonliving objects—including humans, other animals, plants, microbes, soil, water, and air—in a particular environment or physical area.

Environment: the broad range of natural and social conditions of the spaces and communities where human beings live.

Environmental Health: all of the physical, chemical, biological, and social factors external to a person that have the potential to affect human health.[a]

Zoonosis: the process by which pathogens that affect animals mutate in ways that enable them to affect humans who are in regular contact with animals.

---

[a]World Health Organization, *Environmental Health*. Available online at: http://www.who.int/topics/environmental_health/en/.

---

the various living and nonliving organisms in a particular environment. When an environment is in ecological balance, microbial, plant, and animal populations coexist in a relatively steady state with mostly consistent population numbers. A significant change in any part of a particular ecology can disrupt ecological balance. For example, human activity that destroys a specific plant species might lead to the extinction of certain animal species while giving an evolutionary advantage to other animal species. In turn, this change in the ecological balance among animal species can determine which microbes or plants thrive and which struggle. Eventually, a new ecological balance may emerge, only to be disrupted at a later point by some other significant change within the ecosystem.

Ecological balance is crucial to explaining how ecological changes can have major consequences for human health. A change in one element of a specific ecosystem can have ripple effects throughout the system that ultimately affect human health. Human activities and development have played an especially critical role in disrupting ecological balances in ecosystems at every level, from the local to the global. As human societies have grown in size, density, and social complexity over time, they have become more and more likely to upset the balance of ecosystems. In the process, the increasing social complexity of human societies has led to serious outbreaks of disease that sometimes threaten to undermine the stability of human societies.[16]

Major Causes of Ecological Disruptions with Serious Health Consequences

A number of causes have disrupted the ecological balance in ways that have had significant consequences for human health. Human settlement and economic activity in new geographic areas can disrupt existing ecosystems and expose human beings to new pathogens.[17] Historically, industrialization and urbanization were among the most important development processes that disrupted ecological balance in ways that had significant consequences for human health. As humans came to settle in proximity in towns and, eventually, cities with denser populations, the prevalence and deadliness of infectious diseases increased, partly due to the lack of sanitation infrastructure to deal with accumulating human waste and garbage. Smallpox, measles, and bubonic plague are examples of diseases that emerged when human societies became more integrated and complex. These diseases threatened the health of the populations in these societies in dramatic and devastating ways.[18]

The agricultural revolution has been another major cause of ecological disruptions that have led to new health problems among human populations. It has brought humans into greater contact with animals and has increased opportunities for pathogens that affect animals to mutate in ways that enable them to affect humans who are in regular contact with animals.[19] This process is known as **zoonosis**. Zoonotic diseases include Lyme disease, ebola, yellow fever, monkey pox, West Nile virus, rabies, hanta viruses, and various influenza strains.[20] Global fears about the 2009 "swine flu" (H1N1) pandemic are a recent manifestation of the kinds of health problems that originally stemmed from the agricultural revolution that brought humans and animals into closer and more regular contact. Similar dynamics exist in the case of "avian influenza" (H5N1), an incredibly deadly flu strain that has been estimated could kill upward of 62 million people if it ever mutated in such a way that it became easily transmissible between humans.[21]

A final major cause of ecological disruptions that have had far-reaching consequences for human health involves the increased interactions among previously separated societies. These interactions have had the effect of disrupting the balance in local ecosystems, and major outbreaks of disease resulted when particular groups of humans were exposed to pathogens to which they had not previously been exposed. In this regard, it is important to underscore that ecological balance can be very specific to particular ecosystems. Ecological balance emerges between *particular* groups of human beings and *specific* pathogens in different geographic locations. Thus, the ecological balance can be disrupted when groups of humans come into contact with one another for the first time and introduce new pathogens into an environment.

This sort of ecological disruption was exemplified by European colonization of the Americas, which introduced smallpox, measles, and influenza into the environment and decimated the indigenous population. Roughly two-thirds of the indigenous population died.[22] In some cases, the introduction of these pathogens was an unintended consequence of European colonization. In other cases, Europeans intentionally introduced pathogens with the goal of killing indigenous peoples, and, thus, these actions by the European colonizers have been called genocide by disease.[23]

As this case illustrates, colonialism, exploration, tourism, migration, and other forms of human movement across the globe are major causes of ecological disruptions. In an era of globalization, with an increase in movement of peoples across territorial borders, the likelihood of ecological changes leading to global health problems rises as well. As the virologist Stephen S. Morse has said, "Viruses have no locomotion, yet many of them have traveled around the world."[24] The same logic holds for other microbes. Germs respect neither territorial borders nor boundaries of class, ethnicity, or culture. At the end of the day, microbes do not recognize presumed boundaries within or between ecosystems at the local, regional, or global level.

Examples of the Health Consequences of Ecological Imbalance

Examples of ecological disruptions that have had far-reaching effects on human health abound. A high-profile example involves the ebola virus outbreaks that had horrifying effects on the communities where they erupted. Ebola hemorrhagic fever is a devastating disease that causes fever, headache, vomiting, bleeding in the eyes and gums, and bloody diarrhea. In cases of outbreaks, it has had a mortality rate of upward of 70 percent[25]; in at least one outbreak, 100 percent of those who contracted the illness died.[26]

Rare but deadly, ebola outbreaks have occurred mostly in remote forested areas in Central Africa with little human settlement, including areas in the countries of the Democratic Republic of the Congo (formerly Zaire), Gabon, Uganda, and the Sudan.[27] Other mammals, including chimpanzees and gorillas, are also susceptible to the ebola virus, and it is thought that several species of the fruit bat may be vectors for the disease.[28] In these remote areas, poverty, conflict, and poor governance have driven many impoverished people deep into the rain forest in search of habitation and food, one source of which was bush meat. Bush meat has been hunted in these remote areas and then transported and sold in urban markets. These dynamics have brought people in this region into contact with animals with which they do not typically interact and may have facilitated the zoonotic jump of the ebola virus into humans.[29] It is thought that the ebola virus can make the jump from other animals to humans when people eat meat from infected chimpanzees or otherwise come into contact with the blood of infected animals.[30] Subsequently, the lack of a good public health infrastructure, poor sanitation practices when caring for sick loved ones or burying the dead, and substandard medical practices, including the reuse of hypodermic needles in treatment, have led to human-to-human transmission of the deadly virus.[31]

Other examples of ecological disruptions with serious health consequences include less deadly but more widespread illnesses. Take, for example, Lyme disease. The increasing prevalence of this disease in some locations stems, at least in part, from the suburbanization that moved human settlement into areas where human beings previously did not live. This human development brought people into closer contact with animals that carry the tick-borne bacteria that cause the disease at the same time that these processes eliminated the natural predators of deer, one of the major carriers of the disease. In short, human development activities unsettled an ecological balance that allowed the microbes that carry the Lyme disease–causing bacteria to thrive at the same time that it contributed to an increase of the animal populations that serve as vectors for this illness. As these examples illustrate, understanding the links among the environment, ecology, and human health is essential in any examination of global public health.

Drinking Water, the Environment, and Global Health

Access to clean water is a fundamental determinant of human health. The creation of public water systems, water treatment mechanisms, and public sewers has cut down on deadly waterborne illnesses and saved countless lives; these public health interventions are among the most important of the 20th century. Unfortunately, much of the world's population does not have access to clean water or adequate sanitation. Globally, over 1 billion people—roughly 16 percent of the world's population—do not have access to improved water. Almost 40 percent—2.6 billion people—do not have access to improved sanitation.[32]

Not surprisingly, unsafe water supplies and inadequate sanitation are major causes of illness and mortality worldwide. The statistics are sobering. According to WHO estimates, diarrhea causes approximately 1.8 million deaths across the globe each year. Almost 40,000 people in the developing world die *each week* due to lack of access to clean water.[33] The great majority of these cases—88 percent—are caused by unsafe water, sanitation, or hygiene. Most of the fatalities are among children, and almost all of these cases occur in the developing world.[34] Unsafe water supplies and inadequate sanitation are major causes of other illnesses, including scabies, typhoid fever, and trachoma, and

UNDER THE MICROSCOPE

Corn-fed Agriculture and the Diseases of Globalization

Not all cases of ecological disruption involve microbes. Indeed, some of the most widespread and significant health problems resulting from ecological disruptions involve noncommunicable illnesses. A prominent example involves the growth of large-scale industrialized agriculture, which has had fundamental consequences for human health across the globe. The ascendance of corn as a dominant monoculture crop in American agriculture provides a profound illustration of the far-reaching effects of industrialized agriculture. Due to a complicated set of factors—including mechanization leading to the displacement of labor-intensive small farms with large corporate farms, government policies that subsidize the production of corn over other crops, genetic engineering that increases yield, and consumer preferences—a corporate model of monoculture agriculture has led commodity corn to dominate much of the American agriculture landscape. In the first part of the 20th century, a typical American farm had multiple crops and animal species. Today, small-scale farms have been largely displaced by large agribusinesses that produce more and more corn and soybeans and less of everything else.[a]

The dominance of commodity corn in the agricultural landscape of the United States has had numerous effects on the environment and far-reaching consequences for human health.[b] This water-intensive model of agriculture depletes and pollutes local water supplies with the resultant ill effects on human health. The processes that led to the dominance of monoculture farming have contributed to the aggregation of farms and displaced small-scale farmers in the United States, undermining the viability of many small towns in agricultural regions and affecting community health in these areas. Moreover, the subsidization of large-scale farming in the United States makes it difficult for farmers in developing countries to compete on a global scale, thereby exacerbating poverty-related health problems in rural areas across the globe.

Because the commodity corn that is produced is generally not suitable for human consumption, it is used primarily as feed for meat-producing cattle. In turn, because this

[a]Michael Pollan, *The Omnivore's Dilemma: A Natural History of Four Meals* (New York: Penguin Press, 2006): 27–28.

[b]*Ibid.*: 15–119.

diseases caused by parasites, including Ascaris, Trichuris, and hookworm.[35]

One of the paradoxes of efforts to improve public health infrastructure in the developing world is that an improvement in one area may have negative health consequences in other respects. Take the example of major water development projects, such as dam construction. Such projects may have important, if indirect, health benefits. Foremost among these benefits, dam construction expands access to hydroelectricity, which has a number commodity corn is so inexpensive, it has contributed to the emergence of large-scale factory-farmed meat as the primary source of meat in the United States and elsewhere. Large-scale factory-farmed meat leads to air and water pollution from animal waste. Factory-farmed animals are routinely treated with antibiotics due to the prevalence of bacterial illnesses that result from their poor and unsanitary living conditions. The combined effect of this antibiotic use and the water and air pollution resulting from the waste of factory-farmed animals is an increase in the prevalence of bacterial illnesses such as *E. coli* in humans.[c]

Additionally, the large-scale production of meat contributes to global warming; the methane produced by cattle is a bigger contributor to climate change than either the exhaust produced by all modes of transportation (air travel, trains, automobiles) globally or the effects of industry.[d] Finally, this industrialization of agriculture, especially the emergence of commodity corn as a predominant species, has harmed human health by facilitating the expansion of a fast-food diet throughout much of the world. Subsidized commodity corn is used in a number of ways that have detrimental effects on human health. It is the primary feed for the mass-produced meat used in fast-food burgers. It is used to produce high-fructose corn syrup, an ingredient in countless food products, including soda, candy, snack foods, bread, cereals, and even meat.[e] These foods are calorie-rich and inexpensive, which may partially explain their popularity. However, they have serious negative effects on human health and have contributed significantly to the spike in obesity, diabetes, and heart disease in developing and developed countries.

This growing dominance of corn in the industrialized agricultural system in the United States clearly illustrates the ways in which ecological disruptions can have consequences for human health on a global scale. Advances in human technology, economic incentives, government policy, and consumer preferences have combined to create a dramatic shift in the agricultural landscape in the United States. However, the effects of this change extend far beyond local ecosystems in rural areas in the United States. Rather, these changes have altered both rural and urban landscapes across the globe and have contributed to the rise in the diseases of globalization in developing and developed countries.

---

[c] *Ibid.*: 67–79.

[d] Nathan Fiala, "The Greenhouse Hamburger," *Scientific American* 300: 2 (2009): 72–75.

[e] Pollan: 103–104.

of health benefits: (1) it can be used to facilitate the kind of economic development that is correlated with better health outcomes, (2) it can contribute to the development of public health infrastructure (like hospitals), and (3) it can be used to expand access to clean water, for instance, by facilitating the creation and running of water treatment facilities.

The upside of such water development projects is often undermined by negative, if unexpected, health consequences. For example, the Aswan High Dam project in Egypt in the 1950s ultimately led to an increase in schistosomiasis, a parasitic disease with symptoms ranging from mild fatigue to life-threatening heart disease, epilepsy, kidney failure, or cancer.[36] This unintended consequence occurred, at least in part, because international actors promoting the project did not consider the ecological effects of the dam, which slowed the flow of the Nile and led to environmental conditions favoring a species of schistosome parasites that cause more serious disease. Similar ecological changes with ill-health effects for local populations occurred with the construction of the Sennar Dam in the Sudan and the Akosombo Dam in Ghana in the 1970s.[37] These cautionary examples illustrate that efforts to promote public health must consider the ecological foundations of human health.

Although the global burden of disease stemming from waterborne risk factors is significantly higher in the developing world, waterborne illness is also a major problem in the developed world. Serious, often debilitating, and sometimes deadly outbreaks of waterborne illness still occur in developed countries. For example, deadly outbreaks of cryptosporidium, toxoplasma, and E. coli have occurred in recent decades in the United States. In addition to non-water-related causes (including contaminated meat), inadequate or deteriorating water treatment facilities and waste runoff from industrialized meat operations that pollute the water supply have contributed to such outbreaks.

Outbreaks of waterborne disease have been exacerbated by basic evolutionary processes. For instance, water treatment practices, which have done so much to improve health outcomes in the developed and the developing world, have also led to new problems. Chlorine-resistant forms of various pathogens, including E. coli and cryptosporidium, have emerged. These evolved pathogens circumvent existing water treatment efforts and signal the possibility that more virulent forms of waterborne microbes may emerge.[38] This reality again underscores the importance of the concept of ecological

balance—in this case, *microbial ecological balance*. Human efforts to improve access to clean water alter ecosystems *at the microbial level* by killing off certain strains of pathogens and by creating an environment in which other, more deadly strains may thrive. Ultimately, these ecological processes may generate new threats to clean water.

The threat of chlorine-resistant pathogens underscores the need for effective water filtration and sewage treatment. However, the fact that much of the public health infrastructure in developed countries is aging heightens the risk that waterborne illnesses may be a growing problem in the developed and the developing world. For instance, in the United States, much of the underground water and sewage infrastructure, which provides the public with access to clean water and effective sanitation, is over one hundred years old and in need of repair or replacement. Damaged and deteriorating pipes have led to the spilling of human waste into lakes, streams, and other natural bodies of water and, in doing so, have contaminated the country's supply of drinking water.[39] Replacing this infrastructure would cost hundreds of billions of dollars. It will be incredibly difficult for the U.S. government to generate the necessary support for funding such ambitious public infrastructure programs, especially in an era of economic downturn.[40]

Waterborne pathogens are not the only threat in the nexus between drinking water and human health. Industrial activities throughout the developed and the developing world produce chemicals. These waterborne toxins pose serious threats to human health. Negative consequences include short-term health problems, including nausea, vomiting, and lung irritation. Industrial water pollution can also cause chronic conditions, including cancer, birth defects, liver and kidney damage, and immunological problems.[41] A prominent example of a waterborne environmental risk factor involves mercury contamination of major water sources due to industrial activity. Mercury exposure

UNDER THE MICROSCOPE

The Negative Health Consequences of Bottled Water

Bottled water is marketed as a healthy, clean, and safe choice of drinking water. Millions of people across the globe drink bottled water every day, often believing that they are making a healthy choice when they do so. Sales of bottled water have become a major business, with estimates suggesting that bottled water generated almost $80 billion in global sales in 2009. Industry projections suggest that global sales might reach $100 billion by 2014.[a] Americans alone consume more than 7 billion gallons of bottled water annually, an amount that leads them to dispose of almost 50 million water bottles every day.[b]

Despite marketing claims to the contrary, drinking bottled water has many problematic effects on public health. For one thing, bottled water is typically just tap water and, in most countries, does not have to meet higher safety standards than those for basic tap water. Indeed, bottled water is not generally covered by the same regulatory schemes as tap water.[c] Moreover, plastic water bottles contain potentially harmful chemicals that may contribute to numerous health problems, including diabetes and cancer.[d]

Furthermore, the production of bottled water has major negative environmental and health effects. The production of water bottles requires massive amounts of plastic—2 billion pounds per year. In turn, the production of all this plastic requires millions of barrels of oil and an immense amount of water, more than the amount of bottled drinking water being generated. Moreover, this process produces toxic waste as well as an incredible amount of trash in the form of the bottles themselves.[e]

Thus, the belief that bottled water is a healthier alternative to tap water is generally a misguided one. So long as people have access to an improved water source, tap water will usually be just as safe as bottled water. Exceptions to this generalization would be in areas without access to improved water, in conflict zones, or in locations where water treatment facilities have been compromised due to a natural disaster.

---

[a]*Bottled Water: Global Industry Guide—New Market Research Report* (April 12, 2011). A summary of the highlights of the report is available online at: http://news.wooeb.com/NewsStory.aspx?id=720100.

[b]Robert D. Morris, *The Blue Death: Disease, Disaster, and the Water We Drink* (New York: HarperCollins Publishers, 2007): 285–286.

[c]*Ibid.*

[d]David Biello, "Plastic (Not) Fantastic: Food Containers Leach a Potentially Harmful Chemical," *Scientific American*, February 19, 2008.

[e]*Ibid.*

contributes to a range of health problems, most notably potential neurodevelopmental delays in infants born to mothers consuming contaminated seafood.[42]

It is apt to conclude this section with the words of Dr. Robert D. Morris, an environmental epidemiologist specializing in the field of drinking water and health:

> If we do not provide pure water and sanitation for the world's poor, their misery and disease will make their way to our doorstep. If we do not take on the difficult, politically treacherous task of developing realistic plans for sustainable water supplies, we will find a world at war over water. If we do not take on the stewardship of our planet with evangelistic fervor, we will accumulate an ecological budget deficit that future generations can never repay.[43]

Health outcomes throughout the developed and developing world depend on access to clean water, a resource that is threatened by human activities that contaminate the environment and disrupt ecological balance in various ecosystems. Ultimately, this objective requires us to *think globally* in every sense of the word. We must be attentive to the ecological processes that shape the microbial world as well as the economic, political, and social processes that lead to interdependence among people across the globe, whether they are wealthy or poor or whether they live in developed or developing countries.

Climate Change and Global Health

According to a recent report commissioned by the *Lancet*, climate change is the biggest global health threat in the 21st century. In a general sense, *climate change* simply refers to any significant, long-term change in global temperature and weather patterns. Climate change can have natural or human causes. In the present era, climate change, also known as *global warming*, refers to the expected increase in average global temperatures by several degrees in the coming decades and the resultant changes in weather patterns. Doctors and climatologists who collaborated on the *Lancet* report concluded that climate change will exacerbate almost every health problem imaginable.[44]

The WHO echoed these warnings in a December 2009 report on global health risks. The WHO has identified numerous potential health risks stemming from climate change, including deaths from thermal extremes and weather-related disasters (tornadoes, hurricanes, floods, and tsunamis), an increase in waterborne illnesses and infectious diseases, growing mortality and illness due to a lack of access to clean water and sufficient food, and a higher incidence of injury and death in violent conflict over increasingly scarce resources.[45]

Although the WHO concurs with the *Lancet* report in identifying climate change as a serious threat to global health, its current data do not yet support a claim that climate change is *the* biggest global health threat. Indeed, the top five risks of mortality across the globe—high blood pressure, tobacco use, high blood glucose, physical inactivity, and obesity—are noncommunicable illnesses that are not related to global warming.[46] Nevertheless, the WHO has concluded that climate change is already responsible for a significant number of deaths globally. According to WHO estimates, roughly 3 percent of deaths from diarrhea, 3 percent of deaths from malaria, and almost 4 percent of deaths from dengue fever in 2004 can be attributed to climate change. Overall, the WHO estimates that 0.2 percent of deaths worldwide in 2004 could be attributed to climate change. Notably, 85 percent of these deaths were among children.[47] As these figures illustrate, children are most likely to be harmed by health threats stemming from climate change, as is generally the case with environmental threats to health. Furthermore, it is expected that lower-income countries will be hit hardest by climate change due to ongoing struggles with scarce resources and the absence of strong public health infrastructure.

Although current data do not yet appear to support the claim that climate change is the single biggest public health threat of the 21st century, the WHO acknowledges that it is hard to quantify the health consequences of climate change. Furthermore, there is evidence that the dire predictions in the *Lancet* report have already begun to manifest themselves. Viral diseases that were previously limited to tropical areas are starting to show up in new regions due to an increase in average temperatures in these areas. For example, an outbreak of chikungunya, a viral disease transmitted by Asian tiger mosquitoes, occurred in northern Italy in 2007. This disease, which is related to dengue fever, is typically limited to tropical areas in the Indian Ocean region. Its emergence in northern Italy represents the first case of a tropical disease epidemic in a developed European country.[48] As this case illustrates, climate change has expanded the habitat of Asian tiger mosquitoes into southern Europe, where they are now thriving. As average temperatures warm, mosquitoes can be expected to expand their range, and an increase in mosquito-borne illness will be an inevitable result. Thus, illnesses once considered "tropical," such as chikungunya and dengue fever, are likely to spread to areas where they have not previously been seen.

Malaria represents another interesting case in this regard. Historically, malaria has not been limited to the tropics. This parasitic disease was present in temperate zones in Europe and the United States until it was eradicated through the spraying of dichloro-diphenyl-trichloroethane (DDT) and the draining of wetlands. Malaria is a debilitating and often deadly disease that is endemic to over 100 countries. In 2007, malaria was expected to infect approximately 50 million people, roughly 1 million of whom would die. Most malarial deaths are in children under five.[49] Malaria is most prevalent in much of Africa, and its most devastating effects are likely to strike the poor, as they do not have access to antimalarial medications and treatments and often live far from medical facilities where they can seek treatment. The parasite has developed resistance to many of the drugs used

to treat it. In the process, it has mutated in ways that have led to the emergence of more virulent and deadly strains. The WHO has prioritized malaria as a pressing global health problem, and the Bill and Melinda Gates Foundation has channeled millions of dollars to fight the disease. Unfortunately, climate change may add a new obstacle to the global fight against malaria. With global warming, there is a risk that mosquitoes carrying the malaria parasite will expand their range, reintroducing the disease to areas where it has been eradicated and compounding a health problem that is already one of the most serious global health challenges.[50]

There is also concern that climate change will increase the incidence of waterborne illnesses. Cholera provides a frightening example. Rising water temperatures create environmental conditions that allow cholera bacteria to thrive. Increased flooding due to global warming also creates conditions that favor the cholera bacterium. Under these conditions, cholera populations are more likely to survive, and human populations living in low-coastal areas are more likely to be exposed to these deadly bacteria.[51] Cholera is a preventable and treatable disease. Proper sanitation measures can prevent human-to-human transmission, and antibiotics can be used to treat infected people. Thus, major cholera outbreaks are not likely to occur in developed areas with a strong public health infrastructure. However, increased exposure to cholera bacteria among poor populations living in areas without access to clean water, good sanitation systems, and effective treatments could lead to serious outbreaks of this deadly disease.

Global warming also may lead to an increased number of deaths and injuries from catastrophic storms and weather-related disasters, including tornadoes, tsunamis, hurricanes, and floods. These storms are often described as natural disasters. The implication of describing these weather-related disasters as natural is that they are seen as being beyond human control. However, human influences may shape the frequency and intensity of such storms. By increasing the temperatures of both the atmosphere and water and by raising sea levels and reducing natural barriers that protect coastlines, climate change may contribute to the conditions that produce catastrophic storms. Scientists argue that in addition to affecting atmospheric and water temperatures that produce serious storms, climate change also has the potential to increase the number of earthquakes, avalanches, and volcanic eruptions as melting glaciers destabilize the earth's geology.[52]

The climate change/global health nexus provides a fundamental illustration of the ecological foundations of human health. Human economic and social activities are one of the primary causes of global warming. Human industrial activities, agricultural practices, and consumption patterns have played a major role in generating the greenhouse gases that exacerbate climate change. The increase in average temperatures and the resultant shift in weather patterns have significantly disrupted the ecological balance in local, regional, and global ecosystems. As a result, pathogens that previously had been isolated in particular ecosystems are now expanding their range and exposing human beings to new or reemerging illnesses. Climate change is leading to greater food and water scarcity in specific environments, making it more likely that violent conflict over scarce resources will lead to an increase in death and injury in conflict zones. Many scientists have also predicted an increase in injuries and deaths from weather-related disasters. In short, human health cannot be separated from the health of the global environment. Whether climate change becomes the biggest global health threat of the 21st century remains to be seen. Regardless, climate change certainly poses a major challenge to global health that must be addressed by proponents of public health at the local, national, and global levels.

Conclusion

The concept of ecological balance underscores the theme of the interconnectedness of human health. Human health in one area of the world is affected by the economic and social practices of human populations elsewhere around the world as well as the public policies of various governments. Human health is also interconnected with the animal, plant, and microbial worlds. Ecological disruptions to one part of an ecosystem may ultimately have important health consequences for human beings. Thus, one cannot fully understand or promote global public health in an effective way without paying attention to the fundamental ways in which human health is connected to the health of the environments in which people live and the extent to which there is ecological balance among all of the animals, plants, and even microbes that coexist with humans in these ecosystems.

Human health has been grounded in an ecological context throughout history. The ecological foundations of human health have become even more important in an era of globalization. As noted by political scientist Dennis C. Pirages:

> The dynamics of contemporary globalization are linking together peoples, pathogens, and ecosystems that historically have been separated by geographic, political, and cultural barriers. Although there has always been a limited "natural" movement of organisms among the world's diverse ecosystems, the contemporary flow of people, plants, pests, and pathogens through ever more porous borders is producing a planetary mixing of unprecedented magnitude. This growing ecological globalization holds significant consequences for the future well-being of the human race.[53]

Human health has always been inseparable from the health of the ecosystems in which people live. With globalization, the fact that humans live in a *global ecosystem* becomes a more pressing reality.

Because we live in a globalizing world, human health is increasingly being shaped by global forces as well as local forces. Therefore, one cannot isolate the study and promotion of human health from the health of other living beings in the ecosystems in which humans live. Humans ignore the effects of their behaviors and activities on local, regional, and global ecosystems at their own peril.

Discussion Questions

1. For the purpose of exploring the connections between the environment and health, how should the concept of the *environment* be defined? What are the relative advantages and disadvantages of different definitions?
2. How do the concepts of the *environment* and *ecology* differ? What is the relationship between these two concepts?
3. What is the concept of *ecological balance*? How is it connected to human health?
4. What are some of the major human causes of disruption to ecological balance? How have these disruptions affected human health?
5. What are the "diseases of globalization"? How have ecological changes contributed to the spread of the diseases of globalization?
6. How does the issue of access to clean water illustrate the connections among environmental health, ecological balance, and human health?

7. Why do some scientists argue that climate change is the most important global health challenge of the 21st century? Do you agree with their thinking? Why or why not?
8. Some of the health effects of climate change are not quantifiable. Moreover, many of these health problems are predicted to increase in the future but are not necessarily reflected in the current global burden of disease. Do the limitations of providing accurate current data about the connections between health and global warming undermine the argument that climate change is a serious threat to global health? Why or why not?

Web Resources

Center for Health and the Global Environment: http://chge.med.harvard.edu/

Gateway to the UN System's Work on Climate Change: http://www.un.org/wcm/content/site/climatechange/

World Health Organization Department of Public Health and the Environment: http://www.who.int/phe/en/index.html

World Health Organization Programme on Climate Change and Human Health: http://www.who.int/globalchange/en/

World Water Council: http://www.worldwater council.org/

PART II

Medical Aspects of Global Health

CHAPTER 4

Global Health and Communicable Diseases

Introduction

This chapter examines communicable diseases as transnational threats to human health. The chapter begins by introducing students to basic concepts of microbiology, including routes of disease transmission and critical issues pertaining to disease treatment and prevention. The chapter then provides an overview of the global burden of communicable diseases. Next, the chapter reviews the emerging threat of antimicrobial resistance and highlights the complex interplay of individual, social, and environmental factors in contributing to this problem. The chapter concludes with an in-depth examination of three communicable diseases: human immunodeficiency virus (HIV)/acquired immunodeficiency syndrome (AIDS), tuberculosis, and influenza. A recurring theme throughout the chapter is that communicable diseases do not recognize national borders and, as a result, require transnational collaboration to effectively deal with the threat they pose to global health.

Introduction to Microbiology

Definitions and Basic Concepts

A microorganism is a life form that is invisible to the unaided eye. There are several classes of microorganisms, specifically, viruses, bacteria, fungi, and protozoa. Potential pathogenic (disease-causing) microorganisms can be transmitted from one individual to another by one of several modes of transmission. In many instances, potential pathogens merely *colonize* the host without causing illness. However, when a pathogenic organism resides in a host body site at levels high enough to overcome the host's immune system, disease is the result. The severity of the disease depends on the virulence of the invading microorganism, the health status of the host, and the host's access to timely and effective treatment.[1]

Although illnesses caused by microorganisms contribute significantly to the global burden of disease, microorganisms also perform many vital functions that help sustain higher life forms. For example, microorganisms aid in maintaining the oxygen level in the atmosphere. Moreover, the mere existence of a microorganism within another life form is not synonymous with disease. Many microorganisms, referred to as *normal floras*, live in specific sites of higher organisms (such as the bacteria that reside in the mouths, gastrointestinal tracts, or upper respiratory tracts of humans) and cause no adverse effects. In fact, these normal floras sometimes benefit the host organism by competing with other potential pathogenic bacteria for key nutrients, thereby preventing the pathogenic organisms from establishing residence at levels high enough to induce disease. However, normal floras may also cause disease if they enter a typically sterile site of the body. As an example, the normal floras of the gastrointestinal tract may cause severe illness in the host if they relocate to other areas of the abdominal cavity as the result of some trauma.[2]

Viruses are a group of agents that are only able to replicate inside the living cells of other organisms; made up of only genetic information in the form of either deoxyribonucleic acid (DNA) or ribonucleic acid (RNA), a protein coat, and sometimes a lipid membrane, these agents are not themselves cells. Once it has infected a host cell, a virus is able to direct that cell to produce new copies of viral material, most often with resultant injury or death to the host cell. Viruses account for the largest proportion of communicable diseases worldwide. Much of this illness is mild in severity. For example, viruses are the causative agents in the vast majority of upper respiratory tract infections (URTIs)—the "common cold." Viruses also cause many other typically benign, self-limited conditions, such as conjunctivitis (pinkeye), mild forms of diarrhea, and varicella (chicken pox). Viral agents such as HIV, hepatitis B virus (HBV), hepatitis C virus (HCV), and human papillomavirus (HPV) are responsible for other illnesses associated with much greater morbidity and mortality. Respectively, these viruses can lead to the development of AIDS, chronic hepatitis, liver cancer or failure, and cervical or penile cancer in infected individuals. Most viral agents, particularly those that cause benign illnesses such as URTIs, do not respond to currently available antimicrobial agents. For some viral agents, however, antiviral agents that have been developed for clinical use exist. Importantly, these include therapies available for the treatment of infections due to HIV, HBV, and HCV as well as herpes virus.

Unlike viruses, the other microbial classes are made up of organisms that are single- or multicelled agents able to replicate independently of another living organism. **Bacteria** are single-celled microbes that are considered prokaryotic, meaning that, unlike higher life forms, their genetic material is not contained in a true nuclear membrane. For the purposes of this text, it is more important to emphasize that bacteria are microorganisms that are able to replicate themselves independently of a host and that they do so quite rapidly, on the order of minutes.[3] Additionally, bacteria tend to be the microorganisms against which most clinically available antimicrobials are active. Examples of infectious diseases caused by bacteria include many cases of pneumonia and meningitis as well as tuberculosis.

Fungi and **protozoa** are microbiologically distinct from bacteria in that they are considered eukaryotic, meaning their genetic material is contained by a nuclear membrane; they can be single-celled (protozoa) or multicelled (fungi) organisms.[4] Like bacteria, they are able to self-replicate and are responsive to clinically available antimicrobial agents. Examples of diseases caused by fungi include benign conditions such as tinea corporis (ringworm) and vaginal candidiasis (vaginal yeast infection) and more significant diseases including lung infections caused by organisms such as histoplasmosis. Examples of conditions due to protozoa include certain subacute and chronic diarrheal illnesses as well as trichomoniasis, a sexually transmitted infection.

Additionally, disease may result from host infection by multicellular parasites that live inside their hosts and infect a range of body parts, including blood, skin, the intestines, and lymph vessels. As these organisms are large enough to be observed by the naked eye during certain stages of their life cycle, they are technically not considered microorganisms. They are mentioned here, however, because they are an important cause of communicable illnesses globally. Examples of organisms in these classes include tapeworms and flatworms. Disease burden from these organisms tends to be more significant in developing countries due to poor sanitation and inadequate public health infrastructure, among other factors.

A final concept relevant to the host-microbial interaction is that of the immune-compromised host. Immune-competent individuals combat infectious agents through several barrier

---

DISEASE-CAUSING MICROORGANISMS

Bacteria: single-celled microbes, with genetic material that is not contained by a nuclear membrane, that are able to rapidly reproduce themselves independently of a living host.

Fungi: multicelled microorganisms, the genetic material of which is contained by a nuclear membrane, that are able to replicate independently of a living host.

Protozoa: single-celled microorganisms, the genetic material of which is contained by a nuclear membrane, that are able to replicate independently of a living host.

Viruses: a group of agents that are only able to replicate inside the cells of living organisms and that cause illness by directing infected cells to produce new copies of viral material, typically resulting in death or injury to the host cell.

---

mechanisms, primarily intact and functioning dermatological and immune systems. Any condition that disrupts the integrity of these systems makes an individual more vulnerable to communicable diseases. Although any microorganism is likely to establish active infection in such a host, many infectious agents tend to occur only in immune-compromised individuals, causing what are called **opportunistic infections**. For example, many fungal agents are innocuous to a healthy individual but can lead to overwhelming infections such as pneumonia and meningitis in the immune-compromised host. Further, agents that are able to cause infection in any host, regardless of immune status, tend to lead to more severe and difficult-to-treat illnesses in an immune-compromised host. As an example, tuberculosis can lead to greater morbidity and mortality in individuals who are immune-compromised due to HIV.

Routes of Communicable Disease Transmission

Communicable diseases can be transmitted from one individual to another through various routes, as summarized in Table 4.1.[5]

Most modes of transmission are *horizontal*, meaning they pass from one individual to another, as opposed to *vertical* transmission, which involves the passage of an infectious agent from mother to fetus. Important examples of infectious agents that can be transmitted vertically include HIV and HBV. Communicable diseases can also be classified as zoonotic in nature, meaning they are spread to humans from contact with infected animals. Rabies and Lyme disease are examples. Communicable disease prevention strategies are rooted in an understanding of these routes of transmission.

Microorganisms can be spread via respiratory droplets expelled from one individual (usually via coughing or sneezing) and then inhaled directly by another individual. Tuberculosis is a disease that results from such transmission. Respiratory spread can also occur indirectly through contact with an object contaminated with a respiratory droplet, such as a viral URTI being transmitted via an individual whose hand has touched a contaminated surface. Communicable diseases may also be spread via contact with saliva that contains pathogenic microorganisms. Infectious mononucleosis is a typically benign condition

TABLE 4.1 Routes of Transmission for Communicable Diseases

Route of transmission	Disease examples
Respiratory spread	Influenza, tuberculosis
Salivary spread	Infectious mononucleosis, rabies
Fecal-oral spread	Infectious diarrhea
Skin-to-skin transfer	Syphilis, impetigo
Blood-borne transmission	Hepatitis B virus infection, HIV
Genital tract transmission	HIV, herpes simplex virus
Eye-to-eye transmission	Trachoma
Zoonotic transmission	Lyme disease, rabies
Vertical transmission	Hepatitis B virus infection, HIV

Source: Adapted from L. Corey, "Epidemiology of Infectious Diseases," in John C. Sherris, ed., *Medical Microbiology: An Introduction to Infectious Diseases,* 2d ed. (New York: Elsevier, 1990): 184.

transmitted in this manner. Viral URTIs are commonly spread in this fashion. Rabies, a less common but far more severe illness, is transmitted to a human via saliva from the bite of an infected animal. Infection can also spread when contaminated eye secretions from one individual are introduced into the eye of another. Benign viral conjunctivitis is one example of this. Blindness resulting from infection of the eye with *Chlamydia* (a disease called trachoma) is also spread in this manner.

Infectious diseases also can be transmitted by the fecal-oral route, whereby pathogenic microorganisms contained in the fecal matter of one individual are ingested by another individual, typically by drinking from contaminated water supplies. The majority of diarrheal illnesses globally are transmitted in this fashion, most notably in regions with limited access to clean drinking water. Fecal-oral disease transmission can also occur through the consumption of contaminated food, especially when food handlers do not observe proper hand-washing techniques. Certain diseases, such as syphilis, are transmitted via direct skin-to-skin contact. Additionally, the viral agent that causes chicken pox is transmitted from the skin of an infected individual to the respiratory tract of another via droplets from the skin that become aerosolized. Lastly, the skin can be a portal of entry for organisms such as helminthes that reside in soil contaminated by fecal waste, an issue more common in developing countries. Blood-borne transmission of communicable disease occurs when contaminated blood from an infected individual is introduced into the bloodstream of another individual, with the sharing of needles used for illicit drug use being an example. HIV, HCV, and HBV can be transmitted in this manner. Several microbes, such as HIV,

TYPES OF DISEASE AND INFECTIONS

Nosocomial Infections: infections acquired during an admission to an acute health care facility or while residing in a chronic care facility.

Opportunistic Infections: infections that tend to occur in only immune-compromised individuals.

Zoonotic Disease: a disease resulting from a pathogen that is mutated in ways that enable it to be transmitted from animals to humans.

HBV, and *Chlamydia*, are transmitted sexually via genital secretions.

Obviously, many microorganisms can be spread by more than one route. As previously noted, HIV and HBV can be transmitted by the blood-borne route as well as contact with contaminated genital secretions. Rabies, a **zoonotic disease**, is passed from an infected animal to a human via contaminated saliva. In discussing disease transmission, it is also important to consider the location where an infection was acquired. Although many communicable diseases result from the spread of microorganisms in the community setting, others are acquired during an admission to an acute health care facility or while residing in a chronic care facility. These **nosocomial infections** are important in that they are more likely to be associated with antimicrobial-resistant organisms. Their occurrence also highlights the importance of infection-control measures in health care facilities.

Antimicrobial Therapy

With the discovery of penicillin in 1929 by Alexander Fleming and the subsequent demonstration of its clinical utility in the 1940s, the era of antimicrobial therapy was born. This revolution in medicine led to a dramatic decline in morbidity and mortality associated with communicable diseases. By definition, true antibiotics are produced biologically by molds and bacteria. As those medications currently used in clinical practice to treat infectious agents are produced synthetically rather than biologically, the term *antimicrobial agent* is more appropriate. The majority of antimicrobial drugs in clinical use are those that are active against bacteria. However, antimicrobial agents that help treat and control infection due to protozoa, fungi, and, to a lesser extent, viral agents such as HIV, HCV, and HBV also exist.

There are two basic classes of clinically available antimicrobials: **broad-spectrum antimicrobials**, which are effective against a large number of organisms, and **narrow-spectrum antimicrobials**, which treat a much smaller group of organisms. Therapy with a broad-spectrum agent when the symptoms suggest that a narrow-spectrum drug would likely be adequate can contribute to the problem of antimicrobial resistance. Therefore, appropriate use of these more potent agents is critical in efforts to slow the growth of this problem.

The judicious use of antimicrobials is also critical due to the risk of secondary infections that may emerge in the treated host. Even when used appropriately, antimicrobials not only affect the targeted pathogenic microbe but also may suppress the normal floras of the host. As these normal floras often compete against potential pathogens and, thus, suppress infection, their disruption may make the host vulnerable to additional infections. A classic example is the suppression of the normal gastrointestinal floras in a hospitalized patient treated with antimicrobials for a bacterial pneumonia. The patient may then become susceptible to infection of the gastrointestinal tract with the bacterium that causes a nosocomial colitis (infection of the colon), a condition with high morbidity and fatality in severe cases.[6]

Notably, regular access to effective antimicrobial therapy is not uniform across countries or people. Low-income populations in both developed and developing countries often have limited access to health care services. Low levels of national economic development are also associated with underfunded regulatory authorities and poor handling and manufacturing practices that can yield substandard antimicrobials.[7] Additionally, there is a large number of individuals who sell medicine illegally in many low- and middle-income countries.[8] The net effect of these factors is that many individuals in these countries take incomplete courses of often poor-quality antimicrobials, a significant risk for the emergence of antimicrobial resistance. A similar dynamic shapes health-seeking behavior of people in high-income countries who do not have access to affordable health care. In such circumstances, people may not complete the recommended course of antimicrobial therapy in order to "save" expensive medicines (and to avoid additional doctor's visits) in the event of future illness, thereby contributing to the rise in antimicrobial-resistant pathogens.

Vaccinations

The control of communicable diseases with vaccination programs represents one of the greatest public health achievements in modern history. The World Health Organization's (WHO) Smallpox Eradication Program was launched in 1967. In 1977, the single last natural case of smallpox was seen in Somalia, and a final laboratory-acquired fatality occurred in the United Kingdom in 1978.[9] In ten years, this program effectively eradicated one of the major communicable disease contributors to global morbidity and mortality. Similar vaccination programs have markedly reduced the global incidence of poliomyelitis (polio), a common cause of irreversible paralysis, with only four countries (Afghanistan, India, Nigeria, and Pakistan) having significant levels of disease in 2008, down from 125 countries in 1988.[10]

Vaccination programs take advantage of **herd immunity** to effect eradication of disease. Herd immunity is based on the concept that, for those organisms spread by person-to-person contact, it is not necessary to immunize every individual in the community to stop transmission of that organism. Rather, a certain level of prevalence of immunity in the community makes it difficult for that organism to spread to nonimmune, susceptible hosts. Thus, although vaccination of every individual in a community is the ideal goal of an eradication program, a more realistic target is the vaccination of as many individuals within a community as possible.

Individuals combat disease largely through the function of the immune system. When exposed to an infectious microbe, the immune system is triggered to produce cells and chemicals that lead to the control and, ultimately, death of those organisms. In addition to host survival, one result of the successful eradication of an invading organism is the development in the host of **active immunity**, whereby antibodies and "memory cells" are created that are primed to attack those same organisms should they again invade in the future. Vaccinations borrow from this concept to induce **passive immunity** in a host. When only a portion of a microorganism or an attenuated variant of a live pathogenic microbe is injected, the host is triggered to develop immunity to that organism without having to first experience a disease state. Such vaccination practices are associated with known adverse effects—including fever, local swelling, and pain—though most of them are minor to moderate in severity. Rarely, more serious or life-threatening reactions may occur, such as vaccine-associated polio with attenuated live poliovirus vaccines. Informed patient or parental decision making must weigh the risk of these rare but potentially serious adverse events against the greater likelihood of morbidity and mortality resulting from naturally occurring illness due to these microorganisms.

Several obstacles prevent the widespread use of all clinically available vaccinations. In developing countries, economic factors limit the availability of vaccinations. As an example, of the estimated 27 million children not vaccinated worldwide in 2003, 9.46 million were from the WHO African Region and 9.56 million were from the WHO South-East Asia Region, compared with 1.48 million from the WHO Region of the Americas.[11] Further, market forces negatively affect the development and uptake of new vaccinations in low- and middle-income countries more so than in high-income nations.[12] In both developed

KEY TERMS IN IMMUNITY AND SUSCEPTIBILITY TO COMMUNICABLE ILLNESSES

Active Immunity: a form of immunity in which a host is exposed to a microorganism and develops antibodies and "memory cells" that are primed to attack those same organisms should they invade again in the future.

Antigenic Drift: minor mutations in a virus that make the virus less vulnerable to a host's immune response and can lead to local or regional outbreaks of illness.

Antigenic Shift: major mutations in a virus that make the virus significantly less vulnerable to a host's immune response and can lead to pandemics.

Broad-spectrum Antimicrobials: antimicrobials that are effective against a large number of organisms.

Herd Immunity: immunity that is achieved in a community when a certain level of prevalence of immunity makes it difficult for a microorganism to spread to nonimmune, susceptible hosts.

Narrow-spectrum Antimicrobials: antimicrobials that are effective against a small group of organisms.

Passive Immunity: a form of immunity induced by vaccinations whereby a portion or weakened version of a microorganism is introduced into a host that leads to the development of antibodies and "memory cells" that are primed to attack the targeted microorganisms should they invade again in the future.

and developing countries, public buy-in plays a critical role in determining the effectiveness of vaccination initiatives. Public fears about negative health effects of vaccinations (both perceived and real) and skepticism about the motivations of public health actors can reduce vaccination rates in particular countries and communities.

To ensure the continued success of global vaccination programs, governments and the pharmaceutical industry will need to collaborate to support the development and distribution of vaccinations to all countries and to educate the general public about the potential benefits and harms of vaccinations. It also will be essential for policy makers, medical professionals, and public health practitioners to be familiar with the cultural and social contexts in which they are operating, in order to understand the concerns and perspectives of target communities, to take into account legitimate concerns about vaccinations (especially relatively new and untested vaccines), and to increase the likelihood of the necessary levels of participation in vaccination programs to achieve the desired herd immunity.

UNDER THE MICROSCOPE

Public Resistance to Vaccination Campaigns

In both developed and developing countries, utilization is determined to a significant degree by public acceptance of vaccinations. The recent controversy regarding the possible association of vaccinations and autism is one example of the manner in which widespread administration of immunizations is affected by public resistance. In response to a 1998 study of only twelve patients that suggested a possible association between initial administration of the measles-mumps-rubella (MMR) vaccination and autism,[a] the media and parent advocacy groups have paid considerable attention to this issue. The publisher of the study later retracted the finding after it was discovered that the lead author had a significant conflict of interest and acted in an unethical manner during the study.[b] Despite this fact and the now overwhelming data discounting an association between MMR administration and the development of autism,[c] considerable public fear continues to serve as a limitation to the uptake of MMR vaccination.

Cultural resistance to vaccination programs also limits the efficacy of global vaccination programs in developing countries. For example, some political and religious groups in various Indian communities assert that the WHO polio vaccination campaign is actually a hidden family-planning campaign targeted at Muslim families. As a result, many families in these communities have refused to allow their children to be vaccinated against polio; notably, cases of polio subsequently have surged in these areas. Cultural resistance to the WHO campaign to eradicate polio also manifested in 2003 in several Nigerian states, where community leaders claimed a link between the polio vaccination and sterility.[d] Similarly, members of target communities in southern Africa have been reluctant to participate in HIV vaccination trials due to fear that the HIV/AIDS epidemic is, in fact, a result of a Western conspiracy to infect local populations with the deadly disease. The legacy of colonialism and historical episodes of unethical Western medical interventions in the region fuel such conspiracy theories and serve as obstacles to efforts to implement global vaccination campaigns.

[a]A.J. Wakefield, S.H. Murch, A. Anthony, J. Linnell, D.M. Casson, M. Malik, M. Berelowitz, A.P. Dhillon, M.A. Thomas, P. Harvey, A. Valentine, S.E. Davies, and J.A. Walker-Smith, "Ileal-lymphoid-nodular Hyperplasia, Non-specific Colitis, and Pervasive Developmental Disorder in Children," *Lancet* 351: 9103 (1998): 637–641.

[b]General Medical Council, *Fitness to Practise Panel Hearing* (January 28, 2010). Available online at: http://www.casewatch.org/foreign/wakefield/gmc_findings.pdf.

[c]F. DeStefano, "Vaccines and Autism: Evidence Does Not Support a Causal Association," *Clinical Pharmacology and Therapeutics* 82: 6 (2007): 756–759.

[d]Mandip Jheeta and James Newell, "Childhood Vaccination in Asia and Africa: The Effect of Parents' Knowledge and Attitudes," *Bulletin of the World Health Organization* 86: 6 (2008): 419.

Global Burden of Communicable Diseases

Globally, nearly one-quarter of all deaths in both males and females is attributable to communicable diseases. The two leading causes of burden of disease are communicable diseases, specifically lower respiratory infections, and diarrheal illnesses. However, the burden of communicable diseases is not evenly distributed across the globe. Individuals in lower-income countries, particularly young children, suffer the majority of morbidity and mortality associated with disease due to infectious agents.[13]

As seen in Figure 4.1, the majority of deaths globally in children under the age of five is attributable to specific categories of communicable illnesses, with the other 45 percent due to noncommunicable diseases, injury, and neonatal (referring to the first twenty-eight days of life) deaths. Importantly, of the estimated 37 percent categorized as neonatal deaths, nearly one-third are due to infectious diseases.

Table 4.2 shows the five categories of injury or illness that contribute most significantly to disease burden in each of the six WHO regions. In Africa, each category is a communicable disease. The South-East Asia and the Eastern Mediterranean regions similarly experience a significant burden due to communicable diseases. Conversely, in the American, Western Pacific, and European regions, none of the five major categories is a communicable illness.[14]

Antimicrobial Resistance

The growing emergence of antimicrobial resistance is a significant public health concern worldwide. The decreased efficacy of drug therapy in combating infectious diseases is associated with increased population morbidity and mortality as well as lost productivity. Further, antimicrobial resistance is associated with rising health care expenditures due to prolonged illness, more frequent and prolonged hospitalizations, and the need for enhanced,

FIGURE 4.1 Distribution of Causes of Death Among Children Under Five Years and Within the Neonatal Period, 2004

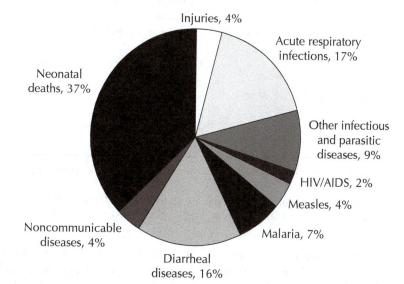

Source: Reproduced from the World Health Organization, *The Global Burden of Disease: 2004 Update* (2008): 14. Available online at: http://www.who.int/healthinfo/global_burden_disease/GBD_report_2004update_full.pdf.

TABLE 4.2 Leading Causes of Burden of Disease (DALYs) by WHO Region, 2004

Disease or injury	DALYs (millions)	Percentage of total DALYs	Disease or injury	DALYs (millions)	Percentage of total DALYs
African Region			**Region of the Americas**		
1 HIV/AIDS	46.7	12.4	1 Unipolar depressive disorders	10.8	7.5
2 Lower respiratory infections	42.2	11.2	2 Violence	6.6	4.6
3 Diarrheal diseases	32.2	8.6	3 Ischemic heart disease	6.5	4.6
4 Malaria	30.9	8.2	4 Alcohol use disorders	4.8	3.4
5 Neonatal infections/other[a]	13.4	3.6	5 Road traffic accidents	4.6	3.2
Eastern Mediterranean Region			**European Region**		
1 Lower respiratory infections	12.1	8.5	1 Ischemic heart disease	16.8	11.1
2 Diarrheal diseases	8.3	5.9	2 Cerebrovascular disease	9.5	6.3
3 Ischemic heart disease	6.2	4.3	3 Unipolar depressive disorders	8.4	5.6
4 Neonatal infections/other[a]	6.1	4.3	4 Alcohol use disorders	5.0	3.3
5 Birth asphyxia/trauma	5.5	3.9	5 Hearing loss, adult onset	3.9	2.6
South-East Asia Region			**Western Pacific Region**		
1 Lower respiratory infections	28.3	6.4	1 Cerebrovascular disease	15.8	6.0
2 Diarrheal diseases	23.0	5.2	2 Unipolar depressive disorders	15.2	5.7
3 Ischemic heart disease	21.6	4.9	3 Chronic obstructive lung disease	11.9	4.5
4 Unipolar depressive disorders	21.1	4.8	4 Refractive errors	10.6	4.0
5 Prematurity/low birth weight	18.3	4.1	5 Road traffic accidents	9.6	3.6

[a]This category also includes other noninfectious causes arising in the perinatal period apart from prematurity, low birth weight, birth trauma, and asphyxia.

Source: Reproduced from the World Health Organization, *The Global Burden of Disease: 2004 Update* (2008): 45. Available online at: http://www.who.int/healthinfo/global_burden_disease/GBD_report_2004update_full.pdf.

costly hospital infection-control measures.[15] Historically, the majority of the antimicrobial resistance has emerged in the hospital setting.[16] More recently, however, community-acquired infections due to drug-resistant organisms have been witnessed more regularly. Perhaps the most noteworthy of such infections are those due to multi-drug-resistant tuberculosis (MDR-TB).[17] Another example is the increasing incidence of skin and soft tissue infections due to community-acquired methicillin-resistant *Staphylococcus aureus* (MRSA).[18] Importantly, the selection of drug resistance also can increase the virulence of an infectious microbe, often leading to more severe disease presentations.[19]

Antimicrobial resistance develops as the result of selection pressure on microbial organisms. Susceptible microorganisms are unable to survive when exposed to lethal doses of antimicrobials, but other microorganisms adapt mechanisms that allow them to overcome the lethal effects of these medications. These adaptations develop as the result of spontaneous mutations of the microorganism's genetic material. The greater the cumulative degree of exposure to antimicrobial agents, the more likely these antimicrobial-resistant organisms will be preferentially selected for survival. Further, given the inherently short life span and rapid turnover of microbes, these drug-resistant microorganisms are able to quickly increase in prevalence within a population. The prescription of antibiotics to "treat" URTIs illustrates the nature of this problem. In many countries, including the United States, URTIs are the most common diagnosis for which antibiotics are prescribed, despite the fact that the overwhelming majority of URTIs are caused by viral agents. Because antibiotics do not affect viruses, treatment does not alter the natural progression of the illness. However, those bacteria that colonize the treated individual will be unnecessarily exposed to antimicrobials, creating an opportunity for the selection of resistant organisms. Further complicating the matter is that physicians often choose broad-spectrum rather than narrow-spectrum antibiotics for treatment, creating the potential for resistance to more potent antimicrobials.

Several risk factors drive the development of antimicrobial resistance within a population. The most important of these factors is the overutilization of antimicrobials in both the medical care of humans and the agricultural industry. Estimates suggest that as much as 50 percent of antimicrobial prescribing in human medicine and 80 percent in veterinary medicine and farming is unnecessary.[20] Multiple clinician and patient factors contribute to the overprescribing of antimicrobials in the clinical setting. Physicians cite numerous reasons for overprescribing antimicrobials, including time constraints for patient visits, fear of litigation, and the perception of patient or parental desire for antimicrobials.[21] Marketing strategies by the pharmaceutical industry also have a direct impact on physician antimicrobial prescribing practices.[22] Surveillance of outpatient antimicrobial use demonstrates that prescription practices differ significantly when comparing countries, even those of similar socioeconomic status.[23] For example, data show that antimicrobial use in the United States is significantly higher and trends toward greater use of broad-spectrum antibiotics when compared to the majority of European countries.[24] Reasons for patient or parental request for antimicrobials include lack of knowledge, pressure from child-care settings, clinicians failing to offer alternative treatments, and previous experience with symptom recovery while on antimicrobials for URTI symptoms.[25] The latter factor is critical in that inappropriate use of antimicrobials for URTIs only serves to reinforce patient belief that such treatment is necessary for subsequent infections.

In response to this problem, many countries have seen leading national medical societies promote more judicious antibiotic use and devise clinical guidelines for a variety of commonly seen clinical conditions, including URTIs. Surveillance data suggest that such awareness campaigns have been associated with overall decreased use as well as the use of more narrow-spectrum agents.[26] Similarly, regional and local medical institutions have developed organizational measures to reduce inappropriate use of antimicrobials for hospitalized patients. Systematic review of the literature has shown that institutional interventions can successfully decrease inappropriate antibiotic use.[27] Specific examples of successful measures include physician education, inclusion of clinical indications for appropriate use on physician antimicrobial order form, computer decision support systems, and enhanced collaboration with pharmacists and infectious disease specialists.[28]

Inappropriate human use of antimicrobials might also occur in the absence of clinician involvement. Individuals frequently self-administer antimicrobials, most commonly in the setting of upper respiratory symptoms.[29] These antimicrobials are typically obtained either through the storage of "leftover" antibiotics from previously non-completed prescription courses or by purchase from retail pharmacies without a prescription.[30] The practice of self-administration of leftover antibiotics is problematic for two reasons. First, the majority of self-treated infections are likely viral in nature and, thus, antimicrobials are not medically warranted. Second, these leftover drugs are available only because the original prescription course was not completed. Both of these factors apply pressure to microbes in a manner that promotes resistance.

Unregulated access to antimicrobial medications also contributes to the emergence of antimicrobial resistance across the globe. Even where legislation prohibiting such practices has been enacted, unregulated access is a problem in both developed and developing countries, and is particularly acute in the latter. In the absence of well-developed public sectors that can effectively regulate the prescribing and dispensing of medications, individuals in developing countries often have ready access to antimicrobials without a prescription. When individuals gain access to antimicrobials without consulting a medical professional, they are not instructed in the proper use of these medicines. Moreover, because they often face economic constraints, individuals may fail to complete the full course of treatment in order to save medicine for future use. Additionally, many antimicrobials available in low- and middle-income countries are either substandard or counterfeit. Further complicating the issue, antimicrobials can easily be purchased without a prescription via the Internet, undermining the ability of governments and medical professionals to regulate their use. This challenge illustrates the fundamental ways in which communicable illnesses—and efforts to combat these illnesses—are shaped by the forces of globalization.

Another factor contributing to the problem of antimicrobial resistance is the inappropriate use of antimicrobials in the agricultural industry. In fact, the largest use of antimicrobials globally is for the production of animals and animal products for human consumption.[31] For example, nontherapeutic agricultural use accounts for 60–80 percent of total antimicrobial production in the United States.[32] As much as 80 percent of this nontherapeutic use is likely unnecessary,[33] with a considerable portion being used for growth promotion.[34] This statistic is especially problematic when one considers that all classes of antibiotics are represented in agricultural use, potentially leading to antimicrobial resistance for a broad range of therapeutic agents.[35] Such agricultural practices have been temporally associated with the emergence of infections due to a number of antimicrobial-resistant bacteria.[36] The transmission of these organisms from animals to humans might occur through direct consumption of an infected animal or animal products or indirectly through contaminated water sources or contact with other animals, such as birds that have become infected. In response to this public health crisis, the European Union enacted legislation in 1998 forbidding the agricultural use of antimicrobials that are used for human therapeutic treatment as growth promoters. Subsequently, scientists observed a decrease in the levels of antimicrobial-resistant bacteria not only in farm animals but also within the general human population.[37] Despite such favorable outcomes, other countries, including the United States, have been slow to adopt similar legislation, due in large part to concerns about the potential for negative economic ramifications for the farming industry.

Whether antimicrobial resistance emerges in developing or developed countries, microbial organisms can quickly spread globally due to current travel and migration patterns. Drug-resistant microbes do not recognize national borders, and the effects of governmental policies and social practices that contribute to the emergence of antimicrobial resistance are transnational in nature. Accordingly, effective solutions to this global problem require cooperation from a wide range of state and non-state actors across the globe. Education of medical providers as well as the general public regarding the appropriate clinical use of antimicrobials is of paramount importance. Closer governmental scrutiny of nonprescribed antimicrobials is also warranted. Organizational efforts by hospitals to support appropriate decision making regarding antimicrobial use as well as to identify and prevent the spread of infections will be a key component of a successful intervention strategy. Stricter governmental regulation of antimicrobial use in the agricultural industry is important. Measures to prevent infection, such as global implementation of effective immunization programs, are critical. Furthermore, because the pharmaceutical industry globally has moved away from prioritizing the development of new antimicrobials due to economic incentives that led drug manufacturers to prioritize the development and marketing of more profitable medicines, governments may need to consider providing financial incentives, such as tax breaks or direct subsidies, to encourage pharmaceutical companies to invest in research and development on new antimicrobials capable of fighting drug-resistant microbes.[38] Moreover, governments must make political and economic investments to improve the living conditions of people living in poverty. Such investments would reduce the prevalence of communicable illnesses, thereby decreasing both the need for antimicrobials and the risk of the emergence of antimicrobial resistance.

HIV/AIDS

HIV infects human CD4+ T-cells, a cell line vital for the proper functioning of the immune system. CD4+ T-cell replication of HIV ultimately leads to CD4+ T-cell death and release of the viral copies in a manner that leads to infection of more CD4+ T-cells. When this CD4+ T-cell suppression reaches a critical level, the infected host is rendered more susceptible

to opportunistic infections as well as more severe clinical presentations of common infectious diseases such as bacterial pneumonia. Additionally, the host is at increased risk for certain cancers, such as lymphoma and Kaposi's sarcoma (a type of skin cancer). When the CD4+ T-cell count of an HIV-infected person reaches this critical level, or when the person is diagnosed with one of several opportunistic infections or malignancies, the individual is diagnosed as having AIDS.[39] HIV can be transmitted from one host to another through sexual transmission (both heterosexual and homosexual contact) and via the blood-borne route, predominantly by the sharing of needles among injection drug users.[40] The virus can also be passed from mother to offspring, either through contaminated breast milk or during pregnancy or delivery.

Consistent with other communicable illnesses, HIV/AIDS is a disease whose impact is felt most greatly by poor people, with a disproportionate burden of disease among children. At the global level, a statistically significant relationship exists between low incomes and HIV-prevalence rates.[41] As of 2008, an estimated 33.4 million people globally were living with HIV, 22.4 million of whom were from sub-Saharan Africa. In 2008 alone, 2.7 million people were newly infected with HIV—430,000 of whom were children under the age of 15 years, and 1.9 million of whom were from sub-Saharan Africa. That same year saw an estimated 2 million AIDS-related deaths, 280,000 occurring in children under the age of 15 years. Again, HIV-related deaths were highest in sub-Saharan Africa, representing 1.4 million of such cases. Consistent with these higher rates of disease, HIV/AIDS accounts for the greatest burden of disease in the African Region (see Table 4.2). High prevalence and incidence rates are also noted in other developing countries in Asia and Latin America.[42] Even in more developed countries, poverty is a significant risk factor for HIV. A recent study demonstrated that poverty is the single most important risk factor associated with HIV infection among inner-city heterosexuals.[43]

Poverty leads to an increased risk of HIV transmission in several ways. First, people living in poverty are likely to have lower levels of education and higher illiteracy rates. Thus, they are less likely to possess knowledge about the transmission of HIV and the role of condoms in preventing such transmission. Individuals who are poor are also more likely to work in the commercial sex industry, with data from some developing regions suggesting a prevalence of HIV among sex workers that is as much as twenty times higher than that of the general population.[44] Individuals of lower socioeconomic status are also more likely to practice the high-risk behavior of injection drug use. Outside sub-Saharan Africa, this behavior is estimated to account for nearly one-third of new HIV infections.[45] Limited access to health care services among poor people is another contributing factor to an increased incidence of HIV. These individuals are not only unable to utilize critical preventive measures but also unable to be tested and thus informed of their HIV status, a serious problem given that knowledge of HIV-positive status may significantly increase condom use, thereby decreasing the risk of transmission.[46] One study estimated that 83 percent of Kenyans living with HIV in 2007 were unaware of their HIV status.[47]

Women and children in developing regions are particularly vulnerable to the threat of HIV infection. Heterosexual exposure is currently the primary mode of transmission in sub-Saharan Africa.[48] Biologically, heterosexual intercourse is more likely to result in HIV infection in women than in men. Further, cultural norms often make it difficult for women in many regions to refuse sex with a male partner.[49] Women are also more likely than men to work as commercial sex workers, with condom use often discouraged by clients. Children in low-income countries are also disproportionately burdened by HIV infection. Many HIV-positive women in developing countries do not have access to care that can decrease transmission during pregnancy or delivery or to replacement feeding that can decrease HIV transmission associated with breast-feeding.

Several strategies have been shown to decrease HIV transmission. Prevention programs promoting condom use during sexual intercourse, antiretroviral (antimicrobials active against HIV) therapy during pregnancy, syringe and needle exchange programs for injection drug users, replacement feeding for newborns and infants, and male circumcision[50] have all been shown to decrease HIV transmission rates. However, education about the effectiveness of these interventions, as well as access to them, is often limited for individuals living in poverty. For example, less than 8 percent of injection drug users receive HIV prevention services.[51] Moreover, prevention measures often fail to reach high-risk groups in many developing countries in Africa.[52] Globally, there are reasons for guarded optimism. Drug abuse treatment, outreach programs to help reduce injection drug use and high-risk sexual behavior, and syringe and needle exchange programs have been shown to stabilize and even reverse AIDS epidemics among injection drug users in several large cities in the United Kingdom, the United States, Brazil, Australia, and Bangladesh.[53] Globally, coverage for services to prevent mother-to-child HIV transmission rose from 10 percent in 2004 to 45 percent in 2008, with evidence of a drop in 2008 of new infections among children.[54] However, despite successful prevention programs in some countries, much of this success still has not reached low-income countries that are most significantly affected by the disease.

Individuals in low-income countries at a greater risk of infection with HIV are also less likely to receive treatment for their disease. Beginning with azidothymidine (AZT) in 1986, more than thirty antiretroviral agents have been developed to date. Treatment of HIV-positive individuals with one or more (typically a combination) of these agents has dramatically changed the natural history of the disease, with a significant decrease in morbidity and mortality in resource-rich countries. Access to these agents has historically been limited in low- and middle-income countries. Due in large part to an initiative launched in 2003 by the Joint United Nations Programme on HIV/AIDS (UNAIDS) and the WHO, access to antiretroviral agents in these countries rose tenfold by 2008.[55] Nevertheless, lack of access as well as lack of education about the availability of these agents continues to be a problem in many poor regions, with more than half of infected individuals going untreated. This problem is even more striking for children in these resource-poor countries, where treatment reaches only an estimated 15 percent of infected children.[56] Further, limited access to health care services often results in infected individuals presenting with an advanced stage of the disease, one that is typically more difficult to treat. Lastly, inconsistent access to care can lead to administration of antiviral therapy in a sporadic manner, a practice that contributes to the development of drug-resistance by the virus.

The association between poverty and HIV/AIDS is not unidirectional. HIV/AIDS also has an adverse economic impact at both the population and household levels. A study of eighty developing countries during the period 1990–1997 demonstrated a direct relationship between the extent of HIV prevalence and the severity of reduction in the growth of gross domestic product (GDP).[57] As HIV/AIDS typically affects working-age people, this disease often leads to decreased productivity and increased absenteeism for the sick and their caregivers. A less productive workforce yields diminished tax revenues and is less attractive to foreign investors. Additionally, a population with high HIV prevalence requires greater health expenditures, diverting investments away from areas of potential economic growth.[58] At the household level, HIV/AIDS often results in a poverty trap for individuals. Affected individuals are often unable to consistently work, as are their family members who must care for them. Further, families are often forced to sell already-limited assets to help pay for medical expenses. Such economic hardship, in turn, has a negative effect on the education of children. Many individuals, as a result of their inability to work and the expense of treating their illness, lack the funds necessary to send their

children to school. Also, children are often required to work and, thus, drop out of school. Additionally, the teacher workforce is often negatively affected by the HIV epidemic.[59]

Although HIV/AIDS is a disease whose greatest burden is in the developing world, the spread of disease in these regions has global implications for health. Without regular access to health care services, an HIV-positive individual may receive intermittent rather than continuous therapy with antiretroviral agents. This practice can lead to the emergence of drug-resistant strains of the virus. The HIV epidemic in many poor regions also contributes to the increasing prevalence of other communicable illnesses, such as malaria and tuberculosis. This resultant increase in other communicable diseases in these resource-poor regions is, in turn, associated with the emergence of drug-resistant strains of other microorganisms. For example, there is a growing prevalence worldwide of MDR-TB, defined as tuberculosis that is resistant to the two most potent first-line agents used to treat it. MDR-TB has been shown to be almost twice as common in HIV-positive individuals with tuberculosis compared to HIV-negative individuals with tuberculosis.[60] More worrisome is the problem of extensively drug-resistant tuberculosis (XDR-TB), defined as tuberculosis that is resistant to the two first-line agents as well as additional second-line agents. The largest number of cases of XDR-TB has been reported from South Africa, owing to the rapid spread of HIV among people in the region.[61] With global migration and tourism, the emergence of drug-resistant microorganisms in one region becomes a communicable disease threat globally.

Tuberculosis

Tuberculosis is a communicable disease caused by the bacteria *Mycobacterium tuberculosis*, a slow-growing organism that is spread from one individual to another by the respiratory route. Initial infection with *M. tuberculosis* causes disease primarily of the lung and chest cavity but may also lead to injury of the abdominal cavity and bony spine as well as meningitis. Initial infection may also be associated with no significant symptoms but result in a condition referred to as latent tuberculosis. In this condition, the host is able to control the infection, but the microorganism establishes residence in the lymph nodes (typically in the chest) of the host. The organism can lie dormant for many years, even decades, only to reactivate and cause secondary disease, typically in a host that has become immunocompromised from, for example, HIV co-infection or simply the process of aging.[62] Tuberculosis is associated with significant morbidity and mortality, particularly in developing countries. Thirty percent of the global prevalence of tuberculosis is accounted for by cases in the WHO African Region as compared to 3 percent in the WHO Region of the Americas. Further, the tuberculosis mortality rates per 100,000 population in the WHO African Region are more than fifteen times greater than those seen in the WHO Region of the Americas.[63]

Reasons for this global disparity are quite similar to those discussed in the section on HIV/AIDS. Because tuberculosis is spread from one host to another by the respiratory route, crowded living conditions are associated with an increased risk of disease transmission. Poor education about the disease, as well as limited access to health care services for appropriate identification and treatment, often results in undertreatment in developing countries. Socioeconomic barriers to access are particularly common due to the required course of treatment, typically multiple antimicrobials for a minimum six-month duration. Even when individuals in developing countries are able to visit a health care facility, they may not receive appropriate treatment because of a shortage of antituberculosis medications. Some studies suggest that shortages occur more than 40 percent of the time. In turn, shortages may lead infected individuals to purchase nonprescription antimicrobials that they take until the symptoms have resolved rather

than until a cure has resulted. This practice makes the infected individual susceptible to disease relapse and leads to the emergence of drug-resistant organisms.[64]

In the mid-1990s, the WHO developed the Directly Observed Therapy, Short-course (DOTS) strategy as the internationally recommended approach to the control of tuberculosis. The strategy emphasizes national and international partnerships to ensure appropriate financing of programs that aid in case finding, observed treatment and support of identified patients, and data recording and evaluation to assess trends in disease burden. The DOTS strategy is primarily funded by national governments through budgets for national tuberculosis control programs (NTPs) and general health care services, with additional funding from loans as well as the Global Fund to Fight AIDS, Tuberculosis, and Malaria. The WHO estimates that between 1995 and 2008, 36 million patients were successfully treated in DOTS programs, with an estimated 2 million–6 million lives saved.[65] However, the significant morbidity and mortality attributable to tuberculosis that continues to be observed in developing countries underscores the challenges that remain.

Further, despite the fact that funding for tuberculosis control in high-burden countries has increased each year since 2002, expansion of DOTS programs to meet diagnosis and treatment goals has resulted in growing funding gaps.[66] Thus, increased financing will be necessary to sustain and expand on the success of the DOTS strategy globally. Given the threat of the global spread of tuberculosis from one region to another, such investments would benefit not only the recipient high-burden countries but also the larger global community. For example, in 2007, foreign-born persons accounted for nearly 60 percent of new cases of tuberculosis in the United States.[67] A 2005 study suggested that, because of the burden of disease in Mexico, Haiti, and the Dominican Republic, as well as the large number of immigrants from those regions residing in the United States,

U.S.-funded efforts to expand the DOTS programs in those countries would produce a net cost savings to the United States.[68] In short, despite the fact that the prevalence of tuberculosis is much higher in the developing world, this communicable illness is a public health challenge for the developed world as well. The growing risk of MDR-TB and the fact that this disease can readily cross national borders in a world of globalization make it critical that governments and non-governmental organizations (NGOs) collaborate to fight the illness in the zones of global poverty where it thrives.

Influenza

Influenza is a communicable disease that typically presents with fever, chills, muscle aches, cough, sore throat, fatigue, and headache. In most individuals, it is a self-limited condition that resolves with no significant consequences. However, influenza can be associated with more concerning manifestations such as pneumonia, with death occurring in the most severe cases. Typically, more severe presentations occur in young children, the elderly, or individuals with chronic medical conditions that render them more susceptible to infection. Influenza is caused by one of three classes of influenza viruses (A, B, or C). Although humans are the predominant hosts of the influenza viruses, the viruses may also circulate among other mammalian species (for example, swine) and avian species. The vast majority of human illness is due to influenza A strains and, to a lesser extent, influenza B strains. Influenza A viruses can be further categorized by subtype of the two major proteins that appear on the envelope that encases the virus—hemagglutinin (H) and neuraminidase (N). The nomenclature for a particular strain of influenza A virus would then be H1N1 or H3N2.[69]

A basic knowledge of these viral envelope proteins is critical in understanding the emergence of epidemics and pandemics associated with influenza. When a human is exposed to the influenza virus, host antibodies form against these proteins. These antibodies serve as the first line of defense against repeat infection should an individual again be exposed to a similar viral strain in subsequent years (active immunity). These viral proteins also serve as the basis for the annual influenza vaccine. Vaccination with an inactivated or attenuated form of the virus induces passive immunity in the host. Because viruses are replicated at a rapid rate by the host cells, they are capable of frequent mutations in the structure of these envelope proteins. These mutations often result in a lesser susceptibility of the virus to host immune defenses, as the altered protein may no longer be recognized by the previously produced antibodies. If these mutations are minor, the process is referred to as **antigenic drift**, a condition that results in the local outbreaks or regional epidemics that characterize the "flu season" that occurs each year. However, when these mutations are more significant, a process known as **antigenic shift** occurs, whereby a much larger portion of the population lacks sufficient immunity to the virus. In this case, a pandemic may result.[70]

Owing to antigenic drift, a flu season typically occurs during the winter months, one season in the southern hemisphere and a second season in the northern hemisphere. These flu seasons are regional epidemics that typically begin abruptly over a two to three week period and last for approximately three months. The severity of each epidemic depends in large part on the degree of antigenic drift and, thus, the number of susceptible individuals in the population. These annual epidemics result in an estimated 3 million–5 million cases of severe illness, and about 250,000–500,000 deaths worldwide.[71] In the United States, annual influenza-associated deaths in the years 1976–2007 ranged from as few as 3,349 to as many as 48,614.[72]

Large-scale influenza epidemics or global pandemics resulting from antigenic shift occur much less frequently, typically on the order of decades. However, these epidemics are associated with much greater morbidity and mortality. The influenza pandemic of 1918 was associated with antigenic shift in both the H and the N antigens of influenza A, resulting in a particularly virulent form of the virus. The case-fatality rates associated with the pandemic were greater than 2.5 percent, compared to the less than 0.1 percent seen in other pandemics, with an estimated 50 million–100 million deaths worldwide. Unlike most epidemics or pandemics, the 1918 pandemic affected a disproportionately large number of healthy young adults.[73] More recently, the swine influenza pandemic of 2009–2010 serves as a cautionary reminder of the potential for antigenic shift among influenza viruses and for rapid global spread of the disease. The outbreak of a new strain of influenza A H1N1 (swine influenza) began in Mexico in April 2009 and quickly spread; the WHO declared a global pandemic in June of that year.[74] A study evaluating the international air-travel patterns from Mexico during that time period suggested a strong correlation with importations of the new H1N1 strain to other regions of the globe.[75] Like the 1918 pandemic, the novel strain identified in 2009 tended to disproportionately affect young, healthy adults when compared to other influenza epidemics. However, the strain was considerably less virulent, with 18,398 confirmed deaths worldwide as of July 2010.[76]

Avian influenza (H5N1) also poses a potentially critical threat to global health. Typically, influenza viruses are species-specific, meaning those that infect birds tend not to infect humans. However, eighteen documented cases, including six deaths, in Hong Kong in 1997 demonstrated that direct contact with diseased poultry could lead to infection among humans. Subsequently, a larger number of cases (440) were reported in Asia, with 262 deaths as of August 2009.[77] To date, there is no evidence of human-to-human transmission of the avian influenza virus. Though the overall reported cases and fatalities are low to date, concern that this interspecies transmission might serve as another potential source for a deadly global

pandemic exists. First, the migratory patterns of birds could lead to rapid global spread of the disease. Additionally, the possibility that mutating viral strains may develop the ability to cause human-to-human transmission is a risk. Should antigenic shift lead to a particularly virulent strain of influenza A H5N1, the global consequences could be quite dramatic.

Several antimicrobial agents are available for clinical use against influenza, including strains of avian influenza. However, not all individuals with suspected or confirmed cases of influenza warrant treatment. Typically, treatment is limited to individuals at high risk for significant morbidity or mortality associated with infection with influenza, namely, the elderly, young children, those with chronic medical conditions that affect the respiratory system or render them relatively immunocompromised, and those individuals whose illness severity requires hospitalization.[78] These restrictions are important not only to ensure that adequate supplies are available for those most likely to benefit but also to decrease the risk of the development of antimicrobial resistance. The widespread administration of influenza vaccinations is another critical component of global disease prevention. Each year, the WHO, in collaboration with national agencies such as the U.S. Centers for Disease Control and Prevention (CDC), monitors influenza activity and performs global surveillance of the viral strains responsible for the majority of current disease activity.[79] The CDC uses this information to predict those strains likely to cause infection during the next flu season and then designs the annual influenza vaccine accordingly, with vaccine development requiring several months for completion. Obviously, due to antigenic drift, the prediction is more accurate in some years than in others. Rates of effectiveness can be as low as 5 percent to as high as 90 percent, though typically they tend to perform closer to the higher end of this range.[80]

As history has shown, influenza is an illness that can spread rapidly with no regard for national borders and can result in considerable global morbidity and mortality. As a result, it presents a significant communicable disease threat to all countries. Such a threat mandates close collaboration among international organizations, national governments, and NGOs to ensure appropriate funding and support of influenza surveillance and control programs. The priorities of these programs should include, but not necessarily be limited to, ongoing surveillance of disease activity, increased national epidemic and pandemic preparedness (including the assurance of adequate vaccine and pharmaceutical supplies), programs that expand the use of existing vaccines and support the accelerated introduction of new vaccines, and establishment of appropriate communication networks between national programs.[81] Public education about the relative benefits and risks of immunizations, as well as appropriate utilization of health care resources during periods of high disease activity, is also critical.

Conclusion

The mortality, morbidity, and disability associated with communicable illnesses result in a significant global burden of disease, particularly in resource-poor regions of the world. Conditions of poverty increase the likelihood of infectious disease acquisition due to heightened transmission risk and inadequate preventive measures. Individuals who are poor are less likely to receive appropriate therapy for these communicable illnesses, which in turn can contribute to the selection of antimicrobial-resistant microorganisms. Foreign investments in preventing and treating HIV/AIDS, tuberculosis, and other communicable illnesses would yield important global benefits by decreasing not only the prevalence of communicable illnesses but also the emergence of drug-resistant strains of microbes that emerge when people do not have the resources to treat illnesses properly. Additionally, foreign investments designed

to mitigate the conditions of poverty in both developing and developed countries would likely generate public health benefits not only for people living in zones of poverty but also for people across the globe. Due to increasing global mobility associated with migration and tourism, communicable diseases and the microorganisms that cause them do not recognize national borders. Therefore, transnational collaboration will be necessary to decrease the health, economic, and social costs associated with the global burden of communicable illnesses.

Discussion Questions

1. As concerns the response to commonly available antimicrobial therapy, how do viruses differ from bacteria?
2. What are the modes of transmission for the microorganisms that cause communicable diseases? How does poverty affect disease transmission?
3. What factors limit the success of vaccination programs in developing regions? Are these the same barriers to universal implementation of such programs in more developed regions?
4. What factors contribute to the emergence of antimicrobial-resistant microorganisms? Do you agree with the assertion that antimicrobial resistance is a more significant problem in developing countries? Why or why not?
5. Why should developed countries consider financial assistance to developing regions to help combat the epidemic of HIV/AIDS and tuberculosis? In what ways do developed countries benefit from this investment?
6. Do you agree with the assertion that transnational collaboration is critical in the development and implementation of strategies to limit the impact of a global influenza pandemic? Why or why not?

Web Resources

The GAVI Alliance (The Global Alliance for Vaccines and Immunisation): http://www. gavialliance.org/

The Global Fund to Fight AIDS, Tuberculosis, and Malaria: http://www.theglobalfund.org/

U.S. Centers for Disease Control and Prevention: http://www.cdc.gov/

World Health Organization Global Health Atlas: http://www.who.int/healthinfo/ global_burden_disease/en/

CHAPTER 5

Global Health and Noncommunicable Illnesses

Introduction

In contrast to communicable diseases, which are transmitted from one individual to another via an infectious agent, noncommunicable diseases occur in the absence of infectious agents and, thus, are not transmissible between individuals. This chapter begins with an overview of the global burden of noncommunicable diseases. Next, it looks at the determinants of noncommunicable illness. Whether any one individual manifests a specific noncommunicable disease is determined by a complex interplay among individual, social, and political variables that serve as risk factors for that condition. To illustrate the interconnected causes of noncommunicable illness, the chapter explores the cases of cardiovascular disease, obesity, and tobacco abuse in detail. In doing so, it examines significant differences between developed and developing countries in the burden of noncommunicable diseases as well as critical disparities between wealthy and poor individuals across the globe.

Global Burden of Noncommunicable Diseases

Noncommunicable diseases are associated with considerable morbidity and mortality worldwide. Globally, noncommunicable diseases account for 57.9 percent of deaths among males and 61.5 percent of deaths among females, according to 2004 data. As demonstrated in Figure 5.1 and Table 5.1, the noncommunicable illnesses that contribute most significantly to these deaths are cardiovascular diseases, including heart disease and cerebrovascular disease (stroke), with nearly 30 percent of all deaths worldwide resulting from these conditions. Cardiovascular diseases account for the greatest proportion of deaths in high- and middle-income countries. However, they also are responsible for an estimated 15 percent of deaths in low-income countries. Chronic obstructive lung disease, cancer, and diabetes mellitus are examples of other noncommunicable diseases that are significant causes of death, particularly in middle- and high-income countries. Further, it is estimated that by 2030, the relative contribution of deaths due to communicable illnesses will continue to decline as mortality resulting from noncommunicable conditions such as cardiovascular disease, chronic obstructive lung disease, diabetes mellitus, and cancer rises. This anticipated shift in cause-specific mortality will be attributable, in large part, to increasing rates of tobacco smoking and obesity in low- and middle-income countries.[1]

As represented in Table 5.2, noncommunicable illnesses are also significant contributors to the global burden of disease as measured by disability-adjusted life years (DALYs). In

FIGURE 5.1 Distribution of Global Deaths by Leading Cause Groups, 2004

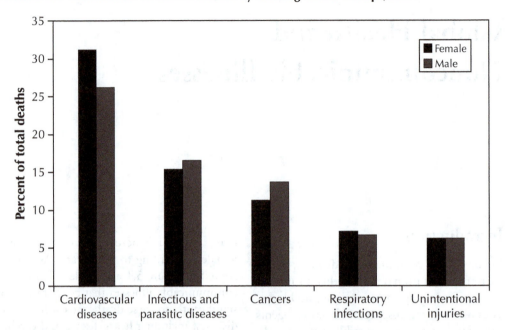

Source: Adapted from the World Health Organization, *The Global Burden of Disease: 2004 Update* (2008): 10. Available online at: http://www.who.int/healthinfo/global_burden_disease/GBD_report_2004update_full.pdf.

high- and middle-income countries, heart disease and cerebrovascular disease are among the three most significant contributors to the overall burden of disease. When comparing disease burden as assessed by DALYs with mortality data, the contribution of noncommunicable diseases appears to be of lesser importance in low-income countries where communicable illnesses account for the majority of disease burden. The reason for this apparent discrepancy is that DALYs assess not only mortality but also potential life lost due to premature mortality and the years of productive life lost due to disability. Thus, use of mortality data alone tends to underestimate the contribution of those diseases that cause significant morbidity and mortality among children and young adults. The data presented in Table 5.2 also emphasize the contribution to disease burden in middle- and high-income countries of other categories of noncommunicable diseases, including diabetes mellitus, chronic obstructive lung disease,

mental health disorders such as depression and alcohol abuse, and neurological conditions such as dementia.

Mental health disorders also contribute considerably to disease burden in low-income countries, where depression ranks as the eighth most significant source of DALYs.[2] Importantly, mental health disorders tend to be undertreated due to inadequate diagnosis and limited access to health care, even in developed countries. Further, these disorders are strongly associated with poverty in a bidirectional manner. Those individuals living in poverty may be at higher risk for developing mental health conditions in large part due to the stressors of their living conditions. Conversely, individuals with serious mental health disorders, such as schizophrenia, are more likely to live in poverty because they not only have a hard time finding consistent employment but also are more vulnerable to substance abuse.

TABLE 5.1 Leading Causes of Death by Country Income Group, 2004

Disease or injury	Deaths (millions)	Percentage of total deaths	Disease or injury	Deaths (millions)	Percentage of total deaths
World			**Low-income countries**[a]		
1 Ischemic heart disease	7.2	12.2	1 Lower respiratory infections	2.9	11.2
2 Cerebrovascular disease	5.7	9.7	2 Ischemic heart disease	2.5	9.4
3 Lower respiratory infections	4.2	7.1	3 Diarrheal diseases	1.8	6.9
4 Chronic obstructive lung disease	3.0	5.1	4 HIV/AIDS	1.5	5.7
5 Diarrheal diseases	2.2	3.7	5 Cerebrovascular disease	1.5	5.6
6 HIV/AIDS	2.0	3.5	6 Chronic obstructive lung disease	0.9	3.6
7 Tuberculosis	1.5	2.5	7 Tuberculosis	0.9	3.5
8 Trachea, bronchus, lung cancers	1.3	2.3	8 Neonatal infections/ conditions	0.9	3.4
9 Road traffic accidents	1.3	2.2	9 Malaria	0.9	2.3
10 Prematurity and low birth weight	1.2	2.0	10 Prematurity and low birth weight	0.8	3.2
Middle-income countries[a]			**High-income countries**[a]		
1 Cerebrovascular disease	3.5	14.2	1 Ischemic heart disease	1.3	16.3
2 Ischemic heart disease	3.4	13.9	2 Cerebrovascular disease	0.8	9.3
3 Chronic obstructive lung disease	1.8	7.4	3 Trachea, bronchus, lung cancers	0.5	5.9
4 Lower respiratory infections	0.9	3.8	4 Lower respiratory infections	0.3	3.8
5 Trachea, bronchus, lung cancers	0.7	2.9	5 Chronic obstructive lung disease	0.3	3.5
6 Road traffic accidents	0.7	2.8	6 Alzheimer's and other dementias	0.3	3.4
7 Hypertensive heart disease	0.6	2.5	7 Colon and rectum cancers	0.3	3.3
8 Stomach cancer	0.5	2.2	8 Diabetes mellitus	0.2	2.8
9 Tuberculosis	0.5	2.2	9 Breast cancer	0.2	2.0
10 Diabetes mellitus	0.5	2.1	10 Stomach cancer	0.1	1.8

[a]Countries grouped by gross national income per capita—low income ($825 or less), high income ($10,066 or more).

Source: Adapted from the World Health Organization, *The Global Burden of Disease: 2004 Update* (2008): 12. Available online at: http://www.who.int/healthinfo/global_burden_disease/GBD_report_2004update_full.pdf.

TABLE 5.2 Leading Causes of Burden of Disease (DALYs), Countries Grouped by Income, 2004

Disease or injury	DALYs (millions)	Percentage of total DALYs	Disease or injury	DALYs (millions)	Percentage of total DALYs
World			**Low-income countries**[a]		
1 Lower respiratory infections	94.5	6.2	1 Lower respiratory infections	76.9	9.3
2 Diarrheal diseases	72.8	4.8	2 Diarrheal diseases	59.2	7.2
3 Unipolar depressive disorders	65.5	4.3	3 HIV/AIDS	42.9	5.2
4 Ischemic heart disease	62.6	4.1	4 Malaria	32.8	4.0
5 HIV/AIDS	58.5	3.8	5 Prematurity and low birth weight	32.1	3.9
6 Cerebrovascular disease	46.6	3.1	6 Neonatal infections/ conditions	31.4	3.8
7 Prematurity and low birth weight	44.3	2.9	7 Birth asphyxia and birth trauma	29.8	3.6
8 Birth asphyxia and birth trauma	41.7	2.7	8 Unipolar depressive disorders	26.5	3.2
9 Road traffic accidents	41.2	2.7	9 Ischemic heart disease	26.0	3.1
10 Neonatal infections/ conditions	40.4	2.7	10 Tuberculosis	22.4	2.7
Middle-income countries[a]			**High-income countries**[a]		
1 Unipolar depressive disorders	29.0	5.1	1 Unipolar depressive disorders	10.0	8.2
2 Ischemic heart disease	28.9	5.0	2 Ischemic heart disease	7.7	6.3
3 Cerebrovascular disease	27.5	4.8	3 Cerebrovascular disease	4.8	3.9
4 Road traffic accidents	21.4	3.7	4 Alzheimer's and other dementias	4.4	3.6
5 Lower respiratory infections	16.3	2.8	5 Alcohol use disorders	4.2	3.4
6 Chronic obstructive lung disease	16.1	2.8	6 Hearing loss, adult onset	4.2	3.4
7 HIV/AIDS	15.0	2.6	7 Chronic obstructive lung disease	3.7	3.0
8 Alcohol use disorders	14.9	2.6	8 Diabetes mellitus	3.6	3.0
9 Refractive errors	13.7	2.4	9 Trachea, bronchus, lung cancers	3.6	3.0
10 Diarrheal diseases	13.1	2.3	10 Road traffic accidents	3.1	2.6

[a]Countries grouped by gross national income per capita—low income ($825 or less), high income ($10,066 or more).

Source: Adapted from the World Health Organization, *The Global Burden of Disease: 2004 Update* (2008): 44. Available online at: http://www.who.int/healthinfo/global_burden_disease/GBD_report_2004update_full.pdf.

Cardiovascular Disease

As just presented, cardiovascular diseases are the leading causes of death worldwide, accounting for nearly 30 percent of all annual deaths. Although cardiovascular diseases rank higher as contributors to mortality and disease burden in high-income countries than they do in low-income countries, these conditions actually disproportionately affect individuals living in low- and middle-income countries. In fact, 80 percent of all cardiovascular disease deaths occur in low- and middle-income countries.[3] Additionally, cardiovascular deaths have a greater impact on disease burden in low- and middle-income countries, as they tend to occur among younger members of the population who might otherwise be likely to contribute to the economic growth of the population. In high-income countries, nearly 80 percent of cardiovascular deaths occur among those over the age of sixty compared with only 42 percent in low- and middle-income countries.[4] In developed countries, disparities between the wealthy and the poor also exist, with data demonstrating that minority groups and individuals of lower socioeconomic status experience higher rates of death due to heart disease than do those of higher socioeconomic status.[5] Further, a gender disparity in burden attributable to cardiovascular diseases also may exist in some countries. For example, in the United States, women have higher mortality rates attributable to cardiovascular disease than men.[6]

As with most health conditions, whether an individual develops cardiovascular disease is determined by a complicated interplay among many individual, social, and political variables. Several traditional individual-level risk factors, both biological and behavioral, have been shown to increase one's risk of cardiovascular disease. These include a family history of cardiovascular disease, age, biological sex, smoking, and the presence of other medical conditions, such as diabetes mellitus, hypercholesterolemia, hypertension, and obesity.[7] The sex-specific risk of cardiovascular disease changes with aging. Among individuals younger than sixty years of age, men have a twofold risk of cardiovascular disease as compared with women, a disparity that decreases with age until the disease rate is equivalent between men and women by the eighth decade of life.[8] An additional biological risk factor has been proposed, with data suggesting that premature birth and small birth weight may increase subsequent risk of cardiovascular disease.[9]

Though factors such as age, biological sex, and familial risk are not modifiable, many factors that contribute to the development of cardiovascular disease, including the presence or absence and adequacy of treatment of other health conditions, reflect individual behaviors that are themselves rooted in socioeconomic conditions and political contexts. For example, an individual's decision to smoke is influenced by several social and political factors. Individuals of lower socioeconomic status and with less educational attainment are more likely to smoke,[10] and the children of smokers are more likely to smoke.[11] Conversely, smoke-free legislation, economic disincentives such as taxes, and public health campaigns can reduce tobacco use. Medical conditions that impact cardiovascular disease outcomes, such as diabetes mellitus, hypercholesterolemia, hypertension, and obesity, have genetic predispositions but are also greatly influenced by behavioral factors such as diet and level of physical activity. These behavioral factors are, in turn, affected by social determinants. For example, the highest obesity rates are observed among people in the lowest income brackets and with the lowest levels of education, who are also likely to be physically inactive and have poor diets.[12] Additionally, studies have highlighted the impact that neighborhoods have on disease states such as obesity, diabetes mellitus, and hypertension. As one specific example, it has been shown that obesity is associated with poor access to healthy foods and neighborhood green space for exercise.[13]

Other social and political factors can impact one's risk of cardiovascular disease. Employment status has been shown to be associated with cardiovascular disease risk. The Whitehall study in Britain demonstrated that, among British civil servants, employment grade was associated with adverse cardiovascular outcomes in a continuous and downward-sloping gradient. In other words, individuals with lower job rank were more likely to have cardiovascular disease; when comparing groups of workers across job-rank categories, workers in the lower category consistently had higher rates of heart disease than workers in the next highest ranking group.[14] Because the study was conducted among civil servants, all of whom earned above living wage and had access to health care services, the implication is that psychosocial pathways contribute to this increased cardiovascular risk. Additionally, higher educational attainment and employment status obviously contribute directly to one's financial well-being, potentially mitigating socioeconomic contributions to adverse health as well as likely improving one's ability to purchase health care services. Further, in countries where health insurance is linked to employment, health care access is often directly determined by one's employment status.

The incidence of cardiovascular disease in low- and middle-income countries is increasing and is anticipated to continue increasing at a higher rate than in high-income countries. The most significant reason for this disparity is the differential distribution of risk factors among these populations. For example, more than 80 percent of tobacco use now occurs in low- and middle-income regions, with particularly high rates in Russia, Indonesia, and China.[15] Even in developed countries, individuals of lower socioeconomic status and with less educational attainment are more likely to smoke. Diabetes mellitus is another cardiovascular risk factor with unequal global distribution, with the greatest burden of diabetes experienced by Asian countries, most notably India and China.[16] This increased burden among Asian populations is due in large part to a greater genetic susceptibility but may also be associated with metabolic effects of undernutrition during fetal development and subsequent "catch-up" growth in early childhood.[17] Further, the prevalence of diabetes mellitus in developed countries is higher among minority

populations.[18] As a final example, though the prevalence of obesity is increasing throughout the world, these rates are rising at a much greater level in many developing countries than they are in developed countries. Additionally, except among the poorest of countries, where limited access to food is associated with malnutrition and thus protective against obesity, lower socioeconomic status is a risk factor for the development of obesity.[19]

Individuals living in poverty are not only at a greater risk for developing cardiovascular disease but also more likely to experience greater morbidity and mortality as a result of this condition. This disparity is largely due to inadequate access to health care services. As there are many underlying medical conditions that serve as risk factors for the development of cardiovascular disease, for example, hypertension, Type II diabetes mellitus, and hypercholesterolemia, regular access to health care for the proper diagnosis and treatment of these conditions is critical in the primary prevention of cardiovascular disease. Individuals living in low-income countries have limited access to care for such medical treatment. In sub-Saharan Africa, for example, health care delivery systems are not organized in a manner that allows for delivery of effective care for many chronic illnesses such as diabetes mellitus and hypertension. Patients have been shown to have poor attendance rates, health centers are typically understaffed, and there tends to be an erratic supply of affordable medications such as insulin and blood-pressure-lowering agents.[20] As a result of such limited access, affected individuals often present at a more advanced disease stage where they are more likely to suffer severe disease consequences, for example, cardiovascular complications like myocardial infarction (heart attack) or stroke. Additionally, undiagnosed or inadequately treated individuals living in these regions are more likely to experience such events at a younger age, increasing overall disease burden to the affected population.

Limited health care services have additional negative implications for cardiovascular health. Patients are much less likely to receive acute interventions at the time of a cardiovascular event that might limit the extent of damage to the heart or brain and, thus, mortality or subsequent morbidity or disability. Further, individuals who have suffered a cardiovascular event such as a myocardial infarction have been shown to greatly benefit from the receipt of secondary preventive measures. These measures—for example, treatment with aspirin therapy and specific blood-pressure-lowering agents—decrease the likelihood of experiencing a recurrent event. As might be expected, individuals in low-income regions are much less likely than those in other regions to receive such care.[21] Data have also shown that women in these regions are particularly vulnerable to recurrent cardiovascular events.[22] This finding is consistent with data from developed countries, where access to appropriate care for cardiovascular disease is limited not only for minorities and those living in poverty but for women as well.[23]

Obesity and Overweight

The global morbidity, disability, and mortality associated with being overweight or obese are significant. Both of these conditions are defined by the **body mass index (BMI)**, a measure calculated by dividing one's weight in kilograms by height in meters squared (kg/m^2). An individual with a BMI of 25–29.9 kg/m^2 is classified as **overweight**. An individual with a BMI of 30 kg/m^2 or greater is classified as **obese**. An obese individual may be further categorized as having **severe obesity**, a group at particular high risk of adverse outcomes, if his or her BMI is greater than 40 kg/m^2. Being overweight or obese is associated with a long list of adverse health conditions, including diabetes mellitus, hypertension, hyperlipidemia, cardiovascular disease (both heart disease and stroke), chronic kidney disease, fatty liver disease, and venous thromboembolic disease (blood clots), along with several types of cancer, for example, breast, colon, uterus, and prostate. Being overweight or obese also increases morbidity and disability due to cholelithiasis (gallstones), obstructive sleep apnea, gastroesophageal reflux disease (heartburn), osteoarthritis of the hips and knees, gout, and chronic low back pain. In women, polycystic ovarian syndrome, a condition that often results in female infertility, is associated with obesity. Importantly, being overweight or obese often contributes to an increased risk for mental health disorders such as depression and social isolation.

Globally, prevalence rates of obesity have increased dramatically over the last several decades. Further, it is important to note that the magnitude of increase in obesity prevalence has been dramatic in many regions. The United States is a case in point. As depicted in Figure 5.2, no region in the United States had a prevalence of obesity greater than 14 percent in 1989. In contrast, in 2009, Colorado was the only state with a prevalence of obesity less than

---

MEASURES OF OBESITY

Body Mass Index (BMI): a measure of obesity calculated by dividing one's weight in kilograms by height in meters squared (kg/m^2).

Obesity: a weight classification that applies to individuals with a BMI greater than 30 kg/m^2.

Overweight: a weight classification that applies to individuals with a BMI of 25–29.9 kg/m^2.

Severe Obesity: a weight classification that applies to individuals with a BMI of greater than 40 kg/m^2.

FIGURE 5.2 U.S. Obesity Trends, by State, 1989–2009

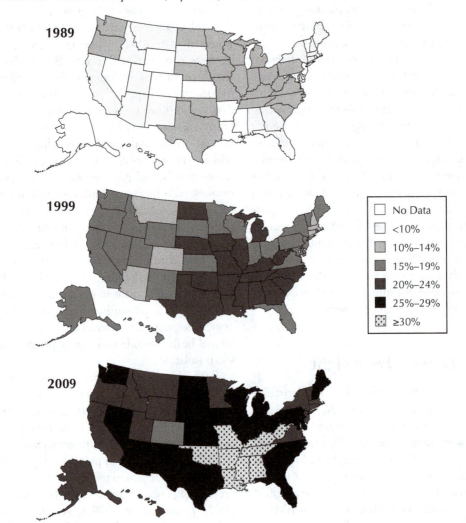

*Data represent percentage of state population that meets criteria for obesity diagnosis.

Source: Reproduced from the Centers for Disease Control and Prevention, *U.S. Obesity Trends, Trends by State 1985–2009* (2009). Available online at: http://www.cdc.gov/obesity/data/trends.html#State.

20 percent. Additionally, 2009 data reveal that nine states had an obesity prevalence greater than 30 percent, and an additional twenty-four states had an obesity prevalence of 25–29 percent.[24] Similar patterns have been observed in other developed regions.

More recently, increases in obesity prevalence have been observed in developing countries as well. In fact, the problem is so widespread that 2005 data suggested that just over 23 percent of the world's adult population was overweight and almost 10 percent was obese, translating to 937 million overweight adults and 396 million obese adults worldwide. Further, if recent trends continue unabated, it is estimated that these numbers will grow to 2.16 billion overweight and 1.12 billion obese individuals worldwide by the year 2030.[25] The problem is certainly not isolated to adults, with the foundation of the growing epidemic based largely on the rising numbers of overweight and obese children. In the United States, the prevalence of overweight and obese children and adolescents more than tripled to nearly 20 percent between

1976 and 2008.[26] As childhood overweight and obesity tend to persist into adulthood, this trend will only worsen the epidemic.

To understand the growing global obesity epidemic, it is necessary to review the determinants of obesity. An individual's risk for becoming overweight or obese is determined by the interaction between individual biological and behavioral variables as well as social and likely political factors. In the simplest of terms, obesity results from an excess energy balance of calories consumed to calories utilized by an individual. However, many individual- and population-level variables contribute to this caloric mismatch in affected individuals.

At the individual level, both behavioral and, to a lesser extent, biological variables contribute to one's risk for obesity. To date, more than twenty genetic loci suspected of increasing an individual's susceptibility to obesity have been discovered. Though the overall contribution to the development of obesity is probably relatively small, these genes likely impact central nervous system regulation of appetite as well as fat metabolism by adipocytes (fat cells).[27] One specific genetic hypothesis proposes that evolutionary pressures have selected for survival "thrifty genes" that historically allowed for survival during times of famine. Based largely on variability of geographic origin and historical risk for famine, particular ethnic groups are more likely to express these genes and subsequently be at risk for obesity when exposed to a Western diet and lifestyle.[28] Similarly, infants born small for gestational age are at increased risk for rapid postnatal weight gain and subsequent obesity, diabetes mellitus, and cardiovascular disease. Recent data have suggested that there may be a genetic and environmental interaction that accounts for such findings.[29] Thus, factors such as maternal smoking and poor maternal nutrition might indirectly impact subsequent obesity risk for the developing fetus.

Obviously, individual behaviors such as dietary choices, both meal portions and composition, and level of physical activity affect obesity risks. However, these individual behaviors are, in turn, shaped by many population-level variables. Individual level of physical activity is determined by both occupational and recreational factors. Leisure-time activity can have a significant effect on the development of obesity. A combination of more time spent in sedentary activities, such as watching television or working on a computer, and less time participating in physical activities increases the risk for obesity. Trends over the last several decades among children and adolescents reflect a shift toward more sedentary leisure activities, which has greatly contributed to the worsening obesity epidemic. Multiple social factors, including neighborhood safety and access to recreational facilities and community park space, determine levels of participation in physical activities.[30] Increasing urbanization often leads to more sedentary jobs as well as greater reliance on motorized transportation, resulting in greater risk for obesity among those low- and middle-income regions experiencing such economic changes.

Carbohydrate-rich diets, sugar-sweetened beverages, and increasing portion sizes are dietary variables that contribute to obesity. Social and environmental factors shape these dietary patterns. Decreasing parental presence for meals, increasing consumption of fast food, and limited neighborhood access to healthy foods have been shown to increase individual obesity risk, with individuals of lower socioeconomic status more likely to have limited access to healthy food choices.[31] Further contributing to the obesity problem among children, many youth have access to sugar-sweetened beverages and high-calorie foods in school.[32] With globalization of the Western lifestyle, individuals living in low- and middle-income countries are increasingly exposed to these dietary patterns that are associated with higher levels of obesity. Further, these individuals may be at even greater risk for developing obesity given the aforementioned genetic vulnerabilities. Additionally, prevailing cultural norms will influence the extent to which the obesity epidemic becomes a problem in developing regions. For example, different cultural perceptions of body size in many developing countries may hinder efforts to slow the obesity epidemic. In many developing regions, larger body size is often associated with affluence, good health, and attractiveness.

UNDER THE MICROSCOPE

Obesity and Excise Taxes on Sugar-sweetened Beverages

The rapidly increasing obesity epidemic poses considerable health and economic risks globally. In response, the WHO adopted the Global Strategy on Diet, Physical Activity, and Health in 2004. National and regional food taxation policies that influence household purchasing choices have been included as one key component of this strategy.

Sugar-sweetened beverages (SSBs) have been identified as an important potential target for intervention. Studies have demonstrated that consumption of SSBs has increased dramatically in recent years and that SSBs contribute significantly to per capita daily calorie consumption, with estimates that as much as 10–15 percent of calories may be derived from SSBs among some populations.[a] Further, because liquid calories have a reduced effect on satiety versus calories consumed as solid foods, SSBs may contribute more significantly to the obesity epidemic than other sources of added sugars.[b]

Given the critical role SSBs play in the worsening obesity epidemic, policies to implement excise taxes on SSBs have been proposed. As opposed to a sales tax, which is a percentage of the overall sales cost that is paid directly by the individual consumer at the point of purchase, an excise tax is imposed on a specific quantity of product, typically at the level of the manufacturer or retailer. The manufacturer or retailer then passes these costs on to the consumer in the form of increased retail costs.

Sales taxes are typically designed to generate revenue rather than influence consumption, and studies have demonstrated that sales taxes on beverages do not impact consumption or obesity.[c] Oftentimes, consumers will purchase discounted generic sodas or even

[a]Gail Woodward-Lopez, Janice Kao, and Lorrene Ritchie, "To What Extent Have Sweetened Beverages Contributed to the Obesity Epidemic?" *Public Health Nutrition* 14: 3 (2011): 499–509.

[b]D.M. Mourao, J. Bressan, W.W. Campbell, and R.D. Mattes, "Effects of Food Form on Appetite and Energy Intake in Lean and Obese Young Adults," *International Journal of Obesity* 31: 11 (2007): 1688–1695.

[c]Eric A. Finkelstein, Chen Zhen, James Nonnemaker, and Jessica E. Todd, "Impact of Targeted Beverage Taxes on Higher- and Lower-income Households," *Archives of Internal Medicine* 170: 22 (2010): 2028–2034.

Conversely, weight loss is often negatively perceived as a possible sign of communicable illness, particularly HIV.[33]

As a result of the large number of chronic medical diseases associated with obesity, the economic consequences of this condition at the individual and population levels are significant. Because obesity disproportionately affects individuals living in poverty, the potential economic consequences at the household level are especially of concern. Individuals often have limited access to necessary medical care and frequently cannot afford medications to treat associated conditions like diabetes mellitus and hypertension, resulting in a greater likelihood of adverse outcomes such as cardiovascular events.

purchase larger serving sizes in an effort to get a better price. With excise taxes, typically proposed as a penny per ounce tax on beverages with added sweeteners, increased manufacturing costs are passed on to consumers in a more uniform manner that would be predicted to reduce consumption of all SSBs.

Evidence exists that excise taxes can influence household purchasing practices in a manner that would likely lead to positive health outcomes at the population level. For example, excise taxes on cigarettes have been associated with decreased population consumption, as has been shown from a rich body of global research. Published studies have demonstrated the efficacy of such policies in South America, North America, Europe, Africa, Asia, and Australia.[d]

Several U.S. states and cities have proposed the implementation of SSB excise taxes. However, these proposals have been met with considerable resistance, particularly from the sugar industry and SSB manufacturers and retailers. These groups have invested considerable funds to influence public opinion in regions where such taxes have been considered, the result of which has been an increase in lobbying expenditures by the beverage industry and the withdrawal of such proposals by public officials. Despite these obstacles, excise taxes on SSBs remain a viable option in the strategy to curb the obesity epidemic. Recent public opinion polls have demonstrated support for an SSB excise tax, particularly if at least some portion of the generated revenues is earmarked to help fund obesity prevention programs.[e]

---

[d]Belén Sáenz de Miera-Juárez and Roberto Iglesias, "Taxation and Tobacco Control: The Cases of Brazil and Mexico," *Salud Pública de México* 52: Suppl. 2 (2010): S172–S185; Centers for Disease Control and Prevention, "Federal and State Cigarette Excise Taxes—United States, 1995–2009," *Morbidity and Mortality Weekly Report* 58: 19 (2009): 524–527; Tibor Szilágyi, "Higher Cigarette Taxes—Healthier People, Wealthier State: The Hungarian Experience," *Central European Journal of Public Health* 15: 3 (2007): 122–126; Mireille Y. Cheyip, G. Nelson, M.H. Ross, and Jill Murray, "South African Platinum Mine Employees Reduce Smoking in 5 Years," *Tobacco Control* 16: 3 (2007): 197–201; Chun-Yuan Ye, Jie-Min Lee, and Sheng-Hong Chen, "Economic Gains and Health Benefits from a New Cigarette Tax Scheme in Taiwan: A Simulation Using the CGE Model," *BMC Public Health* 6: 62 (2006): 1–9; Sally M. Dunlop, Donna Perez, and Trish Cotter, "Australian Smokers' and Recent Quitters' Responses to the Increasing Price of Cigarettes in the Context of a Tobacco Tax Increase," *Addiction* 106: 5 (2011): 1–9.

[e]Field Research Corporation, *Soda Tax Poll 2010*. Available online at: http://www.yaleruddcenter. org/resources/upload/docs/what/policy/SSBtaxes/CCPHAPollSodaTax3.10.pdf.

These adverse outcomes can, in turn, lead to disabilities that limit one's ability to work.

Particularly in developing countries, the net result of such circumstances is often the creation of a vicious cycle of poverty, in which conditions such as obesity contribute to the greater likelihood that poor individuals will remain in poverty.[34] Obesity also results in considerable economic burden to populations, in terms of both health care expenditures and negative effects on productivity in the workplace. In the United States, annual medical expenditures per person were nearly $1,500 (42 percent) greater for obese individuals than for normal-weight individuals in 2006, yielding an estimated net excess spending of

$147 billion annually, up from $74 billion in 1998. Canada and Germany have experienced similar findings of excess spending attributable to obesity.[35] Obesity has also been shown to contribute to work impairment, including higher rates of absenteeism, with estimated excess costs due to health-related lost productivity time among obese workers totaling more than $11.7 billion as compared with nonobese employees in a recent U.S. survey.[36]

Given the health and economic global burdens posed by the rapidly increasing obesity epidemic, measures to slow and perhaps reverse the trend are imperative. Studies have demonstrated that lifestyle (dietary and physical activity) and medical (both pharmacotherapy and surgical) interventions to prevent diabetes mellitus and cardiovascular disease among obese individuals are cost-effective.[37] However, efforts to prevent the condition of obesity are likely to be even more cost-effective than interventions to prevent complications among obese individuals, particularly in low- and middle-income regions, where national health care budgets are limited. Therefore, efforts to promote a healthier lifestyle at the population level are critical.

Consistent with this aim, the World Health Organization (WHO), in 2004, adopted the Global Strategy on Diet, Physical Activity, and Health. The overall goal of the strategy is "to promote and protect health by guiding the development of an enabling environment for sustainable actions at individual, community, national and global levels that, when taken together, will lead to reduced disease and death rates related to unhealthy diet and physical inactivity."[38] The strategy calls for partnership between intergovernmental bodies (such as the United Nations, national governments, non-governmental organizations, and professional societies) and the private sector to formulate policies and action plans that will result in lasting changes that contribute to healthier living worldwide. One key component of the strategy is the recommendation that governments provide accurate and balanced information to the public so that individuals may make informed choices about matters that may affect health. Additionally, national food and agricultural policies that promote and protect public health are encouraged—including, but not limited to, fiscal measures such as food taxation policies that influence household food purchasing choices. The strategy also stresses the need for public policies that provide opportunities for sports and recreation activities for the entire population. Further, the strategy urges governments to make long-term investments in surveillance, research, and evaluation of major risk factors that contribute to unhealthy lifestyles.

The WHO strategy has been met with resistance by certain key players, most notably the global sugar industry and high-income countries such as the United States. Fiscal and food policies that serve as disincentives to large-scale sugar consumption have obvious negative ramifications for the sugar industry as well as adverse consequences for U.S. corporations involved in the global food trade.[39] Despite such resistance among powerful state and non-state actors, all important global partners will need to make the promotion of public health a priority in order to slow the worsening worldwide obesity epidemic.

Tobacco Abuse

Tobacco abuse is another condition that contributes significantly to global morbidity, disability, and mortality. Chronic tobacco use has been shown to increase one's risk for cancers of the lungs, mouth, throat, upper airway, esophagus, stomach, pancreas, bladder, and kidney. In women, it has also been associated with cervical cancer. Cardiovascular diseases such as heart disease and stroke are also significantly more common among smokers than nonsmokers. Tobacco smoking leads to chronic obstructive lung disease and increases one's risk for bronchitis as well as pneumonia. Maternal smoking during pregnancy has been shown to have negative implications, such as miscarriage, for pregnancy outcomes as well as for the developing fetus, most notably prematurity and low birth weight. As has been previously discussed, these conditions, in turn, may increase subsequent risk for obesity and cardiovascular disease in adulthood. Maternal smoking during pregnancy has also been associated with a subsequent increased risk for sudden infant death syndrome (SIDS). Additionally, considerable morbidity and mortality is associated with exposure to secondhand smoke (SHS). Among children, exposure to SHS has been associated with respiratory conditions including asthma as well as pneumonia. Exposure to SHS during infancy also increases the risk for SIDS. Limited evidence also suggests that childhood exposure to SHS is associated with dysfunction of vascular endothelial cells (cells that form the inner lining of blood vessels), raising the possibility that such exposure may contribute to the subsequent development of cardiovascular disease.[40] Similar concerns have been raised about childhood SHS exposure and the subsequent risk for lung cancer.[41] SHS exposure among children also contributes to middle ear disease as well as increased school absenteeism. Among adults, data support a relationship between SHS exposure and the risk for cardiovascular diseases, respiratory illnesses such as pneumonia, lung cancer, and all-cause mortality.[42]

Despite the known medical hazards of tobacco smoking as well as exposure to SHS, the consumption of tobacco products is increasing worldwide, with a shift in use from predominantly high-income countries to middle- and low-income countries. In fact, more than 80 percent of the world's 1 billion smokers reside in middle- and low-income countries. Given tobacco's widespread consumption as well as the number of severe medical conditions with which it is associated, it should not be surprising that its use is currently among the most significant contributors to the global burden of noncommunicable illness and, as shown in Figure 5.3, is a risk factor for leading global causes of mortality. Data show that tobacco use contributes to more than 5 million deaths globally each year and accounts for one of every ten adult deaths. Approximately one-half of all persistent smokers will die prematurely. Further, it is estimated that by 2030 tobacco use will contribute to more than 8 million worldwide

deaths annually if current consumption trends continue, with more than 80 percent of these deaths occurring in low- and middle-income countries.[43]

Several factors influence an individual's likelihood of smoking. As previously discussed, in high-income countries, individuals of lower socioeconomic status and with less educational attainment are more likely to smoke. Though more affluent individuals in low- and middle-income countries have historically had a greater likelihood of smoking tobacco, recent trends suggest that the burden of smoking is now disproportionately experienced by poor individuals in these regions as well.[44] Individuals with mental health disorders are another group at risk for chronic tobacco abuse; notably, the risk for mental health disorders is higher for individuals with lower socioeconomic status. Additionally, in both developed and developing regions, children of smokers more commonly smoke as adolescents and adults than do children of nonsmokers.[45] Conversely, parental disapproval of smoking has been shown to reduce the likelihood of adolescent smoking initiation.[46] In both developed and developing regions, mass media marketing of tobacco products through direct advertising as well as through product placement in cultural and entertainment events has been linked to increased tobacco use among both adults and adolescents.[47] In fact, the effects of tobacco advertising and promotion often override parental influences on smoking behavior by adolescents.[48] The tobacco industry invests in such marketing efforts to adolescents and young adults with the realization that the initiation of smoking often leads to chronic tobacco abuse. The nicotine contained in cigarettes and other forms of tobacco is highly addictive. The properties of nicotine are such that individuals exposed to consistently high levels of the drug will crave it and experience unpleasant withdrawal symptoms when abstaining from use. Thus, those individuals who begin using tobacco products tend to become chronic abusers.

Similar to the condition of obesity, tobacco abuse is associated with considerable economic consequences at both the household level and the

FIGURE 5.3 Tobacco Use as a Risk Factor for Leading Global Causes of Death, 2005

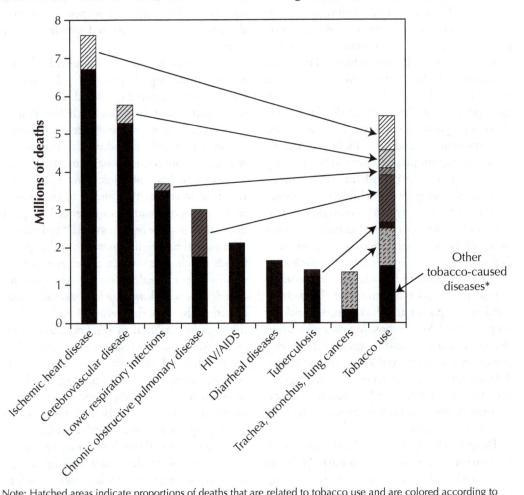

Note: Hatched areas indicate proportions of deaths that are related to tobacco use and are colored according to the column of the respective cause of death.

*Includes mouth and oropharyngeal cancers, esophageal cancer, stomach cancer, liver cancer, and other cancers, as well as cardiovascular diseases other than ischemic heart disease and cerebrovascular disease.

Source: Reproduced from the World Health Organization, *WHO Report on the Global Tobacco Epidemic, 2008: The MPOWER Package*: 8. Available online at: http://www.who.int/tobacco/mpower/mpower_report_full_2008.pdf.

population level. Much of the household-level burden is experienced disproportionately by those living in poverty. For example, recent data show that at the household level in Indonesia, the lowest-income group spends 15 percent of its total expenditure on tobacco.[49] Such spending limits resources available for household spending on food, education, and health care. In fact, parental tobacco abuse in low-income countries is associated with childhood malnutrition.[50] Additionally, individuals often have limited earning potential due to diminished

health status associated with tobacco abuse. As a result, households in which one or more family members abuse tobacco are vulnerable to getting stuck in a cycle of poverty.

Like the condition of obesity, tobacco abuse also results in considerable economic burden to populations, in terms of both health care expenditures and negative productivity effects in the workplace. In the United States for the period 1995–1999, estimated annual smoking-related costs were $157.7 billion, with more than $75 billion in direct medical costs and $82 billion in indirect costs from lost productivity.[51] Data from this period suggest that the total annual costs, including both direct health care expenditures and indirect costs such as decreased productivity, of tobacco use in many developing regions are considerable, estimated to be as much as $5 billion per year in China and $1.7 billion per year in India.[52] As a number of the adverse health effects of tobacco abuse are often not seen until after many years of exposure, it is anticipated that the economic burden attributable to smoking seen in low-income countries will grow considerably in the coming decades.

Because of these considerable health and economic consequences, global measures to slow the tobacco abuse epidemic are necessary. Owing to the addictive nature of the nicotine contained in tobacco products, individuals who smoke find it difficult to quit, even though the majority would like to do so. To address this issue, several behavioral and pharmacological interventions have been devised. These therapies, however, are of limited effectiveness and often not implemented until after adverse health consequences have already developed, underscoring the importance of measures that prevent the initiation of tobacco use. Preventive measures focus on education as well as government policies that limit mass media marketing, restrict public smoking, and serve as financial disincentives to the purchase of tobacco products. Educational interventions have been shown to decrease the initiation of tobacco use among adolescents. However, it has also been demonstrated that educational campaigns to prevent smoking are less likely to reach individuals of lower socioeconomic status.[53] In developed countries like the United States, where legislation has restricted advertising to youth and has limited product placement in media such as television programs, a decrease in the prevalence of smoking has been observed. Similarly, financial disincentives, including the imposition of taxes on tobacco products, have been associated with decreased tobacco use.[54] Lastly, smoke-free air laws have resulted in decreased SHS exposure risk while not adversely affecting the restaurant and hospitality industries.[55]

As the prevalence of tobacco use in developed countries has decreased over the past several decades as a result of such interventions, the tobacco industry has directed marketing and sales efforts to developing regions. This strategy reflects, in large part, the fact that low- and middle-income countries are much less likely than high-income countries to have legislated policies that significantly tax tobacco products, restrict advertising, require health risk labeling on tobacco products, or mandate smoke-free air in specified public areas. As mentioned previously, this shift has resulted in a redistribution of smoking prevalence such that 80 percent of the world's 1 billion smokers now reside in middle- and low-income countries.

To appropriately address the global tobacco epidemic, an internationally coordinated response is required. To that end, the WHO in 2003 negotiated the WHO Framework Convention on Tobacco Control, a treaty that has been signed by 168 of the 192 WHO member states to date.[56] The treaty emphasizes price and tax measures as well as nonprice interventions intended to reduce the global supply of and demand for tobacco products. Importantly, these efforts will need to address the potential economic ramifications for, and allay concerns of, regions that benefit from the production and distribution of tobacco. Due to these constraints, any successful reduction in global tobacco use that is achieved is very likely to be gradual and would allow for tobacco-dependent economies to transition to alternative commodities, particularly with appropriate governmental support.[57]

Conclusion

The data on global morbidity and mortality attributable to noncommunicable illnesses demonstrate that although noncommunicable diseases have historically been more prevalent in developed countries, developing regions now experience the greatest burden attributable to these conditions. Although the aging of populations that is seen with economic growth in developing regions explains some of this shift, a significant portion is attributable to the economic and social dynamics of globalization. In particular, globalization of the Western lifestyle and diet is contributing significantly to the growing worldwide epidemics of obesity and tobacco abuse. These epidemics, in turn, contribute to the worsening global burden of cardiovascular disease. Similarly, in great part due to the obesity epidemic, other noncommunicable illnesses such as diabetes mellitus are increasing at an alarming rate in both developed and developing regions. By 2030, nearly 5 percent of the global population will develop diabetes mellitus, and approximately one-third of the U.S. population will do so by 2050.[58] This alarming increase in the prevalence of noncommunicable illnesses around the world is not sustainable. The rising levels of noncommunicable disease in developing and developed countries not only pose major challenges to the health of populations across the globe but also generate significant threats to economic and social well-being in many societies.

Thus, transnational collaboration is necessary to slow and perhaps reverse these trends. Improved access to early, effective treatment for conditions such as diabetes mellitus, hypertension, and tobacco abuse is necessary to reduce the prevalence of other chronic conditions such as end-stage renal disease and cardiovascular diseases that can result from these illnesses. Treatment of underlying conditions is cost-effective when one considers the economic burden of the secondary illness. In the United States, for example, whereas the cost of medication for the early treatment of diabetes is as little as $15–$150 monthly, the total per person/per year outpatient expenditures for patients with end-stage renal disease is approximately $30,000.[59] Further, appropriate early management of these conditions will allow affected individuals to remain in the workforce and contribute to the economic growth of the population.

An even more cost-effective approach would be the prevention of many noncommunicable illnesses through policies that promote and support access to healthy foods and participation in routine physical activity as well as reduce the abuse of tobacco, alcohol, and drugs. Prevention and early treatment measures must be inclusive of especially vulnerable groups such as women, minorities, and those living in poverty. Governments will need to organize health care systems in a manner that anticipates these growing noncommunicable disease epidemics. This need is particularly critical in developing countries that still must be prepared to deal with significant disease burden due to communicable illnesses. Lastly, governments must also be attentive to cultural and economic considerations in formulating policies intended to address public health threats from noncommunicable diseases in order to minimize public resistance to such policies and to increase the likelihood of success.

Discussion Questions

1. Are noncommunicable diseases primarily a concern for high-income countries? Why or why not?
2. What are the determinants for cardiovascular disease? Are most determinants for cardiovascular disease modifiable? Why or why not?
3. What factors have contributed to the worsening global obesity epidemic?
4. What are possible barriers to the reduction of global tobacco abuse? How might these barriers be addressed?
5. What are the implications of the global obesity and tobacco abuse epidemics for health care systems in developed countries? In developing countries?

Web Resources

NCDnet—Global Noncommunicable Disease Network: http://www.who.int/ncdnet/en/

WHO Framework Convention on Tobacco Control: http://www.who.int/fctc/en/

WHO Noncommunicable Disease Surveillance: http://www.who.int/ncd_surveillance/en/

WHO Strategy on Diet, Physical Activity, and Health: http://www.who.int/dietphysicalactivity/en/

PART III

The International Relations of Global Health

CHAPTER 6

Economic, Ethnic, and Gender Inequities in Global Health

Introduction

Different levels of economic development and inequitable distribution of economic resources fundamentally shape health outcomes for individuals, communities, and populations across the globe. Additionally, inequities in individual and population health stem from a variety of cultural, political, and social variables. Gender norms also contribute to inequities in global health. Accordingly, this chapter explores inequities in global health at multiple levels: territorially based inequities among different regions and countries of the world, poverty-based inequities that cut across territorial borders, racial and ethnic inequities within countries, and gender inequities in the health status of men and women.

Economic Development and Territorially Based Inequities in Global Health

National Economic Development and Population Health

The achievement of higher levels of national **economic development** tracks closely with significant improvements in population health. The growth of the modern state in the 20th century was accompanied by unprecedented improvements in human health. As Richard Skolnik notes, "It is an astonishing fact that half of all the increase in human life expectancy over recorded time occurred in the 20th century."[1] It is not a coincidence that this century involved the buildup of public infrastructure that either directly or indirectly contributed to improved living conditions and health outcomes among populations living in areas that attained high levels of economic and social development. Millions of lives have been saved due to large-scale public health interventions, including the creation of public water systems and public sewers.[2] In fact, the relationship between economic development and population health is mutually reinforcing. Investments in public infrastructure help fuel economic development that, in turn, contributes to improvements in public health. A healthier, longer-living population sustains high levels of economic development, which enables a country to make long-term investments in population health.

Many reasons help explain the strength of the positive relationship between national wealth and population health. Economic development increases the amount of financial resources available to national governments to direct toward investments in public health. Such investments might include funding or subsidization of health care for individuals, the use of financial resources to implement and enforce regulations that contribute to improvements in population health (for example,

KEY TERMS IN THE INTERNATIONAL POLITICAL ECONOMY OF GLOBAL HEALTH

Economic Development: growth in income and improvements in standard of living in a country, region, or community.

Gross Domestic Product (GDP): the market value of all final goods and services produced within a country during a specified period.

Human Development: a concept of development that takes not only national income but life expectancy, literacy rates, poverty rates, and other indicators of quality-of-life of individuals in particular countries into account.

North-South Gap: a term used to describe the significant economic, political, and social divisions between developed countries (largely concentrated in the northern hemisphere) and developing countries (largely concentrated in the southern hemisphere).

Per Capita Gross Domestic Product (GDP): the market value per person of all final goods and services produced within a country during a specified period.

Political Liberalization: a process of political change involving the adoption of democratic reforms, increased governmental transparency, the protection of the rule of law, and the expansion of individual political freedoms as means for reducing poverty in the developing world.

Poverty Trap: a self-perpetuating condition that keeps individuals, households, or populations in poverty.

State Capacity: the ability of a state to govern itself effectively and to implement important public policy objectives, such as social and economic development.

Structural Adjustment Policies: policy changes involving privatization and deregulation required by the World Bank and the International Monetary Fund as a condition for receiving low-interest development loans.

World Bank: an international financial institution that provides low-interest loans to developing countries for the purpose of reducing poverty.

---

regulations governing workplace, food, or drug safety or environmental regulations), or public investments in infrastructure (like safe roads and public water systems) that improve public health. Higher levels of national wealth also make it more likely that individuals and families will have access to employer-funded health care. More simply, a healthy national economy creates socioeconomic benefits in the form of higher levels of education and income for individuals and families, which contribute to better health outcomes, as discussed in Chapter 2.

If national wealth and population health are positively correlated, the reverse, unfortunately, is also true. Major health problems within a country can lead to **poverty traps** that hinder national economic development. In turn, low levels of economic development make it difficult for countries to promote

UNDER THE MICROSCOPE

The Inequitable Effects of Natural Disasters

When natural disasters strike, people living in poverty are more likely to suffer negative consequences. The inequitable effects of natural disasters are felt at country, community, and neighborhood levels. The negative effects of natural disasters are often amplified in developing countries. At the community level, low-income populations living in areas of concentrated poverty often suffer catastrophic injury at higher rates than people living in wealthier neighborhoods.

Developing countries and low-income populations are more vulnerable to the negative effects of so-called natural disasters for many reasons. Developing countries often have weak state capacity to respond to calamitous events. Moreover, they typically do not have adequate public infrastructure to meet basic needs in the face of serious natural disasters or to respond to major public emergencies. The lack of effective regulations on safety standards in public buildings or housing contributes to the negative consequences when natural disasters strike. In low-income communities, the housing of people in poverty is more likely to be made from substandard materials that are vulnerable to collapse and destruction in the face of hurricanes, earthquakes, flooding, and other natural disasters. People living in poverty also do not have the income or other resources to seek necessary medical care, emergency housing, or transportation out of a disaster zone.

The comparative mortality outcomes from the 2010 earthquakes in Haiti and Chile serve as a stark example of this problem. The 8.8-magnitude earthquake in Chile resulted in a death toll numbering in the hundreds, whereas the 7-magnitude earthquake in Haiti led to an estimated 220,000 deaths.[a] While some of this disparity can be attributed to geological differences between the two regions as well as energy differences between the two earthquakes, socioeconomic factors also played a role. Chile's national income is significantly higher than Haiti's. In 2010, the per capita GDP in Chile was $14,780 compared to $1,040 in Haiti.[b] Differences in state capacity and public infrastructure, including emergency response planning and building code regulations, also contributed to these disparate outcomes.[c]

---

[a]Stephen Kurczy, Leigh Montgomery, and Elizabeth Ryan, "Chile Earthquake Facts: Chile vs. Haiti, in Numbers," *Christian Science Monitor*, March 2, 2010.

[b]United Nations Development Programme, *International Human Development Indicators.* Available online at: http://hdr.undp.org/en/statistics/data/.

[c]Tim Padgett, "Why Chile Is Better than Haiti at Handling Earthquakes," *Time*, March 1, 2010.

public health and, in fact, can exacerbate preexisting health challenges, leading to a vicious cycle of poverty and disease. A strong negative relationship exists between health indicators and **state capacity**, a state's ability to govern itself effectively and to implement basic public policy objectives.[3] According to Andrew T. Price-Smith, disease serves as a stressor on state capacity and increases deprivation in a population, thereby leading to more demands on the state to meet basic needs and provide public services and, ultimately, it may undermine or reverse development gains.[4]

In countries with a high incidence of communicable disease, there are considerable negative implications for economic growth. For example, between 1965 and 1990, countries with high rates of malaria experienced an average growth in per capita GDP of 0.4 percent per year, whereas average growth in other countries was 2.3 percent per year.[5] Although it does not fully explain the disparity in economic growth, the negative effects that high rates of malaria have on trade, tourism, and foreign domestic investments are likely a significant factor. Decreased demand for agricultural imports from regions with high rates of communicable illness also contributes to this problem.[6]

Not surprisingly, a strong correlation between national wealth and health status exists. Data from the United Nations Development Programme (UNDP) illustrate the strength of this correlation. According to 2010 data, the ten countries with the highest **per capita gross domestic product** (GDP in U.S. dollars), the market value per person of all final goods and services produced within a country during a specified period, included Liechtenstein ($94,569), Qatar ($77,178), Luxembourg ($76,448), Norway ($58,278), United Arab Emirates ($56,485), Kuwait ($50,284), Singapore ($50,266), Brunei Darussalam ($49,915), the United States ($46,653), and Hong Kong ($45,049). Each of these countries achieved high rankings on measures of life expectancy, ranging from 76 years in Qatar to 82.5 in Hong Kong.[7]

In contrast, the ten countries with the lowest per capita GDP were Zimbabwe ($187), the Democratic Republic of the Congo ($326), Liberia ($400), Burundi ($403), Guinea-Bissau ($554), Eritrea ($648), Niger ($677), the Central African Republic ($766), Sierra-Leone ($825), and Togo ($846). Four of these countries were among the countries

that ranked lowest globally on measures of life expectancy—Zimbabwe (47 years), the Central African Republic (47.7 years), the Democratic Republic of the Congo (48 years), and Sierra Leone (48.2 years). The other countries with the lowest per capita GDP also had relatively low average life expectancy: Togo achieved the highest ranking on this measure, with life expectancy of 63.3 years, a figure still significantly below measures for more developed countries.[8]

As these data suggest, a strong correlation between national wealth and population health exists. However, the relationship between wealth and health does not tell the entire story. UNDP data on wealth and health also contain interesting gaps that indicate other factors are at play in shaping population health outcomes. Japan, with a per capita GDP of only $33,649, achieved the highest ranking on measures of life expectancy, at 83.2 years. Numerous additional countries, including Switzerland, Iceland, Australia, France, Italy, Sweden, Spain, and Israel, had higher life expectancy than the countries that were ranked in the top ten based on per capita GDP; only Hong Kong was ranked in the top ten on both measures.[9]

At the other end of the spectrum, several low-income countries that had higher per capita GDP when compared with other low-income countries performed the worst on measures of life expectancy. Afghanistan, with a per capita GDP of $1,419, ranked the lowest worldwide on life expectancy, at 44 years. The ongoing war in Afghanistan certainly plays a role in this outcome. Next to Afghanistan, Lesotho and Swaziland had the lowest life expectancy, at 45.9 and 47 years, respectively, despite having higher per capita GDPs ($1,608 for Lesotho and $5,058 for Swaziland) than many other developing countries. High prevalence of HIV/AIDS in these countries likely plays a role in these outcomes. Notably, these countries are still quite poor in comparison to high-income countries, but they have significantly higher GDPs than the very poorest countries. Yet, their relatively higher levels of national wealth did not contribute to higher life expectancies for their populations. Such gaps make clear that national wealth alone is not sufficient for measuring or promoting population health.

Human Development and Population Health

Critics argue that measures of national wealth are an imperfect indication of the quality of life or well-being of individuals within a country. In response, the United Nations Development Programme came up with the concept of **human development**. Rather than assuming that national income is the best measure for human well-being within countries, the concept of human development suggests that other indicators, including life expectancy, literacy rates, and levels of poverty, need to be taken into account when trying to assess the well-being of individuals in particular countries.

Although the human development index incorporates a variety of indicators in addition to national wealth, country rankings on the human development index do not vary dramatically from measures of national wealth as a general rule. There is considerable overlap among the countries that rank highest on both indicators. Countries categorized as high-income tend to rank high on the human development index. Conversely, countries categorized as low-income tend to be located toward the bottom of the scale on the human development index.

For example, in the Human Development Report 2009, Norway had the highest ranking on the UNDP's human development scale, and Niger had the lowest ranking. Norway's per capita GDP was US$58,278 in comparison to per capita GDP of only $294 in Niger. In both cases, the countries were at the extremes of the scale in terms of relative national wealth. The discrepancy between life expectancy in each country was equally stark: 80.5 years in Norway compared to just 50.8 years in Niger. Government expenditures on health also dramatically differed, with the Norwegian government spending $3,780 per capita in comparison to only $14 by the government in Niger. These figures suggest a very strong correlation between national wealth and health status.[10] This correlation is especially strong at the extreme ends of the spectrum, with the wealthiest countries tending to have high rankings on leading health indicators and the poorest countries having the worst outcomes.

Although there is a strong relationship between national wealth and population health, these correlations are not perfect. A comparison of the 2009 data from the Human Development Report for four countries—the United States, Cyprus, China, and Mexico—effectively demonstrates the imperfect correlation between relative wealth and population health. Among these countries, the United States had the highest per capita GDP at $45,592 and a life expectancy of 79.1 years. The U.S. government spent $3,074 per capita on health. In Cyprus, the per capita GDP was $24,895, yet life expectancy was slightly higher, at 79.6 years. That year, Cyprus spent $759 per capita on health. During this time period, Mexico had a per capita GDP of only $9,715, a life expectancy of 76 years, and government health expenditures of just $327 per capita. Despite much lower national income and government spending on health, the life expectancy in Mexico was not dramatically lower than in the United States. Similarly, China had a per capita GDP of just $2,432, a life expectancy of 72.9 years, and government health expenditures of just $144.[11] These figures indicate that the correlation between national income and health outcomes is not perfect and that other factors are in play in determining the health status and well-being of populations across the globe.

As these figures suggest, a human development lens applied to global health provides some interesting insights and leads to a number of important questions.[12] On the one hand, measures of national wealth and human development indicators tend to follow the same trajectory. As a general rule, wealthy countries score high on measures of human development, whereas poor countries produce low levels of human development. On the other hand, important gaps between national wealth and human development exist. These gaps can signify the existence of inequities within societies that are not captured by measures of a country's income alone.

What, then, explains the fact that health outcomes may not be significantly worse in countries with much lower national incomes and government health expenditures than in wealthier countries? Health policy is one variable that may help explain that national income and health outcomes do not correlate perfectly. Some countries with relatively low national income may, despite their relative poverty, spend health care dollars in a more efficient, effective, and equitable manner than wealthier countries. We explore the relationship between national health care policy and population health outcomes further in Chapter 10.

Moreover, national income does not account for inequities within societies, and, thus, it is not a perfect predictor of health outcomes. A high per capita GDP might mask vast inequities between the wealthiest and the poorest members of a society. Similarly, bad health outcomes within disadvantaged groups in particular societies will bring down measures of average life expectancy even if such inequities are not captured by aggregate measures. Subsequent sections of this chapter explore the inequities *across* and *within* societies that are not captured by measures of national wealth.

Poverty and Economic Inequities Across and Within States

Poverty and health are linked in fundamental and complicated ways. Strong connections between wealth and health status exist at the global, regional, state, and individual levels. The previous section focused on national-level indicators of health, which illustrate the strong, if imperfect, correlation between wealth and health. Although the relationship between national wealth and health is powerful, we need to move away from a country-based analysis in order to gain a fuller understanding of the ways in which wealth shapes health outcomes. As we will see, a state-centric lens does not provide a complete picture of the nature of economic inequities in global health.

A North-South Gap in Global Health

Structural features of the global economy and international political system create dynamics that produce and reinforce inequities between developed and developing countries, contributing to systemic inequities in global health that transcend the territorial borders of specific countries. As shown in the previous section, measures of population health vary dramatically among states. Much of this variation can be attributed to different levels of national economic development. However, it is not enough to look at the state as a unit of analysis in order to understand the ways in which economic inequities shape population health outcomes. Rather, these economic inequities are rooted in broader economic and social forces, including the legacy of colonialism and globalization processes, which transcend the borders that divide states. Variations among states matter, to be sure. But a more general divide between developed and developing countries is also significant.

This division between developed and developing countries is often referred to as a **North-South gap** and is characterized by significant differences in levels of social and economic development as well as varying degrees of political influence and power on the global stage. The North-South gap describes real and important divisions between developed and developing countries that break down largely along geographical lines. The vast majority of developed countries are geographically located in the northern hemisphere. Conversely, most developing countries are located in the southern hemisphere. Hence, scholars often describe the divisions between developed and developing countries as a North-South gap.

Despite the geographic distribution of this gap, the most notable feature of the north-south division of the international system is inequitable access to global economic resources. Five and a half billion of the world's approximately 6.7 billion people—82 percent—live in developing countries.[13] Almost 1.4 billion people live on less than $1.25 per day, the figure that the **World Bank** uses to define the poverty line. Most of the people surviving on less than $1.25 per day live in developing countries. Poverty rates are significantly higher in some regions. For instance, whereas 20 percent of the population in East Asia lives on less than $1.25 per day, over 50 percent of the population in sub-Saharan Africa lives below the poverty line.[14] The inequitable distribution of global economic resources is also reflected in the high concentration of wealth in developed countries. For instance, the UNDP has estimated that populations in high-income countries have over eighty times as much income as people in low-income countries.[15]

Although poverty levels remain high throughout the developing world, it is important to note significant reductions in global poverty. According to the World Bank, the number of people living below the poverty line has fallen from 1.9 billion in 1981 to 1.4 billion in 2005. This decline represents a significant reduction in the percentage of the world's population living below the poverty line—from 52 to 26 percent[16]—and is particularly notable given that the world's population has been increasing during this time period. Despite the reduction in the number and percentage of people living in abject poverty, the number of people living in moderate poverty—on less than $2 per day—increased during the same time period from 2.5 billion people to 2.6 billion people. Because the world's population has been growing, this increase in the absolute number of people living in moderate poverty still represents a reduction in the proportion of the world's population living in moderate poverty, from 70 to 48 percent.[17] Declining rates of global poverty are a welcome development. Nevertheless, both the absolute number and the proportion of the world's population

living in either abject or moderate poverty remain incredibly high.

Not surprisingly, the economic inequities between developed and developing countries contribute to significant gaps in global health. On the whole, developing countries have worse outcomes across the board on most health indicators. They have lower life expectancy; higher rates of maternal, infant, and child mortality; higher rates of malnutrition; and higher prevalence of communicable illnesses. The high concentration of poverty-related disease in the developing world is especially notable. For example, diarrhea is the second major cause of death among children globally, and most of these deaths—over 99 percent—occur in the developing world.[18] The fact that preventable childhood deaths from diarrhea occur almost exclusively in the developing world is a striking figure. It indicates clear evidence of a pattern throughout the developing world, suggesting that the causes of poverty-related illness cannot be located only in specific countries. Rather, scholars, practitioners, and policy makers must be attentive to the systemic roots of poverty and poverty-related health challenges.

The necessity of paying attention to the systemic roots of the North-South gap raises the question of what causes the fundamental divide between developed and developing countries. The history of colonialism in the developing world certainly has played a significant role. The negative legacy of colonialism is far reaching. Colonial powers created administrative structures and political borders in colonized territories that did not correspond to the ethnic, social, or cultural composition of these areas. As a result, new states that were created during the process of decolonization were based on arbitrary boundaries that have contributed to ongoing civil conflict and power struggles in these countries decades later. Colonial administrative practices also disrupted traditional modes of governance while excluding the majority of indigenous populations from colonial governing institutions. Thus, when colonial rule ended, much of the indigenous population had not had access to the education and administrative experience essential for effective governance of large modern states. Moreover, colonial governance was antidemocratic and antithetical to the rule of law. Therefore, it should not be surprising that the departure of colonial powers left in place political structures and systems that were not grounded in democracy or the rule of law. Obviously, the structure of colonialism also created lasting economic dependencies—in which former colonial powers continue to exert control over natural resources, markets, and financial resources in former colonies—that reinforce inequities between developed and developing countries.

Although virtually all scholars acknowledge the historical role of colonialism in creating and perpetuating inequities between developed and developing countries, consensus does not exist among scholars, practitioners, and policy makers regarding the ways in which global economic structures and processes affect this gap today or on the question of how the international community should respond. Marxist scholars argue that neocolonialism or imperialism is to blame. In this view, the political and economic relationships between developing and developed countries are characterized by ongoing subordination, exploitation, and domination.

In a similar vein, many scholars and practitioners (Marxist and otherwise) point to globalization as the driving force underlying many inequities between developed and developing countries. Critics of globalization argue that the increasing interconnectedness of the global economy puts pressure on all countries to reduce wages, to eliminate or forgo environmental and workplace safety regulations, to limit human rights protections, and to implement cutbacks in the provision of basic social services, including health services, in an effort to attract or keep corporate investment. These pressures can have particularly strong effects in developing countries, which already have lower levels of economic development, relatively weak state capacity, and limited public infrastructure. **Structural adjustment policies**

required by the World Bank as a condition for low-cost development loans also contribute to such pressures.[19]

Other scholars believe that economic liberalization, a concept introduced in Chapter 1, is precisely what is needed to foster social and economic development. According to this perspective, economic liberalization generates higher national wealth, which, in the aggregate, increases the resources available to national governments, communities, families, and individuals. These resources can strengthen state capacity, thereby enabling states in the long run to build up public infrastructure and to govern more effectively. Additionally, proponents argue that the wealth generated by economic liberalization expands the resources available to families and individuals for spending on goods and services, like health and education, that confer important socioeconomic improvements. In a similar vein, other scholars believe that **political liberalization** is essential for reducing the gap between developed and developing countries. In this view, inefficient, corrupt, and illiberal governments share a significant portion of the blame for poverty in developing countries. Proponents of this view advocate political reforms involving the adoption of democratic reforms, increased governmental transparency, the protection of the rule of law, and the expansion of individual political freedoms as means for reducing poverty in the developing world.[20]

Despite the lack of scholarly consensus on how to respond, the concept of a North-South gap helpfully draws attention to systemic inequities in global health. Nevertheless, this approach is also problematic. Grouping the world into two single categories obscures important differences across, between, and within countries. For one thing, a North-South gap suggests a strictly geographic dividing line between developed and developing countries that is not accurate. For example, Australia and New Zealand are developed countries geographically located in the global south. In a similar vein, reducing the world to two categories of development is overly simplistic.

For instance, many countries from the former Soviet bloc, including Belarus, Georgia, Armenia, Kazakhstan, Azerbaijan, Uzbekistan, and Kyrgyzastan, score lower on measures of human development than some countries in the global south. Russia itself is ranked lower on the scale of human development than many southern hemisphere countries. Thus, despite the fact that a North-South gap suggests a geographic division between developed and developing countries, it does not, strictly speaking, indicate that this division is rooted in territorially based inequities. Rather, it involves poverty-based inequities rooted in the global economic system.[21] For these reasons, we must look *inside* states as well as *beyond* them in order to understand the nature of poverty-based inequities in global health.

Poverty and Economic Inequities Within Societies

Economic inequities *within* states are just as powerful a determinant of health outcomes as inequities between developed and developing countries. Low-income populations in developed countries face many of the same economic constraints that negatively impact their health that low-income populations in developing countries face. Likewise, high-income populations in developing countries share many of the same socioeconomic advantages as their counterparts in developed countries and achieve similar health outcomes.

Regardless of overall levels of national development or a country's position in the global economy, individuals living in poverty tend to have worse health outcomes in every country and region of the world. A variety of reasons help explain the strong relationship between poverty and relatively poor health. Individuals living in abject poverty often do not have access to adequate food and suffer the effects of malnutrition. If they do not have access to clean water, low-income populations are more likely to contract waterborne illnesses. Individuals living in poverty may live in substandard housing, which can lead to a variety of health problems, including chronic respiratory illness due to indoor cooking without adequate ventilation (an illness with particularly high prevalence among women in poor communities) or communicable illnesses resulting from a lack of access to basic sanitation infrastructure.

The ways in which poverty contributes to and exacerbates the global burden of communicable diseases are illustrative. People living in poverty are more likely to reside in crowded conditions, putting them at increased risk for exposure to infectious agents, such as tuberculosis, that are transmitted via the respiratory route. Lack of access to clean drinking water and poor sanitation and hygiene increase the risk for the spread of waterborne agents that lead to diarrheal illnesses. In regions of high malaria risk, poor people have less access to insecticide-treated bed nets that serve to decrease the spread of disease by mosquitoes. Individuals living in poverty, particularly women, are less likely to use condoms to prevent the spread of HIV due to limited access to condoms, a lack of education about the efficacy of such practices, and cultural obstacles to condom use.[22] Once exposed to infectious agents, individuals living in poverty are more likely to develop disease, often with more severe clinical manifestations. The most notable reason for this increased susceptibility is that people who are poor are often malnourished, a condition that adversely impacts an individual's immune system and skin integrity, two of the most important barriers to infection. Notably, malnutrition is more prevalent in developing countries. More than four out of five children who are underweight for their age live in developing regions in Africa or South Asia.[23] This fact helps explain why communicable illnesses make up such a large proportion of the burden of disease in developing countries.

Additionally, individuals living in poverty are less likely to have access to adequate health care services. As a result, they are less likely than individuals in higher-income brackets to receive preventive care or appropriate treatment in the case of illness. For example,

UNDER THE MICROSCOPE

Reflections on Global Health Aid to Developing Countries

I lived in Botswana for six months in 2009. Prior to my arrival, most of what I knew about public health in southern Africa involved the HIV/AIDS crisis. Because this crisis has had such devastating consequences throughout the region, discussion of HIV and AIDS dominates much of the news on southern Africa. Similarly, international aid efforts to the region have been largely directed to HIV/AIDS projects. My first weeks in Botswana confirmed the importance of HIV/AIDS—you could not travel a block in the capital city, Gaborone, without seeing an AIDS-related billboard or an HIV clinic, and the city is full of American medical students doing short rotations at Princess Marina Hospital, the primary public medical facility in the city.

Yet, it did not take me long to realize that the public health situation in Botswana is more complicated than the media, dominated by coverage of the AIDS crisis, suggest. Despite the fact that Botswana is a middle-income country, it is a highly inequitable society with enormous gaps between the wealthy and the poor in terms of income and health care access. AIDS has hit the poorest and most vulnerable people in the society especially hard, and international programs focused on dealing with the AIDS crisis address this reality. Although these contributions have obvious importance to individuals suffering from HIV/AIDS, the international community has paid less attention to the poverty-related health challenges faced by the poor on a daily basis—lack of access to adequate nutrition, high rates of child and maternal mortality, and substandard housing and working conditions.

On a drive from Gaborone to the Khutse Game Reserve, we passed through the town of Molepolole. At the edge of town, we saw a state-of-the-art medical facility, one I presumed had been partially funded through global health aid. It was located in proximity to low-income neighborhoods with substandard housing. It was a stark visual reminder of the gap between the extremes of wealth and poverty in the developing world. My observations led me to question whether the international community has been providing the type of public health aid most needed by the populations it purports to serve. Certainly,

many children living in poverty do not receive appropriate oral rehydration therapy for diarrheal illness—a simple, inexpensive treatment shown to decrease morbidity and mortality due to diarrheal illnesses. In fact, in developing countries, less than 40 percent of children receive such therapy, with those in the lowest percentiles of household income being particularly vulnerable.[24] Many children living in poverty fail to receive care for other communicable diseases as well. One survey in rural Tanzania found that children from low-income families with malaria were less likely than their counterparts from higher-income families to be evaluated by a health care professional and less likely to receive antimalarial drugs even when being evaluated by a clinician.[25] Low-income populations often do not receive expensive, long-term treatments for chronic illnesses, such as diabetes, because the treatments are unaffordable and because these individuals do not have regular access to health care facilities. As a the government of Botswana welcomes global health aid, and international programs have helped to bring the HIV/AIDS crisis under control. However, general poverty-related public health challenges have not been adequately addressed by HIV/AIDS funding. Notably, international organizations and major aid donors (public and private) have dominated the process by which public health priorities have been determined in Botswana and elsewhere in the developing world.

A related criticism is that local health care workers and other individuals with skills to contribute to improving public health infrastructure get drawn into working for international programs directed toward the AIDS crisis rather than working on public health more generally. According to Laurie Garrett, this dynamic represents a sort of internal brain drain where well-intentioned international actors place a high demand on local financial and human resources in ways that may not be the best for long-term, sustainable solutions to public health problems in the developing world.[a] In short, Garrett's criticisms suggest that there may be a fundamental gap between the international community's assessment of public health priorities in the developing world and actual public health needs in these countries.

The global emphasis on the HIV/AIDS crisis has developed despite the fact that HIV/AIDS is not the leading cause of death in the developing world. Rather, a number of other risk factors, including high blood pressure, smoking, high cholesterol, and childhood underweight, cause a greater number of deaths throughout the developing world. Thus, a preliminary evidence-based assessment of the causes of death in the developing world lends some support to the argument that the overarching emphasis on HIV/AIDS in global health funding initiatives might be misplaced.

My own observations of daily life in Botswana certainly made me wonder whether the international community should be devoting more resources to sustainable development and general poverty alleviation measures rather than disease-specific funding.

—Debra L. DeLaet

[a]Laurie Garrett, *The Coming Plague: Newly Emerging Diseases in a World out of Balance* (New York: Penguin Books, 1994): 456.

result, people living in poverty are more likely to suffer greater morbidity and mortality from both communicable and noncommunicable illnesses.

Several factors contribute to this disparity in the receipt of appropriate medical treatment. Due to limited education, individuals living in poverty often fail to recognize the clinical severity of an illness, making it less likely that they will seek medical evaluation and treatment. For example, one survey in western Nepal demonstrated that poor education was associated with a greater likelihood of parental failure to recognize the severity of respiratory illness in their children and to seek medical care.[26] Across the globe, the working poor also may not have adequate health insurance and may not be able to take off work in order to get the care they need.

People living in poverty often forgo accessing medical care due to the considerable distance they must travel to receive such care.

Individuals and families living in poverty often do not have means of transportation to hospitals, doctors' offices, or other medical facilities. This problem is especially acute for more serious health issues that require care at medical facilities offering advanced care. For instance, hospital-based clinics are typically located in urban centers at some distance from rural populations living in poverty. Thus, the rural poor have difficulty accessing treatments that are available only in hospital-based settings.

Moreover, care is often perceived to be of higher quality in hospital-based facilities in urban centers.[27] One example of the lower quality of care offered by rural primary facilities is that they are less likely than urban hospital-based centers to stock vital medications, such as antibiotics.[28] Where available in rural areas, antimicrobials are often of lesser quality due to poor governmental regulation of handling and manufacturing of these products. Preventive services such as vaccinations are also less likely to be available to low-income populations. In many countries, this disparity in quality among health centers is a direct result of an allocation of national and regional budgetary resources that favors urban centers. Further, an underdeveloped private-sector health care system in these countries often results in many public-sector resources being utilized by wealthier individuals in that country, further limiting access for low-income populations who are unable to financially compete for these resources. Many families living in poverty are then left to prioritize spending for health care services, with adult males often receiving care at the expense of women and children.[29]

Health challenges may also create poverty traps for individuals and households, contributing to the likelihood that low-income populations will get stuck in poverty. Ill health undermines people's ability to be economically productive and to pursue education that would enable them to improve their economic opportunities. Also, catastrophic illness can result in the loss of employment and can bankrupt individuals who do not have adequate health care. Indeed, illnesses and injuries are among the most common reasons that individuals fall

into poverty. People affected by disease are less likely to be able to work, with resultant loss of income. Additionally, they are often forced to sell assets to help pay medical expenses. Children who are sick also face negative socioeconomic consequences. For example, infectious illnesses during early childhood can have a negative impact on both physical and cognitive development. An appropriate level of iron in the blood is necessary for the cognitive development of a young child. Because certain intestinal parasites, such as hookworms, are associated with decreased iron absorption, infection with these parasites leads to cognitive delay in children.[30] In another example, infection due to malaria is a significant contributor to school absenteeism among low-income populations in many developing countries.[31] Illness also increases a person's risk for malnutrition (and vice versa), with an obvious effect on the ability to work or to attend school.

The types of inequities discussed here are not reflected in aggregate measures of national wealth and population health. In every country in the world, high-income populations have a high probability of good health outcomes because of socioeconomic advantages that give them access to preventive care, appropriate treatments in the event of illness, education, and good nutrition. Conversely, people living in poverty—in developed as well as developing countries—face numerous constraints in their efforts to stay healthy.

Racial and Ethnic Inequities in Global Health

Race refers to a classification of human beings into distinct population groups historically based on presumed biological and genetic differences. In contrast, **ethnicity** refers to a classification of human beings into distinct population groups based on the self-identification of people according to shared language, history, culture, or other social factors. Although these terms are often used interchangeably, they reflect a deep tension regarding the nature of differences among

---

KEY DEFINITIONS PERTAINING TO RACE, ETHNICITY, AND GLOBAL HEALTH

Ethnicity: a classification of human beings into distinct population groups based on the self-identification of people according to shared language, history, culture, or other social factors.

Race: a classification of human beings into distinct population groups historically based on presumed biological and genetic differences, usually manifested in visible physical differences such as skin color.

---

human populations. Historically, the concept of race has been used to suggest that innate physical variations among populations, most notably skin color, are at the root of social and cultural differences among groups of people. At one level, such categorization might be seen as a harmless way to describe real differences—cultural, linguistic, social—that appear to be associated with skin color. At another level, such categorization has had nefarious consequences. Historically, the concept of race has been used to rationalize slavery, colonialism, genocide, and a wide range of human rights abuses. Indeed, critics argue that the very idea that fundamental biological and genetic distinctions divide the human species is itself at the heart of racism. Critics of the concept of race also note that all human beings are members of the same species. As such, humans largely share the same genetic material across population groups. Indeed, some geneticists note that human beings are genetically more homogenous than other mammal species and that more genetic variation exists within specific populations than among these populations.[32] For these reasons, many social scientists prefer to use the term *ethnicity* rather than *race* when describing significant differences among human populations.

The controversy over the concept of race notwithstanding, it provides an important framework for discussing significant economic and social inequities in the world. Whether or not the concept of race itself captures real differences among human populations, racism and racial inequities are very much real phenomena. Accordingly, scholars and practitioners still rely on this category to investigate inequities faced by disadvantaged racial and ethnic groups. For our purposes, the category of race remains very important in the medical literature on disparities in health among population groups. Moreover, it should be noted that some scholars use the term *race* because they see it as interchangeable with *ethnicity*, not because they want to signify innate physical differences among populations. We will follow that convention by referring to both racial and ethnic inequities throughout this section.

Health Disparities Among Disadvantaged Racial/Ethnic Populations

Significant disparities in health have been demonstrated among disadvantaged racial and ethnic groups across the globe. Racial and ethnic populations experience inferior physical and mental health outcomes in terms of both morbidity and mortality in all geographic regions in which such comparative data are available. In most cases, such inequities are faced by racial and ethnic minorities within countries, but, in some cases, racial and ethnic populations that face health disadvantages actually constitute the majority of a population. Blacks in South Africa, where the legacy of apartheid fundamentally shapes population health outcomes, are a prominent case in point. The available data are particularly robust in developed countries, but evidence from developing regions supports similar conclusions.

While a comprehensive review of data from developed regions is beyond the scope of this section, several examples highlight these inequities. According to 2009 data, the life expectancy among whites in the United States was 76.2 years for males and 80.9 years for females, as compared to 70.9 years for males and 77.4 years for females among African-Americans.[33] The infant mortality rate was 5.32 per 1,000 live births for whites and 12.71 per 1,000 live births for African-Americans.[34] Similarly, African-Americans, Asian-Americans, Pacific Islanders, and Hispanics have a higher overall childhood mortality rate than their white counterparts.[35] Data from other developed countries, such as Canada and Brazil, also demonstrate racial and ethnic inequities in infant and childhood mortality rates.[36]

Using health-related quality-of-life measures such as healthy days, defined as "the overall number of days during the previous 30 days during which a person reported good (or better) physical and mental health," it appears that racial and ethnic minorities in the United States also experience greater morbidity.[37] Similarly, with the exception of Asian-Americans, racial and ethnic minorities are much less likely than whites to report their health status as "excellent" or "very good," as is demonstrated in Figure 6.1. These self-reported measures of disparities in health status are consistent with the extensive body of evidence demonstrating racial and ethnic inequities in health outcomes for specific medical conditions. To cite only a few examples, studies have shown that racial minorities in the United States experience poorer outcomes for cardiovascular disease, asthma, and cancer.[38] This is

FIGURE 6.1 Self-reported Health Status by Race, 2005

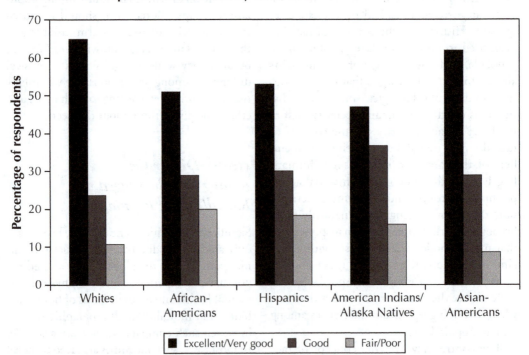

Source: Adapted from Holly Mead, Lara Cartwright-Smith, Karen Jones, Christal Ramos, and Bruce Siegel, "Racial and Ethnic Disparities in U.S. Health Care: A Chartbook" (The Commonwealth Fund, 2008). Available online at: http://www.commonwealthfund.org/usr_doc/mead_racialethnicdisparities_chartbook_1111.pdf.

particularly true for African-Americans, who are significantly more likely than other racial and ethnic groups to suffer a chronic medical condition or disability, even after adjusting for income.[39] These findings have been replicated in other developed countries. For example, racial and ethnic minorities in the United Kingdom, Australia, South Africa, and Brazil are more likely to develop end-stage kidney disease as a result of an increased incidence of hypertension and diabetes mellitus.[40] As a final example, among both children and adults, racial and ethnic minorities have been found to experience an increased burden of mental health disease, including depression and anxiety, in countries such as the United States, Canada, and the United Kingdom, to name just a few.[41]

Though considerably sparser, data from developing countries across global regions also demonstrate similarly increased morbidity and mortality for disadvantaged racial and ethnic populations. For example, studies in sub-Saharan Africa reveal that, consistent across all countries studied, ethnic inequalities exist in the infant and under-five mortality rates. In Asia, a recent study from Vietnam found that ethnicity was the main socioeconomic determinant for neonatal mortality.[42] In lower-income countries in Central and Latin America, overall health inequities have been demonstrated among indigenous and black people in comparable geographic and social locations.[43] Just as in the case of developed countries, disease-specific differences in health outcomes have been demonstrated in developing countries. For example, the risk for lung cancer in Nepal has been shown to differ by ethnicity.[44] Data also demonstrate an increased risk for mental health disorders among racial and ethnic minorities in developing countries.[45]

The Causes of Health Disparities Among Disadvantaged Racial/ Ethnic Populations

Because race and ethnicity are so intimately linked with socioeconomic status, it is difficult to fully tease out the contribution of race

and ethnicity to population-level health outcomes. Nevertheless, studies have suggested that as much as one-half of mortality differences among racial and ethnic groups may be attributable to socioeconomic factors.[46] The corollary is the suggestion that a significant portion of health status is determined by factors specifically unique to race and ethnicity. This section explores the factors that may lead to disparities in health outcomes for disadvantaged racial and ethnic populations.

Research has suggested that many social variables likely contribute to racial and ethnic inequities in health. First among these includes determinants directly related to the neighborhoods in which these populations live. For example, as was discussed in Chapter 5, obesity is associated with poor access to healthful foods and neighborhood green space for people of lower socioeconomic status, an association more likely to affect minority groups due to their higher rates of poverty.[47] In the United States, African-American and Hispanic children are more likely to develop asthma in part due to their increased likelihood of living in public housing and the resultant exposure to such asthma triggers as cockroaches.[48] Disadvantaged racial and ethnic groups are also much more likely to be exposed to violence, with negative ramifications for physical and mental health.[49] Similarly, indigenous populations across the globe tend to experience higher injury and death rates due to accidents associated with cramped living conditions, unsafe housing, lack of space and facilities for safe play, and exposure to a high volume of fast-moving traffic.[50] The social environment in which disadvantaged racial and ethnic populations live and the associated self-perception of inequalities lead to an increase in risk taking and unhealthy behaviors.[51]

Social factors also likely contribute to racial and ethnic inequities in health outcomes as a result of their impact on access to care. Again, the case of the United States is instructive. As shown in Figure 6.2, racial and ethnic minorities in the United States have historically been less likely than whites to have health insurance coverage. As will be discussed in more detail

FIGURE 6.2 Percentage of Americans with Health Insurance Coverage, by Race and Ethnicity

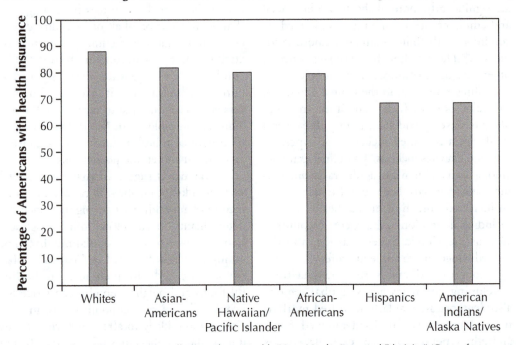

Source: Reproduced from Lesley Russell, "Fact Sheet: Health Disparities by Race and Ethnicity" (Center for American Progress, 2010). Available online at: http://www.americanprogress.org/issues/2010/12/disparities_factsheet.html.

in Chapter 10, this situation has existed due to a health care model that relies heavily on employer-based health insurance and does not provide universal coverage to all residents.

Consistent with this inequity in insurance coverage, racial and ethnic minorities are much less likely than whites to access the health care system. For example, African-Americans, Hispanics, and Asian-Americans are more likely to be without a regular doctor than are whites.[52] Additionally, racial and ethnic minorities are much less likely than whites to receive health care services, including preventive care, such as screening for colorectal cancer and prostate cancer.[53]

Even in countries where universal health care coverage is provided, inequities in access to care for disadvantaged racial and ethnic populations exist. For instance, certain immigrant populations in Australia have been shown to receive lower rates of orthopedic surgery for severe osteoarthritis.[54] Racial and ethnic minorities have been shown to have similarly decreased

access to therapies for end-stage renal disease in Venezuela.[55] Finally, in South Africa, a study revealed that, even after adjusting for other socioeconomic factors, black women were less likely than nonblack women to receive preventive care services during pregnancy and birth,[56] and another study revealed that 40.8 percent of blacks, as compared with 10.9 percent of whites and 6.9 percent of Asians, reported going without necessary medical care at some point in the previous year.[57]

These findings of racial and ethnic inequities in health care among countries with universal health care coverage suggest that factors other than health insurance status affect access to high-quality care. Some of these determinants are likely rooted in socioeconomic factors. For example, a 2008 study demonstrated that transportation barriers are significantly more often responsible for unmet medical care needs for children among Native Americans than for other racial groups.[58] Disparities in access to care can also result from inequities in educational attainment among racial and ethnic minorities. For example, lower levels of health literacy and educational attainment serve as a barrier to the receipt of preventive services such as screening mammography among racial and ethnic minorities in the United States.[59] Ethnic minorities in Vietnam occasionally forgo seeking care for their children because they have not been appropriately educated on recognizing the signs of illness.[60] Geographic determinants have also been associated with inequities in the quality of care delivered to disadvantaged racial and ethnic groups. In the United States, individuals living in predominantly racial and ethnic minority communities are much more likely than whites to report having little choice in where to seek medical care.[61] This inequity is further complicated by findings that show that racial and ethnic health disparities in the United States exist across hospitals rather than within individual facilities.[62] According to this study, whites and racial and ethnic minorities treated within the same hospital were shown to receive the same standard of care; minorities, however, were more likely to present to hospitals that provided lower-quality care.[63] Similar geographic disparities have been demonstrated in South Africa, where medications such as antimicrobials in rural primary facilities are often of lesser quality than in urban hospital-based centers.[64]

Because they are intimately linked with racial and ethnic status, socioeconomic determinants likely account for a significant portion of the inequities in health status and health care access seen among disadvantaged racial and ethnic populations. However, there are almost certainly factors specific to race and ethnicity that also contribute to these disparities. Biological differences in risk for developing certain conditions exist among racial and ethnic groups. For example, individuals of African heritage are much more likely to inherit the mutated gene responsible for causing sickle cell disease. Genetic factors also influence the predisposition of individuals of certain racial and ethnic groups to the development of conditions such as Type II diabetes mellitus and hypertension.

Racial and ethnic minorities may also experience inferior health outcomes as a result of language barriers. In the United States, individuals with limited English proficiency (LEP) often have limited access to care or receive a lesser quality of care. Though Title VI of the Civil Rights Act requires that any health care provider receiving federal funds, including providing Medicaid and Medicare services, must provide adequate language assistance to an LEP patient,[65] language discordance can still limit the quality of care provided. For example, in one study, Spanish-speaking Hispanics noted that communication difficulties made it more challenging to fully explain symptoms, ask questions of providers, follow through with filling of prescriptions, and fully understand physician recommendations; nearly 20 percent reported not seeking medical treatment due to language barriers.[66]

Disadvantaged racial and ethnic populations also tend to be more likely to exhibit mistrust toward health care providers. For example, Malay-Muslims in Singapore expressed concern about the potential for racial discrimination as well as the participant selection process for genetic research.[67] As a result of patient mistrust, disadvantaged racial and ethnic groups may be less likely to seek critical preventive care and treatment. For instance, patient mistrust contributes to lower prostate cancer screening among African-Americans in the United States.[68] Patient race and ethnicity can also influence physicians' perceptions of patients. Data from a 2000 study revealed that patient race was associated with physicians' assessment of patient intelligence, feelings of affiliation toward the patient, and beliefs about the patient's likelihood of risk behavior and adherence with medical advice.[69] These potential barriers of language discordance, patient mistrust of providers, and patient stereotyping by physicians likely exist in no small part due to the underrepresentation of disadvantaged racial and ethnic populations in the physician workforce. In the United States, although African-Americans, Hispanics, and Native Americans constitute more than 30 percent

UNDER THE MICROSCOPE

Reflections on Patient-Physician Language Discordance

I have worked as a primary care provider for pediatric and adult populations since 1995. During this time, I have had the opportunity to work in a variety of settings. I worked at three large academic health centers in Cincinnati and New York City that served a wide variety of patients, but I largely provided care for children and adults with public health insurance, the majority of whom were racial and ethnic minorities. I also worked at a community health center in Cincinnati, where many of the patients were uninsured minorities. Lastly, I worked briefly providing care to a population of patients who were mostly healthy, nonminority young adults with employment-based private health insurance while I was employed by a private practice in an affluent neighborhood in New York City. Prior to entering the workforce, I had the privilege as a medical student to work for a limited period of time with the Indian Health Services in Oklahoma caring for a population of Native Americans. Given this breadth of experience, I feel that I can offer a unique perspective on the challenges faced in accessing high-quality care for racial and ethnic minorities.

It has been my experience that racial and ethnic minorities are at a clear disadvantage when attempting to navigate the health care system. The challenges faced result not only from issues related to our current organization of health care in the United States but also from social and cultural factors. One important example is that of patient-physician language discordance.

Many of the patients for whom I have provided care, and continue to provide care, are individuals with limited English proficiency. I am limited in that I am fluent only in English. In our practice, we see patients who speak Spanish, French, Portuguese, Senegalese, Mandarin, Bengali, and Hindi, to name just a few. Many of my patient encounters, therefore, have language discordance as an obstacle that must be addressed to ensure the best possible delivery of care. To deal with this challenge, we have available to us, at a cost to our institution, language interpreter services. Given the volume of patients and

of the population, these groups accounted for only 8.7 percent of physicians, 6.9 percent of dentists, 9.9 percent of pharmacists, and 6.2 percent of registered nurses, according to 2007 data.[70]

Several overarching themes can be gleaned from this examination of the causes of health disparities faced by disadvantaged racial and ethnic populations. First, social determinants play a critical role in the development of racial and ethnic inequities in health. Only by addressing these disparities in the condition of daily life of disadvantaged racial and ethnic groups can greater equity in the health status of populations be achieved.[71] As concerns health care systems, measures must be taken to improve access, including expansion of health care coverage to the uninsured and underinsured members of the population. Education of patients to improve their understanding of disease processes, treatment options, and methods to most effectively access health care systems is important.[72] Additionally, it is critical to provide better education of health care the diversity of languages for which such services are required, on-site interpreters are impractical. Rather, we employ an off-site service accessed via telephone.

Communication in this manner is less than ideal, for both patient and provider. In a system that places a priority on seeing a high volume of patients in an efficient manner, the time intensity required to ensure mutual understanding of key elements of the patient's history and the provider's prescribed plan of care steals critical minutes from an already-limited visit. This is particularly troubling when providing care to patients with a complexity of medical problems. Additionally, a large portion of communication is subtle, in terms of both spoken word and nonverbal cues, and these subtleties are easily missed during language discordant evaluations. Given the inherent intimacy of the professional relationship between patient and physician, these missed opportunities for information gathering might negatively affect physician decision making. Lastly, even when language discordance is not, strictly speaking, an issue during a patient evaluation, ethnic and cultural differences in spoken word between provider and patient can also affect communication—if I ask for "a lift" in London, I may be surprised to be led to an elevator rather than to one's car.

Underscored in this reflection is the critical importance of effective communication between patient and physician. It is a common medical teaching, one that I have found to be confirmed in my years as a clinician, that 90 percent of arriving at a correct medical diagnosis is based on a detailed patient history of symptoms. How, then, can one provide the best possible care to his or her patients if the starting point is one of limited communication? To remedy this, it is imperative that, when necessary, clinicians be provided with language interpreter services. Also, having available culturally appropriate and language-specific reading materials for patients is critical. Providing education to expand provider language skills is helpful, though, as suggested, any one provider being able to gain fluency in the multitude of languages that may be encountered in practice is likely impractical. Thus, the ultimate goal should be to increase the diversity of trainees in the field of medicine to ensure the most appropriate care for the greatest breadth of patients seen in our health care systems.

—David E. DeLaet

professionals so that communication barriers, both cultural and linguistic, can be addressed and providers might more consistently exhibit cross-cultural competency in the care of patients. Implementing policies that will better ensure medical training for a greater diversity of health care providers would be of obvious benefit in eliminating these language and cultural barriers. Lastly, improving public awareness of the scope of the problem is likely to result in greater support and more realistic achievement of these goals.

Gender Inequities in Global Health

Health Disparities Between Men and Women in Global Health

The health status of men and women across the globe is characterized by significant differentials. Several indicators used to measure health status, including life expectancy, health-adjusted life expectancy (HALE), and disability-adjusted life years (DALYs), demonstrate the health disparities that exist between men and women.

In every region of the world and across all levels of economic development, women have a higher life expectancy than men. In 2007, the global average female life expectancy was 70 years, compared to 65 years for men. Women's higher average life expectancy is especially pronounced in the developed world, where more than twice as many women than men live past the age of 80.[73] A narrower gap between female and male life expectancy exists in low-income countries, where women can expect to live 58 years, compared to 55 years for men.[74] The female health advantage in life expectancy holds true across all regions of the world.[75] The starkest gap in life expectancy between women and men emerges in Central and Eastern Europe and the Commonwealth of Independent States, where women can expect to live roughly 74 years, compared to just 65 years for men. The gap between women and men is smallest in sub-Saharan Africa, where female life expectancy is 52.5, compared to 50.4 for men.[76] According to United Nations Development Programme (UNDP) data for 2007, male life expectancy was higher than female life expectancy in only two countries: Afghanistan (43.5 for women versus 43.6 for men) and Swaziland (44.8 for women versus 45.7 for men).[77] Taken together, World Health Organization (WHO) and UNDP data on life expectancy demonstrate a striking, if surprising, pattern of greater longevity for women that holds across the globe.

HALE estimates follow the same pattern as life expectancy indicators. Women can expect to live more years in full health in every region of the globe, and women's health advantage on this indicator holds across all levels of economic development. However, the gap between men and women is smaller in HALE estimates than in general estimates of average life expectancy. The 2007 HALE for women globally was 61 years compared to just 58 years for men. Women's advantage in HALE estimates is somewhat more pronounced in high-income countries, where females have a

HALE of 72 years compared to 68 years for males. As in the case of general life expectancy, the gap between men and women on HALE indicators narrows at lower levels of economic development. In lower-middle-income countries, females have a HALE estimate of 62 years compared to 60 years for men in good health. The gap is narrowest in low-income countries, where women can expect to live 49 years in full health compared to 48 years of expected good health for men.[78] The female advantage in HALE estimates again holds across all global regions, although the HALE gap between men and women is smaller than the gap in general life expectancy.

The most interesting discrepancies between life expectancy and HALE indicators show up in individual countries. Unlike life expectancy measures, which show a male advantage over females in only Afghanistan and Swaziland, HALE estimates are higher for males in a number of countries: Bangladesh, Botswana, the Central African Republic, Pakistan, Qatar, Tajikistan, Tonga, and Zimbabwe. In numerous other countries—Afghanistan, Bahrain, Benin, Cameroon, Chad, Kuwait, Mali, Mozambique, Nepal, Nigeria, Sudan, Swaziland, Tuvalu, United Arab Emirates, and United Republic of Tanzania—HALE estimates for men and women are identical. The male advantage in HALE is not large in the cases where it exists—typically just one or two years.[79] Nevertheless, the shift is notable and suggests that HALE estimates, which incorporate variables related to quality of life and not just longevity of life, are more likely to capture the effects of variables that have negative effects on women's health.

An examination of lost healthy life expectancy years, which is the difference between total life expectancy and HALE,[80] provides another lens for examining health differentials between men and women. In contrast to life expectancy and HALE indicators, data on lost years of full health suggest a health disadvantage for women. Globally, women lose an average of nine years of HALE compared to seven years for men. This pattern holds across all regions of the world and across all levels of economic development. In every region of the world, women lose eight or nine years of full health compared to six to eight years for men.[81] The estimated number of lost years of full health for females is highest in upper-middle-income countries, where women lose an average of eleven years of good health and males lose an average of nine years. In low-income countries, the number of lost years of good health drops to nine for females and seven for males. Despite women's health advantage in longevity and HALE, these data show that women have higher morbidity than men and will spend a higher percentage of their lives in less than a state of full health.[82]

In addition to differentials in life expectancy measures, men and women experience different burdens of disease, as measured in DALYs, which indicate the number of years of healthy life lost due to particular diseases and injuries. As DALY data show, men and women suffer disproportionately from different kinds of illnesses. Table 6.1 shows the leading causes of burden of disease measured in DALYs by sex. In high-income countries, the top five causes of DALY losses in women include unipolar depressive disorders, migraines, health problems associated with alcohol use, bipolar disorders, and schizophrenia. In low-income countries, the major causes of DALY losses for women are HIV/AIDs, tuberculosis, abortion complications, schizophrenia, and maternal sepsis.[83] Conditions specific to women make up a significant proportion of women's burden of disease. Globally, maternal conditions (including maternal hemorrhage, maternal sepsis, hypertensive disorders, obstructed labor, obstetric fistula, and complications from unsafe abortions) contribute to 2.8 percent of women's DALY losses.[84] Cancers, including breast and cervical cancer, contribute to 1.1 percent of DALY losses for women.[85] Women also have higher disease prevalence for certain illnesses, such as Alzheimer's, osteoporosis, and arthritis, due, in part, to their average higher life expectancy.[86] Injuries contribute disproportionately to men's burden of disease, and men are also more prone to suffer from heart

TABLE 6.1 Leading Causes of Burden of Disease (DALYs) by Sex, 2004

Disease or injury	Percentage of total DALYs	
	Female	Male
Infectious and parasitic diseases	19.6	20.1
Neuropsychiatric disorders	13.9	12.4
Cardiovascular diseases	9.4	10.4
Unintentional injuries	7.1	10.9
Perinatal conditions	8.5	8.1
Sense organ disorders	6.2	5.3
Cancers	4.9	5.3
Maternal conditions	5.4	—
Respiratory diseases	3.6	4.2
Digestive diseases	2.5	3.1
Intentional injuries	1.8	4.6
Diabetes mellitus	1.5	1.1

Source: Adapted from the World Health Organization, *The Global Burden of Disease: 2004 Update*: 60–64. Available online at: http://www.who.int/healthinfo/global_burden_disease/GBD_report_2004update_full.pdf.

disease and coronary artery disease. A significant proportion of the global male burden of disease—2.7 percent of DALY losses—results from war and violence.[87] Men also have significantly higher prevalence rates of drug and alcohol disorders.[88]

The causes of death for males and females also shed light on disparities in the health status of men and women across the globe. Figure 6.3 illustrates the distribution of the major causes of mortality by sex. At the global level, cardiovascular disease is the major cause of death for both men (26.8 percent) and women (31.5 percent). Globally, other major causes of male mortality are infectious and parasitic diseases (16.7 percent), cancers (13.4 percent), unintentional injuries (8.1 percent), respiratory infections (7.1 percent), and respiratory disorders (6.9 percent). After cardiovascular disease, the major causes of death for females include infectious and parasitic diseases (15.6 percent), cancers (11.8 percent), respiratory

FIGURE 6.3 Distribution of Global Deaths by Leading Cause Groups, Males and Females, 2004

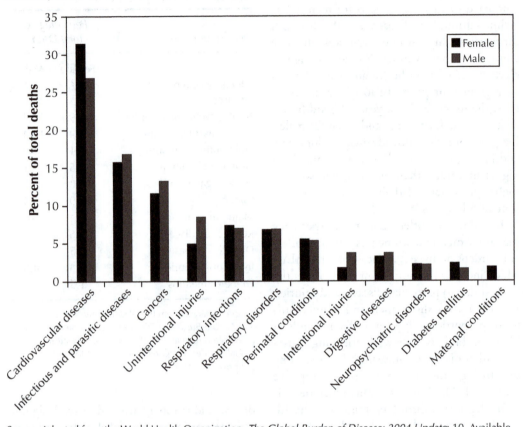

Source: Adapted from the World Health Organization, *The Global Burden of Disease: 2004 Update*: 10. Available online at: http://www.who.int/healthinfo/global_burden_disease/GBD_report_2004update_full.pdf.

infections (7.4 percent), and respiratory disorders (6.8 percent).[89]

Men have higher adult mortality rates across all regions, which can be attributed in large part to high male mortality due to injuries. Although this pattern holds across the globe, sex-based disparities in mortality rates are apparent across regions. Differences are most pronounced in Africa, where females have significantly higher mortality due to communicable illnesses and to maternal and nutritional conditions. Overall, HIV/AIDS causes 40 percent of female deaths in Africa compared to the 14 percent of deaths resulting from maternal conditions. Communicable illnesses are also the major cause of mortality for African men, but they are less likely to die from communicable illnesses than women. Males in Africa have a somewhat higher mortality resulting from injuries than

women. In Europe, cardiovascular disease and injury are major causes of male mortality. Men face much higher mortality rates than women in the Eastern Mediterranean Region due to injuries. In South-East Asia, minimal differences between men and women manifest in mortality rates due to communicable illnesses. Men have slightly higher mortality rates due to noncommunicable illnesses and injuries. In Latin America and the Caribbean, injuries are a major cause of death for men, contributing to higher male mortality rates in this region.

A final indicator that underscores a serious global health disadvantage for women is the surplus male population in the developing world. Approximately 50.3 percent of the world's 6.2 billion people are male, and roughly 49.7 percent are female. Records of live births across all societies indicate a "natural" sex ratio of 103–106 male births for every 100 female births. In China today, this ratio is 124 to 100 in favor of boys. India, South Korea, Singapore, and Taiwan have similarly distorted sex ratios. These sex ratios indicate a surplus male population. Globally, estimates suggest that 100 million women are "missing" from the total global population.[90] The discrepancy results from gender-biased practices in areas of the developing world, most notably sex-selective abortion and the killing of girl children in infancy. These practices stem from cultural preferences for boy children in many societies. The neglect of girl children, dowry violence, and other forms of domestic violence also contribute to surplus male population across the globe. This "gender paradox"—of longer average female life expectancy and HALE but a lower percentage of women in the world's total population—is largely concentrated in the developing world.[91] High-income countries have a higher proportion of women than men in the total population; this relationship is reversed in low-income countries, and it is especially pronounced in the region of South Asia.

The Causes of Health Disparities Between Men and Women in Global Health

The global health disparities between men and women have varying causes. In some cases, these disparities can be described as **sex differentials**. Here, health disparities are rooted in biological causes, including basic biological differences between males and females as well as genetic and hormonal factors. Other health disparities are better characterized as **gender differentials**, in which case men and women experience different health outcomes due to socially constructed norms of masculinity and femininity. Gender differentials in health outcomes between men and women result from health behaviors, cultural practices, and governmental policies shaped by **gender norms**—the culturally prevailing constructs of presumed "normal," "appropriate," or "ideal" behavior and identities of men (masculinity) and women (femininity.) Although it is helpful to distinguish between sex and gender differentials, divergent health outcomes for men and women, in many instances, represent a complex interplay of biology and gender.

Many health disparities between men and women can be attributed to sex differentials. Take women's longer average life expectancy as an example. Women have certain biological advantages that contribute to their greater average longevity. Scientists have offered a variety of potential explanations for the female longevity advantage. For one, sex chromosomes give females a health advantage. To understand this advantage, it is necessary to review some very basic fundamentals regarding sex chromosomes. Female offspring result from two X chromosomes, whereas male offspring are the product of an X chromosome and a Y chromosome. X chromosomes carry

---

KEY DEFINITIONS PERTAINING TO GENDER AND GLOBAL HEALTH

Gender Differentials: health disparities between men and women that are rooted in socially constructed norms of masculinity and femininity.

Gender Norms: the culturally prevailing constructs of presumed "normal," "appropriate," or "ideal" behavior and identities of men (masculinity) and women (femininity).

Sex Differentials: health disparities between men and women that are rooted in basic biological differences between males and females as well as genetic and hormonal factors.

more genes than Y chromosomes, and, as a result, more sex-linked traits, including illnesses, are carried on the X chromosome. Most sex-linked illnesses result from recessive genes carried on the X chromosome. Therefore, males have a 50 percent chance of getting a sex-linked illness if their mother carries one abnormal gene. Conversely, females would need to inherit a recessive gene from both the mother and the father in order to develop the condition. Hemophilia is a classic example of a sex-specific illness that is more common among males for precisely this reason. Women may have certain hormonal as well as chromosomal advantages that contribute to their longer average life expectancy. The male hormone testosterone may increase risk taking and aggressive behavior that lead to high rates of unintentional injury among men. Metabolic differences, which predispose men to higher levels of LDL ("bad cholesterol"), may also contribute to longevity disadvantages for men.[92] For instance, to the extent that metabolic differences lead to higher levels of bad cholesterol among men, they contribute to the higher rate of cardiovascular disease seen in men.

Although sex differentials produce certain health advantages for women, biological factors are responsible for a number of significant health challenges faced by women alone. For example, women's reproductive health issues are fundamentally rooted in biological differences between the sexes. Numerous examples fall under this category. Ovarian cancer, eclampsia, gestational diabetes, pregnancy and birth-related hemorrhage, obstetric fistula, and maternal death during childbirth all involve reproductive and maternal health conditions faced by women alone. Thus, these health challenges have roots in basic biology. Higher rates of depression and migraine headaches among women also can be attributed to hormonal and genetic factors fundamentally rooted in sex differentials. Additionally, autoimmune disorders, such as hypothyroidism and hyperthyroidism, as well as lupus and rheumatoid arthritis, are more common

among women and can be attributed to inherent biological differences.

Men also face a number of health challenges that are primarily biologically based. Obvious examples include prostate and testicular cancer. Males also have a much higher incidence of cardiovascular morbidity and mortality in young and middle adulthood, at least in developed countries. Higher rates of cardiovascular disease among men have been attributed in large part to hormonal differences between males and females. Interestingly, these hormonal differences are essentially neutralized after women become postmenopausal, and women experience a similar incidence of cardiovascular morbidity and mortality in late adulthood.[93]

As these examples illustrate, health disparities between men and women in global health can be partially attributed to sex differentials. However, gender differentials also contribute fundamentally to various disparities in health outcomes between men and women. For example, maternal conditions are sex-specific health challenges rooted in biology. Over 500,000 women die each year due to complications from pregnancy and childbirth; most of these deaths would be preventable with simple and affordable public health interventions.[94] The extent to which these maternal conditions contribute to burden of disease depends very much on socially constructed gender norms that partially determine women's access to perinatal and postnatal care as well as the general social and economic determinants that shape women's health status across the globe. As the example of maternal health suggests, divergent health outcomes in some areas reflect gender biases that lead to underfunding of women's health priorities.

Gender biases that prioritize men's health over women's health also manifest in different ways. Men in most societies have dominated political decision making over health care policy and budgets.[95] Male biases in medical research also have played a role here. For example, a great deal of medical research on cardiovascular disease has historically been based primarily on male subjects, which limits the applicability of research findings to female patients. Due to prevailing conceptions of femininity in many societies that lead women to prioritize the health of the male members of their families and communities more highly than their own health or that of their daughters, women are often less likely than men to seek necessary health care. The uneven distribution of financial resources within households also makes many women less likely to seek professional medical care even if they would otherwise be inclined to do so.[96] Gender differentials also contribute to underreporting of certain diseases for women. For example, due to social stigmas that place high value on sexual "purity" among women, women are often reluctant to undergo testing or to seek treatment for sexually transmitted diseases.

Gender norms also contribute to health disadvantages for women in other ways. In particular, gender norms that devalue girl children and women contribute to all sorts of harmful practices that threaten the health and lives of women and girls across the globe. These harmful practices include sex-selective abortion and female infanticide, feeding practices that prioritize giving more of scarce food to boy children and men, dowry violence, sexual violence, and other forms of domestic violence. Such practices lead to a wide range of health problems for girls and women, including debilitating injury, malnutrition, and death. Unlike maternal conditions, these health problems have no biological basis and are rooted almost entirely in discriminatory gender norms. Gender norms also shape the transmission, experience, and treatment of critical illnesses for women. HIV/AIDS is a case in point. Gender inequalities embedded within societies can make women more susceptible to contracting the disease. For example, gender inequalities can limit women's ability to control their sexuality or to use birth control in sexual relationships (especially within marriage) and, thus, contribute to high HIV prevalence rates among women in many societies. Sexual violence against women also exacerbates the spread of disease. Unequal economic and power relations within families and

societies at large also can limit women's ability to receive effective treatment for the disease.[97]

Additionally, women face gendered health challenges that undermine their well-being without necessarily constituting disease or disability. For instance, women in the developing world, especially in rural areas, commonly have primary responsibility for running households. Women are often responsible for child rearing, growing and cooking food for the family, obtaining water for the household (which often involves walking significant distances), caring for frequently sick children, and facing high mortality rates among their children. These burdens are especially pronounced in high-fertility countries where women are often pregnant and raising several young children at the same time. These sorts of socioeconomic burdens may negatively affect women's physical and mental health without necessarily resulting in diseases or disabilities that show up in general health indicators.[98]

Gender differentials also contribute to specific health challenges faced by men. Although women's longer average life expectancy can be attributed in part to biology, social factors also contribute to a lower average life expectancy for men. For example, fatal injuries are a major cause of male mortality in regions across the globe. Socially constructed gender norms contribute to this phenomenon. A form of masculinity that encourages aggressive, risk-seeking behavior results in a greater propensity of men to engage in behaviors (for example, fast or reckless driving) that could lead to life-threatening injuries. Prevailing forms of masculinity in most societies contribute to high mortality rates among men in other ways as well. High rates of male morbidity and mortality due to injuries result in large part from gendered social and economic norms that place many men at risk of occupational threats to their health. Occupational injuries are a major cause of morbidity and mortality for men in most societies across the globe. The fact that men are more likely than women to work in more dangerous occupations (for instance, construction, mining, or factory work involving heavy or dangerous equipment) can be attributed, at least in part, to socially constructed norms that treat such work as largely masculine endeavors.

Similarly, male burden of disease and mortality stemming from war-related violence is a highly gendered phenomenon resulting from the deep associations between prevailing forms of masculinity and military combat in most societies. For example, in countries with forced military conscription, such policies typically apply only to men. (The case of Israel, where women as well as men face compulsory military service, is a prominent exception.) As a result, men are more likely to be injured or killed as combatants even when they do not have a real choice about participating in military service. This phenomenon stems from gender norms that fundamentally tie responsibility for military service in national defense to a masculine conception of civic duty. Gender norms that presume men are potential combatants and women and children are innocent civilians also contribute to war-related morbidity and mortality for men during war.[99] Many civilian men are likely to be killed as *potential* soldiers simply because they are males of "fighting age."[100]

Many crucial questions remain about the relative effect of sex differentials versus gender differentials on health disparities between men and women. In some cases, it is clear that sex differentials are the primary cause of disparate health challenges. Maternal health conditions, experienced only by women, are a good example. In other cases, such as female infanticide and sex-selective abortion, discriminatory gender norms are obviously the primary determinant of this gender gap in health outcomes—neither practice is fundamentally rooted in biology.

However, in many cases it can be very difficult to disentangle the relative contribution of biological sex versus gender constructs in shaping health outcomes. For instance, high rates of unintentional injury among men are caused, in part, by risk-taking behavior shaped by prevailing conceptions of masculinity. At the same time, hormonal differences rooted in biology also contribute to such behavior. The same thing can be said of the higher rates of war-related injury and death for men. On the one hand, masculine norms that prioritize aggressive, self-sacrificing behavior among men shape these outcomes. On the other hand, we can ask ourselves how much of this behavior is influenced by fundamental biological differences between men and women. Some evidence exists that men are more prone to violence due to higher testosterone levels, biological propensity to greater size and strength, biologically rooted differences in cognition, and other biological or genetic factors.[101] Furthermore, there is evidence that suggests that aggressive behavior itself increases testosterone levels, indicating that the relationship between biological sex and gender works in both directions.[102]

Due to the complex interplay of biology and gender, we cannot reach definitive conclusions about what causes various gender gaps in global health. Clearly, both biology and gender play a role, and interactive effects of both biology and gender are important. Disentangling the relative influence of biological sex and gender goes well beyond the scope of this chapter. For the beginning student of global health, the important thing to remember is that both sex and gender differentials are responsible for the disparities in health outcomes between men and women.

Conclusion

This chapter provided an overview of a range of inequities in global health. These inequities are manifested across numerous borders—territorial, poverty-based, and social borders—that shape the international relations of global health. Territorial borders reveal distinct inequities between high-income countries with good aggregate population health outcomes and low-income countries with comparatively poor aggregate population health outcomes. The strength of this general correlation between levels of national wealth and population health reflects a larger North-South gap in global health that is rooted in broad systemic features and underlying structural inequities in the global economy.

Despite the importance of broad territorially based inequities between countries and between developed and developing regions in general, significant inequities within, between, and across territorial borders are also critical. Differences in population health outcomes across countries are not entirely rooted in levels of national income, and variations in national health systems (as will be discussed in Chapter 10) influence population health, as do social, political and cultural inequities within societies. In particular, poverty-based inequities are a fundamental source of disparities in population health outcomes, as are disparities rooted in socioeconomic inequities among racial and ethnic groups across and within societies. Across the globe, both women and men face important health disparities rooted in both sex and gender differentials. Notably, poverty-based, racial/ethnic, and gendered health disparities cut across national borders, suggesting transnational causes and trends, at the same time as they are manifested in unique ways in particular societies.

The economic, ethnic, and gender inequities in global health considered in this chapter do not represent isolated, discrete categories. Rather, considerable overlap exists in terms of both the disparities in health outcomes and the root causes of these disparities. Territorially based inequities have been shaped by racialized transnational processes and events, such as colonialism. Sexism on a global scale has contributed to poverty-related health challenges faced by women across the globe. The reverse is also true: Health disparities faced by disadvantaged racial and ethnic populations, as well as health disparities between men and women within particular societies, are rooted in broader, transnational economic forces and trends. As a result of the complicated intersections among poverty, race/ethnicity, and gender both within and across societies, it is difficult to disentangle the relative weight of each of these categories.

For our purposes, the critical point is to highlight the importance of all of these inequities. Students of public health need to be aware of the multiple sources and manifestations of economic, ethnic, and gender inequities in global health. The range of inequities in global health—and the complex interplay among various forms of inequities—underscores the importance of drawing on the knowledge of scholars and practitioners from many disciplines in seeking to promote global health. To mitigate inequities in global health, the insights and contributions of medical professionals, social workers, sociologists, economists, cultural anthropologists, public policy experts, and political scientists will be essential in efforts to address the underlying socioeconomic determinants of health in a comprehensive manner on a global scale.

Discussion Questions

1. Do you agree with the assertion that national wealth is directly correlated with better population health outcomes? Why or why not?
2. What factors make individuals living in poverty more susceptible to the morbidity and mortality associated with communicable diseases? What are "poverty traps," and how does a high burden of communicable disease cause poverty traps for individuals as well as populations?
3. What are the major determinants of racial and ethnic disparities in health?
4. What critical interventions might help eliminate racial and ethnic disparities in health?
5. What are some of the specific health challenges faced by women and men across the globe?
6. What factors contribute to gender gaps in global health?
7. What actions might be taken to reduce gender gaps in global health?

Web Resources

Global Alliance for Women's Health: http://www.gawh.org/home.php5

Global Fund for Women: http://www.globalfundforwomen.org/

International Society for Men's Health: http://www.ismh.org/en/

Men's Health World Congress: http://www.ismh.org/en/mens-health-world-congress/

The North-South Institute: http://www.nsi-ins.ca/

United Nations Development Programme Human Development Reports: http://hdr.undp.org/en/

U.S. Centers for Disease Control, Racial and Ethnic Approaches to Community Health (REACH): http://www.cdc.gov/reach/

CHAPTER 7

Global Health and Security

Introduction

Global health has obvious connections to both **national security**, traditionally defined as state security from external military threats, and **human security**, conceptualized in terms of the well-being and health of individuals rather than states. This chapter outlines the ways in which both conceptions of security are related to global health. In the realm of national security, the chapter looks at how public health challenges can destabilize states and contribute to interstate violence. In order to explore the connections between global health and national security in greater detail, the chapter includes a discussion of biowarfare and bioterrorism. Next, the chapter examines the health problems that arise in conflict zones, followed by a look at the connections between global health and human security. In concluding, the chapter discusses the arguments for and against "securitizing" global health challenges.

Global Health Challenges as Potential National Security Threats

Traditionally, the discipline of international relations has been concerned with the issue of national security. In the discipline, a **state** is defined as an entity that meets several criteria: a defined territory, a permanent population, a functioning government, the capacity to conduct foreign relations, and, according to some scholars, recognition by other states.[1] Whether a particular territory fulfills these criteria and should be considered a state is often contested, and disputes over such issues are a major source of conflict in international relations. Addressing the contested nature of statehood in both law and practice goes beyond the scope of this chapter. Nevertheless, because the state is a central actor and concept in the study of international relations, it is important for students to understand the basic meaning of the term.

Because of the field's focus on states, international relations scholars historically have prioritized the study of interstate war, questions related to military security and defense, and foreign relations among states. Such matters are often referred to as "high politics." Other global issues, such as human rights, the environment, and health, traditionally have been relegated to the realm of "low politics." Scholars who emphasize the importance of high politics do not necessarily intend to signal that these other global issues do not matter. Rather, many international relations scholars simply believe that issues of war and peace are the most central to interstate relations, a core focus of the discipline, and should be prioritized accordingly.

The discipline of international relations has evolved considerably since its inception. Increasingly, many scholars recognize that the division of international relations into realms

KEY TERMS IN THE STUDY OF GLOBAL HEALTH AND SECURITY

Bioterrorism: the use of biological weapons to perpetrate acts of violence against civilians with the intent of instilling fear for the purpose of political objectives (a contested term because of disagreement about whether acts of violence against civilians by states as well as non-state actors should be considered terrorism).

Biowarfare: the use of biological weapons as instruments of violence.

Complex Emergency: a humanitarian crisis involving the breakdown of authority in a society due to internal or external conflict and requiring an integrated response by multiple international agencies.

Human Security: a concept of security that emphasizes the quality of life and well-being of individuals.

National Security: state security from external threats, usually military threats.

Securitization: the practice of framing specific phenomena, such as health, as security issues.

State: a territorial entity with a resident population and a functioning government capable of engaging in foreign relations.

of "high" and "low" politics is a false and not terribly useful one. Indeed, these categories have considerable overlap and interconnections. Environmental scarcity and conflicts over resources within states can contribute to international conflicts. Similarly, human rights violations in one state may have destabilizing effects on neighboring states. Environmental, human rights, and public health challenges can all displace people in ways that disrupt the territorial integrity of neighboring states, raising concerns about national defense and potentially precipitating conflict among states. In this way, these global issues are potential determinants of *national security*. Therefore, a broad understanding of the interconnections between high and low politics underscores the reality that global health challenges have the potential to threaten national security.

There are many ways in which global health challenges might threaten national security. Public health challenges in one country are not easily contained and may readily cross territorial borders, affecting intergovernmental relations. Public health crises can contribute to deteriorating or failed states, which, in turn, breeds chaos, conflict, and violence that can spill over borders.[2] Furthermore, states and non-state actors may exploit germs as instruments of violence in the conflicts to which they are parties. Additionally, if national security is broadly conceptualized to encompass economic interests, rather than just narrowly defined military/strategic interests, then the connections between health and national security are even more apparent. For example, European powers in the 19th century feared the effects that "tropical" diseases might have on their imperial power and commercial interests abroad. In response, they set up centers and programs for the treatment of tropical illnesses, demonstrating some of the earliest evidence of state interest in global health issues.[3]

In contemporary global politics, there is growing evidence that states and international organizations conceive public health threats as potential national security issues. In the United States, the Central Intelligence Agency's National Intelligence Council identified infectious diseases as potential threats to national security in its report, issued in January 2000, titled *The Global Infectious Disease Threat and Its Implications for the United States*.[4] In a similar development that same month, the UN Security Council took up the issue of the HIV/AIDS crisis in sub-Saharan Africa. The UN Charter gives the Security Council primary responsibility for the maintenance of international peace and security, but this body does not have charter-based authority over non-security issues in international affairs. Thus, the fact that the Security Council dealt with the issue of HIV/AIDS signals that the international community is willing to frame important global health challenges like HIV/AIDS as security issues.[5] A number of non-governmental organizations (NGOs), including the Center for Strategic and International Studies and the International Crisis Group, have also issued reports that identify global health challenges as potential issues of national security.[6]

These developments indicate that important actors in global politics have started to conceptualize public health challenges as potential threats to national security. A number of factors help explain how such challenges might contribute to intrastate or interstate conflict. If public health challenges displace populations and thereby threaten territorial borders, such population movements might foment discord between neighboring states. Similarly, if public health challenges create extensive fear among populations, they might generate repressive governmental responses that lead to intrastate conflicts. Once again, such conflicts, especially if they involve significant violence, might spill over territorial borders, threatening the security interests of neighboring states and precipitating conflict throughout a region. Public health challenges also clearly affect the material interests of states; because state military

power is fundamentally shaped by the material resources of states, any public health challenge that depletes state resources has the potential to undermine a state's security interests.[7] Thus, we can see that there are mechanisms by which serious public health challenges could produce threats to national security.

But is there actually empirical evidence that such linkages between public health problems and national security exist in practice? Andrew Price-Smith argues that epidemic disease may directly undermine the material power of a state, thereby threatening its national security interests. According to Price-Smith, a high prevalence of communicable illnesses in countries and regions reduces state capacity by increasing poverty, contributing to state failure, and generating instability within countries and regions. In some cases, endemic disease may have more direct effects on national security. Price-Smith asserts that the Spanish influenza epidemic of 1918–1919 helped contribute to the defeat of Austria and Germany in World War I, largely because the disease had higher prevalence and mortality rates among Austrian and German troops and thereby contributed to the capitulation of these powers.[8] It is difficult to imagine a more powerful example of how communicable illness might change the course of world history and politics. It is worth noting that states themselves have taken the potential microbial threat to national security seriously. In the 19th century, European militaries were at the forefront of national efforts to promote sanitary reforms because they saw such measures as necessary to ensure military preparedness.[9] A more contemporary example involves the global HIV/AIDS epidemic. A number of scholars have questioned whether the staggering HIV prevalence rates in many southern African countries undermine the military preparedness and combat effectiveness of the armed forces in these countries.[10]

Price-Smith also provides examples of public health challenges with regional, if not global, national security effects. In particular, he examines the case of Zimbabwe to illustrate the ways in which epidemic disease—in this case,

HIV/AIDS—can contribute to state collapse and violent conflict within a country. Notably, deteriorating state capacity in Zimbabwe has led to a flood of refugees into Botswana and South Africa and thereby affected the territorial integrity and security interests of these neighboring countries.[11] In this way, the Zimbabwe case demonstrates concrete linkages between public health challenges and national security.[12] Similar dynamics involving the deterioration of state capacity, the displacement of populations across territorial borders, and epidemic disease outbreaks in refugee camps are common in war-affected regions, suggesting that a public health/national security linkage may be the norm rather than the exception in zones of conflict.

Despite the importance of these examples, it must be noted that public health challenges do not necessarily *directly* threaten national security in most cases. Even Price-Smith acknowledges that infectious diseases do not normally pose a *direct* threat to national security, especially in industrialized states.[13] Rather, infectious diseases have greater potential to shape national security *indirectly* through a variety of mechanisms—by displacing people across borders, by depleting state material resources, or by undermining state capacity. Such mechanisms are more likely to be in play in relatively poor, less developed countries. Notably, public health challenges already tend to be more pressing in these countries and are more likely to exacerbate—and be exacerbated by—national security tensions.

Biological Warfare and Bioterrorism

One exception to the generalization that diseases do not directly threaten national security in most cases involves the use of biological weapons. **Biowarfare**, the use of biological weapons as instruments of violence, provides a powerful and frightening example of the potential strategic connections that exist between human health and national security. In this case, germs are *intentionally* used as instruments of violence by states or non-state actors. When states or non-state actors employ biological weapons in this way, they usually do so because they believe that they are advancing their strategic interests. Thus, it can be said that states might view germs as a mechanism for protecting national security. At the same time, of course, the use of such weapons clearly undermines the national security of targeted states.

References to biological warfare are prevalent throughout recorded human history, suggesting that states and non-state actors have always used biological weapons to advance perceived strategic interests. Partisans in ancient Greece and Rome poisoned the water and food supplies of their enemies. In medieval Europe, fighting armies used the bodies and human waste of victims of the bubonic plague to spread the disease among their enemies.[14] The United Kingdom deployed biological weapons, specifically smallpox, during its colonization of the Americas, killing a large portion of the indigenous population in the process.[15] During the American Revolution, American military forces accused the British of intentionally infecting the Continental Army with smallpox, although no clear empirical evidence has been uncovered to confirm this assertion.[16] During World War I, Germany allegedly used biological weapons, primarily by infecting animals in an effort to sabotage the Allied war effort.[17]

The international community has sought to ban the use of biological weapons. In 1925, state parties signed the Protocol for the Prohibition of the Use in War of Asphyxiating, Poisonous, or Other Gases, and of Bacteriological Methods of War. This treaty, commonly known as the Geneva Protocol, entered into force in 1928 and outlawed the use of biological weapons. However, the language in the treaty did not apply to non-state actors. Moreover, state parties to the treaty often reserved the right to the defensive use of biological weapons in response to any biological attacks on their territory.[18] The Geneva Protocol was not different from most other instruments of international law in that it lacked concrete enforcement mechanisms. As a result, the strong prohibitory language in the treaty had little real effect on the behavior of state or non-state actors. The 1972 Convention on the Prohibition of the Development, Production, and Stockpiling of Bacteriological (Biological) and Toxin Weapons and on Their Destruction, commonly referred to as the Biological Weapons Convention, bans the development, production, or stockpiling of biological weapons. Once again, however, the treaty does not contain effective enforcement mechanisms.

Given the reality that international laws prohibiting the use, possession, or development of biological weapons do not include effective enforcement mechanisms, it should not be surprising that states have continued to develop, and in some cases use, biological weapons throughout the 20th century and into the 21st century. Japan had a major biological warfare program during World War II. This program, which involved horrific human experiments, was created for the purpose of facilitating germ warfare attacks that the Japanese government believed would advance its national security interests.[19] The Japanese military used cholera, typhoid, anthrax, and other pathogens to carry out attacks on targets in China. Scholars have estimated that approximately 580,000 people died during World War II as a result of Japanese germ warfare and human experimentation.[20] Nazi Germany had a similar biological warfare program and conducted germ experiments on human beings in its infamous concentration camps. However, although the Soviet Union accused Nazi Germany of conducting germ warfare attacks on its territory during the war, to date, these accusations have not been proved.[21]

The Soviet Union carried out its own biological weapons research during World War II. The United States and Britain also had their own wartime biological warfare programs, and the Allies seriously considered military strategies that involved germ warfare attacks on German cities.[22] During the Cold War, both the Soviet Union and the United States maintained biological warfare programs, and each side accused

the other of deploying biological weapons in the proxy wars they fought in Cambodia, Laos, Afghanistan, and Cuba during this conflict. However, each government has disputed the charges.[23] Although the evidence is absolutely clear that both the United States and the Soviet Union (and, subsequently, Russia) have maintained significant biological warfare programs, concrete evidence of biological warfare attacks does not exist. The fact that major powers have maintained biological warfare programs underscores the importance that states place on germs as potential weapons that they can use in their efforts to advance their strategic interests, despite the fact that the development or possession of biological weapons is prohibited under international law.

Although major powers have consistently maintained biological warfare programs, the actual use of these weapons has been relatively rare in comparison with conventional weapons. A number of factors help explain why states rely on biological weapons to a lesser extent than conventional weapons. For one thing, it is not clear that germs are actually effective strategic weapons. Even when actors have the capacity to develop and stockpile deadly germs, the effective deployment of these germs presents an obstacle to their use. Additionally, it can be difficult to contain germs in ways that distinguish between enemy soldiers and a state's own forces or between soldiers and civilians. A related apprehension about the possibility of precipitating a global epidemic may constrain state use of germs as weapons.[24] Some people might even argue that moral considerations make states less likely to deploy biological weapons, though states' clear willingness to maintain biological warfare programs should raise some skepticism about this argument.

At this point, a discussion of **bioterrorism** becomes relevant. Bioterrorism can be defined simply as terrorist acts using biological agents. For this definition to have any meaning, we must also define terrorism, a far trickier proposition. *Terrorism* is a controversial term. Terrorism can be defined as any act of violence that targets civilians and that is intended to instill fear as a means of furthering political objectives.[25] The key controversy in the discipline of international relations is whether the label *terrorism* should be applied only to violence carried out by non-state actors or whether state violence that targets civilians should also be considered terroristic. State governments often apply the label of terrorism to violent acts committed by non-state actors against the state. Media outlets often follow the lead of states by labeling any violence by non-state actors as terroristic. In contrast, media coverage of interstate war does not tend to label state violence as terrorism, even when it intentionally targets civilians. For this reason, critics contend that terrorism is a biased and misleading concept that states manipulate to advance their own strategic interests and that fails to distinguish between legitimate and illegitimate uses of violence by non-state actors. This dilemma is effectively captured by the well-known aphorism, "One person's terrorist is another person's freedom fighter." Despite the controversy evoked by the concept of terrorism, the term *bioterrorism*— which, again, can be defined as terrorist attacks with biological agents—is a subject of serious interest for many scholars, national security experts working within governments, and public health and medical practitioners charged with being prepared to respond to biological weapons attacks. When these actors discuss bioterrorism, they typically are working under a definition that assumes biological attacks carried out by non-state actors.

In working with a definition of bioterrorism that focuses primarily on non-state actors, it is important to explore what might motivate such attacks. Non-state actors may have even stronger incentives to obtain and use biological weapons than state actors. Because non-state actors do not have the same military or financial resources as states, they do not have access to conventional military power. In this context, biological weapons are an attractive alternative for non-state actors that face perceived threats to their interests from states with superior military forces. If non-state actors have greater incentives to rely on germs as weapons, they

may also have fewer disincentives to their use. Non-state actors may be motivated more by ideological considerations than strategic considerations and, as a result, may be less concerned with protecting their own combatants. At the same time, such groups may not recognize the international legal distinction between combatants and civilians that constrains states during war.

The 9/11 Al Qaeda attacks on the World Trade Center illustrate these dynamics, even though these attacks did not involve biological weapons. In this case, Al Qaeda partisans hijacked commercial airplanes that they flew into both World Trade Center buildings in New York City, killing approximately 3,000 people. Al Qaeda selected civilian targets, indicating that the organization did not respect the distinction between civilians and combatants. In fact, the group intentionally targeted civilians precisely because it knew that such an attack would instill significant fear and draw extensive media attention that would provide a vehicle for articulating its political objectives, which were far disproportionate to its actual numbers, resources, or power. Suicide bombers knowingly and willingly gave their lives to this cause. Thus, this example illustrates the appeal that unconventional weapons—in this case, commercial airplanes—have for non-state actors seeking to harm the interests of more powerful state actors.

National security experts who focus on threats from bioterrorism believe that similar dynamics may motivate attempts by non-state actors to use biological weapons against more powerful states whose interests they wish to harm. Indeed, there are examples of deadly, if small-scale, bioterrorist attacks, most notably the 2001 anthrax attacks in the United States. The anthrax attacks are not the only bioterrorist incident on record, though other attacks have been similarly small in nature, killing only a few people.[26]

Nevertheless, the threat of biological attacks remains frightening for a variety of reasons. Bioterrorism attacks can be carried out covertly and can involve efforts to infect humans directly (for example, by releasing biological agents into the atmosphere) or indirectly (for example, by contaminating animals or plant crops).[27] Until public health officials notice any unusual significant pattern in symptoms of patients showing up at emergency rooms or doctors' offices, the public might not even be aware of the threat, making it harder to control. As in the case of a communicable illness that is readily transmissible between humans, it might also be difficult to contain the effects of any biological attack. However, there are reasons to think that the threat from biological weapons may be overstated. It is difficult to produce, maintain, and deploy truly dangerous microbes like smallpox, anthrax, or plague. That said, it must also be noted that developments in biotechnology may increase the likelihood that non-state actors will be able to develop and deploy biological weapons more easily in the future.[28] At present, the most accurate summary we can make is to say that bioterrorism is a potential national security threat with *a high capacity* for producing very serious negative health consequences and a *relatively low probability* of being carried out effectively on a large scale.

Despite consistent references to, and concrete examples of, biological warfare throughout human history, scholars have noted that the use of biological weapons is relatively rare in comparison with the use of conventional weapons. Similarly, there is a gap between fearful rhetoric describing the potential threat of bioterrorism and the reality of relatively few bioterrorist attacks on record. Nonetheless, the historic use of biological weapons underscores the reality that germs can be used as instruments of violence toward very deadly ends and can generate a great deal of fear among populations threatened with biological warfare. In this regard, even when states or non-state actors do not actually deploy biological weapons, the mere threat of biological warfare can be used for strategic purposes.[29] In this way, biological warfare and bioterrorism reflect a clear linkage between human health and national security.

The Health Costs of Intrastate and Interstate War

Both intrastate and interstate war have devastating effects on human health. Violent conflict produces wide-ranging physical and psychological harms to human health. Most obviously, war kills, maims, and injures human beings, both combatants and civilians. Precise estimates on war deaths, which include combatant and civilian deaths resulting from direct wartime violence, are difficult to obtain, and efforts to forge consensus on such estimates can be contentious. Thus, the following figures should be taken for exactly what they are—estimates and not precise counts. Nevertheless, these figures give some indication of the major health consequences of wartime violence. One study estimated that, on average, 458,000 people died per year as a result of war-related causes in the 20th century.[30] Another study cites a lower figure of approximately 378,000 war deaths annually between 1985 and 1994.[31] A subsequent study suggests that both of these estimates are inflated. Instead, due to the changing nature of warfare (with conventional wars fought by large armies being displaced by smaller and more localized wars), this study suggests that the number of wartime deaths each year is on the decline, though it does not provide an estimated annual figure of war deaths for the comparable time period.[32] In addition to war deaths, countless other combatants and civilians are injured or maimed by direct wartime violence. Furthermore, thousands of women are raped in the context of wartime violence each year, though, once again, reliable estimates are difficult to obtain.[33] Regardless of whether one relies on high-end or low-end estimates, it is clear that war produces serious negative health consequences for affected populations.

The indirect health consequences of interstate and intrastate violence are often just as devastating. Violent conflict exacerbates the conditions that produce a wide range of health problems, including communicable illnesses like cholera, other diarrheal diseases, respiratory infections, measles, malaria,[34] and AIDS,[35] as

UNDER THE MICROSCOPE

Disease and Death in the Shadow of War

The case of a major cholera outbreak in a refugee camp in Goma, Zaire (now the Democratic Republic of the Congo), in 1994 provides a stark example of the indirect health consequences of wartime violence. This outbreak occurred in the context of much broader violence in the region. The refugee camp in Zaire was set up for individuals fleeing Rwanda in the aftermath of the horrifying genocide and civil war in that country. In the 1994 Rwandan genocide, Hutus, who represented a majority in the country, killed hundreds of thousands of Tutsis in the span of just 100 days. (Estimates of the number of Tutsis killed in the genocide range from 500,000 to 800,000.) This genocide occurred in the context of broader civil conflict in which the Rwandan Patriotic Front (RPF), comprising mostly Tutsi insurgents, fought against a repressive government dominated by Hutus.

After the RPF overthrew the Hutu regime in July 1994, hundreds of thousands of Hutus, many of whom had participated in the genocide, fled to neighboring countries. An estimated 2 million Tutsi and Hutu refugees were driven out of Rwanda, and an additional 1.5 million were internally displaced within the country's borders. Thousands of these refugees died from diseases that thrived in the squalid conditions of the refugee camps.[a] Refugee camps were created in areas with inhospitable geography for human settlement, insufficient water resources, and the absence of proper infrastructure for maintaining a major humanitarian operation.[b] The cholera outbreak in Goma, Zaire, occurred under these conditions. Due to the isolation of the refugee camp and the lack of adequate roads, international aid agencies could not bring in sufficient supplies of clean water. As a result, refugees retrieved water from Lake Kivu, the lake adjacent to the camp. The particularities

---

[a]United Nations High Commissioner for Refugees, "The Rwandan Genocide and Its Aftermath," *State of the World's Refugees 2000: Fifty Years of Humanitarian Action* (January 2000): 246–247. Available online at: http://www.unhcr.org/4a4c754a9.html.

[b]*Ibid.*

---

well as noncommunicable health problems such as malnutrition and famine.[36] In conflict zones, people become more susceptible to disease, as they are more likely to face malnutrition and stress.[37] One of the mechanisms by which violent conflict indirectly leads to new health challenges is through the displacement of people in conflict zones. Wartime violence often drives people out of their homes and communities within a country's borders (in which case international law refers to these people as *internally*

displaced persons) or across international borders (in which case the displaced people are categorized under international law as *refugees*). This internal and external displacement of people produces conditions conducive to serious outbreaks of disease. Furthermore, violent conflict damages public infrastructure (roads, water systems, and electrical power facilities) as well as health infrastructure (hospitals and clinics) in ways that facilitate the transmission of communicable diseases and prevent their treatment.

of the geography in the region also made the construction of latrines difficult. Thus, human waste from the dense concentration of refugees made its way into the lake. All of these factors led to a deadly outbreak of cholera. The bodies of people who died from the disease ended up in the lake, thereby exacerbating the problem.[c] Out of the 70,000 people who contracted cholera during this epidemic, 12,000 people died, making this case the deadliest outbreak of waterborne illness in the 20th century.[d]

Although the cholera outbreak in the Goma refugee camp was particularly deadly, it is not an isolated case. The squalid conditions of refugee camps are breeding grounds for disease, and the wartime violence that produces mass displacement of people is clearly a cause of the major health problems that emerge under such conditions. Moreover, deteriorating public infrastructure limits the ability of health care professionals to work in conflict zones by limiting access to drugs that might otherwise be used to treat curable illnesses like cholera. Although this case illustrates the ways in which violent conflict can exacerbate conditions that lead to disease, it is important to note that conflict does not necessarily *produce* disease. Obviously, other factors, including the presence of specific microbes and natural conditions under which these germs thrive, are necessary to produce illness in a particular environment.[e] That said, wartime violence and the deterioration of public infrastructure that typically accompanies war produce conditions under which certain microbes thrive, facilitate the human-to-human transmission of these germs, and create obstacles that make it difficult, if not impossible, for medical professionals to treat curable illnesses. In the words of Andrew Price-Smith, "War may act as a powerful amplifier of disease."[f]

---

[c]Robert D. Morris, *The Blue Death: Disease, Disaster, and the Water We Drink* (New York: HarperCollins Publishers, 2007): 262.

[d]Didier Bompangue, Patrick Giraudoux, Martine Piarroux, Guy Mutombo, Rick Shamavu, Bertrand Sudre, Anne Mutombo, Vital Mondonge, and Rinaud Piarroux, "Cholera Epidemics, War and Disasters Around Goma and Lake Kivu: An Eight Year Survey," *PLoS Neglected Tropical Diseases* 3: 5 (2009): e436. Available online at: http://www.ncbi.nlm.nih.gov/pmc/articles/PMC2677153/.

[e]*Ibid.*

[f]Andrew T. Price-Smith, *Contagion and Chaos: Disease, Ecology, and National Security in an Era of Globalization* (Cambridge, MA: MIT Press, 2009): 3.

The deterioration of public infrastructure also makes it more difficult to meet the basic needs of people living in conflict zones, thereby undermining basic health. Wartime violence also does significant damage to the psychological health of people living in conflict zones.

Scholars and practitioners often discuss the indirect costs of war, including costs to human health, under the concept of **complex emergencies** that manifest in the context of wartime violence. According to the UN Office for the Coordination of Humanitarian Affairs, a complex emergency is "a humanitarian crisis in a country, region or society where there is total or considerable breakdown of authority resulting from internal or external conflict and which requires an international response that goes beyond the mandate or capacity of any single agency and/or the ongoing United Nations country programme."[38] In short, complex emergencies involve a wide range of humanitarian challenges that result from the social, political, and economic disruptions of violent conflict, and threats to public health are among the greatest challenges that occur. One study estimates that between 320,000 and 420,000 people die annually due to complex emergencies.[39] Other threats to human health, including malnutrition and mental illness, are heightened in complex emergencies.[40]

Despite the fact that wartime violence clearly produces significant indirect harms to human health, one study notes that these indirect costs of war have decreased over time. Indeed, this study claims that *overall mortality rates* actually decline during war in most conflict-affected countries.[41] The authors attribute this paradox to several factors: (1) overall mortality rates are declining in developing countries, a trend that still holds during wartime; (2) contemporary armed conflict tends to be very localized and does not affect large swaths of territory or portions of the populations in countries where conflict is occurring; and (3) international humanitarian assistance has been effective in bringing down mortality rates due to the indirect effects of war.[42] Although it concludes that the indirect costs of war are shrinking, this report acknowledges that populations in conflict zones are still more susceptible to disease during times of war than in times of peace.[43] More importantly, the report confirms that the number of indirect deaths from war is still higher than the number of direct deaths from war, especially in poor countries.[44] Thus, although proponents of public health should welcome any decline in indirect deaths from wartime violence, the still-significant health costs of war, both direct and indirect, remain a serious challenge in efforts to improve global health and provide a stark illustration of the concrete linkages between public health and national security.

Human Security and Health

Given that the indirect and direct consequences of war for human health remain high, why does it matter that the overall health costs of war are shrinking? Focusing on the shrinking costs of war seems to lessen the importance of war as a matter of grave concern in global politics. Unless one is callous to the real human costs of war (even if these costs are diminishing overall), it might seem strange that any scholar or organization would choose to highlight this empirical trend. However, the debate over the real costs of war begins to make sense if one places it in a broader context of debates within the field of international relations over the issues that should be prioritized by governments, NGOs, and scholars.

In this regard, the conceptual distinctions between *national security* and *human security* are fundamental in explaining why determining the actual costs of war—and whether they are rising or falling—matters a great deal in global politics. Once again, national security refers to the security of states from external, usually military, threats. In contrast, human security is concerned with the well-being of *individual* human beings, and threats to human security can be internal as well as external. Of course, war and external threats from other states can affect individual well-being across borders. However, the state in which one lives can also pose a threat to human security either directly (for example, by abusing human rights) or indirectly (for example, by failing to provide a basic social safety net that helps ensure that the basic needs of human beings residing in the state are being met).

As discussed in the previous section, the discipline of international relations historically has prioritized the issues of war and peace. In part, this prioritization reflects the state-centric approach that has fundamentally shaped this discipline. Yet, it also reflects an underlying assumption that war and state-dominated power politics are the most fundamental and important threats to human civilization. If this assumption is true, then it makes sense for international relations scholars to prioritize the study of war. Similarly, it makes sense for governments to place issues of war, national security, and defense high on their lists of policy and funding priorities. However, if the assumption is not true—if, in fact, there are greater threats to human society than war—then governments would be well served to adjust their policy agendas and national budgets accordingly. In fact, disagreements about the most serious threats to human well-being and appropriate governmental and nongovernmental responses to these threats are precisely what is at stake in the debate over whether security should be conceptualized in *national* or *human* terms.

Human security conceptualizes security in individual terms. What matters is the well-being of individual human beings and not the stability of states. Even if a state is not threatened by external military threats, its population may be highly vulnerable and insecure. Indeed, proponents of human security point out that people across the world are far more likely to be victims of violence perpetrated by their own governments than militarized violence carried out by external actors. The Human Security Report Project explains this perspective succinctly: "National security remains important, but in a world in which war between states is the rare exception, and many more people are killed by their own governments than by foreign armies, the concept of 'human security' has been gaining recognition."[45] Because of its recognition that internal violence represents a far greater threat to human well-being than external military threats, the Human Security Report Project conceptualizes human security as individual freedom from violence, internal as well as external. Notably, it was the Human Security Report Project that put out the report on the shrinking costs of war. This research center, funded by the governments of Norway, Sweden, Switzerland, and the United Kingdom, is seeking to shift the terms of the debate over security in world politics. It wants governments and international agencies to prioritize human security over national security and to adopt noncoercive, nonmilitary means for promoting human security.

Whereas the Human Security Report Project broadens the concept of security to encompass internal as well as external violent threats to human well-being, other organizations and scholars conceptualize human security in an even broader way. In 1994, the United Nations Development Programme (UNDP) put human security prominently on the international policy agenda. The UNDP offered a very broad conception of security as being primarily concerned with individual human beings rather than states and as encompassing economic, health, and social well-being rather than simply freedom from violence. It is worth repeating at some length excerpts of the language used by the UNDP to justify the dramatic shift in the conception of security that the agency was advocating:

> The concept of security has for too long been interpreted narrowly: as security of territory from external aggression, or as protection of national interests in foreign policy, or as global security from the threat of a nuclear holocaust. It has been related more to nation-states than to people . . . Forgotten were the legitimate concerns of ordinary people who sought security in their daily lives. For many of them, security symbolized protection from the threat of disease, hunger, unemployment, crime, social conflict, political repression and environmental hazards . . . For most people, a feeling of insecurity arises more from worries about daily life than from the dread of a cataclysmic event . . . In the final analysis, human security is a child who did not die, a disease that did not spread, a job that was not cut, an ethnic tension that did not explode in violence, a dissident who was not silenced. Human security is not a concern with weapons—it is a concern with human life and dignity.[46]

For the first time, an international organization formulated security in a radically different way than the state-centric conception of national security that had dominated the study and practice of international relations up to this time.

As this rather lengthy discussion illustrates, the difference between national and human security is at base a rhetorical distinction with real political consequences. War and national security have been prominent issues in media coverage of world politics, foreign policy agendas, and scholarship on international relations. A national security perspective mobilizes public opinion and social and governmental resources toward war-related issues. It also suggests that military solutions are the most appropriate solutions for national security problems. In contrast, a human security perspective suggests, at a minimum, that internal violent threats to human well-being be prioritized. An even broader human security perspective, such as that favored by the UNDP, urges governments to prioritize a wide range of threats—economic, political, social, health, and environmental—to the well-being of individual human beings and the communities in which they live. Accordingly, a broad human security perspective suggests that policy agendas and financial resources at both the national and international levels be directed toward meeting basic human needs rather than shoring up the military defenses of states.

The linkages between human security and public health are readily apparent. Indeed, human security and public health, while different paradigms, are in many ways synchronistic models for understanding the most serious threats to human well-being. Both approaches recognize that war is *not* the most significant threat to human society or the lives and well-being of individuals. In both developing and developed countries, disease is the greatest threat to human life. In fact, "infectious disease morbidity and mortality far exceed war-related death and disability in human history."[47] Communicable illnesses, especially upper-respiratory infections, diarrhea, and tuberculosis, kill an average of 17 million people in the developing world each year.[48] As shown in Figure 7.1, this staggering figure far outweighs annual war-related deaths across the globe. Of course, it is a fact of life that people die, and it is not surprising that "natural" health-related problems are major causes of death, especially among the elderly.

But what is notable about these figures is that most of these deaths are preventable, many of them striking children under five years of age. It is also notable that poor people, in the developed as well as the developing world, are more likely to die from these treatable diseases.

Thus, preventable infectious diseases, in terms of sheer numbers, threaten far more people than war across the globe. Moreover, in qualitative terms, there is no reason to suppose that the human suffering involved in dying from malnutrition, diarrhea, or any other preventable health problem is any less than that suffered in war-related deaths. In accordance with these realities, both the human security and the public health paradigms suggest that these health challenges be prioritized at local, national, and global levels. Within these frameworks, public monies would be better spent trying to address the health problems that a huge percentage of the global population faces on a daily basis. Unlike a national security perspective, which tends to emphasize military solutions, human security and public health perspectives suggest that nonmilitary approaches are more likely to advance the well-being of individual human beings and the communities in which they live.

Ultimately, human security does not simply deal with a different aspect of security than national security. Rather, a human security perspective represents an altogether different way of conceptualizing security. It redefines security in human rather than state-centric terms, and it prioritizes nonmilitary solutions to the predominantly nonmilitary threats to human well-being. Thus, a human security perspective represents a radical departure from traditional ways of thinking about international relations. In this regard, the concept of human security is consistent with the core assumptions that have guided the study and practice of global public health. Human health is interdependent. Threats to human health easily cross national borders and require transnational solutions. The poor are especially vulnerable to health threats, and both human security and public health frameworks contend that it is important

FIGURE 7.1   Estimated Annual Deaths from Poverty-related Versus Conflict-related Causes

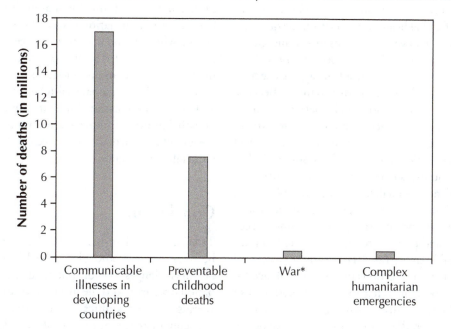

*Rough estimates of annual war-related deaths are based on an annual average of estimated total wartime deaths during the 20th century.

Sources: Estimated deaths from war were drawn from Richard M. Garfield and Alfred I. Neugut, "The Human Consequences of War," in Barry S. Levy and Victor W. Sidel, eds., *War and Public Health* (Washington, DC: American Public Health Association, 2000): 29 and Ziad Obermeyer, Christopher J.L. Murray, and Emmanuela Gakidou, "Fifty Years of Violent War Deaths from Vietnam to Bosnia: Analysis of Data from World Health Survey Programme," *British Medical Journal* 336 (June 2008): 1482–1486. Estimated deaths from complex humanitarian emergencies were taken from Richard J. Brennan and Robin Nandy, "Complex Humanitarian Emergencies: A Major Global Health Challenge," *Emergency Medicine* 13: 2 (2001): 149. Figures on deaths from communicable illnesses in developing countries are from United Nations Development Programme, *Human Development Report* 1994: p. 22. Available online at: http://hdr.undp.org/en/media/hdr_1994_en_chap2.pdf: 27–28. Current estimates of preventable childhood deaths are from World Health Organization, *Reducing Mortality from Major Killers of Children*, Fact Sheet 178. Available online at: http://www.who.int/inf-fs/en/fact178.html.

to address the needs of the poorest and most vulnerable people across the globe out of both pragmatic self-interest and concerns for justice.

The Securitization Debate in Global Health

The tension between national and human security perspectives raises an important question about the merits of "securitizing" global health. In the discipline of international relations, **securitization** involves the practice of constructing and framing specific phenomena as security issues.[49] Actors can attempt to

securitize any international or transnational phenomena, including issues like civil war, terrorism, or immigration. In particular, actors engaged in global politics tend to try to securitize issues that have not been traditionally conceptualized in ways that engage national security concerns, for example, human rights, the environment, and global health. Thus, the objective of securitizing a specific issue is to raise its profile and increase the likelihood that states and other actors will prioritize the issue in question. In practice, then, to securitize an issue involves an effort to evoke national security concerns rather than human security concerns. International organizations, states, and

NGOs have increasingly sought to securitize global health.[50] Despite the fact that securitization of global health is on the rise, the question remains: Does it make sense to frame global public health challenges as security issues?

There are potential advantages to securitizing global health in this manner. Because states are highly motivated by national security concerns, they generally are willing to expend significant state resources on issues perceived to affect national security. Thus, some scholars and practitioners have argued for securitizing global health challenges as a way of raising global awareness of important public health challenges and increasing the amount of economic and political resources directed to public health endeavors.[51] For example, increased spending on infectious disease surveillance for the purpose of trying to prevent bioterrorism could improve disease surveillance in general.[52]

However, the securitization of global health also involves important risks. For one, securitization reinforces a narrow, state-centric vision of the nexus between global health and national security. In doing so, securitization could push states to prioritize military responses to global health challenges as opposed to nonmilitary solutions that might be more appropriate for addressing the economic, social, and political dynamics underlying particular health problems. For instance, Stefan Elbe argues that efforts to securitize HIV/AIDS could give military and intelligence agencies powers that might undermine respect for the human rights and civil liberties of people living with HIV/AIDS.[53] There is also a risk that securitization could dilute the meaning of both national security *and* public health in ways that undermine local, national, and global efforts to develop meaningful, targeted programs designed to advance global health. Robert Ostergard, for example, has argued that securitization risks creating complacency about serious public health problems: "If all human maladies are a security threat . . . , then the potential for complacency or apathy becomes the real threat."[54]

Whether the benefits of securitizing global health challenges outweigh the costs may, in the end, merely be an academic question.

International organizations, states, and NGOs increasingly have framed global health problems as potential national security issues. In an age when national security concerns continue to dominate the foreign policy agendas of many states, more useful questions may be, *To what degree* should global health be securitized? and *How* can the national security dimensions of global health be addressed in ways that best meet the fundamental health needs of the most vulnerable populations?

Conclusion

This chapter demonstrated clear linkages between security and global health. Global health challenges have the potential to threaten national security, and the inverse is true as well. Because violent conflict has such devastating consequences for human health, it is clear that national security threats have the capacity to undermine human health on a local, national, regional, and even global scale. The chapter also highlighted the parallels between human security and public health paradigms for understanding human well-being.

In the process of showing clear connections between security and global health, the chapter also identified tensions between competing conceptions of security. National security and human security frameworks offer dramatically different ways of understanding security. These distinctions are not merely semantic. Instead, they suggest entirely different sets of political priorities and policy approaches for promoting both security and human health. Under a national security framework, the emphasis is on the ways in which public health problems can destabilize states and disrupt the stability of territorial borders, and on pathogens as possible instruments of violence. This approach reflects a state-centric model that emphasizes largely military solutions to health security problems. Conversely, a human security framework contends that fundamental human health needs, including access to adequate food, clean water, and basic health care, affect a significantly higher percentage of the world's population and represent far more pressing health problems. This approach prioritizes nonmilitary solutions and calls for the diversion of military spending to funding for the building up of public infrastructure and basic health care.

No consensus exists among scholars or practitioners as to whether health should be framed as a national security issue or a human security issue. Indeed, critics have reservations about whether it is helpful to place health into any sort of security framework. Nonetheless, the securitization of global health is an increasingly common practice. Therefore, it is essential for students and engaged citizens to understand the important, if complicated, linkages between security and global health.

Discussion Questions

1. Describe the potential linkages between global health and national security. How can global health shape national security, and, conversely, how might national security affect global health?
2. Should global health be considered an issue of national security? Why or why not?
3. Are public health challenges more likely to pose a direct or an indirect threat to national security? Why?
4. Are biowarfare and bioterrorism significant national security threats? Why or why not?
5. How do the direct health costs of war compare with the indirect health costs of war? Which of these health costs (direct or indirect) should be considered a bigger public health priority? Why?

6. How does a human security framework differ from a national security framework in the context of global health? Which framework is more useful for understanding global health issues? Why?
7. How do the health costs of war compare with the overall mortality rates and burden of disease in most war-torn countries? Which issue—war-related health costs or general health problems—should be considered a bigger public health priority? Why?
8. What are the potential risks and benefits of securitizing global health challenges?

Web Resources

Center for Strategic and International Studies Global Health Policy Center: http://csis.org/program/global-health-policy-center/

Center for Unconventional Security Affairs: http://www.cusa.uci.edu/

George Washington Africa Center for Health and Human Security: http://www.gwumc.edu/africa/about_center.html

Global Health Security Initiative: http://www.ghsi.ca/english/statementLondon2009.asp

Human Security Centre: Liu Institute for Global Issues at the University of British Columbia: http://www.ligi.ubc.ca/page165.htm

Human Security Gateway: http://www.humansecuritygateway.com/

Human Security Report Project: http://www.hsrgroup.org/

United Nations Centre for Regional Development: http://www.uncrd.or.jp/

CHAPTER 8

Global Health and Human Rights

Introduction

Article 12 of the International Covenant on Economic, Social, and Cultural Rights codifies a fundamental human right to health under international law. Other international human rights treaties and humanitarian laws assert basic health rights for human beings. This chapter considers the implications of the human right to health under international law. To this end, it provides an overview of the relevant body of international law, including international human rights law, international humanitarian law, and professional codes of ethics that govern medical practitioners and others working in health-related fields. The chapter takes a close look at the gendered dimensions of international human rights law by examining provisions of the Convention on the Elimination of Discrimination Against Women. The chapter also explores the significant gap between the legal articulation of a human right to health and the reality that much of the world's population does not, in practice, have access to the resources, infrastructure, or health care necessary for the fulfillment of health as a human right. Finally, the chapter examines major obstacles to the promotion of global health within a human rights framework.

The Right to Health Under International Human Rights Law

The emergence of a **human right** to health in international law can be traced back to the development of the United Nations system in the aftermath of World War II. The preamble to the Constitution of the World Health Organization, which entered into force in 1948, states: "The enjoyment of the highest attainable standard of health is one of the fundamental rights of every human being without distinction of race, religion, political belief, economic or social condition."[1] Article 25 of the Universal Declaration of Human Rights, adopted by the UN General Assembly in 1948, articulates, in a less direct way, a fundamental human right to health: "Everyone has the right to a standard of living adequate for the health and well-being of himself and of his family, including food, clothing, housing, and medical care." Despite their unambiguous and forceful language, these documents did not clearly codify a human right to health under **international law**. Although the Constitution of the World Health Organization is a binding legal document, its preamble does not necessarily have the force of law.[2] Similarly, UN declarations are not binding sources of

TYPES OF INTERNATIONAL LAW RELATED TO HUMAN RIGHTS

International Human Rights Law: the body of international law that codifies fundamental rights for all persons regardless of race, biological sex, religion, nationality, or other status.

International Humanitarian Law: the rules and norms in international law that govern the conduct of war.

International Law: the body of laws, rules, and norms that governs interactions between and among states and other actors operating in the international sphere.

international law.[3] Nonetheless, these documents signaled the emergence of a global norm conceptualizing health as a fundamental human right.

The human right to health became a binding part of international law in 1976, when the International Covenant on Economic, Social, and Cultural Rights (ICESCR) entered into force.[4] Echoing the language of the preamble to the WHO Constitution, Article 12 of the ICESCR asserts "the right of everyone to the highest attainable standard of physical and mental health." In addition to codifying a general right to health for all human beings, Article 12 identifies specific steps that state parties should take to realize the human right to health. It calls for reductions in stillbirth rates and infant mortality; affirms the importance of promoting the healthy development of the child; prioritizes the improvement of environmental and industrial hygiene; and calls for the prevention, treatment, and control of endemic, epidemic, occupational, and other diseases. Finally, Article 12 calls for state parties to take steps to create conditions that ensure medical treatment and attention in the event of illness. The ICESCR contains other provisions that assert basic health rights. Article 10 calls for special protection for mothers before and after childbirth and indicates that the employment of

children in work that could be harmful to their health should be punishable by law. Article 11 recognizes the right of all human beings to an adequate standard of living, including adequate food, clothing, and housing.

The ICESCR's recognition of a human right to health represents a notable development in **international human rights law**, which codifies fundamental rights for all persons regardless of race, biological sex, religion, nationality, or other status, as well as progress in global efforts to promote the highest attainable standards of human health. Yet, this development also reveals the stark limitations of a rights-based legal framework for promoting global health. Despite the fact that the human right to health has been binding for several decades, it is clear that for much of the world's population, a "right" to health remains illusory. The roughly 7.7 million children who die each year from preventable illness are not realizing a human right to health.[5] Nor are the hundreds of thousands of women who die each year due to complications from pregnancy and childbirth achieving the highest attainable standard of health. The roughly 2 billion people across the globe who do not have access to basic sanitation are unlikely to attain the highest standards of health. And the human right to health is not a reality for the 2 million people who die as a result of indoor air pollution annually.[6] In general, the disparities in health outcomes between the wealthy and the poor underscore the stark gap between rhetoric and reality in international human rights law.

A closer look at specific provisions of the ICESCR helps explain this gap between rhetoric and reality. On the one hand, the ICESCR's language is strong and clear in articulating a human right to health. *All* human beings have a right to health. They have a right to *the highest attainable* standards of health, not merely to minimal health standards. The right to health is framed broadly to encompass mental as well as physical health. The ICESCR also specifically recognizes the right to a decent standard of living, food, and housing—all basic needs that are essential to fulfilling a human right to health. Thus, a cursory examination of the ICESCR's language suggests that the international community has embraced a human right to health in no uncertain terms.

On the other hand, the ICESCR contains only minimal directives for implementing economic and social rights, including the right to health. The language in Article 2 is particularly revealing in this regard:

> Each State Party to the present Covenant undertakes to take steps, individually and through international assistance and co-operation, especially economic and technical, to the maximum of its available resources, with a view to achieving progressively the full realization of the rights recognized in the present Covenant by all appropriate means, including particularly the adoption of legislative measures.

If the language articulating a human right to health is strong and clear, the ICESCR's provisions detailing the precise obligations that states have to implement a right to health are weak and ambivalent. Article 2 binds states to *undertake to take steps*, including passing legislation, intended to help realize the rights articulated in the ICESCR. Not pass legislation. Not take steps to pass legislation. But "undertake to take steps" to pass legislation and other measures intended to promote the rights identified in the document. Article 2 also codifies the idea that states will only be able to take such steps contingent on the resources they have available. This caveat is completely understandable; the lack of resources in less developed countries is, of course, one of the reasons that the health status of populations in developing countries tends to be lower, on average, than the health status of populations in developed countries. That said, this legal qualification demonstrates that the treaty does not create concrete, consistent obligations for states to implement a human right to health.

Similarly, the ICESCR does not contain provisions for effective enforcement of a human right to health. The treaty creates a modest system for monitoring state progress toward achieving economic and social rights. Under Article 16, state parties agree to undertake to submit reports on progress toward implementing measures. Again, note that the requirement is very indirect. States are not required to submit reports; rather, they must *undertake* to submit reports.

In 1985, the UN Economic and Social Council created the Economic, Social, and Cultural Rights Committee to monitor the implementation of the ICESCR. This committee, which has a membership of eighteen independent experts, has the authority to review the reports that state parties to the treaty submit under Article 16. Unfortunately, many states fail to submit these reports. Even when states do submit reports, the committee does not evaluate their progress. Rather, it engages in "constructive dialogue" with states about their records in undertaking to take steps to promote the rights, including the right to health, identified in the ICESCR. The committee can issue concluding observations, make recommendations, evaluate obstacles to implementation, and provide an overview of concerns.[7] In the end, however, the committee's findings and recommendations have no binding force. In short, the ICESCR does not create effective mechanisms for enforcing a human right to health.

The gap between the ICESCR's strong language asserting a human right to health and its weak language on implementation and enforcement reflects the state-centric nature of international law. States make international law and must give their express consent for international laws to be considered binding. As a result, it should not be surprising that states are reluctant to create strong mechanisms for implementation and enforcement that would limit their **sovereignty**, a core principle in international relations asserting that states have the right to govern themselves as they see fit. Sovereignty is reinforced by the principle of nonintervention in international law, which is articulated in Article 2 of the Charter of the United Nations: "Nothing in the present Charter shall authorize the United Nations to intervene in matters which are essentially within the domestic jurisdiction of any state." Traditionally, governing elites have certainly considered health policy as a matter that falls within the domestic jurisdiction of states. As this discussion illustrates, the lack of strong implementation and enforcement mechanisms reflects an international legal system that is based on sovereignty and nonintervention as fundamental principles. If the ICESCR's weak language on implementation and enforcement is thus understandable, it is also illustrative of how low international human rights law sets the bar for the implementation and enforcement of the rights it so eloquently identifies. The devil, as they say, is in the details. At the end of the day, the state-centric nature of international law—even international human rights law—underscores the limitations of a rights-based legal framework for promoting human health across the globe.

The ICESCR is the core international legal document establishing a human right to health. As shown in Table 8.1, a wide variety of other international treaties also contain provisions relevant to a human right to health. The International Covenant on Civil and Political Rights (ICCPR), which entered into force in 1976, contains a number of articles that indirectly suggest basic health rights for human

beings. Article 6 asserts that human beings have an inherent right to life and may not be arbitrarily deprived of life. Article 7 prohibits torture and cruel and unusual punishment. Article 8 prohibits slavery, and Article 9 prohibits arbitrary detention. All of these fundamental civil rights are relevant to bodily integrity, which has obvious connections to physical and mental health, even though the ICCPR does not specify the health implications of these rights.

The 1948 Genocide Convention prohibits acts, including killing or causing serious bodily or mental harm, that are committed with the intent to destroy, in whole or in part, members of particular national, ethnic, racial, or religious groups. These prohibited acts have obvious health implications for members of targeted groups. The 1965 Convention on the Elimination of All Forms of Racial Discrimination calls for the provision of fundamental health rights, including the right to public health and access to medical care, without distinctions or discrimination on racial grounds. The 1984 Torture Convention prohibits torture and other cruel and degrading treatment. In doing so, it further elaborates on the bodily integrity rights codified in the ICCPR. The Torture Convention does not explicitly discuss the health implications of these bodily integrity rights, though they have obvious connections to physical and mental health. The 1989 Convention on the Rights of the Child affirms that children have a fundamental right to the highest attainable standard of health. It includes provisions that call for equitable access to health care for children, prohibitions against work that would be harmful to a child's health, and protections against child abuse.

This progressive development of international human rights law clearly indicates the emergence of a binding human right to health. However, all of these treaties share the limitations of the ICESCR. Although they contain forceful and unambiguous language codifying fundamental human rights, including health rights, they provide only weak or limited

TABLE 8.1 Health Rights in International Human Rights Law

Treaty (date of UN adoption/ date of entry into force)	Health-related protections and rights	Implementation mechanisms
Genocide Convention (1948/1951)	Prohibitions against killing or causing serious bodily or mental harm with the intent to destroy a particular national, ethnic, racial, or religious group	Trials in competent national or international tribunals for persons charged with genocide, potential action by UN organs
Convention on the Elimination of Racial Discrimination (1965/1969)	Prohibitions against racial discrimination in the provision of the rights to public health, medical care, and social security	State reporting requirements, monitoring by the UN Committee on the Elimination of Racial Discrimination
International Covenant on Civil and Political Rights (1966/1976)	Prohibitions against arbitrary deprivation of life, slavery, torture, cruel and unusual punishment, and arbitrary detention	State reporting requirements, monitoring by the UN Human Rights Committee
International Covenant on Economic, Social, and Cultural Rights (1966/1976)	Protections for human right to health, maternal and child health rights, adequate standard of living, adequate food	State reporting requirements, monitoring by the UN Economic, Social, and Cultural Rights Committee
Convention on the Elimination of All Forms of Discrimination Against Women (1979/1981)	Protections for pregnant women and mothers, health and safety in working conditions, nondiscrimination in health care, health needs of rural women	State reporting requirements, monitoring by the UN Committee on the Elimination of Discrimination Against Women
Torture Convention (1984/1987)	Prohibitions against torture, bodily integrity rights	State reporting requirements, monitoring by the UN Committee Against Torture
Convention on the Rights of the Child (1989/1990)	Right to health, access to health care, protection from work that would be harmful to a child's health, protections against child abuse	State reporting requirements, monitoring by the UN Committee on the Rights of the Child

implementation and enforcement mechanisms. The primary mechanisms for implementation of international human rights law include reporting requirements for states that are parties to specific treaties and monitoring by standing UN committees that are associated with each treaty. In general, the monitoring process involves a nonadversarial review of state reports by the relevant UN committee. After reviewing the reports, the treaty-monitoring committees may make recommendations and raise concerns about the degree of a state's compliance with its treaty commitments. However, these recommendations are nonbinding, and concrete enforcement is essentially nonexistent.[8]

The Genocide Convention provides an exception to this general rule. Under Article 6 of the Genocide Convention, persons charged with genocide shall be tried by a competent national or international tribunal. Furthermore,

Article 8 states that any state party to the treaty may call upon competent organs of the UN to take measures to prevent or suppress genocide. These provisions go beyond the reporting and monitoring requirements of other human rights treaties. Nevertheless, they still constitute a weak system of enforcement. Despite the fact that the treaty states that persons charged with genocide "shall" be tried, the treaty does not include language specifying what should happen in the event that persons charged with genocide are not tried. Because the UN Security Council has the legal power to authorize strong measures to respond to threats to international peace and security, including nonmilitary measures like economic sanctions as well as the use of armed force, it is important that the treaty acknowledge the right of competent UN organs to take action against genocide. However, it is important to note that the Genocide Convention only reaffirms that state parties *may* call upon the UN to act in the face of genocide. It does not require them to do so, and it certainly does not require the UN to take concrete measures in response to genocide. Thus, even the Genocide Convention creates only minimal, weak enforcement mechanisms.

Gendering the Human Right to Health: The 1979 Convention on the Elimination of All Forms of Discrimination Against Women

The 1979 Convention on the Elimination of All Forms of Discrimination Against Women (CEDAW) recognizes women's particular health challenges and needs. For instance, CEDAW contains provisions related to reproductive and maternal health issues. Article 11 and 12 of the treaty are especially notable in this regard. Article 11 calls for measures that would prevent discrimination or dismissal of women workers due to pregnancy or maternity leave. It also calls on state parties to offer maternity leave with pay or comparable social

benefits and to provide special protections to women working in harmful conditions during pregnancy. Article 12 calls on state parties to eliminate discrimination in health care in order to ensure equal access to health care services, including family planning. This article calls for state parties to ensure women's access to appropriate health services for pregnancy, birth, and postnatal health needs. In addition to provisions related to reproductive and maternal health, CEDAW contains other health-related protections for women. Article 11 calls for state parties to eliminate discrimination in the right to protection of health and safety in working conditions. Article 14 calls on state parties to pay particular attention to the needs of rural women, including health care needs.

In addition to these special protections related to the particular health needs of women, CEDAW also contains a provision that calls for gender equity for both men and women. Article 5 deals directly with the concept of gender as socially constructed ideals about the proper roles, behaviors, and identities of men and women. It calls for modifications in the social and cultural patterns of conduct of men and women with a view toward eliminating prejudices and practices that are based on the idea of the inferiority or superiority of either sex. Article 5 stands out from other provisions in international human rights law in relation to the concept of gender. Most provisions of international human rights law are gender-neutral in the sense that they merely call for equal treatment for women and men. Other provisions of international human rights law call for special attention to the particular needs of women. In contrast to both of these approaches, Article 5 highlights the importance of paying attention to socially constructed gender norms in any efforts to promote fundamental human rights, and it does so in a way that acknowledges that men as well as women might be harmed by prejudices or practices that are based on the idea of the inferiority or superiority of either sex.

Despite that Article 5 calls for modifications in the social and cultural patterns of conduct of men and women with a view toward eliminating prejudices and practices based on the idea of the inferiority or superiority of either sex, CEDAW does not articulate concrete steps for doing so. Indeed, CEDAW may inadvertently reinforce traditional gender roles that contribute to social and cultural inequities between men and women. Most notably, CEDAW's special protections for women before and after childbirth may reinforce the notion that women are—and should be—primarily responsible for child care. On the one hand, provisions protecting pregnant women and mothers against discrimination are logical given women's biological role in pregnancy and childbearing. On the other hand, provisions that provide for maternity leave with pay or comparable social benefits without parallel provisions for paternity leave reinforce traditional views on parenting that may, in the end, disadvantage women by reproducing social and cultural patterns that contribute to subordinate roles for women in the family and in society at large.

Regardless of any gaps or potential biases in CEDAW, the limitations of international human rights law as a tool for promoting a human right to health are more critical. Ultimately, the treaty does not provide concrete obligations or effective enforcement mechanisms that ensure the fulfillment of the provisions articulating health rights for women. Thus, CEDAW shares the limitations of the ICESCR and is a limited tool for promoting a human right to health for both women and men.

Health Rights Under International Humanitarian Law

International humanitarian law also contains provisions with significant implications for a human right to health. International human rights law codifies fundamental rights for all persons regardless of race, biological sex, religion, nationality, or other status. In contrast, international humanitarian law refers to the legal rules governing the conduct of war.[9]

International humanitarian law sets out norms calling for the humane conduct of war and, in this way, has significant implications for the health of civilians and soldiers during wartime. The historical roots of international humanitarian law can be traced back to customary practices in antiquity as well as early religious traditions that discouraged the targeting of civilians, attacks on women or the wounded, and the infliction of unnecessary suffering during war.

In contemporary international law, the Hague Convention and the Geneva Conventions are the primary treaty bodies that codify international humanitarian law, as shown in Table 8.2. Although neither of these treaty bodies explicitly asserts health *rights*, they contain provisions intended to protect the health of civilians and soldiers during wartime. The 1899 Hague Convention condemned the use of "dum-dum bullets" that inflicted unnecessary suffering as well as the use of armed projectiles designed to diffuse poisonous gases. The 1907 Hague Convention contained the following health-related provisions: calls for the humane treatment of prisoners of war and prohibitions on the use of poisonous weapons, the infliction of unnecessary suffering, and attacks on undefended public buildings including hospitals.

The first Geneva Convention, adopted in 1864, called on states to provide treatment for wounded armed forces without discrimination based on nationality and asserted the neutrality of medical personnel. This treaty is associated with the emergence of the International Committee of the Red Cross, an organization devoted to providing relief to war victims around the world. Subsequent Geneva Conventions elaborated on the norms that should govern the wartime treatment of protected persons, including detainees, the sick, the wounded, and civilians. The four Geneva Conventions, adopted in 1949, constitute the core of international humanitarian law. The First Convention calls for the humane treatment of sick and wounded combatants on land, whereas the Second Convention outlines

TABLE 8.2 Health Rights in International Humanitarian Law

Treaty	Health-related protections and rights	Implementation mechanisms
Hague Convention (1899)	Humane treatment of prisoners of war, prohibitions against the use of poisonous weapons, prohibitions on attacks against public buildings, including hospitals	Calls for parties to issue instructions to bring their military forces into compliance with treaty provisions, provisions stating that belligerent parties violating treaty obligations shall be liable for compensation
Geneva Conventions (1949)	Humane treatment of sick and wounded combatants and prisoners of war, humanitarian protections of civilians during wartime	Third-party access to protected persons to monitor compliance, calls for penal sanctions against persons committing grave breaches of the treaty

similar provisions for the treatment of sick and wounded combatants at sea. The Third Convention regulates the treatment of prisoners of war, and the Fourth Convention governs the protection of civilians in wartime, including prohibitions on rape, murder, and torture. In 1977, state parties adopted two protocols to the Geneva Conventions that expand the humanitarian protections for civilians in wartime. Unlike the primary Geneva Conventions, both protocols specifically prohibit indiscriminate attacks on civilians in international armed conflicts. Protocol II supplements the civilian protections for victims of noninternational armed conflicts, including prohibitions against murder, torture, corporal punishment, rape, slavery, and other humiliating and degrading treatment.

The wide range of protections codified in international humanitarian law has obvious connections to health as a human right. Prohibitions against torture, corporal punishment, and rape, for example, involve bodily integrity rights with serious consequences for physical and mental health. Other provisions, including rules calling for the humane treatment of sick and wounded combatants, suggest that combatants have fundamental health rights in the context of war. In short, international humanitarian law contains forceful and unambiguous language that asserts fundamental rights for individuals in conflict zones. However, as in the case of international human rights law, international humanitarian law contains loopholes and weak enforcement mechanisms that limit its effectiveness as a tool for promoting the health rights of human beings in war zones.

Consider the example of the Fourth Geneva Convention's provisions governing the treatment of detainees. Article 142 calls on state parties to allow religious organizations, relief societies, or other organizations to have access to protected persons for the purposes of assisting them and providing relief. Article 142 recognizes the special status of the International Committee of the Red Cross as a relief organization acting in this capacity. At first glance, this provision might seem to open state parties to a degree of independent monitoring of their respect for the Geneva Convention's provisions. However, Article 142 qualifies state obligations under this provision by specifying that access to protected persons is "[s]ubject to the measures which the Detaining Powers may consider essential to secure their security or to meet any other reasonable need." It also gives detaining powers the right to limit the number of organizations that are given access to protected persons.

Article 146 of the Fourth Convention calls on state parties to "undertake to enact any legislation necessary to provide effective penal sanctions for persons committing, or ordering to be committed, any of the grave breaches of the present Convention." Article 146 also creates an obligation for state parties to search for persons who have committed, or ordered to have committed, grave breaches of the treaty's provisions and bring these persons to trial in their own courts or hand them over to another state party to the treaty for trial. According to Article 147, the grave breaches referred to in Article 146 include willful killing, torture or inhumane treatment (including biological experiments), and the willful causing of great suffering or serious bodily injury; all of these grave breaches have connections to fundamental health rights. Thus, it appears that the Geneva Convention creates concrete obligations for states to protect the health rights codified in the treaty. At the same time, it is important to note the indirectness of this enforcement language—it asks states to "undertake" to pass legislation providing penal sanctions rather than directly committing them to provide penal sanctions. Although the treaty does create concrete obligations for bringing persons who violate Geneva provisions to trial, it does not provide mechanisms for ensuring that states comply with these obligations. There are no specified punishments or consequences for states that fail to fulfill their obligations under Geneva.

Ultimately, international humanitarian law, like international human rights law, contains unambiguous language codifying fundamental health rights. Yet, in each case, there is a gap between legal rhetoric and respect for these rights in practice. States and non-state actors regularly violate international humanitarian law in conflict zones. Allegations of violations of international humanitarian law, including wartime rape, the abuse of detainees, and the targeting of innocent civilians, routinely arise in every war. To be sure, some states uphold international humanitarian law at least some of the time, and the extent to which international humanitarian law is violated varies from conflict to conflict. But most states and non-state actors fail to fulfill all of their obligations to conduct war humanely. For some critics, the idea that war can be conducted humanely remains an oxymoron in any case. Regardless, in the absence of concrete enforcement mechanisms, there remains a significant gap between rhetoric and reality in the implementation of international humanitarian law.

Professional Codes of Ethics and the Human Right to Health

Another important area of international law relevant to the human right to health involves professional codes of ethics. Ethical codes for medical practitioners are particularly relevant here. In 1948, the World Medical Association (WMA) adopted the Declaration of Geneva, which articulates a physician's oath that pledges physicians to work in the service of humanity, to hold the health of the patient as the first consideration, and to maintain the utmost respect for human life. The declaration also contains specific language pertinent to respect for international human rights and humanitarian law. Under this declaration, physicians pledge the following: "I will not use my medical knowledge contrary to the laws of humanity, even under threat."[10] The WMA pledge has its origins in the Hippocratic oath, a historic oath calling on physicians to uphold certain ethical standards in the practice of medicine.

Adopted in the immediate aftermath of World War II, the WMA's Declaration of Geneva reflects the medical community's response to the fact that medical professionals committed atrocities in conducting inhumane medical experiments on human subjects in Germany and Japan.[11] This declaration commits physicians to refuse to participate in such medical experimentation. Taken together with the human rights and humanitarian treaties created in the aftermath of World War II, this declaration indicates that a professional medical code of ethics formally prohibits physicians from violating provisions of international human rights and humanitarian law.

Notably, the WMA Declaration does not have binding force under international law. Physicians may or may not take the WMA pledge or recite the Hippocratic oath, depending on national laws governing medical licensing in particular countries, the guidelines and requirements of professional medical associations, and national standards for medical education. For instance, many countries, including the United States, Canada, and the United Kingdom, require the teaching of ethics in medical colleges, though the form such training takes varies widely from institution to institution.[12] Other countries, such as India, have no such standards, with curriculum decisions left to individual institutions. The result is that fewer institutions offer formal ethical training.[13] Even when physicians are aware of international ethical guidelines governing the practice of medicine, they do not necessarily have a deep understanding of these norms. For instance, a study in India found that whereas 99 percent of physicians were familiar with Medical Council of India's Code of Medical Ethics, only 60 percent of Indian physicians had read the code.[14] Additionally, the extent to which physicians who violate the ethical code embodied in the WMA Declaration face legal or other sanctions (such as the loss of licensure or the loss of the ability to prescribe controlled substances) depends on national laws and the regulatory practices of professional medical associations.

Despite the voluntary nature of the WMA ethical code, it still has normative force. In the United States, for example, physicians are not required to take the Hippocratic oath in order to become licensed doctors. That said, medical schools in the United States increasingly expose students to the Hippocratic oath at some point during their medical education, and students graduating from medical school often recite this oath during formal ceremonies

at the culmination of their medical education.[15] Similarly, many national medical societies, for example, the American Medical Association,[16] the European Foundation of Internal Medicine,[17] and the Medical Council of India,[18] have created codes of ethics that incorporate the principles embodied in the Hippocratic oath and the WMA Declaration.

Other professional medical associations have adopted similar guidelines outlining the ethical commitments and human rights obligations of medical practitioners. In 1998, the International Council of Nurses (ICN) adopted a statement on Nurses and Human Rights that clearly asserts fundamental health rights for all human beings. The ICN statement describes health care as a right of all individuals, regardless of financial, political, geographic, racial, or religious status. It calls for the inclusion of human rights issues in nursing education and indicates that nurses have a responsibility to safeguard human rights.[19] The 1996 Madrid Declaration on Ethical Standards for Psychiatric Practice contains numerous provisions related to health and human rights. Most notably, it prohibits psychiatrists from participating in torture, legally authorized executions, and sex-selective pregnancy terminations.[20] The American Psychological Association has adopted similar standards.

In addition to general guidelines outlining ethical commitments for medical practitioners, professional associations have also adopted specific guidelines governing research involving human subjects. These professional codes of ethics reflect a response to the participation of medical practitioners in unethical human experiments during World War II. Additionally, they represent a reaction to problematic human experimentation that occurred outside wartime during the 20th century. One of the most notable examples of such problematic human research is the Tuskegee experiments. These experiments were carried out by the U.S. Public Health Service between 1932 and 1972 at the Tuskegee Institute, a historically black college in Alabama. Researchers recruited poor African-Americans for participation in a study on the long-term effects of syphilis with the promise of free medical treatment. In the 1940s, doctors discovered that penicillin could be used to effectively treat syphilis. Despite this important discovery, investigators in the Tuskegee study did not inform their human subjects or offer them effective treatment. Numerous subjects died from syphilis, and in many cases, the devastating disease was spread to their wives and children. The study was not ended until the press discovered the nature of the program and its denial of effective treatment for the human subjects.[21]

The troubling involvement of medical practitioners in unethical human experimentation has led to the progressive development of guidelines for the conduct of research involving human subjects. In 1964, the WMA adopted the Declaration of Helsinki on Ethical Principles for Medical Research Involving Human Subjects. This declaration, which has been updated multiple times in subsequent years, prioritizes the health of individual patients over the interests of science and society; demands special protections for vulnerable populations; and must be based on the ongoing, voluntary, and informed consent of human subjects.[22] The Council for International Organizations of Medical Science (CIOMS), in collaboration with the World Health Organization (WHO), adopted similar guidelines for biomedical research involving human subjects, updated most recently in 2002.[23] The CIOMS guidelines make specific reference to the need for biomedical research to be consistent with international human rights law. The guidelines require that human subject research conform to three general ethical principles: respect for the autonomy and self-determination of persons, beneficence (which requires an obligation to maximize benefits and minimize harms), and justice.

Created outside the state-centric system of public international law, these professional codes of conduct provide an interesting illustration of the ways in which nonbinding international norms can have important human rights effects. Although they are not binding forms of international law, they may act as constraints on the behavior of medical practitioners. Professional associations serve as one mechanism by which global ethical norms influence the practice of medicine. These associations may adopt standards that shape governmental policy and practice in various countries. For example, the Department of Health and Human Services in the United States has adopted regulations governing human subject research that incorporates most of the ethical guidelines outlined in the CIOMS guidelines for biomedical research involving human subjects. Notably, this regulatory system has been highly effective, as scholars who seek to conduct human research must gain approval from Institutional Review Boards at institutions that receive federal funding. Thus, it is noteworthy that nonbinding guidelines created by non-state actors can have a major impact on the behavior of professionals covered by these codes of ethics.

Acknowledging the potential importance of these codes of ethics does *not* suggest that they have been terribly effective in promoting ethical behavior among medical practitioners across the board. Indeed, physicians and medical professionals in numerous countries have been implicated in questionable ethical behavior and in the violation of fundamental human rights. For example, military medical personnel at Guantanamo Bay have been accused of inappropriately sharing medical information that was subsequently used by interrogators in ways that violate international legal commitments. Psychiatrists and psychologists at Guantanamo Bay also have been accused of violating their ethical duties by employing interrogation tactics, including sleep deprivation and extreme stress, to try to extract intelligence from detainees.[24] Notably, medical practitioners are often unfamiliar with the international laws that are intended to govern medical practice in military settings.[25]

Medical practitioners in the United States are not uniquely prone to violating ethical codes of conduct. Despite the significant development of ethical codes that call on medical practitioners to respect fundamental human rights, some medical professionals continue to be complicit in human rights abuses across the globe.[26] Such violations of ethical codes of conduct are especially likely in conflict zones and when questions of national security are at stake. Notably, it is precisely at such times that respect for fundamental human rights is the most crucial.

Conceptual and Cultural Challenges to the Human Right to Health

Understanding the limitations of international human rights law as a tool for promoting global health is essential for students and practitioners. Nevertheless, an analysis of the international legal framework is only one piece of the puzzle. To fully understand the obstacles that make it difficult to promote health as a human right, students and practitioners must also delve into deeper philosophical, political, and cultural issues that are at stake in global debates over human rights. Numerous conceptual and philosophical challenges hinder global consensus on human rights and thereby limit the utility of a rights-based framework for promoting human health.

Human Rights as a Contested Concept

One of the most basic conceptual challenges is definitional. How should the concept of human rights be defined? To whom does it apply? At first glance, it might seem that easy answers to these questions exist. Human rights are the rights held by all humans and, by definition, apply to all people equally. However, global consensus on answers to these questions has actually been elusive. Gross violations of

human rights often occur precisely because one group does not see members of another group as fully human. Such was the case in the Rwandan genocide in which Hutu perpetrators frequently referred to the Tutsis as cockroaches. The caste system in India is another example of a categorization of groups of people that treats some groups as fully human and deserving of fundamental rights while other groups are viewed as subhuman and less deserving of basic civil, political, economic, and social rights.

There is also a lack of consensus regarding precisely what constitutes a right. If rights are legal entitlements, then they exist only if they have been codified into law. Conversely, if rights are moral entitlements—rights that all human beings *should* have—then questions remain regarding whose moral system determines the set of rights to which all humans are entitled, no small task given the diversity of moral values in the world. To the extent that rights are deemed to exist, questions remain about the mechanisms by which they are to be fulfilled. Who is responsible for protecting and promoting human rights?

In this regard, philosophical and political disagreements about whether human rights should be conceptualized as positive or negative rights are pertinent. **Positive rights** refer to rights that individuals claim from the state. States must take "positive" action in order to fulfill these rights. In contrast, **negative rights** involve rights that are abused or violated by states. The fulfillment of negative rights requires inaction on the part of states. Whether rights are framed as positive or negative has important implications for the mechanisms by which they should be implemented.

We can examine the right to food as an illustration. If the right to food is a positive human right, then the state must take concrete steps to ensure that it provides citizens with adequate food. Such steps could include providing food directly to people in need or providing people with money to buy their own food. Conversely, if the right to food is a negative right, then the government is obliged to

KEY TERMS IN INTERNATIONAL HUMAN RIGHTS

Human Rights: the moral and/or legal entitlements all people have simply because they are human beings.

Negative Rights: rights that are abused or violated by states and that require the state to refrain from specific actions in order to ensure their fulfillment.

Positive Rights: rights that individuals claim from the state and that states must take action to provide or fulfill.

Relativism: a perspective that suggests that moral values are—or should be—contingent on specific historical, religious, cultural, or other social contexts and, accordingly, asserts that definitions and interpretations of human rights will vary across cultures and societies.

Sovereignty: a core principle in international relations asserting that states have the right to govern themselves as they see fit.

Universalism: a perspective that suggests that moral values are—or should be—the same for every person, everywhere and asserts that fundamental human rights are the same, irrespective of particular historical, religious, cultural, or other social context.

refrain from interfering in the lives of individuals in ways that hinder their ability to provide food for themselves. Formulating the right to food as a negative right might lead to criticisms of a variety of state policies that interfere with people's ability to provide their own food. For instance, state regulations that limit the ability of indigenous peoples to hunt, fish, or engage in traditional agricultural practices could be seen as violating the right to adequate food. Additionally, governmental subsidies to big agricultural corporations that distort markets in ways that make it hard for small-scale farmers to survive might be seen as undermining the right to food.

Similar logic can be applied to the right to health itself. A positive formulation of the right to health suggests that states have legal obligations to ensure that their citizens reach the highest attainable standard of physical and mental health. In this case, the state's obligations might be fulfilled in numerous ways—by the direct provision of health care through a national health system, by subsidizing the purchase of private health insurance plans with government funds, or by adopting regulations intended to promote high standards of health and optimal health outcomes. Such regulations might include taxing unhealthy food choices (such as soda or fast food), prohibiting industrial practices that undermine environmental health (such as regulations on factory farms designed to minimize air and water pollution), or adopting national educational standards that prioritize physical education in an effort to reduce obesity.

A negative formulation of the right to health would emphasize a different set of governmental obligations. In this case, proponents of a human right to health might criticize governmental subsidies that provide incentives for the production of cheap but unhealthy food while putting small-scale farms that produce healthy food in a sustainable manner at a market disadvantage. Conservatives who argue that national health care systems undermine optimal health outcomes by leading to bureaucratic inefficiencies in the provision of health care are conceptualizing health as a negative right. A negative formulation of the right to health might also be critical of governmental regulations of medical and pharmaceutical practices. In the United States, for instance, governmental restrictions on the medicinal use of marijuana could be criticized within a framework that conceptualizes health as a negative right.

Individual Versus Collective Conceptualizations of Rights

Similar disagreements exist about whether human rights should be conceptualized in individual or collective terms. Under a liberal democratic political ideology, rights belong to autonomous individuals and trump any obligations individuals have to the communities in which they live. Conversely, communitarian traditions suggest that human beings depend on the social structures in which they live for survival. Therefore, their obligations to the communities in which they live take priority over any individual rights people claim.[27] Thus, what it means to have human rights depends on whether one embraces a vision of fundamental human rights as *individual* or *collective*.

Individual conceptions of health rights differ from collective conceptions of health rights in significant ways. If a human right to health is individual, then all human beings—regardless of ethnic, social, political, gender, or other status—deserve the same health rights. Women should have the same health rights as men, children should have the same health rights as adults, and members of different ethnic and religious groups should have exactly the same health rights. Conversely, a collective conception of human rights suggests that various groups may have different health rights. In this way, a collective conceptualization of rights might rationalize inequitable health outcomes among different groups.

Female infanticide provides a bleak example of the tensions that may exist between individual and collective conceptualizations of health-related rights. In traditional Indian culture, the parents of a young woman customarily provide a dowry payment to their daughter's husband, or his family, at the time of marriage. The pressure to make these dowry payments, coupled with cultural norms that devalue women and girl children, have contributed to high rates of female infanticide in India. Such pressures are especially strong among poor families for whom making dowry payments, or continuing to support unmarried girl children, is a real financial hardship. As a result, many families have taken to killing girl children at birth.[28] The practice of female infanticide obviously violates the fundamental health rights of individual girl children in cultures where it is practiced. Yet, female infanticide may be consistent with a collective conception of rights that places greater emphasis on respect for different cultural value systems (in this case, a culture that places less value on women and girl children than on men and boys).

Competing Rights Claims

Conceptual difficulties in sorting out competing rights claims also make it difficult to promote universal human rights in a world of difference. If all humans have fundamental rights, what specific rights do they have in practice? How can we sort out legitimate rights claims from mere desires? International human rights law specifies the kinds of rights that all humans are supposed to have, but it does not necessarily settle all the difficult questions. For example, the International Covenant on Economic, Social, and Cultural Rights specifies a human right to adequate food. What does that right imply in practice? Does it mean that everyone should have the means to provide for his or her own subsistence, for example, by having access to enough land to grow food? Does it mean that governments

UNDER THE MICROSCOPE

Intellectual Property Rights and Access to Medicine

The 1994 Agreement on Trade-Related Aspects of Intellectual Property Rights (TRIPS) formally establishes intellectual property rights as a critical element of the international trade system. Under this agreement, state members of the World Trade Organization are required to adopt strong protections for intellectual property rights. To this end, member states agree to respect specified patent protections. An examination of this agreement helps explain why some critical medicines are undersupplied in the developing world.

Proponents of the TRIPS agreement contend that intellectual property rights provide researchers and pharmaceutical companies with incentives to research and develop lifesaving medications. Because developing new medicines is an incredibly expensive endeavor, pharmaceutical companies can be reluctant to fund research and development of new drugs if they are not confident that they will profit from their efforts. Patent protections help ensure that companies can profit from developing lifesaving medications and, therefore, give these companies the incentives to fund research and development. The logic for patent protections is rooted in basic economics. A company that spends huge sums researching and developing new drugs will need to charge prices that cover its costs and generate sufficient profit to make its efforts worthwhile. In the absence of patent protections, another pharmaceutical company might copy the innovation but charge significantly lower prices because it has not incurred any research and development costs. Given this market logic, it would be irrational for pharmaceutical companies to spend research and development money on drugs from which they might never realize a profit. Patent protections essentially allow pharmaceutical companies to exercise a monopoly over patented medicines for a specified period of time. As a result, they can charge prices that allow them to cover their research and development costs and profit from their investment. Proponents of intellectual property rights argue that this system actually makes it more likely that pharmaceutical companies will develop new lifesaving medicines.[a]

[a]Jorn Sonderholm, "Intellectual Property Rights and the TRIPS Agreement: An Overview of Ethical Problems and Some Solutions," *World Bank Policy Research Working Paper Series* (March 1, 2010). Available online at: http://siteresources.worldbank.org/EXTDEVDIALOGUE/Images/537296-1238422761932/5968067-1269375819845/Property_Rights_Jorn.pdf.

are responsible for providing their citizens with food if people cannot provide for themselves? Must the food fulfill particular nutritional qualities? As another example, take the right to the highest attainable standard of mental health. The assertion of a right to mental health does not indicate what requirements must be met to achieve this right. Does a right to mental health mean that all human beings should have guaranteed access to therapy? Or do different communities have alternative approaches to mental health? Given

Conversely, critics contend that patent protections limit poor people's access to life-saving medications. Because pharmaceutical companies may price drugs at levels significantly higher than the costs of producing them (in order to recover research and development costs), the drugs are often priced out of reach of low-income individuals. As a result, critics argue that patent protections undermine the human right to health. A human right to health suggests that health belongs to all people, everywhere. However, patent protections result in discriminatory effects in that they produce classes of people—lifesaving medications for those who can afford them, and lack of access for those who cannot. This problem is exacerbated by the fact that incentives may not exist for diseases that are prevalent in low-income countries, such as malaria, but not high-income countries. When prevalence rates for an illness are highest among poor populations, pharmaceutical companies simply may not have any incentive to develop new drugs—even with patent protections—because a for-profit market does not exist.[b]

Potential solutions to this dilemma exist: varying pricing structures for different regions based on levels of economic development; exceptions to patent protections that enable countries to license companies to produce generic versions of patented medications in cases of public emergencies (a practice that is authorized in the 2001 Doha Declaration, an interpretation of TRIPS put forth by developing countries); donor commitments to long-term subsidies for medications under development that meet specified criteria; and the provision of financial awards (by either governments or non-state actors) to the first company to develop a lifesaving medication. Each of these solutions has potential advantages and disadvantages. Both varying price structures and exceptions to patent protections might lead to illicit transnational smuggling of low-cost generic drugs. From a rights-based perspective, these approaches also are problematic because wealthy people in developing countries might have access to inexpensive medicine, whereas low-income populations in developed countries would only have the option of expensive medicine. Prize schemes may not provide enough of an incentive for pharmaceutical companies to engage in research and development, because only one company will receive an award.[c]

The case of intellectual property rights illustrates the ways in which the right to property and the right to health may come into conflict as well as the potential tension among different conceptions of health rights.

---

[b] *Ibid.*
[c] *Ibid.*

differences across societies, who gets to decide how a right to mental health should be interpreted in practice?

The difficulties in sorting out what a general assertion of rights means in practice are exacerbated by potential tensions among different sets of human rights. For example, individual rights to privacy and autonomy may clash with a right to health. In the case of HIV/AIDS, a right to health might suggest that HIV testing should be mandatory both to promote treatment for infected individuals and to limit the spread of the disease. However, many practitioners believe that HIV testing should be voluntary in order to respect the autonomy of persons and to reduce the likelihood that individuals who test positive will be discriminated against.[29] Other potential trade-offs between privacy and health rights exist. In the case of individuals who test positive for HIV, should their rights to privacy take priority over the rights of their spouses or partners to have knowledge that may be crucial to protecting their health? Similarly, governmental policies intended to protect public health may violate the autonomy and freedom of movement of individuals who carry certain diseases. For instance, the forced hospitalization and quarantine of individuals who carry tuberculosis in South Africa has been criticized for violating the liberty of individual patients.[30] These examples clearly illustrate the ways in which a human right to health can create significant tension with other human rights and can thereby create obstacles to the promotion of health as a human right.

Another example involves potential tension between the right to property and a right to health. If governments are responsible for promoting the highest attainable standards of mental and physical health for their citizens, then they need financial resources for funding health care. Governments will need to tax their citizens in order to obtain the monies for spending on health care programs. Perhaps not surprisingly, governmental efforts to raise taxes on citizens often generate significant political opposition. At least some of the time, such opposition is framed in rights-based terms. Conservatives, for example, commonly argue that governmental taxation infringes on a fundamental human right to property by unduly taking hard-earned money from individuals and transferring it to others through spending on governmental programs.

In a similar vein, intellectual property rights have the potential to come into conflict with a right to health. Critics contend that patent rights that limit the access of poor people to lifesaving medications violate the human right to health. However, defenders of patent rights argue that, though they may limit the health rights of specific individuals in the short run, intellectual property rights actually promote better health outcomes in the long run. Patent rights provide researchers with incentives to research and develop lifesaving technologies and medications.[31] Thus, the case of intellectual property rights illustrates not only the ways in which the right to property and the right to health may come into conflict but also the potential tension among different conceptions of health rights.

Universalist Versus Relativist Perspectives on Human Rights

The ongoing tension between relativism and universalism in debates over international human rights provides another crucial piece of the puzzle in understanding the gap between rhetoric and reality in the promotion of health as a human right. As we will see, this tension is connected in integral ways to the conceptual challenges that hinder global consensus on human rights, outlined in the previous section. **Universalism** is a perspective that suggests that moral values are—or should be—the same across time and space. Applied to human rights, universalism suggests that fundamental human rights are the same, irrespective of particular historical, religious, cultural, or other social context. **Relativism** is a perspective based on the belief that moral values are—or should be—contingent on specific historical, religious, cultural, or other social contexts. A relativist perspective on human rights suggests that definitions and interpretations of human rights vary across cultures and societies.

Numerous examples illustrate the ways in which relativism challenges the notion of health as a universal human right. Assertions of universal health rights may clash with cultural and religious systems that reject mainstream medicine. Take the case of Jehovah's Witnesses. Most Jehovah's Witnesses believe that it is against religious principle in this faith tradition to accept blood transfusions, even in life-threatening situations. Members of the sect seek to prevent their children from receiving transfusions that may be necessary to save their lives. Legal judgments in the United States and Canada have prioritized the rights of children to health and life over the religious rights of their parents. Yet, resistance to forced blood transfusions among Jehovah's Witnesses remains incredibly high, and parents go to great lengths to keep their children out of the hands of medical professionals and social workers to avoid this forced medical treatment. In their view, the life of the soul is much more important than the life of the body, and the violation of this religious injunction is considered a serious offense.[32] Other conservative Christian traditions also reject medical treatment in favor of prayer, resulting in significant numbers of infant and child deaths within these groups.[33] Such cases clearly demonstrate the tensions between relativist and universalist perspectives on human rights as well as the potential clashes between different sets of rights—in this case, the right to freedom of religion and the right to health.

Even strong proponents of a universal human right to health will be well served to pay attention to the importance of competing cultural values and interpretations of rights in a world of difference. Indeed, sensitivity to cultural context is probably essential for any efforts to promote health as a human right to be successful. Heavy-handed efforts to impose law from above, absent cultural sensitivity, may be counterproductive in many cases. For example, the international movement to eradicate female genital mutilation (FGM) has often generated cultural resistance in societies targeted by anti-FGM efforts due to perceptions that such efforts are arrogant and insensitive to the cultural values in societies where FGM is widely practiced.[34]

Cultural sensitivity may be necessary to produce effective results in promoting global health norms. Indeed, international organizations working in developing countries have found that it is often helpful to work *with* traditional cultural perspectives in implementing health programs rather than trying to override this traditional knowledge with expert medical opinion from outside these communities. Traditional beliefs about health play a fundamental role in shaping health-seeking behavior, and such beliefs can be very difficult to change. Because health is such a complicated phenomenon, learning about the causes of illness and effective treatments can be very difficult. Thus, people understandably rely on their experiences and inherited knowledge to shape their understanding of health. In this regard, the fact that traditional beliefs and culture play a critical role in shaping health-seeking behavior should not be surprising. Traditional belief systems may play a particularly significant role for low-income populations that have limited access to public education and formalized medical care.[35]

Given this reality, a model that works with rather than against traditional understandings of health may be more likely to promote effective communication with the populations that public health practitioners are seeking to help. For example, since the 1970s, the WHO has advocated that public health organizations should collaborate with traditional healers in Africa. Such collaboration may be beneficial for a variety of reasons. In countries with very little public health infrastructure and few trained medical personnel, the majority of the population often relies on traditional healers. Given this reality, it is arguably better to have traditional healers with some biomedical training than without any training. Additionally, proponents of collaboration with traditional healers often value a holistic approach to health, which addresses spiritual as well as physical needs, that is highly valued in societies where traditional healers are an important part of the culture.[36]

UNDER THE MICROSCOPE

Intercultural Communication in Global Health

It is common knowledge within mainstream Western medicine that invisible microbes are a major cause of illness. However, such knowledge is not necessarily taken for granted among populations in undeveloped regions of the world. Indeed, convincing these populations that something they cannot see is the cause of serious illnesses, such as waterborne illness or HIV/AIDS, can be a hard sell. In response to these challenges of intercultural communication, public health experts have sometimes tried to work with traditional knowledge to produce results.

For instance, an HIV prevention program in South Africa involved training traditional healers to help teach local populations about methods of preventing the spread of HIV. Rather than relying on strictly technical information about the etiology of AIDS, the trainers used culturally appropriate terms that made more sense to the traditional healers and the populations with whom they worked. Trainers described HIV transmission to traditional healers in the following way: "White blood cells were described as healers' apprentices who guard the master healers, T-cells. During sex, the enemy, HIV, sneaks in and kills the master healers, takes their places, and tricks the apprentices into thinking they are still taking orders from their superiors. The enemy orders the apprentices to let in more and more HIV, until finally the enemy takes over the whole body."[a] A study of the traditional healers who had completed the training program found an increase in the healers' knowledge about HIV prevention and also indicated that the healers were willing to communicate effective prevention strategies to their patients. By working in a culturally sensitive way with local populations, public health practitioners were able to promote a human right to health in a way that was mindful of a particular cultural context.

---

[a]Matthew Steinglass, "It Takes a Village Healer: Anthropologists Believe Traditional Medicine Can Remedy Africa's AIDS Crisis. Are they Right?" *Lingua Franca* 11: 3 (2001): 3.

Conclusion

As this chapter has shown, international law contains unambiguous and forceful language codifying fundamental health rights. Yet, the highest attainable standard of physical and mental health remains an elusive goal for much of the world's population. Competing perspectives on the precise elements of a human right to health, divergent interpretations over what the right to health means in practice, a lack of agreement about how to best implement the right to health, and relativist perspectives create significant obstacles to global efforts to promote health as a human right. Furthermore, the absence of clear implementation directives and concrete enforcement mechanisms indicates a significant gap between legal rhetoric and reality.

It is also important to note that a rights-based legal framework may be in tension with a global health approach. As discussed in this chapter, a human rights framework may bring to light tensions among competing sets of rights. For

Despite the potential advantage of working with rather than against traditional culture in efforts to promote public health, there are potential pitfalls to such collaboration. Some studies have indicated that traditional healers do not consistently follow the practices for treating illness that they were taught in training sessions. Indeed, they often favor treatments that are viewed as harmful practices among Western medical practitioners. For example, despite training programs, some traditional healers in Africa continue to treat diarrhea with herbal enemas (considered a harmful practice) rather than oral rehydration therapy, which is favored by Western medical practitioners and the WHO.[b] In this context, some critics argue that collaboration with traditional healers reinforces their legitimacy and encourages communities to seek care that does not represent best practice and, indeed, in some cases involves harmful practices. In this way, critics argue that collaboration with traditional healers ultimately undermines the long-term goal of promoting public health. Paul Farmer, a well-known physician and medical anthropologist with a deep commitment to promoting public health in the developing world, also argues that programs emphasizing collaboration with traditional healers divert attention from the critical need for developed countries to ensure that the world's poor have access to adequate and scientifically based medical care.[c]

The conceptual and philosophical tensions illustrated by this examination of the complicated relationship between Western medicine and traditional healers underscore the difficulty of promoting a human right to health in a world of difference. Both within states and across state borders, fundamentally different conceptions of human rights exist. Even if there were global consensus, conceptual and cultural challenges create obstacles to efforts to promote health as a fundamental human right. These challenges go a long way toward explaining the gap between a legal right to health under international law and the reality that most human beings have not achieved the highest attainable standard of mental and physical health in practice.

[b]*Ibid.*: 5–6.
[c]*Ibid.*: 6.

example, religious rights or property rights may be in tension with a human right to health. Moreover, in practice, a public health model, even though it recognizes the underlying socioeconomic determinants of health, has tended to prioritize interventions intended to address health-seeking behavior. In contrast, human rights advocates have tended to prioritize structural changes to social, political, and legal systems over measures focused on the amelioration of health concerns in the short term.[37] In a similar vein, medical professionals who have played a critical role in establishing and advancing the field of public health have different professional training and experiences than legal professionals who have dominated international human rights work.[38]

If there is peril in a rights-based approach, there is also promise. Even if states do not have concrete obligations to promote health as a human right under international law, the mere fact that a human right to health exists under international law changes the political landscape in important ways. Non-state actors can use international legal principles in their efforts to promote global health—through monitoring, education, and advocacy at the local, national, and global levels. Despite the state-centric nature of international law, non-state actors can put pressure on states to adopt measures designed to promote global health and to direct resources toward global health programs. Non-state actors can also circumvent states. For example, non-governmental organizations (NGOs) like Doctors Without Borders, Save the Children, and Physicians for Human Rights work independently of states to promote fundamental health rights for populations in need. Thus, the progressive development of a human right to health is a notable political achievement in world politics, even though the international community still needs to make great strides in order to realize this right in practice.

Discussion Questions

1. International human rights law identifies a human right to health. Is such a right enforceable? Why or why not?
2. Does it matter that there is a significant gap between the human right to health under international law and the reality that, in practice, so many humans do not enjoy the highest attainable standard of physical and mental health? Why or why not?
3. How are human rights considerations relevant to understanding gender inequities in global health outcomes? Can a human rights framework help reduce gender inequities in global health outcomes? Why or why not?
4. Are professional codes of conduct for medical practitioners useful in promoting health as a human right? Why or why not? Can you think of other professions where professional codes of conduct related to health rights might be appropriate?
5. When a human right to health conflicts with another human right, which right should take priority?
6. How does the tension between positive and negative conceptions of human rights relate to global health considerations?
7. Is a universalist perspective on human rights necessary for promoting health as a human right? Why or why not?
8. Do human beings have a right to refuse lifesaving medical treatment on religious grounds? Why or why not? Can a right to refuse medical treatment be reconciled with ethical codes of conduct for medical practitioners that require doctors to prioritize the health and life of the patient?
9. Do parents have a right to refuse lifesaving medical treatment for their children on religious grounds? Why or why not?
10. From the vantage point of Western medical science, do the advantages of collaboration with traditional healers outweigh the disadvantages? Why or why not?
11. Is a relativist perspective on human rights always in tension with the idea of health as a human right? Why or why not?

Web Resources

Center for Economic and Social Rights: http://www.cesr.org/

Center for Public Health and Human Rights at the Johns Hopkins Bloomberg School of Public Health: http://www.jhsph.edu/humanrights/

Convention on the Elimination of Discrimination Against Women: http://www.un.org/womenwatch/daw/cedaw/cedaw.htm

Doctors Without Borders: http://www.doctorswithoutborders.org/

Global Lawyers and Physicians Working Together for Human Rights: http://www.globallawyersandphysicians.org/

Health and Human Rights: An International Journal: http://www.hhrjournal.org/index.php/hhr/index/

Health and Human Rights Info: http://www.hhri.org/

Human Development Reports: http://hdr.undp.org/

International Committee of the Red Cross: http://www.icrc.org/

International Covenant on Economic, Social, and Cultural Rights: http://www2.ohchr.org/english/law/pdf/cescr.pdf

Physicians for Human Rights: http://physiciansforhumanrights.org/

Public Health and Social Justice: http://www.publichealthandsocialjustice.org/

World Health Organization Health and Human Rights Program: http://www.who.int/hhr/en/

PART IV

Promoting Global Health

CHAPTER 9

Promoting Global Health from the Top Down: International Organizations

Introduction

This chapter examines the strengths and weaknesses of efforts to promote global health through international organizations, with a focus on the United Nations (UN) organs and programs. In particular, the chapter looks closely at the role of the World Health Organization (WHO) as an important example of global health promotion efforts within the UN system. The chapter examines the global campaign to eradicate smallpox, a success story coordinated and led by the WHO, as an example of an effective top-down effort to promote global health. The chapter concludes with an analysis of the health-related provisions of the Millennium Development Goals (MDGs). In doing so, it considers the value of global norms as a tool for promoting global health. As it looks at the role of international organizations, the chapter examines the political and legal obstacles that arise when seeking to promote global health in a top-down fashion.

Range, Functions, and Powers of International Organizations in the Promotion of Global Health

A wide range of **international organizations**, including UN bodies, multilateral development banks, and regional organizations, are involved in global efforts to promote public health. Despite the prominence and visibility of these international organizations, they generally have limited functions and powers. For the most part, international structures of governance reflect at most a weak form of **confederalism**.[1] In this way, the international system remains state-centric, and international organizations have only the powers and authority that member states voluntarily give them. International organizations are also constrained in their efforts to promote global health by the fact that their programmatic budgets typically depend on significant voluntary financial contributions by member states. This confederal dynamic fundamentally shapes the nature and effectiveness of top-down efforts by international organizations to promote global health.

The international organizations that play a role in top-down efforts to promote global health can be grouped into several categories. First, UN organs, specialized agencies, and programs play a major role in international efforts to promote global health. Within the UN system, a variety of institutions and programs with missions related to the promotion of global health exist. The WHO is the most prominent UN specialized agency involved in global health promotion endeavors and has coordinating authority over health-related issues addressed by the UN system.[2] Some UN programs address very specific challenges in global health. For example, the Joint United Nations Programme on HIV/AIDS (UNAIDS)

KEY TERMS IN THE STUDY OF INTERNATIONAL ORGANIZATIONS

Confederalism: a system of government in which the powers of the "central government" are derived exclusively from its constituent member states; it is a weak form of government with only minimal authority over its member states.

Global Norms: shared ideas and knowledge about specific global phenomena that structure expectations and behaviors in a particular issue area.

International Organization: an organization whose members are states represented by national governments; a more technical term for these organizations is *international governmental organizations.*

Multilateral Development Bank: an international organization that finances development programs in developing countries through low-cost, long-term loans and grants.

Regional Organization: an international organization whose membership is limited to a specific geographical region.

coordinates UN programming and activities in the global fight against AIDS. The World Food Programme, in addition to providing food aid in humanitarian crises, promotes programs intended to address hunger and chronic undernutrition.

Other UN programs have broad mandates that include provisions related to the promotion of global health. For instance, the United Nations Children's Fund (UNICEF), the UN agency whose mission is to promote the rights of the child globally, plays an important role in advocating for fundamental health rights for all the world's children. The UN Population Fund (UNFPA) works on global health promotion, with a focus on reproductive, sexual, and maternal health as well as poverty-related health challenges. Another example involves the work of the UN Development Programme (UNDP), which is responsible for coordinating the UN's global development network. In this capacity, poverty reduction is one of the UNDP's major objectives, and this goal has obvious connections to critical poverty-related global health challenges. The UNDP also has identified HIV/AIDS as a global development

challenge and, accordingly, does work in this area. Additionally, the UNDP coordinates global efforts to promote the MDGs, which include many health-related development targets.

UN organs involved in responding to natural disasters, international and civil conflicts, and other humanitarian emergencies also engage in activities pertinent to global health promotion. A number of UN organs and programs act in this capacity. Natural disasters, violent conflicts, and humanitarian crises create many serious health challenges, including disruptions to access to clean water, basic sanitation, and adequate food; disease outbreak; injuries and death resulting from violence; and threats to mental health.[3] Various UN institutions respond to these different health challenges. For instance, the Office of the UN High Commissioner for Refugees (UNHCR) coordinates international actions designed to protect and meet the basic needs of refugees, including shelter, clean water, sanitation, and basic health care. The World Food Programme (WFP) provides food assistance to victims of natural disasters, war, and other humanitarian crises. One can even argue that UN peace-keeping missions are relevant to global health promotion to the extent that they mitigate morbidity and mortality resulting from violent conflict.

In the second category, **multilateral development banks**, through their work on economic development and poverty reduction, have mandates related to global health promotion. Multilateral development banks include global actors, notably the World Bank, as well as regional actors, including the African Development Bank, the Inter-American Development Bank, and the Asian Development Bank. These banks are "owned" by their member states and primarily serve to direct money from developed countries to developing countries in the form of long-term loans or grants. The mission of multilateral development banks typically involves technical and financial assistance directed toward poverty-reduction programs. For example, the World Bank provides low-interest loans and interest-free credit and grants to developing countries for poverty-reduction programs, including activities directed toward public health. Critics of the World Bank argue that the conditions imposed on recipient countries as a requirement for loans or grants often create undue hardship for populations in these countries, fail to take account of particular local needs and contexts, produce negative effects on the environment, and undermine the sovereignty of these countries.[4] An in-depth consideration of the work of multilateral development banks, an important topic in its own right, goes beyond the scope of this chapter. Nonetheless, it is important for students to be aware of multilateral development banks as important international actors with mandates related to global health promotion as well as the fundamental criticisms thereof.

In the third category, **regional organizations**, like the European Union (EU), the Organization of American States (OAS), and the African Union (AU), play a role in promoting health within their respective systems of regional governance. The institutional structures of regional organizations vary significantly, and each regional organization takes a unique approach to health governance. Within the EU, the European Parliament created a European Centre for Disease Prevention and Control in 2004. This agency has responsibility for coordinating disease surveillance, early warning systems, and outbreak control among EU member states in an effort to prevent the spread of infectious diseases throughout the region. In 1902, the OAS created the Pan-American Health Organization as a specialized organization with responsibility for fostering collaboration among its member states on public health issues. Other regional organizations, including the Association of South-East Asian Nations and the Arab League, do not have major institutional organs specifically devoted to the promotion of public health. Instead, other regional organizations have health offices operated under the auspices of the WHO. Regional WHO offices exist in six areas: Africa, the Americas,[5] the Eastern Mediterranean, South-East Asia, Europe, and the Western Pacific.

In addition to these regional WHO offices, regional organizations typically have institutions focused on human rights as well as programs directed at economic and social development, areas with important connections to poverty-related global health challenges. In addition, other regional organizations have committees devoted to addressing health issues. For instance, the AU has its Committee on Health, Labour, and Social Affairs; the Arab League, under the auspices of its council, has its Health Committee. Moreover, regional organizations have been involved with programs intended to address specific health challenges. For example, the AU has sought to facilitate collective action among its member states to address the challenges of HIV/AIDS, malaria, and tuberculosis in Africa. Thus, regional organizations are involved in a range of activities that have a bearing on the promotion of public health.

This chapter focuses primarily on UN institutional organs and specialized agencies as the international organizations that play the most prominent role in global health promotion.

Unlike regional organizations, the UN system is truly global in scope. Moreover, the work of the UN represents, for better or worse, the promise and peril of top-down measures to promote global health. The UN has the potential to coordinate global health programs and initiatives that dramatically reduce major threats to public health, as in the case of the eradication of smallpox. At the same time, the UN faces important legal, political, and social constraints in its efforts to promote global health. Regional organizations vary somewhat in their capacities, capabilities, and levels of success in achieving common goals among states. Despite these variations, all regional organizations are plagued by a similar set of constraints as the UN. Thus, the UN represents a useful example of the possibilities and limitations of top-down efforts at global health promotion through international organizations.

World Health Organization

The International Health Conference adopted the Constitution of the WHO in July 1946, and the organization came into being in 1948 once the requisite number of states ratified the Constitution. The WHO succeeded the League of Nations Health Organization, the permanent international health organization created by the League of Nations in 1920 to deal with global outbreaks of epidemic and pandemic disease, including the devastating influenza pandemic that occurred during World War I. The WHO serves as the specialized agency with primary authority for coordinating health programs and activities within the UN system. In this capacity, the WHO plays perhaps the most critical role in UN efforts to promote global health. Membership in the WHO is open to all states, and, currently, 193 states are members of the organization, indicating near-universal participation in the organization among states.[6]

Whereas its League of Nations predecessor focused more narrowly on the prevention and control of global disease outbreaks, the WHO has a wide-ranging public health agenda. The WHO defines health very broadly as a "state of complete physical, mental, and social well-being and not merely the absence of disease or infirmity."[7] Accordingly, its agenda focuses not only on the prevention of the transnational spread of communicable illness but also on economic and social development efforts intended to promote standards of living necessary for achieving this broad definition of health. The preamble to the Constitution of the WHO asserts that the "enjoyment of the highest attainable standard of health" is a fundamental human right and also notes the fundamental connections among health, peace, and security.

Article 2 of the WHO Constitution outlines numerous functions that the organization has in pursuit of this broad health agenda. These functions include, but are not limited to, the following: serving as coordinating authority on international health work; collaborating with the UN, other specialized agencies, governmental entities, and non-state organizations working on global health; helping governments strengthen their health services; providing technical assistance and, in emergency settings, aid upon governmental request; providing administrative and technical services, such as epidemiological services; working on the eradication of diseases; promoting improved access to nutrition, housing, sanitation, and other health-related economic and social goods; promoting cooperation among scientific and professional groups in health-related fields; making recommendations regarding **global norms** governing international health matters; and gathering and sharing information on public health. As indicated by this long list of functions, the WHO works in a variety of capacities in its efforts to promote health, broadly defined.

The WHO comprises three organs—the World Health Assembly (WHA), the Executive Board, and the Secretariat, each with distinct membership, decision-making structures, powers, and responsibilities. Each member state of the WHO has a delegation of 1–3 members in the WHA. Each state delegation gets one vote in the Assembly, and decisions on important questions, including the adoption of conventions and agreements as well as amendments to the Constitution, require a two-thirds majority. Decisions on other questions require a simple majority of members present and voting. By a simple majority vote, the Assembly also may require that other categories of questions require a two-thirds majority.

The WHA meets in a regular annual session, typically in May, and may also schedule special sessions at the request of the Executive Board or a majority of WHO members. The WHA has a wide range of functions, including setting policy and international standards, reporting on health-related recommendations made by the main bodies of the UN, promoting and conducting research in the field of health, creating other institutions and committees to carry out work that falls under the mandate of the WHO, and adopting regulations related to sanitation and quarantine procedures intended to prevent the transnational spread of disease. The WHO Constitution also gives the Assembly the authority to adopt conventions or other agreements, with a vote by a two-thirds majority, related to the organization's mandate. These agreements are to have binding force on member states when a member ratifies it according to its constitutional procedures.

The membership of the Executive Board is made up of thirty-four technical experts appointed by the Assembly. In making appointments to the Executive Board, the Assembly elects members to designate the thirty-four technical experts. To ensure equitable regional representation on the Executive Board, the WHO Constitution requires that at least three members be elected from each of the regional WHO organizations. The Executive Board is required to meet at least twice annually. As defined in Article 28 of the WHO Constitution, its primary functions are to implement the WHA's decisions and policies, to serve as the executive organ of the WHA, to provide advice to the WHA upon request

or on its own initiative, to set the agenda for WHA meetings, and to take emergency measures in cases calling for immediate action, such as fighting global epidemics or providing health aid to victims of natural disasters or humanitarian emergencies. The Board may create committees serving the purposes covered by the WHO's mandate as directed by the WHA, and either the WHA or the Board has the authority to convene conferences on any matter falling within the competence of the organization.

The Secretariat is led by a director-general, nominated by the executive and appointed by the WHA. The director-general serves as the chief administrative officer of the organization. Article 37 of the WHO Constitution specifies that the director-general, in administering the organization and supervising the staff of the Secretariat, is supposed to remain independent of the governments of member states. Approximately 8,000 administrators, technical experts, and support staff serve in the Secretariat, which includes people working at the WHO headquarters, in the regional offices, and in member countries.[8]

In addition to creating a three-tiered organizational structure, the WHO Constitution creates obligations for member states. Specifically, the Constitution requires each member state to submit an annual report documenting its actions and progress toward improving the health of its population. These reports are to include discussion of actions with respect to WHO recommendations; documentation of health-related laws, regulations, and reports adopted by the reporting state; statistical and epidemiological information; and other information requested by the Board.[9]

As this overview indicates, the WHO has an intricate bureaucratic structure and a wide range of functions and responsibilities. However, a close inspection of the WHO structure and its underlying legal framework demonstrates that its powers, in practice, are limited. Like other UN organs, the WHO is constrained in its actions by the state-centric nature of international law and organization. For the most part,

UNDER THE MICROSCOPE

The WHO Framework Convention on Tobacco Control

The WHO Framework Convention on Tobacco Control (FCTC) was adopted by the WHA in 2003 and entered into force in 2005. This treaty seeks to promote international cooperation on the regulation and control of tobacco and has widespread membership, with 174 state members as of 2011. Globalization dynamics contributed to the need for international cooperation on tobacco control. As powerful multinational tobacco corporations increased their marketing and sale of tobacco products worldwide, an epidemic of tobacco-related illnesses and deaths spread across the globe. In 1998, approximately 3.5 million premature deaths were attributed to illnesses caused by tobacco use. The rise in smoking across the globe led experts to predict that by 2030 premature deaths from tobacco abuse will reach 10 million annually if trends in tobacco use are not reversed.[a] The tobacco epidemic has had particularly devastating effects in developing countries, which have experienced a rise in noncommunicable illnesses associated with tobacco use at the same time that they continue to face high prevalence rates of communicable illnesses. The growing nature of this problem led to the initiation of a novel campaign to regulate the control of tobacco through international law. The result was the FCTC, the first global health treaty negotiated under the umbrella of the WHO system.

The FCTC contains provisions designed to reduce demand for and supply of tobacco products. Articles 6–14 cover provisions designed to reduce demand for tobacco products and include measures to encourage the use of taxation policies to reduce demand, prohibitions on the sale of tobacco products to minors, the adoption and implementation of measures designed to limit exposure to smoke, regulations on the contents of

[a]World Health Organization, *History of the World Health Organization Framework Convention on Tobacco Control* (2009). Available online at: http://whqlibdoc.who.int/publications/2009/9789241563925_eng.pdf.

the long list of WHO functions and powers can be categorized into seven basic activities: (1) coordination of global health initiatives, (2) advocacy/consensus-building, (3) dissemination of knowledge/information, (4) disease surveillance, (5) certification of quality standards, (6) standard setting and the development of global norms, and (7) technical assistance and training. In all of these capacities, the WHO does *not* have enforcement power. Rather, it must work with states and requires their consent and voluntary participation in an effort to promote effective global health initiatives.[10]

Despite the fact that the WHO does not have enforcement power and must rely on the cooperation of its member states, the cooperative model on which the WHO is based offers many advantages. The multinational and collaborative nature of the WHO helps ensure its global legitimacy. Most ministries of health in member countries view the WHO as a credible tobacco products, regulations governing the packaging and labeling of tobacco products, the adoption of measures to raise public awareness about the risks of tobacco use, and efforts to adopt programs intended to reduce dependence on tobacco products. Provisions intended to regulate the supply side of tobacco are contained in Articles 15–17 and include measures calling on member states to prohibit the illicit trade of tobacco products, to criminalize the sale of tobacco products to minors, and to fund programs designed to create alternative economic opportunities for populations for whom the tobacco industry is a primary source of income.

Implementation mechanisms in the FCTC include reporting requirements by parties to the treaty. A large majority of parties to the framework are complying with reporting requirements, and a review of these reports indicates that most FCTC members are taking steps to implement key provisions of the treaty. Eighty percent of members have created educational programs designed to raise public awareness about tobacco-related health risks. A similarly high percentage of members have put prohibitions on the sale of tobacco to minors in place. Adoption of other recommendations included in the treaty, including calls for bans on advertising, the establishment of smoke-free public spaces, or the creation of economic alternatives for populations whose income comes from tobacco production, is not as high.[b]

The FCTC illustrates the potential opportunities and challenges of efforts to promote global health through international organizations. Treaties like the FCTC typically do not include strong enforcement mechanisms. Nevertheless, such treaties can play a critical role in helping to generate global norms, to coordinate transnational advocacy, and to prompt the passage of national legislation. The WHO may not be able to force states to comply with the FCTC, but it is notable that the international campaign that led to the adoption of this international agreement prompted many countries to adopt stronger regulations on the use and sale of tobacco products even in the absence of strong enforcement mechanisms.

---

[b]Haik Nikogosian, "WHO Framework Convention on Tobacco Control: A Key Milestone," *Bulletin of the World Health Organization* (2010). Available online at: http://www.who.int/bulletin/volumes/88/2/10-075895/en/.

organization and, accordingly, are inclined to believe and act on the WHO's recommendations and technical advice. The fact that the WHO has offices in various regions across the world helps facilitate a rapid global response in preparing for or responding to global epidemics. The WHO's reliance on technical experts on its Executive Board also lends legitimacy to the norms and technical standards adopted by the organization. The cooperative as opposed to the coercive nature of interactions between states and the WHO also makes it more likely that states will collaborate in a meaningful way on global health initiatives.[11]

Nevertheless, the organizational structure of the WHO creates obstacles to its efforts to promote global health. It is a highly bureaucratic and stratified organization. Significant resources are spent on promoting policies, global norms, and standards, which involves workshops, meetings, and training sessions for expert consultants, rather than spending directly on the health needs of populations. Like most bureaucracies, the WHO can be a slow-moving, inefficient institution. The implementation of WHO policies often requires approval from multiple departments and divisions. On the one hand, such approvals are important because they help ensure that policies are technically sound and have the appropriate political support. On the other hand, these bureaucratic hurdles can delay the implementation of important policies and may make it less likely that the WHO will innovate.

The WHO ultimately must defer to its member states, which results in its being a highly political institution. Director-generals seek to define their own particular visions for the organization, with resulting shifts in priorities and emphasis. The WHO at times can be out of touch with practical constraints on the ground in countries where it operates. The WHO headquarters are in Geneva, Switzerland. The policy-making functions of the WHA take place at a great distance from the realities in the field, where local health workers may not have the education or resources to effectively use training materials provided by WHO consultants. Dr. John Murray, an independent consultant who has worked for the WHO in Asia and Africa, has said, "WHO publications are often seen in perfect condition, stacked neatly on shelves, gathering dust."[12] At the same time, technical experts and administrators headquartered in Geneva often do not have crucial knowledge about local cultural contexts or political realities that is essential for an initiative to succeed in a targeted area.

Furthermore, the WHO's reliance on voluntary participation by states becomes especially important in the area of financing. Because the WHO does not have a regular budget for the implementation of its programs, it must rely on voluntary contributions from member states. In the developing countries where it does much of its work, significant funds are generally not available. Thus, the WHO must rely on voluntary contributions from developed countries and other non-state actors to carry out its work. These state and non-state actors may have different priorities than the WHO, leading to political tensions about how to best spend global health aid. Because the WHO does not have its own budget for implementing its policies, it may lose its ability to influence donor countries and non-governmental organizations (NGOs). Indeed, the WHO's dependence on voluntary contributions from other actors makes it susceptible to losing control over agenda setting and its general authority to coordinate global health initiatives.

A Success Story: The Global Eradication of Smallpox

Despite the political obstacles it faces, the WHO has contributed to notable successes in the promotion of global health. Perhaps the most prominent global health success story is the eradication of smallpox,[13] in which the WHO played a key role. In the mid-1960s, there were an estimated 10 million–15 million cases of smallpox each year. The disease was endemic in over fifty countries, and it killed approximately 1.5 million–2 million people annually. By the end of the 1970s, just over a decade later, smallpox had been eradicated from the globe; no new cases of smallpox have been reported since 1978.[14] The success of the global smallpox eradication campaign was by no means guaranteed. Importantly, the WHO played a critical role in pushing the initiative toward success. Although the eradication of smallpox represents a major success for the WHO in global health promotion, it also illustrates the political, legal, and structural challenges faced by the WHO as outlined in the previous section.

Early efforts to eliminate smallpox can be traced back to the creation of a primitive vaccine in 1798. Subsequently, numerous national governments used improved versions of the vaccine to eliminate the disease among their populations. In the 1950s, early proposals to target smallpox for eradication emerged in the WHA. Although these proposals were well received, efforts to put together a concrete plan of action stalled for a variety of reasons. Initially, many WHO officials saw only a minimal role for the WHO and preferred to emphasize the role of national governments in eradication efforts. Between 1960 and 1965, the WHO spent only around $500,000 on smallpox eradication efforts annually even though a comprehensive global vaccination program would have cost $98 million dollars. Similarly, the WHO did not devote staffing resources to the campaign, either at headquarters or in the regional offices. Member states did not initially donate adequate financial resources for a successful global campaign.[15] In short, a lack of political will and leadership among both WHO officials and member states resulted in relative inaction by the international organization.

Moreover, bureaucratic complexities and political disagreements within the organization resulted in slow movement on smallpox eradication efforts. Some actors within the WHO system placed a lower priority on smallpox than on other diseases, such as malaria.[16] Even though proposals to embark on a smallpox eradication campaign were well received by the WHA in the 1950s, action stalled as various departments and offices within the WHO system tried to reach agreement on what the plan should look like. The Executive Board sought to create a top-down campaign centralized in Geneva Headquarters, whereas representatives from the WHO regional offices argued that the global campaign would need to take into account specific local contexts.[17] Also, the emerging smallpox eradication campaign involved a complicated array of international, national, local, and nongovernmental actors, creating challenges for the WHO in its efforts to coordinate this international initiative.[18]

Eventually, the WHO worked through some of these internal and international political challenges and initiated a new global campaign to eradicate smallpox in 1965 when it created the Smallpox Eradication Unit. This unit went on to provide crucial global leadership and coordination. Additionally, shifting political circumstances in the United States

helped move the WHO campaign forward. Under President Lyndon Johnson, the United States agreed to provide increased financial support. The U.S. Communicable Disease Center[19] partnered with the WHO on the initiative, providing critical support and leadership from a major world power. Dr. M.G. Candau, director-general of the WHO at the time, recommitted the WHO to the smallpox eradication initiative, began to provide much-needed leadership, and initiated policies designed to encourage collaboration with target countries that would be essential for success. The growing political support for the smallpox eradication campaign was affirmed by the WHA in 1966 when it adopted the Intensified Smallpox Eradication Programme, which allocated $2.4 million to the program.[20]

Another significant policy shift involved the adoption of more proactive vaccination strategies in the early 1970s. Previously, the WHO had relied heavily on general vaccination programs to promote eradication. However, after recognizing the persistence of the disease in countries plagued by civil conflict and natural disasters, the WHO adopted more aggressive methods involving surveillance and containment. The WHO encouraged governments to adopt methods that involved active surveillance of villages and remote areas for signs of the disease. WHO and local health workers worked together to quickly isolate infected individuals and vaccinate populations in the area when they found active cases of infection. The highly aggressive nature of these methods led some observers to characterize the approach as militaristic,[21] and national militaries, paramilitaries, and local police forces used force to counter opposition to the vaccination campaign in some instances.[22]

The ultimate success of the smallpox eradication campaign resulted, in part, from features of the disease and technical developments that made smallpox a good target for eradication. The fact that smallpox involved human-to-human transmission rather than another vector for transmitting the disease eliminated concern that a nonhuman reservoir for the disease would remain in place. The symptomatic rash made it easy to diagnose and, as a result, to isolate infected individuals to prevent transmission of the disease. Coupled with isolation of infected individuals, the widespread vaccination of populations in endemic areas enabled public health workers to prevent further spread of the disease. A freeze-dried variant of the vaccination became available in the 1950s, making it possible to store it effectively for long periods of time in places that might otherwise not be able to store vaccination that required refrigeration. Also, the invention of the bifurcated needle reduced program costs significantly.[23] Furthermore, the smallpox vaccination confers long-term protection, for a minimum of ten years and upward of thirty years.[24]

The success of this campaign also very much depended on the leadership and the successful negotiation of political obstacles toward cooperation across state borders on global health promotion. Without increased political and financial commitment from developed countries (in this case, the United States played a particularly significant role), and without leadership and policy innovations within the WHO, the campaign to eradicate smallpox likely would have failed. The success of the campaign also depended on effective collaboration among WHO officials and experts in the field, national governments, and local health workers. Notably, specific vaccination strategies were adapted to address specific national and local contexts, a flexibility that was essential to the success of the initiative.[25]

In the end, the global campaign to eradicate smallpox cost approximately $298 million. The estimated annual costs of the program were $23 million.[26] With an estimated 1.5 million–2 million lives saved per year, the global smallpox campaign cost roughly twelve dollars per life saved. An additional, and perhaps unexpected, benefit of the global campaign to eradicate smallpox is that it contributed to a growing global commitment to routine vaccination, a practice that saves millions of lives each year.[27]

Millennium Development Goals

In September 2000, the UN General Assembly adopted the Millennium Declaration.[28] This declaration commits UN member states to work together to eradicate extreme poverty across the globe. The Millennium Declaration's language is strong and unambiguous: "We will spare no effort to free our fellow men, women and children from the abject and dehumanizing conditions of extreme poverty, to which more than a billion of them are currently subjected. We are committed to making the right to development a reality for everyone and to freeing the entire human race from want."[29] The General Assembly identifies a number of methods for achieving this goal, including the promotion of good governance at both the national and international levels, the removal of obstacles to financing for development, and the provision of debt relief to poor countries. The UNDP has primary responsibility for coordinating the Millennium Development Campaign and, in this capacity, collaborates with other UN organs, member states, and NGOs.

The Millennium Declaration outlines a series of commitments for eradicating global poverty with a target deadline of 2015.[30] From this list of commitments, the UN has identified eight specific objectives that have become known as the Millennium Development Goals (MDGs): (1) to eradicate extreme poverty and hunger; (2) to achieve universal primary education with equal access for boys and girls; (3) to promote gender equality and empower women; (4) to reduce child mortality; (5) to improve maternal health; (6) to combat HIV/AIDS, malaria, and other diseases; (7) to ensure environmental sustainability; and (8) to develop a global partnership for development. For each of these goals, the UNDP further articulated specific targets that identify quantifiable benchmarks by which member states will measure their progress toward reaching the MDGs.

Notably, three of the MDGs (MDG 4, reducing child mortality; MDG 5, improving maternal health; and MDG 6, combating HIV/AIDs, malaria, and other diseases) are explicitly related to global health. Other MDGs include targets that are directly connected to global health. For instance, MDG 1 (eradicating extreme poverty) includes a target of halving the proportion of the world's population who suffer from hunger by 2015. The malnutrition and undernutrition associated with hunger have obvious connections to human health. All of the targets of MDG 7 (ensuring environmental sustainability) have important connections to human health. Target 1 urges countries to integrate the principles of sustainable development and to reverse the loss of environmental resources. This target identifies greenhouse gas emissions, ozone depletion, and climate change as critical issues. Target 2 called for a significant reduction in the rate of biodiversity loss by 2010—a target date that the international community missed, with a growing number of species facing extinction under current conditions. These environmental challenges affect human health in significant ways, as was discussed in Chapter 3. Target 3 calls for the halving of the proportion of people without access to clean water and basic sanitation by 2015. Finally, Target 4 calls for a significant improvement in the lives of slum dwellers by 2020; the lack of basic infrastructure and the extreme poverty in slums are serious obstacles to the health of the people who live in these substandard conditions. MDG 2 (achieving universal education) and MDG 3 (promoting gender equality/empowering women) do not include specific health-related targets. Nevertheless, clear connections among education, gender equality, and poverty-related health challenges exist. Thus, it can be said that all of the MDGs are connected in important ways to global health.

The MDGs reflect the most specific and ambitious global plan to address poverty to date. Indeed, this high-profile campaign to coordinate efforts among international organizations, national governments, and NGOs toward the common goal of eradicating extreme poverty is unprecedented. As discussed

earlier, global health challenges are at the core of the MDGs. If the international community makes significant progress toward the MDGs, it will, in the process, be taking major steps toward promoting a human right to health. The UNDP has estimated that achievement of the MDGs would save tens of millions of lives.[31] Millions more would benefit from improved health and quality of life.

Because the MDGs involve specific, quantifiable targets, progress toward their fulfillment can be measured. Unfortunately, an assessment of global progress toward the achievement of the MDGs indicates that, to date, the implementation of concrete actions to fulfill the MDGs has not matched the ambitious rhetoric of the Millennium Declaration.[32] To be sure, there have already been important successes in the Millennium Development Campaign. The UN Statistics Divisions has compiled data by regional grouping to assess progress toward the MDGs. Notably, some regions have already met or are close to meeting important targets. For example, both Eastern and South-Eastern Asia are on target to meet the goal of halving the extreme poverty rate by 2015. Northern Africa is on target to reduce hunger by half. Both South-Eastern Asia and the Latin American/Caribbean regions are on target to meet their goals for halting or reversing the spread of tuberculosis. Many regions should meet some of the MDG targets if current trends continue.[33]

However, as shown in Table 9.1, the overall record is mixed. Progress has been strongest in Northern Africa, throughout Asia, and in the European states of the Commonwealth of Independent States. The Latin America and Caribbean Region has made significant progress toward some targets. However, notable gaps in progress are present in all regions. The situation looks particularly bleak in sub-Saharan Africa, which is not on track to meet any of the MDG targets.[34] For example, only 15 percent of the population in sub-Saharan Africa lives in a country that is on track to meet its malnutrition targets.[35] Moreover, deficits in progress toward the MDGs are particularly notable

TABLE 9.1 Progress Toward Health-related MDGs by Region, 2011

	GOAL 4: Reduce child mortality	GOAL 5: Improve maternal health		GOAL 6: Combat HIV/AIDS, malaria, and other diseases	
	Reduce mortality of children under 5 years by two-thirds	Reduce maternal mortality by three-fourths	Access to reproductive health	Halt and begin to reverse the spread of HIV/AIDS	Halt and reverse the spread of tuberculosis
Northern Africa	Target met or expected to be met by 2015	Insufficient progress	Insufficient progress	No progress or deterioration	Target met or expected to be met by 2015
Sub-Saharan Africa	Insufficient progress	No progress or deterioration	Insufficient progress	Target met or expected to be met by 2015	Insufficient progress
Eastern Asia	Target met or expected to be met by 2015	Target met or expected to be met by 2015	Target met or expected to be met by 2015	Insufficient progress	Target met or expected to be met by 2015
South-Eastern Asia	Insufficient progress	Insufficient progress	Insufficient progress	Insufficient progress	Target met or expected to be met by 2015
Southern Asia	Insufficient progress	Insufficient progress	Insufficient progress	Target met or expected to be met by 2015	Target met or expected to be met by 2015
Western Asia	Insufficient progress	Insufficient progress	Insufficient progress	Insufficient progress	Target met or expected to be met by 2015
Oceania	Insufficient progress	No progress or deterioration	Missing or insufficient data	Target met or expected to be met by 2015	Target met or expected to be met by 2015
Latin America & Caribbean	Target met or expected to be met by 2015	Insufficient progress	Insufficient progress	Insufficient progress	Target met or expected to be met by 2015
Caucasus and Central Asia	Insufficient progress	Target met or expected to be met by 2015	Insufficient progress	No progress or deterioration	Insufficient progress

Source: United Nations Department of Economic and Social Affairs, Statistics Division, *Millennium Development Goals: 2011 Progress Chart.* Available online at: http://www.un.org/millenniumgoals/pdf/(2011E)_MDReport2011_ProgressChart.pdf.

in important health targets. On the target of reducing mortality for children under five years of age, developing countries have fallen significantly short.[36] Again, sub-Saharan African countries, in particular, have not made much progress toward MDG targets. Progress is also far short of the MDG targets for improvements in maternal health and for halting or reversing the spread of HIV/AIDS in most regions.[37]

Perhaps most ominously, there has been either no progress or even deterioration in progress toward health-related MDG targets in many regions. For example, the Western Asian Region has fallen behind on all targets related to Goal 1, eradicating extreme poverty and hunger. Sub-Saharan Africa and Southern Asia have had no or deteriorating progress on the Goal 2 target to reduce maternal mortality. In both sub-Saharan Africa and the Commonwealth of Independent States, efforts to halt or reverse the spread of tuberculosis have either stalled or declined. Many regions are characterized by no or deteriorating progress on Goal 7's environmental targets as well.[38]

The bottom line is that the international community, despite important progress in some areas, is not on target to meet the MDGs by 2015. Scholars have estimated that an estimated $20 billion–$70 billion annually would be necessary to achieve the MDGs. The World Bank has estimated that an additional $20 billion–$25 billion in global health aid would be required to meet the health-related targets of the MDGs, approximately four times the amount of current development assistance on health.[39]

The UNDP has encountered numerous political and legal constraints that have hindered more rapid progress toward fulfillment of the MDGs. For one, the UNDP, like other UN organs, is confronted with the reality of the state-centric nature of the international system. Under international law, declarations are nonbinding instruments. Thus, despite the unambiguous language of the Millennium Declaration, which unequivocally commits states to the goals of development and the eradication of poverty, it does not create any binding obligations on states. The UN does not have any authority to coerce states to fulfill the aspirations to which they have committed. In this regard, there is a gap between the rhetoric and the reality of the Millennium Development Campaign.

In a similar vein, the UNDP has only limited powers for encouraging the fulfillment of the MDGs. As the institution with the primary responsibility for coordinating the Millennium Development Campaign, the UNDP has the authority and responsibility to raise awareness about the MDGs, to advocate that member states adopt and implement the MDGs, and to help design policies, strategies, and plans that countries can follow in pursuit of the MDGs. To this end, the UNDP may organize training, conduct research, and develop planning and management information tools. The UNDP also is able to help countries report on their progress toward the MDGs. As this list indicates, the UNDP has only minimal powers that are grounded in a cooperative rather than a coercive model. Thus, just like the WHO, the UNDP must rely on the voluntary cooperation of states to work toward fulfilling the MDGs.

The mixed record, to date, of the health-related aspects of the Millennium Development Campaign also reflects the reality that top-down health promotion initiatives involve a multiplicity of actors—from the global to the local levels. Each of these levels of action is shaped by unique sets of cultural, political, economic, and other social factors. For instance, the question of how much any individual country should spend in order to achieve health-related MDG targets must be balanced against the question of how much it can afford to spend. While international development assistance can be used to fill financial gaps within countries, it can also complicate matters in that international donors often attach aid conditions that create bureaucratic burdens and limit the flexibility of countries to adopt approaches that they deem most appropriate. International aid also can create a dependency that makes it harder for a country to develop its own permanent, sustainable health programs and infrastructure.[40] Given such complexities, it is understandably difficult for UN organs to coordinate appropriate and effective strategies for implementing policies designed to fulfill the MDGs.

These complexities also make it difficult to determine which actors are responsible for any successes or failures in making progress toward the MDGs. For example, one of the major challenges of improving global health outcomes is that effective, low-cost interventions—including childhood immunizations, condom use for the prevention of HIV transmission, and prenatal care—are not reaching the people who need them most.[41] The lack of reach of these affordable interventions might result from inadequate funding or training by global actors, lack of political commitment to implementing these interventions by national actors, or simply inability (due to financial or time constraints) or unwillingness of populations (due to lack of accurate information about treatment or different cultural perspectives on treatment) to take advantage of low-cost interventions. In fact, a combination of these factors often limits the effectiveness of global health promotion efforts. The existence of obstacles on many different levels underscores the challenges faced by UN actors in their health promotion endeavors.

Global Health Promotion from the Top Down: Possibilities and Challenges

The examination of the WHO and the MDGs illustrates the potential advantages and disadvantages of working through international organizations to promote global health. Despite the political and legal obstacles faced by international organizations in their global health promotion activities, UN organs and programs have contributed to successful public health interventions that have saved millions of lives. The successful campaign to eradicate

smallpox, in which the WHO played a significant role, is perhaps the most notable success story.[42] UN actors, including the WHO, UNICEF, and the UNDP, have been involved in other successful efforts to eradicate or control the effects of devastating diseases, such as a guinea worm eradication campaign and global efforts to control river blindness (onchocerciasis) in Africa.[43] The WHO has contributed to successful national campaigns to fight serious illnesses within particular countries. For instance, the WHO helped promote Directly Observed Therapy, Short-course (DOTS) for tuberculosis in China, which has helped prevent an estimated 30,000 tuberculosis deaths annually.[44] The WHO and UNICEF also collaborated with the Egyptian government on a program designed to expand the use of oral rehydration salts in an effort to reduce diarrheal deaths among children. This program reduced infant mortality by an estimated 36 percent and child mortality by an estimated 43 percent.[45] In such cases, UN agencies have contributed to the success by channeling international funding, disseminating knowledge about best practices in medicine, and providing basic technical training.

UN organs also have been involved in notable public health failures and face significant challenges in their efforts to promote global health. An example of a failed UN-sponsored public health policy involved early WHO efforts to reduce morbidity and mortality associated with malaria. In the 1960s, the WHO and other UN agencies began coordinating malaria eradication initiatives involving billions of dollars of expenditures by states, international organizations, and non-state actors.[46] As part of its broader malaria eradication campaign, the WHO adopted a policy that trained health practitioners in African countries to assume every childhood fever resulted from malaria and to treat it with chloroquine. Instead of mitigating the effects of malaria, this policy contributed to the emergence of drug-resistant strains of malaria-causing parasites.[47] As a result, more dangerous and deadly forms of malaria emerged that continue to threaten millions of lives each year. The WHO and other UN agencies continue to work with states and NGOs on global initiatives to combat malaria, but this disease remains a vexing problem in global health.

A variety of challenges stymie top-down efforts to promote global health through international organizations. In the case of the WHO's early malaria eradication initiatives, the unique features of local ecologies hindered efforts to develop a global strategy for malaria control. For example, the spraying of DDT as a method for controlling mosquito populations that carry malaria-causing parasites was not an effective strategy in the dense rain forests of Southeast Asia. Poverty and a lack of adequate public health infrastructure in societies with endemic malaria also contributed to the improper use of antimalarial drugs and incomplete treatment that facilitated the emergence of drug-resistant strains of the parasites that cause malaria.[48] As this example illustrates, global efforts to promote public health can be hindered by a disconnection between global norms, priorities, and strategies set by international organizations and specific local needs.

In a similar vein, efforts by international organizations to promote global health in developing countries may have unintended negative consequences. For instance, the magnitude of the HIV/AIDS crisis in southern Africa, where numerous countries have staggering HIV infection rates, indicates an acute need for significant international aid to combat the disease. Accordingly, the UN has initiated a major, multiagency campaign to combat the global AIDS crisis, led by the Joint United Nations Programme on HIV/AIDS (UNAIDS), with an annual budget of over $400 million.[49] In 2008, $15.6 billion in global health aid was directed toward HIV/AIDS.[50]

Despite the obvious need for global aid to combat HIV/AIDS, such programs have not escaped critical scrutiny. Critics charge that the global funding dynamic for HIV/AIDS can be characterized as a form of aid "funneling," in which international actors have converged upon the AIDS crisis as a high-profile funding opportunity that diverts funding from other critical public health challenges in developing countries, including basic access to health care, access to adequate food and clean water, and maternal and child health. Critics also contend that global health aid creates an internal brain drain within developing countries, whereby local health care workers and other individuals with skills to contribute to improving public health infrastructure get drawn into working for international HIV/AIDS programs rather than contributing to the development of local public health infrastructure.[51] In this way, global health aid may actually undermine the creation of long-term sustainable, local solutions to public health problems in the developing world.

Another obstacle to health promotion efforts by international organizations is a potential trade-off between short- and long-term goals in the provision of global health aid. In developing countries, the health needs of poor populations are critical and immediate. Thus, UN programs are often intended to address the most basic health needs of vulnerable populations. In doing so, however, a question arises regarding whether health aid may enable corrupt or ineffective governments by failing to create pressures for political change in these countries. Similarly, as demonstrated in the box "Women's Health Initiatives in the UN System," UN programs focused on the immediate health needs of populations typically fail to consider the ways in which discriminatory gender norms that are deeply embedded in societies fail to generate the kinds of structural changes that ultimately will be necessary to improve women's health.

These concerns parallel a criticism made of peacekeeping operations in conflict zones. On the one hand, UN peacekeeping has been lauded as a mechanism that has saved countless lives in conflict-ridden societies. On the other hand, critics charge that peacekeeping may prolong violent conflicts and, as a result, lead to greater loss of human life in the long run.[52] Similar concerns can be raised about

UNDER THE MICROSCOPE

Women's Health Initiatives in the UN System

Women's health emerged on the UN's agenda in the 1960s. The first international women's health initiatives focused on women's fertility behavior as a means of population control. At this time, the UN also began to focus on maternal and child health, and international women's health initiatives remained focused on fertility and maternal and child health in subsequent decades.[a]

By the 1980s, UN institutions broadened their focus by considering ways in which the status of women shapes population health. The final report of the 1985 UN Women's Conference in Nairobi asserted that because of women's central role in providing clean water, fuel, and sanitation to families and communities, efforts to improve the situation of women could help reduce mortality, morbidity, and population growth. The Nairobi report also identified basic reproductive rights as a critical part of an international agenda for women.[b]

The UN broadened the women's health agenda even further in the 1990s. The 1994 UN Conference on Population and Development reaffirmed the importance of reproductive and health rights on the women's health agenda. The final conference report also highlighted the social and economic vulnerabilities that make women especially susceptible to HIV/AIDS and called for equal relationships between men and women as a means for promoting sexual and reproductive health. Finally, the report identified violence against women, including domestic violence and rape, as a threat to women's health and

---

[a]Mayra Buvinic, André Médici, Elisa Fernández, and Ana Cristina Torres, "Gender Differentials in Health," in Dean T. Jamison, Joel G. Breman, Anthony R. Measham, George Alleyne, Maria Claeson, David P. Evans, Prabhat Jha, Anne Mills, and Phillip Musgrove, eds., *Disease Control Priorities in Developing Countries*, 2d ed. (New York: Oxford University Press; Washington, DC: The World Bank, 2006): 196.

[b]Paragraphs 28 and 29 of the *Report of the World Conference to Review and Appraise the Achievements of the United Nations Decade for Women: Equality, Development, and Peace.* Available online at: http://www.un.org/womenwatch/confer/nfls/Nairobi1985report.txt.

---

global health aid. Whereas such aid has been absolutely critical to reducing morbidity and mortality in the short term, questions remain about whether the provision of aid by international organizations creates dependencies in recipient countries that preclude or delay the adoption of policies that would create indigenous, long-term solutions to serious health challenges. In such settings, ethical questions arise about whether it is a greater priority to help people in immediate need or to create pressure for long-term, sustainable change.

Finally, the UN is fundamentally constrained by the political, economic, and strategic interests of its member states. Because the UN ultimately recognizes the sovereignty of also named female genital mutilation as a harmful traditional practice that undermines women's rights and women's health.

The 1995 Fourth World Conference on Women in Beijing also put forth a broad platform of women's health rights. Highlighting women's unequal access to basic health resources, the Platform of Action from this conference asserts a human right to health for women. It criticizes gender biases in national health policies and health systems and contends that decreases in public health spending disproportionately harm women. The Platform of Action also reaffirms the importance of women's sexual and reproductive health and repeats calls for attention to gender-based violence as a threat to women's health. Finally, the platform draws attention to discrimination against girls—including son preference, access to nutrition, and access to health services—as a practice that undermines the health of girl children.[c] It also echoes the calls in previous UN reports for attention to gender-based violence, including such violence perpetrated during armed conflict, as a threat to women's health.

Most recently, the 2002 MDGs prioritize women's issues that are pertinent to health. Goal 5 calls for the improvement of maternal health, with the specific objective of reducing the maternal mortality ratio by three-quarters. To this end, the MDGs call for an increase in the proportion of births attended by skilled health personnel. Specific women's health issues addressed in the MDGs are not as broad as some of the global health initiatives coming out of UN-affiliated agencies in the 1990s. However, the MDGs also prioritize a number of health-related goals, including the eradication of extreme poverty and hunger and combating HIV/AIDs, malaria, and other diseases that create disproportionate health burdens for women.

To date, women's health initiatives within the UN system have focused on identifying women's health issues without seriously engaging with the gender constraints that shape women's health-seeking behavior and health outcomes. In order to address women's health in a comprehensive way, future global initiatives related to women's health will need to consider socially constructed gender roles, identities, and behaviors (and not just biological sex) as determinants of women's health.

---

[c]Paragraphs 89–93 of the *Platform of Action of the Fourth World Conference on Women* (1995).

its members, it seeks to promote cooperation among states in its global health promotion endeavors. Rather than attempting to compel states to implement specific public health programs or seeking to enforce a human right to health, the UN works within the state system to generate and share public health funding, global norms, and technical knowledge.

Also of note, UN agencies involved in the promotion of global health typically have relatively small budgets financed by voluntary contributions from states. In this regard, state cooperation with the UN is essential, and the UN is unlikely to push programs that deviate significantly from state preferences, especially those of powerful and wealthy states.

Conclusion

This chapter demonstrated that there is both promise and peril in top-down efforts to promote global health. The promise of working through international organizations on health promotion involves the global reach and legitimacy of these institutions. This advantage holds especially for the UN system. As an international organization with near-universal membership, the UN is in a better position than any other organization to lead initiatives that are truly global in scope. UN organs have been at the forefront of the development of health-related global norms and programs and are legally and politically positioned to collaborate with states in raising awareness about global health challenges, raising funds for health-related development assistance, and for coordinating the activities of other international organizations, states, and NGOs on global health initiatives. The cooperative, as opposed to coercive, nature of UN engagement with states on global health initiatives helps ensure meaningful collaboration. Because states are such dominant actors in the international system, any successful global health initiative will require meaningful collaboration with and effective contributions from national governments. The successful global campaign to eradicate smallpox demonstrates the great potential of international health initiatives based on effective collaboration between international organizations and states.

However, there are also perils inherent in top-down efforts at global health promotion. Like UN activities in other issue areas, UN organs and agencies involved in global efforts to promote public health have generally limited functions and powers. In general, UN global health promotion efforts are centered on several activities: norm creation and dissemination, advocacy, consensus-building, technical assistance, and coordination of global activities in public health promotion (which can include contributions from states and NGOs as well

as other international organizations). Notably, UN programs related to the promotion of global health involve voluntary participation by states and require state consent. As a result, the extent to which UN-led global health initiatives succeed or fail depends very much on the political will of UN member states. Whereas idealist theorists of international relations often promote a vision of the UN as an institution that transcends state interests, ultimately the UN is a political body that must consider the political, economic, and strategic interests of the diverse states that make up its membership. For better or worse, this reality fundamentally shapes any effort to promote global health through international organizations.

Discussion Questions

1. What are the advantages of working through international organizations to promote global health?
2. What obstacles do international organizations face in their efforts to promote global health?
3. Do the benefits of working through international organizations like the UN outweigh the costs of doing so? Why or why not?
4. What factors contributed to the success of the global campaign to eradicate smallpox?
5. What are some of the characteristics that distinguish successful global health initiatives from unsuccessful ones? What can the UN and other international organizations do to increase the likelihood that their efforts to promote global health will be successful?
6. Are global norms like the MDGs effective tools for promoting global health? Why or why not?
7. What are some of the major challenges that the UN and other international organizations face in their efforts to promote global health? How can the

international community address these challenges?

8. Why must international organizations like the UN cooperate with states in their efforts to promote global health? On balance, is this cooperative model beneficial or detrimental to international efforts to promote global health?

Web Resources

African Development Bank: http://www.afdb.org/

Asian Development Bank: http://www.adb.org/

Constitution of the World Health Organization: http://www.who.int/governance/eb/constitution/en/index.html

European Centre for Disease Prevention and Control (ECDC): http://www.ecdc.europa.eu/en/

Inter-American Development Bank: http://www.iadb.org/

Joint United Nations Programme on HIV/AIDS (UNAIDS): http://www.unaids.org/en/

Millennium Development Goals: http://www.un.org/millenniumgoals/

Pan-American Health Organization (also serves as the WHO's Regional Office for the Americas): http://new.paho.org/hq/

Report of the Fourth World Conference on Women: http://www.un.org/womenwatch/daw/beijing/pdf/Beijing%20full%20report%20E.pdf

Report of the International Conference on Population and Development: http://www.un.org/popin/icpd/conference/offeng/poa.html

United Nations Centre for Regional Development: http://www.uncrd.or.jp/

United Nations Children's Fund (UNICEF): http://www.unicef.org/

United Nations Development Fund for Women (UNIFEM): http://www.unwomen.org/

United Nations Development Programme (UNDP): http://www.undp.org/

United Nations High Commissioner for Refugees (UNHCR): http://www.unhcr.org/

United Nations Population Fund (UNFPA): http://www.unfpa.org/

United Nations World Food Programme (WFP): http://www.wfp.org/

The World Bank: http://www.worldbank.org/

World Health Organization (WHO): http://www.who.int/en/

WHO Regional Office for Africa: http://www.afro.who.int/

WHO Regional Office for Europe: http://www.euro.who.int/

WHO Regional Office for South-East Asia: http://www.searo.who.int/

WHO Regional Office for the Americas: http://www.paho.org/

WHO Regional Office for the Eastern Mediterranean: http://www.emro.who.int/index.asp

WHO Regional Office for the Western Pacific Region: http://www.wpro.who.int/

CHAPTER 10

Promoting Global Health from the Top Down: States

Introduction

Given their predominance in the international system, states play a critical role in shaping health outcomes across the globe. As large political entities that encounter countervailing political pressures and encompass a wide variety of competing social interests, states face significant obstacles in efforts to promote health. Moreover, the diversity among states in terms of political systems, economic resources, social structures, and culture leads to different approaches to health promotion in different countries. In an effort to explore these differences, this chapter compares and contrasts competing national approaches to promoting health as well as health outcomes under these diverse systems, specifically those in Rwanda, South Africa, Cuba, South Korea, the United Kingdom, and the United States.

States and the Promotion of Global Health

States play a critical role in shaping health outcomes for the populations living within their borders. States shape population health outcomes in multiple ways: (1) through the adoption of policies that determine the type of national health system that will prevail in a country, (2) through policies that influence the level and quality of a country's public health infrastructure, (3) through targeted programs

intended to address specific health challenges, (4) through monitoring and surveillance activities, and (5) through aid to other countries that affects population health outcomes internationally as well as domestically.

One of the primary ways in which states influence population health outcomes is by shaping the nature of **national health systems**. The World Health Organization (WHO) defines a health system to include "all activities whose primary purpose is to promote, restore, or maintain health."[1] Such activities include, but are obviously not limited to, the delivery of formal health services, administration of both prescription and nonprescription medication, the practices of traditional healers, and home care of the sick. As this broad definition indicates, the actions of both states and non-state actors determine the nature of a particular health system, and the relative influence of governments versus private actors varies across countries. In addition to the provision of health care and medicine, a national health system includes public health promotion and disease prevention measures, health-related education endeavors, and other interventions. For example, regulatory policies that affect health-seeking behaviors within a population or that create health-enhancing effects in homes, workplaces, and public spaces constitute part of a national health system under this definition. Policies to diminish environmental hazards, reduce workplace injuries, improve road safety, and decrease smoking among a population fall under the health system umbrella.[2]

States also influence health outcomes by providing (or failing to provide) public infrastructure that contributes to population health. Governments adopt many policies that affect the economic, political, and social determinants of health. For example, education policy and redistributive economic policies that affect personal or household income can have important health effects, even when health is not the primary objective addressed by these policies. Additionally, policies directed toward the provision of public goods, like roads, clean air, and clean water, contribute in significant ways to the health and well-being of a country's population.

In addition to shaping the nature of health systems and providing public infrastructure, states may adopt targeted programs intended to mitigate specific health challenges. Numerous examples of successful national programs to address significant health challenges exist. For instance, national immunization campaigns against measles in several countries in southern Africa, including Botswana, Lesotho, Malawi, Namibia, South Africa, and Zimbabwe, led to the virtual elimination of measles from the region and substantially reduced the number of deaths resulting from this major cause of child mortality. National governments in these countries played a primary role in creating, funding, and implementing these campaigns.[3] Notably, national governments often collaborate with international organizations and non-governmental organizations (NGOs) to tackle particular health problems. The successful global campaign to eradicate smallpox, discussed in detail in Chapter 9, is a prominent case in point.

States can play a critical monitoring and surveillance role directed toward preventing or controlling levels of both communicable and noncommunicable illnesses. National governments typically have agencies responsible for surveying the incidence of disease and monitoring disease outbreaks for the purpose of preventing major epidemics or pandemics of deadly illness. These monitoring bodies collaborate with other governmental agencies (for example, departments of public health in subnational units of governance or in local communities) as well as with actors throughout civil society, including schools, hospitals, and other public places where disease may spread, in an effort to prevent disease outbreak or to promote health practices intended to prevent illness. These bodies also collaborate with their counterparts in other countries as well as with international organizations and NGOs involved in disease control and prevention endeavors.

The U.S. Centers for Disease Control and Prevention (CDC) is a widely known example of a monitoring and surveillance body that has played an important role in preventing the spread of illness in the United States and abroad. For example, the CDC monitors developments in the prevailing strains of influenza each year as well as the prevalence and mortality associated with the disease. It also communicates and collaborates with monitoring and surveillance bodies in other countries in an effort to track the global spread of influenza. Given the potentially devastating effects of a new global flu pandemic, such monitoring activities are critical. The CDC also does epidemiological work in other countries. A prominent recent example is the CDC's involvement in a coordinated global response to the 2010 cholera outbreak in Haiti. The CDC collaborated with the U.S. Agency for International Development, the Haiti Ministry of Health, the Pan American Health Organization, the United Nations Children's Fund, and other state and non-state actors to contain the spread of this outbreak.[4]

Finally, states provide development and health aid to other countries in an effort to affect population health outcomes both at home and abroad. President Barack Obama's global health initiative is an illustrative example. In May 2009, President Obama put forth a far-reaching global health initiative that asked Congress to provide $63 billion for the provision of medicine and preventive care to millions of people in developing countries. President Obama's initiative targets, among other things, neglected "tropical diseases" such as hookworm infections and river blindness, which are a major cause of morbidity in the developing world.[5] In providing development and health aid, states may be motivated by a mix of principle and pragmatism. On the one hand, states may provide such aid because of a genuine commitment to humanitarian policies on the part of key actors within a government or because they are responding to public pressure from groups motivated by principled considerations. On the other hand, states are also motivated to respond to public health challenges in other countries out of self-interest due to the reality that one of the best ways to prevent the transnational spread of deadly illnesses is to address these illnesses in the zones of poverty where deadly infectious diseases often thrive. President Obama's rhetoric in support of his administration's global health initiative illustrates the influence of both principled and pragmatic objectives: "We cannot fix every problem. But we have a responsibility to protect the health of our people, while saving lives, reducing suffering, and supporting the health and dignity of people everywhere."[6]

Health Care Systems

This section focuses on those activities directly associated with the delivery of health care services. Specifically, it discusses basic concepts relating to the financing of health care, health care reimbursement, levels of health care delivery, and the organization of health care providers and institutions. The section also examines the role of governments in legislating policies that affect health care financing, reimbursement, and organization.

Financing Health Care

The overall structure of **health care financing**—the mix of methods by which health care services are funded and paid for by governments,

employers, and individuals—varies considerably from one country to the next. However, there are several basic methods of financing upon which these larger structures are built. The simplest method of payment is one that occurs out of pocket, whereby a provider delivers a service to an individual in exchange for cash or other goods or services. This method of payment is more common among individuals living in low-income countries,[7] though some individuals in more developed countries do not have health insurance coverage and must pay out of pocket for any services rendered. More commonly, reimbursement for health care services is made by health insurance plans, of which there are two major types—public plans and private plans.

Among private plans, there are both individual insurance plans and employer-based insurance plans. Individual plans are those that are directly purchased by an individual from a health insurance provider. Typically, an individual pays a monthly premium to the health insurer, which in turn reimburses health care providers for services rendered to the insured individual. Employer-based plans are those in which an employer pays a premium to purchase health insurance coverage for a group of employees. These premiums are benefits to employees that are not taxed by the government. As such, the government indirectly subsidizes these employee benefits. Further, employers often pay lower wages to employees to offset these health care premium expenditures. Such wage adjustments are likely to have greater adverse impact on lower-wage earners than on higher-wage earners. It is also important to understand that with many private insurance plans, individuals are often responsible for not only the monthly premium but also a deductible, which is the amount the insured individual must first pay out of pocket per a specified time period before the health insurer pays for services. Additionally, individuals may be responsible for co-payments, which are out-of-pocket payments that must be made by the individual at the time of service before the health insurer pays its portion. Co-payments, for example, are often required at the time of medication purchase, with the insured being responsible for a portion of the cost of the drug. Similar to wage reductions made by employers in response to the provision of employment-based insurance, these out-of-pocket payments are likely to have greater impact on lower-income employees than on higher-income employees. A final point worth noting as concerns private commercial insurers is that most are for-profit agencies, meaning that only a portion of collected premiums is actually spent on reimbursement for the delivery of health care services or administrative functions related to the processing of those payments.

In contrast to private insurance plans, public plans are not directly financed by individuals or employers but rather by the government through taxes. Such plans may be either public assistance models or social insurance models. In a public assistance plan, taxpayers who contribute to the financing may not be eligible for benefits. An example is the Medicaid system in

the United States, a plan that provides health insurance to qualified low-income populations. The majority of taxpayers who finance the system are too wealthy to qualify for benefits. In contrast, a social insurance plan requires an individual to make a specified level of contributions prior to becoming eligible for benefits. An example is the Medicare plan in the United States, in which individuals who have contributed payroll taxes during their years of employment become eligible for health insurance coverage upon reaching 65 years of age.[8] In some countries, a small group of individuals receive public health insurance benefits as part of their active enrollment in the military, with the U.S. Department of Veterans Affairs being an example.

Health Care Reimbursement

While the preceding discussion addressed the financing of health care, this section reviews **health care reimbursement**, the methods by

---

KEY TERMS RELATED TO HEALTH CARE FINANCING AND REIMBURSEMENT

Bundling Model of Reimbursement: a method of health care reimbursement in which physicians, medical groups, or hospitals are paid a prespecified amount for a group of services regardless of the number of medical visits, tests, or interventions involved with the provision of these services.

Capitation: a method of health care reimbursement in which a health insurer pays a health care provider a prespecified amount per time period (typically a month) for every insured individual for whom the physician agrees to provide care.

Fee-for-service Reimbursement: a method of health care reimbursement in which prespecified fees are charged to an individual or health care insurer for each service provided during a health care encounter.

Health Care Financing: the mix of methods by which health care services are funded and paid for by governments, employers, and individuals.

Health Care Reimbursement: the methods by which health care providers and institutions are reimbursed.

which health care providers and institutions are reimbursed. In the simplest method, physicians are paid on a **fee-for-service** basis, meaning that prespecified fees are charged to an individual or health care insurer for each service provided during a health care encounter. For example, a physician charges a fee for a health care visit as well as additional fees for any laboratory tests performed or immunizations administered during that visit. If one considers a health care encounter to involve financial risk to one of the involved parties, a fee-for-service method of reimbursement poses risk to the patient or health care insurer. Additionally, health care providers have financial incentives to provide a larger number of services under fee-for-service payment schemes, a situation that serves to inflate health care costs.

Alternatively, a **bundling model** may be used to finance health care. Under this model, reimbursement is made for services that have been bundled. For example, a physician might be paid a prespecified amount for all services rendered in association with a specific surgical procedure, including the surgery itself as well as any required follow-up visits. Similarly, a hospital might be paid only a prespecified amount for any services delivered for a single hospitalization. For instance, hospitals in the United States are reimbursed by health insurers based on units referred to as diagnosis-related groups (DRGs). The amount paid varies based on the complexity of the condition or conditions for which the patient is admitted. The hospital is reimbursed the same amount regardless of the number of hospital admission days or types of testing or interventions performed during the admission. Obviously, such reimbursement arrangements shift financial risk from the patient and insurer to the health care providers. As a result, this method of payment discourages physicians from ordering unnecessary diagnostic evaluations and therapeutic interventions. Conversely, it might lead to increasing demand for services by patients who are not responsible for costs beyond insurance premiums, direct service co-payments, and deductibles, regardless of the number of services delivered at one

visit. Additionally, this payment model may also result in providers ordering fewer tests and interventions that could potentially be beneficial to patients.

The most extreme form of bundling of services is **capitation**. Capitation is a reimbursement arrangement between a health insurer and a health care provider in which the provider is paid by the insurer a prespecified amount per time period (typically a month) for every insured individual for whom the physician agrees to provide care. Again, the provider assumes the greater financial risk, as payments from the insurer do not increase above the prespecified amount regardless of how many patients are seen or services are rendered during that time period. Under this model, providers are again discouraged from providing unnecessary services but may also perform fewer tests or interventions that might benefit patients.

Levels of Health Care

Health care systems can be divided into multiple levels of care. **Primary care** encompasses the management of common chronic medical conditions such as hypertension, diabetes mellitus, and hypercholesterolemia; the treatment of mild acute illnesses and minor injuries; and the delivery of preventive care such as immunizations and routine cancer screening like mammography and Papanicolaou (pap) smears. This level of care is relatively low cost and typically delivered in the outpatient setting by general practitioners such as family physicians, internists, and pediatricians. **Secondary care** refers to the management of more complicated medical conditions, such as chronic obstructive lung disease (emphysema) or chronic kidney disease, or more severe acute illnesses (for example, congestive heart failure or acute kidney failure, conditions that are often managed by physicians with subspecialty training such as cardiologists and nephrologists). Depending on the specific illness, these conditions can be managed in either the outpatient or inpatient setting and are generally more costly than primary care interventions. **Tertiary care** is highly

TYPES AND LEVELS OF HEALTH CARE DELIVERY

Complementary and Alternative Medicine: a term used by medical professionals to describe traditional medical practices that are applied outside their indigenous settings.

National Health System: all activities, including health care policy, formal health services, the administration of prescription and nonprescription medications, public health promotion, preventive measures, the practices of traditional healers, and home care of the sick, whose purpose is to promote, restore, or maintain health.

Primary Care: a generally low-cost level of care that focuses on common chronic medical conditions and preventive care and that is typically delivered in the outpatient setting by general practitioners such as family physicians, internists, and pediatricians.

Secondary Care: a generally more costly level of health care that involves the management of more complicated conditions and that is typically provided by specialists in either inpatient or outpatient settings.

Tertiary Care: highly specialized, typically costly care most often delivered by subspecialty-trained physicians at regional academic medical centers for severe medical illnesses or uncommon medical conditions.

Traditional Medicine: health care informed by the beliefs, theories, and experiences of particular cultures and societies.

---

specialized, typically costly care most often delivered by subspecialty-trained physicians at regional academic medical centers for severe medical illnesses or uncommon medical conditions. The relative contribution of each of these levels of care within a health care system varies considerably from one country to another.

Though not generally considered a formal part of health care systems in most countries, other categories of health care used by a large number of individuals in certain regions are worth mentioning. **Traditional medicine** is defined by the WHO as "the sum total knowledge, skills, and practices based on the theories, beliefs, and experiences indigenous to different cultures that are used to maintain health, as well as to prevent, diagnose, improve or treat physical and mental illnesses."[9] Specific examples include acupuncture, massage therapy, faith healers, and the use of herbal supplements.

Compared with other levels of health care services, traditional medicine tends not to be as rigorously studied in a scientific manner and is, thus, much less rooted in evidence than other levels of care. In part due to inadequate education about the limitations of traditional medicine practice as well as lack of access to more evidence-based health care services, traditional medicine is the primary type of health care for as much as 80 percent of the population in some regions of Asia and Africa. When practiced outside indigenous cultures, such interventions are referred to as **complementary and alternative medicine** (CAM). Use of CAM is increasing in many developed countries, with 70–80 percent of the population in some regions estimated to use some form of CAM. In fact, the herbal supplement industry is now a largely unregulated, multi-billion-dollar industry in many developed countries.[10]

Organization of Health Care Providers and Institutions

Though a detailed discussion of the multitude of ways in which health care providers and institutions can be organized is beyond the scope of this text, a brief introduction to several basic concepts allows for a better understanding of comparative national health systems. At the level of individual health care providers, physicians can work as solo practitioners or, much more commonly, as part of either a small, single-specialty practice or a larger, multispecialty group practice. For example, clinicians may organize as a group of several general practitioners who share office space as well as medical and administrative staff. Alternatively, some practices organize as multispecialty groups in which generalists as well as multiple subspecialty-trained physicians organize to provide coordinated primary and secondary care for patients. These single- or multispecialty groups may be private entities or may be owned and operated by larger hospital corporations or even governments. Individual physicians in such practices may be salaried employees or may be partners in the practice, both liable for debts and entitled to profits of the practice. As an additional complexity, physicians and physician groups may see patients in the outpatient setting, in the inpatient setting, or in both. Those physicians who provide both outpatient and inpatient services may align with only one hospital for the care of their hospitalized patients or may provide inpatient care in multiple hospital settings. Similar to physician groups, independent hospitals and hospital groups may be operated as private entities, which may be either for-profit or not-for-profit, or public entities. Also like physician groups, hospitals may be organized as independent institutions, or they may form business alliances in which resources are pooled and administrative and operating costs are shared.

In some countries, health care systems are highly integrated and well organized, with primary care being delivered by generalists who practice only in the outpatient setting and refer to subspecialists who then provide secondary care or tertiary care as necessary upon referral by the generalists. Often, these same countries organize care regionally and integrate care services in a manner that limits redundancy and thus reduces administrative and operating costs. One key component of the effective coordination of care is the existence of a patient medical record system that is available across a spectrum of patient care sites. Ideally, this record would be in an electronic form that allows sharing of individual patient information from one health care setting to another. Conversely, other countries have more fragmented care in which patients may be evaluated by subspecialists without referral from a primary care physician and may receive care in more than one hospital. Further, competition by non-integrated physician groups and hospitals for patients often leads to redundancy in operating and administrative costs. Lack of integration can also lead to inadequate exchange of patient medical information and, thus, often excessive delivery of diagnostic and therapeutic services. These factors together can serve to unnecessarily inflate health care expenditures.

Role of Governments in the Development of National Health Care Systems

As discussed throughout this section, there is considerable variability among countries in the financial and organizational components of health care systems. This variability is due in large part to differences among countries in health care legislation. In some countries, policies mandate a system of financing that is largely public in nature while simultaneously restricting all but a small contribution of private financing. In other countries, the absence of such strict policies leads to a less integrated, more competitive market consisting of largely private funding. Health care policies also largely determine the structure of provider and institutional reimbursement and may even dictate the relative proportion of generalist and subspecialist providers that make up the national workforce. The result is that a country's degree of spending for health care services is largely determined by the legislative policies of its government and the health care system such policies yield. As has been suggested, provider reimbursement schemes can lead to inflation of health care spending driven by either patients or providers, depending on the prevailing market method. The methods that predominate are, in turn, largely set either directly or indirectly by governments. Additionally, secondary and tertiary care delivered by subspecialists tends to be more costly than the primary care services of a generalist. National policies that emphasize primary and preventive care and foster the development of a health care system that is bottom-heavy in generalists rather than top-heavy in subspecialists might serve to contain health care spending. This outcome is even more likely in countries where care is coordinated between generalists and specialists as well as the outpatient and inpatient settings on a regional basis.

Governmental agencies are also largely responsible for the oversight of the pharmaceutical and health care technology industries operating within countries. These agencies are primarily responsible for ensuring patient safety as concerns the research and development and ultimately the clinical utilization of pharmaceuticals and medical devices. However, governments can also influence national spending on pharmaceuticals by taking an active role in negotiating prices and regulating profits, along with placing regulations on pharmaceutical marketing strategies that inflate costs. Governmental policy can also influence end-of-life care issues such as the delivery of high-cost, often futile medical interventions. It has been shown that such end-of-life care often consumes as much as 10 percent of total health care budgets in many countries.[11] Legislation also directly shapes end-of-life care such as the practice of physician-assisted suicide. Lastly, legislation can impact physician and institutional exposure to risk from medical malpractice suits. Although policies governing medical malpractice are of great importance to individual patients, providers, and institutions when dealing with such claims, their overall effects on health care expenditures at the population level are variable and likely to contribute little to overall health care expenditures.[12]

Comparing National Approaches to Health and Health Care

This section compares national health systems in six countries to demonstrate the ways in which different models of financing, reimbursing, providing, and organizing health systems influence population health outcomes. The comparative country cases in this section underscore that a unique set of historical circumstances, economic resources, political systems, social structures, and cultural influences shapes each national health system. The section begins with a case study of Rwanda, a low-income country. Then, we examine two middle-income countries, South Africa and Cuba, with distinctive national health systems that contribute to divergent population health outcomes. We conclude with case studies of three high-income countries, the Republic of Korea, the United Kingdom, and the United States, to illustrate the ways in which unique approaches to national health systems can lead to dramatically different population health outcomes despite similar levels of national wealth.

Rwanda

Rwanda is a low-income country[13] with a population of almost 11 million people. It faces the standard health challenges common to most developing countries. Approximately 37 percent of Rwandans live in extreme poverty that is concentrated in rural areas. The country has high rates of infant, child, and maternal mortality. HIV prevalence is 3 percent, and malaria is a major cause of morbidity.[14]

Since 1999, Rwanda has provided national health insurance through a community-based health insurance scheme called the Mutuelle de Santé. Ninety-two percent of the population is covered. Premiums for the health insurance plan cost $2 per year, and patients also pay a 10 percent fee for each treatment. Under this plan, an elected village committee has the authority to determine whether some individuals are too poor to pay, in which case the cost of coverage is subsidized by donor funds. Approximately 10 percent of the population has had health care fees waived under this community-based health insurance model, but critics have suggested that an additional 5–20 percent of the population cannot afford the minimal health care premiums or fees.[15]

The Rwandan government spends approximately $12–$14 per person on health care each year. Government expenditures cover approximately one-third of health care spending, and the remaining two-thirds is provided through international donors and direct payments by patients.[16] In 2000, the Rwandan government put a health model into place under which each district was responsible for providing care to roughly 20,000 people. The health care available under Rwanda's national plan is fundamental and basic. It covers treatment for those illnesses that contribute most significantly to mortality in Rwanda: diarrhea, pneumonia, malaria, and malnutrition. The national health system helps ensure that local clinics have WHO essential medicines in stock as well as laboratories capable of conducting routine tests and screenings.

Rwanda would not be able to fund even its small-scale national health care system without external funding. NGOs such as Partners in Health play a critical role in bringing funding, medical personnel, and necessary medications into the country. Indeed, over 50 percent of the funding for Rwanda's national health care system comes from foreign aid; the United States is the largest governmental donor, and the Global Fund to Fight AIDS, Tuberculosis, and Malaria has provided significant funding. The Rwandan government has sought to maximize the efficiencies of international donations by integrating and coordinating donor funds within a single fiscal framework.[17]

The health system in Rwanda faces additional challenges as well. An insufficient number of trained health care professionals are available to provide health care. Whereas the WHO suggests a minimum of ten doctors per 100,000 people to run an effective health system, a majority of health districts in Rwanda have only two doctors per 100,000 people.[18] One of the challenges in health care staffing is that many personnel leave positions in the health care system to work in higher-paying jobs for international NGOs and donor agencies,[19] a sign that these international actors can undercut their efforts to promote health in developing countries. Moreover, Rwandans living in poverty may resist paying even the minimal premium of $2 and may not be able to afford the small co-pays that are required for procedures.[20] Notably, premiums are the same regardless of income status, and, as a result, the system puts a disproportionate burden on Rwanda's poor, the people who can least afford to spend money on their health.[21] These factors lead many Rwandans to rely on traditional medicine rather than the national health system.[22] Furthermore, Rwanda is unable to fund high-end tests and treatments, such as cancer screenings, that are considered routine in developed countries. The health system is not well positioned to deal with the diseases of globalization—heart disease, cancer, and obesity—that are likely to constitute a higher proportion of the burden of disease as the country develops, and few medical specialists are present in the country.[23]

Despite ongoing challenges related to high rates of poverty and economic underdevelopment, Rwanda has made significant strides in health outcomes. It now has the highest levels of immunization coverage in Africa and has realized significant declines in infant, child, and maternal mortality. Data also indicate that HIV prevalence rates are declining.[24] Since Rwanda instituted national health coverage, its average life expectancy has increased from

48 to 52 years, a notable increase given that the country still suffers from a high prevalence of HIV/AIDS.[25] In sum, Rwanda has been able to effectively address some of the most pressing health concerns of its population, an impressive accomplishment in a low-income country still recovering from the 1994 genocide and ongoing civil conflict. However, Rwanda's performance on core health indices is still much lower than the aggregate performance of most high- and middle-income countries.

South Africa

South Africa is an upper-middle-income country[26] with a population of just over 49 million people. Owing in large part to the country's history of apartheid, the health system in South Africa historically has been a fragmented one. The South African health system has both public and private health care sectors, and each sector operates independently in terms of the financing as well as the organization of services, including distinct facilities and a separate provider workforce. As far back as 1889, the private sector has been financed through health insurance organizations known as medical schemes, which are voluntary employment-based social insurance programs funded through employee and employer tax contributions.[27] There has been considerable growth of the private sector in the subsequent 120 years such that there are currently 125 medical schemes, leading to redundancy in operating and administrative costs.[28] Because enrollment is voluntary, many employees, particularly those in the lower earnings category, opt out of these employment-based plans and either pay out of pocket for services or receive care through the public sector depending on level of income.

In contrast to the growth of private-sector financing, the public sector was largely neglected until the end of apartheid in the 1990s. In 1994, the African National Congress (ANC) put forth a health plan intended to extend coverage and improve the financing and organization of the public sector. The public sector is now financed predominantly by taxes and external grant support, with equitable distribution to each of the nine provincial health departments.[29] Approximately 15 percent of the population of South Africa is insured through a medical scheme, with an additional 21 percent of individuals paying out of pocket for services delivered in the private sector; the remaining 64 percent of the population receives health care in the public sector.[30]

In terms of reimbursement, providers and for-profit hospitals in the private sector are paid on a fee-for-service basis. Beginning with the aforementioned 1994 ANC health plan, free care for children under the age of six years and pregnant women became available at the levels of primary health care and district hospitals. At that same time, user fees were removed at the primary care level for all individuals not in medical schemes.[31] User fees are also waived for higher levels of care including tertiary care at public hospitals for the disabled and the indigent. Reimbursement of public-sector providers occurs in the form of salaries and additional allowances paid for by the government.[32] Proportionate health care expenditures are heavily weighted in favor of the private sector. Although individuals evaluated and treated in the private sector make up only 15 percent of the population, approximately 55–60 percent of all national health care expenditures are diverted to providing private-sector care.[33]

Just as the financing of health care has been fragmented, the organization of services in South Africa has been poorly coordinated, particularly in the public sector. In response to this ineffective coordination at the national level, the ANC has included efforts to decentralize health care coordination and allow for greater autonomy at the provincial level in its approach to health care. These efforts have included the construction and upgrade of more than 1,000 new primary care sites and the development of an essential drug program. However, stewardship at the provincial level has been lacking, and many operational decisions remain centralized. Additionally, maintaining a sufficient provider workforce in the public sector has been quite challenging due to the potential for higher earnings and a better work environment in the private sector. One study estimates that 75 percent of specialists, 50–70 percent of generalists, and 40 percent of nursing staff are employed in the private sector, particularly in urban areas.[34] In an effort to address such provider shortages, the ANC has implemented a community service program that mandates that newly graduated health professionals serve a two-year period in the public sector.[35] Nevertheless, ongoing provider shortages limit access to care for the poor, in part due to excessively long wait times.

Because of such shortages, particularly in more rural areas, patients often need to travel great distances to receive care, another factor that limits health care access for the poor. Even those who travel long distances to be seen in public hospitals may be denied care. Recent surveys reveal that only half of those who visited a public hospital obtained a fee exemption despite being eligible for one.[36] Because poor individuals in South Africa are also more vulnerable to experiencing disease burden associated with the growing HIV and tuberculosis epidemics, such limited access has significant ramifications for public health and national economic growth. Limited access to care also contributes in part to the continued reliance of many members of the population on traditional health practitioners and spiritual faith healers for care, with surveys suggesting that as much as 39 percent of the population employs the services of such providers. In an effort to standardize such practices and protect the interests of individuals who use these services, the ANC recently passed the South African Traditional Health Practitioners Act. Although the intention is not to incorporate such practices into the mainstream health care system, the goal is to foster cooperation where appropriate.[37]

Cuba

Cuba is an upper-middle-income country[38] with a population of over 11 million people. Cuba has a nationalized health system, and the government both finances and administers health care. The health care budget comes almost entirely from state resources, and national government exerts centralized control over many facets of the health system. As an example, the government facilitates national networks in health communications, technology, and research. At the same time, aspects of the Cuban health system are decentralized. For example, over 90 percent of health care expenditures comes from municipal budgets.[39] Moreover, primary care is provided at regional and provincial facilities in an effort to expand access to care among Cubans living outside city centers. Tertiary care is more likely to be provided at larger hospitals in urban centers.[40] In short, the Cuban national government maintains control over financing and setting policy priorities for health care, but care is administered through clinics and hospitals at the municipal and regional levels.

Since 1976, the Cuban Constitution has affirmed a right to health protection and care and has called for the fulfillment of this right through the provision of free medical and hospital care. Under the Cuban health system, citizens have free access to routine medical examinations, dental care, vaccinations, medicines, and other basic preventive and curative care.[41] Some other health care services and procedures are paid for at subsidized prices by patients who can afford to pay, whereas these services and procedures are free for low-income individuals. Inefficiencies and limited resources in the Cuban system also lead many patients to turn to traditional medicine, and the government has formally incorporated traditional medicine practices and treatments, including acupuncture and herbal remedies, into the national health care system.[42]

Two historic moments have fundamentally shaped the Cuban health system: the Cuban Revolution in 1959 and the collapse of the Soviet Union in 1991. Prior to the Cuban Revolution, the Cuban health system relied on both the public and private sectors. The private health sector in prerevolutionary Cuba comprised many actors, including private hospitals, private pharmaceutical companies, and mutual aid societies, which involved prepaid health plans that provided comprehensive medical coverage to members.[43] Under this prerevolutionary system, Cuba had comparatively positive health outcomes and performed well on major health indices, including life expectancy, infant mortality, and maternal health conditions. Health outcomes in Cuba were generally better than in other Latin American countries.[44] However, the system was characterized by significant inequities and had worse outcomes among low-income and rural populations.

By 1961, the new government had nationalized the health care system, including voluntary mutual aid societies, private hospitals, and other private substate actors. Initially, health outcomes worsened under the new system partly due to the trade embargo imposed by the United States in reaction to the communist revolution and also as a result of the outmigration of a significant portion of the country's medical professionals. Over time, the patient–doctor ratio improved, and health outcomes under the national system again returned to high levels. Indeed, Cuba's performance on core health indicators, including life expectancy, infant mortality, and maternal health, improved steadily and eventually exceeded prerevolutionary performance on key health indicators. Furthermore, Cuba did not lag far behind the United States in health outcomes for much of the 1970s and 1980s.[45]

The Cuban health system faced a fundamental setback at the end of the Cold War. Between the Cuban revolution in 1960 and the collapse of the Soviet Union in 1991, the Cuban government relied heavily on Soviet subsidies to fund its health care system. The disintegration of the Soviet Union meant that these subsidies dried up. In the 1990s, the United States tightened its trade embargo on the country in both the 1992 Cuban Democracy Act (which prohibited all subsidiary trade, including food but with ostensible exemptions for medicine) and the 1996 Helms-Burton Act (which undermined the previous exemptions on medicines). Due to this combination of factors, health outcomes in Cuba worsened considerably.[46] The country was hit by famine in the early 1990s,

and the prevalence of poverty-related infectious diseases, including tuberculosis and hepatitis, increased during this period. Subsequently, the United States loosened its embargo and is now a major source of imported food as well as humanitarian assistance. Since the mid-1990s, health indicators in Cuba have been improving, and Cuba continues to perform nearly as well as the United States on many indicators. In general, Cuba's health system produces health outcomes on par with many high-income developed countries, and, in fact, Cuba has a higher doctor to patient ratio than many high-income countries.[47]

Another important feature of the Cuban health system is a significant black market in health care. Due to inefficiencies in the state-controlled system and a limited supply of critical medicines, supplies, and services, underground trade in health care has emerged. Additionally, corruption is a feature of the system, with doctors taking unauthorized payments in return for quicker or higher-quality health services. This black market in health care undermines the equity-oriented goals that undergird the nationalized health system in the country and result in access to high-quality care and specialized treatment going to the highest bidder.[48] In a similar vein, medical tourism has become a major source of foreign currency, and critics charge that foreign tourists are able to buy access to quality health care in Cuba that is not available to Cuban nationals, again undermining the core goal of equity in the Cuban health system. In fact, critics charge that a two-tiered system is emerging, with high-quality treatment and access to the best medical institutions available for foreign medical tourists and Cubans who can pay, and lower-quality care at substandard facilities for many Cubans, especially the poor.[49]

Although it produces comparatively good health outcomes at the population level, the state-controlled health system also generates problematic practices. In particular, the Cuban health system is criticized for undermining civil and political rights even as it prioritizes a right to health. The Cuban Ministry of Health sets target outcome quotas that are supposed to guide treatment. For example, the ministry has target quotas for infant mortality. If quotas on infant mortality are close to being met or exceeded, physicians may feel pressure to recommend abortion, even against a patient's wishes, if a screening suggests a pregnancy may have a high probability of a bad outcome. In general, patients do not have a right to refuse treatment.[50] Cuba's practice of quarantining patients with HIV/AIDS also has come under critical scrutiny.[51] These examples indicate that the right to health in Cuba is conceptualized largely as a collective right that emphasizes aggregate population health outcomes rather than as an individual right that takes patient concerns and preferences into account.

The Republic of Korea (South Korea)

The Republic of Korea is a high-income country[52] of just fewer than 49 million people. In its current format, the South Korean health care system ensures universal health coverage for a restricted number of health care services and relies on a combination of public and private financing to purchase these basic services. Additional health care services may be purchased on an individual basis through out-of-pocket payments, either directly or in the form of supplemental private insurance. In terms of health care providers, the majority of both clinicians and hospitals are in the private sector.

In 1977, the National Assembly of South Korea passed health care legislation creating the first of many compulsory social insurance programs. This legislation mandated that employees of corporations with more than 500 employees contribute toward social health insurance. Subsequent legislation over the ensuing decade led to inclusion of smaller corporations and ultimately the self-employed such that universal coverage was achieved by 1989.[53] For people employed by corporations, mandatory premium payments, determined at a fixed percentage rate of income, are split evenly between employee and employer. For the self-employed, mandatory premium rates are determined by a formula that takes into account income, motor vehicle ownership,

age, and gender.[54] Family-based membership is also provided for by this legislation. To ensure coverage for low-income populations, the government, in 1977, also created a Medical Aid program, a public assistance insurance plan financed by general revenue of the central and local governments.[55] According to 2008 data, 62.5 percent of the population was enrolled in employer-based social insurance schemes, 34.2 percent was enrolled in self-employed social insurance schemes, and 3.3 percent was covered by the Medical Aid program.[56] Though this mandatory social insurance and public assistance arrangement ensured universal coverage, there initially was considerable redundancy in administrative costs owing to the numerous insurance schemes that existed from which to purchase services. In 2000, the National Assembly passed legislation that consolidated these schemes in creating the National Health Insurance (NHI), a public nonprofit organization that purchases insured services for the entire population, including those covered by the Medical Aid program. Data reveal that administrative costs declined by more than 50 percent in the subsequent six years after enactment of this legislation.[57]

In order to both provide universal health coverage and control national health care spending, the government restricts the package of services covered by the NHI. These services are mainly restricted to curative services, biannual check-ups, and vaccination services. Additionally, individuals are required to make co-payments at the point of care. These co-payments account for 20 percent of inpatient and 35–50 percent of outpatient service costs.[58] Additionally, patients must pay for all provided services that are not covered by the NHI. Given the cost risk of these uncovered services, many individuals elect to purchase supplemental private insurance plans. In fact, nearly three-quarters of the population had supplemental private insurance in 2008.[59] Most recent estimates based on 2008 data reveal that the sources of national health care financing were the following: 38.6 percent from the NHI, 16.9 percent from government sources in the form of subsidies for self-employed premiums and the Medical Aid program, 21 percent in the form of out-of-pocket payments for uncovered services, 13.7 percent in the form of co-payments for covered services, 4.4 percent from private insurance, and an additional 4.6 percent from voluntary payments by firms.[60]

All services provided by practitioners and hospitals, both those covered and those not covered by the NHI, are reimbursed on a fee-for-service basis. For covered services, the NHI controls the setting and annual revision of these negotiated fees. This practice serves to control governmental spending on health care. However, it incentivizes practitioners and hospitals to increase fees for uncovered services, services for which the government does not regulate pricing. In essence, there is a shifting of costs from the government to the individual for the receipt of services not included in the benefits package. Such cost-shifting and uncovered service fee escalation increase the risk for disparities in care, with lower-income individuals being less able to afford comprehensive care. Hospitals also have incentives to increase service intensity because of these reimbursement structures, with South Korea having comparatively lengthy hospitalizations per episode of illness. Pilot programs introducing DRG reimbursement methods have been shown to reduce length of stay, antibiotic use, average number of tests, and overall costs without compromising quality of care.[61] However, there has been considerable resistance on the part of providers to accept such forms of capitation.[62]

Health care providers and hospitals in South Korea are largely private institutions, with only 10 percent of health care being delivered in the public sector. Private and public facilities provide many of the same services, though only the private hospitals provide services not covered by the NHI. They also typically charge higher fees than those of the public institutions. Considerable competition exists among private facilities.[63] Overall coordination of care in the South Korean health care system is relatively poor, with no requirement for referral by a generalist to a specialist for care, thereby limiting the role of primary care.[64] Additionally,

there tend to be geographic disparities in provider density, with a relative shortage in rural regions.[65]

Coordination of care is further complicated by the fact that many people in South Korea seek the care of practitioners of traditional Korean medicine (TKM). TKM is a discipline of Asian medicine that encompasses many therapies, including various acupuncture methods, moxibustion, and other herbal remedies. Recent data suggest that 7.6 percent of total medical insurance costs are directed toward TKM services. TKM doctors provide these services to patients in any one of more than 8,000 TKM hospitals and clinics throughout the country. TKM doctors are licensed only after completing six years of coursework at one of eleven TKM schools. The government provides formal oversight of TKM education and health care practices. Further, established in 1994, the Korea Institute of Oriental Medicine promotes standardization and quality control of practices as well as active research and support for policy.[66]

The United Kingdom

The United Kingdom is a high-income country[67] with a population of nearly 62 million people. The format of the existing health care system in the United Kingdom ensures universal health coverage through financing that is predominantly from public sources. A small component of financing occurs in the form of out-of-pocket payments on the part of health care consumers. Additionally, a limited number of individuals choose to purchase supplementary private insurance. In contrast to the system in the Republic of Korea, the government plays a significant role in cost-containment efforts intended to limit overall health care expenditures. Reimbursement to health care providers predominantly occurs through public mechanisms.

Similar to the Republic of Korea, the United Kingdom provides universal health coverage. The National Insurance Act of 1946 led to the creation of the National Health Service (NHS) in 1948. The NHS is a publicly funded, single-payer health system that provides universal health care to residents of the United Kingdom. According to 2004 data, the NHS accounts for an estimated 86.3 percent of total national health care expenditures. The remaining 13.7 percent is private expenditures in the form of out-of-pocket payments and premiums for supplemental health insurance coverage.[68] Funding for the NHS comes from several sources, including 76 percent from general taxes, 19 percent from national insurance contributions, and 5 percent from user charges.[69] National insurance contributions are employee contributions, typically matched by employers, made as a percentage of weekly earnings for individuals 16–65 years of age with an income above a prespecified threshold. Many state benefits, including basic state pensions, are paid for by national insurance contributions, though a portion is applied to NHS funding.[70]

Unlike the considerable cost-sharing model that exists with the NHI in the Republic of Korea, the vast majority of publicly covered services in the United Kingdom are free at the point of care. The minimal user charges that are incurred are for dental services, ophthalmic services, and co-payments for prescription drugs. Children, the elderly, pregnant women, and low-income individuals are typically exempt from such user charges. Unlike the system in the Republic of Korea, insurance is not linked to employment. Therefore, a separate insurance plan for the poor and unemployed is not necessary. Because of these factors, the system is likely to be more equitable than that in the Republic of Korea. Approximately 11.5 percent of the population elects to purchase supplemental private health insurance to receive some preferential benefits, such as greater choices of specialists and decreased waiting time for specialty care.[71]

Similar to the NHI in the Republic of Korea, the NHS works to control health care spending while simultaneously providing universal coverage. It does so, in part, by determining what services it should cover in response to recommendations made by national quality research organizations and agencies. The National Institute for Health and Clinical Excellence (NICE) is an independent organization established by the government in 1999 that examines in a transparent manner existing clinical outcomes and cost-effective analysis data on pharmaceuticals and treatments. It then makes recommendations as to whether a specific treatment or intervention should be included among the NHS-covered services in England and Wales, and if so, for what subpopulation of people. The Department of Health, Social Services, and Public Safety in Northern Ireland and the NHS Quality Improvement for Scotland and the Scottish Medicines Consortium perform similar roles for their respective regions. Although specific drugs or interventions may not be included, the NHS covers all levels of care, including primary and preventive services provided by a general practitioner, inpatient and outpatient secondary care provided by a specialist, inpatient and outpatient drugs, and mental health services and rehabilitation.

The method of provider and institutional reimbursement also serve to control total health care expenditures in the United Kingdom. Unlike the fee-for-service method of payment that predominates in the Republic of Korea, reimbursement in the United Kingdom relies largely on the bundling of services. General practitioners, though typically self-employed, have historically been reimbursed by local primary care trusts or partnerships based on a system of capitation for the list of patients on his or her panel.[72] More recently, an agreement allowing for additional annual income for general practitioners based on the delivery of high-quality care was negotiated.[73] Specialty physicians are typically members of hospital staff and receive salaries based on contracts negotiated with district health authorities and general practitioners, though they can receive reimbursement on a fee-for-service basis for care delivered through the small private sector. Hospitals, most of which are public facilities, also receive global health budgets that are based on contracts negotiated with district health authorities.[74] Such reimbursement schemes reduce incentives for the performance of unnecessary, expensive diagnostic and therapeutic interventions.

The organization of health care providers and institutions provides other mechanisms of cost containment. The delivery of care is managed at the regional level by a strategic health authority. All individuals are allowed to select a general practitioner in their designated practice area with whom they then enroll. The general practitioners not only provide primary care but also serve as "gatekeepers" to the receipt of more specialized care. Except in the case of emergencies, an individual can be evaluated and treated by a specialist only upon referral from a general practitioner.[75] Because hospitals are predominantly public institutions that are also organized in a regional manner, there tends to be considerably less redundancy of administrative costs and expensive advanced-technology medical equipment when compared with other health care systems, such as that of the United States.

The prevalence of the use of CAM in the United Kingdom has been estimated to be as high as 20 percent among the general population, with herbal therapy, homoeopathy, acupuncture, massage therapy, and reflexology being the most popular CAM modalities.[76] Additionally, there are an estimated 50,000 CAM practitioners in the United Kingdom and an additional 10,000 practitioners of traditional Western medicine who also practice some form of CAM.[77] Currently, chiropractic and osteopathy are two CAM professions subject to statutory regulation in the United Kingdom. In order to practice with either profession, an individual must register with the regulatory body for the General Chiropractic Council or the General Osteopathic Council. Proposals by the Department of Health in 2004 called for the statutory regulation of herbal medicine and acupuncture practitioners as well, though the formalization of these regulatory bodies is still pending. The expectation of the government is that other CAM professions will work toward voluntary self-regulation. Currently, it is at the discretion of primary care trusts and their contracted general practitioners to assess the suitability of CAM for patients under their care through the NHS.[78]

The United States of America

The United States of America is a high-income country[79] with a population of just over 307 million people. Its existing health care system is financed through a private and public payer mix with largely fragmented care delivered by providers and institutions that are reimbursed through both fee-for-service and capitation methods of payment. An exception among high-income countries, the United States does not mandate universal health insurance coverage. In an effort to extend coverage to all legal residents, the Obama administration pushed for the Patient Protection and Affordable Care Act, which Congress passed in March 2010. However, the shift in the balance of power in Congress that resulted from the 2010 midterm elections may impede the implementation of this legislation.

The financing of health care in the United States occurs through a mix of public and private sources. In 2004, general government expenditures on health as a percentage of total health care expenditures were 44.7 percent, with 55.3 percent of total health care expenditures accounted for by private sources.[80] In the United States, individuals may have both public and private insurance plans. For example, an elderly individual may receive coverage from both Medicare and a supplemental private insurance plan. Private plans may be employment-based or individually purchased plans. Unlike countries that rely on employment-based private insurance to help finance health care, such as the Republic of Korea, the United States does not mandate employers to offer such coverage. Rather, larger businesses typically offer these benefits to employees in order to compete with other employers for their services. In the U.S. system, hundreds of for-profit private insurance plans compete to provide these benefits, leading to considerable administrative costs.[81] These administrative costs include aggressive marketing strategies, expenditures that contribute to overall health care financing budgets but do not deliver a health care benefit to the insured.

UNDER THE MICROSCOPE

The Patient Protection and Affordable Care Act in the United States

With the support of a Congress controlled by the Democratic Party, President Barack Obama signed the Patient Protection and Affordable Care Act (PPACA) into law on March 23, 2010. To address the challenges of the large number of uninsured members of the U.S. population and escalating health care costs, the law contains several key provisions intended to expand coverage to all citizens while simultaneously controlling overall health care expenditures.

The law works to extend coverage to uninsured or underinsured individuals through several avenues. It expands Medicaid eligibility by lowering the household income threshold to 133 percent of the federal poverty level. Additionally, it seeks higher participation rates for individuals and families eligible for Medicaid and CHIP through state-level measures to improve enrollment outreach, the application process, and renewal procedures. The law also stipulates that parents are permitted to keep adult children on their health care plans until the age of 26 years, thereby providing coverage for a population that often is uninsured. The law further mandates that health insurance plans can neither impose lifetime limits on coverage nor exclude coverage or charge higher premiums to individuals with preexisting medical conditions—strategies that have historically limited access to care for these at-risk populations. Perhaps most controversially, the law includes mandates that all individuals not otherwise covered through a public insurance health plan purchase and maintain health insurance or pay a penalty. Individuals who do not qualify for Medicaid but whose household income is below 400 percent of the federal poverty level may apply for subsidies to assist with purchasing insurance; companies that employ 50 or more people but do not offer insurance to employees will be required to contribute if an employee requires such a subsidy from the government. Finally, the law targets potential areas of underinsurance, for example, providing more comprehensive prescription coverage and preventive service delivery to Medicare beneficiaries.

Governmental sources of financing include the Medicare program, Medicaid, military health care, and the Children's Health Insurance Program (CHIP). Created as part of the 1965 Social Security Act, Medicare is a social insurance program that provides health insurance coverage to people 65 years of age and older if they or their spouse have contributed to Medicare taxes through employment for a minimum of ten years. Individuals with specific disabilities, most notably end-stage kidney disease requiring dialysis treatment, are also covered under Medicare. Administered by the federal government, the program is funded through federal income taxes. Medicare covers various inpatient and outpatient services. Since 2006, it also has provided partial prescription drug coverage. For each level of Medicare coverage, out-of-pocket payments in the form of premiums and deductibles are required.[82] Thus, many individuals choose to purchase supplemental private insurance to cover these

The PPACA attempts to address rising health care expenditures through several vehicles. First, it establishes specific target growth rates for Medicare spending and calls for the creation of an Independent Payment Advisory Board responsible for ensuring that Medicare expenditures stay within the limits specified by the PPACA. The law also encourages the establishment of Accountable Care Organizations (ACOs). ACOs are affiliations of health care providers that are held jointly accountable for achieving improvements in the quality of care and reductions in spending. To qualify as an ACO, a group of health care providers must have the capacity to deliver the full continuum of care to at least 5,000 Medicare beneficiaries and to be held accountable for the costs and quality of their care. The law also encourages private insurers to contract with ACOs for their insured population. Participation is voluntary, with ACOs receiving bonuses if they meet expenditure savings goals and achieve quality measures in areas of patient experience, care coordination, patient safety, preventive health, and health of at-risk and frail elderly populations.[a] The PPACA also places increasing emphasis on the utilization of Comparative Effectiveness Research (CER). The Federal Coordinating Council for Comparative Effectiveness Research is responsible for allocating funding and coordinated CER across the federal government. CER allows for health care providers and patients to decide on the best and most cost-effective treatments while improving the performance of health care systems.[b]

The PPACA has experienced considerable opposition, particularly from leaders in the Republican Party. With the Republican Party regaining control of the House of Representatives after the 2010 midterm elections, the law is in jeopardy of being repealed before many of its provisions are enacted. Further, legal challenges to the constitutionality of insurance mandates have already been brought in district courts in Michigan, Virginia, Florida, and the District of Columbia, with conflicting results. It is expected that this issue will ultimately be brought before the U.S. Supreme Court.

---

[a]U.S. Department of Health and Human Services, "Accountable Care Organizations: Improving Care Coordination for People with Medicare." Available online at: http://www.healthcare.gov/news/factsheets/accountablecare03312011a.html.

[b]U.S. Department of Health and Human Services, "Comparative Effectiveness Research Funding." Available online at: http://www.hhs.gov/recovery/programs/cer/index.html.

gaps in coverage. Many low-income individuals may be dual-eligible for Medicaid as well as Medicare, with Medicaid covering gaps in Medicare coverage.

Also created by the 1965 Social Security Act, Medicaid is a public assistance form of health care coverage for low-income individuals and their families. Each state administers its own Medicaid program, and these programs are jointly funded by both federal and state taxes. Although determination of eligibility is at the level of the states, it is in large part based on income relative to the defined federal poverty level, the existence of specific medical conditions or disabilities, and age (with children and adolescents below the age of 19 years from low-income families being a prioritized group). Unlike Medicare, Medicaid does not require out-of-pocket payments.[83] Similar to the Medicaid program, CHIP is dually funded by the state and federal governments to provide health insurance to children in families with incomes too high to qualify for Medicaid but too low to afford private health insurance. Again, this income is specified by each state relative to the federal poverty level.[84] Lastly, a small portion of the population receives public insurance coverage as a result of their current or past service in the U.S. military.

As previously mentioned, private expenditures exceed governmental sources of funding for health care in the United States. In 2007, 67.5 percent of individuals had some type of private insurance plan: 59.3 percent had employment-based plans, and 8.9 percent had directly purchased plans. Conversely, 27.8 percent of individuals had some type of government plan—13.8 percent had Medicare, 13.2 percent had Medicaid, and 3.7 percent had military health care coverage. Individuals with no insurance coverage represented 15.3 percent of the population, equating to 45.7 million people. This number includes 11 percent of children under the age of 18 years who were not insured. Low-income populations and minority groups are more likely to be uninsured. In 2007, 24.5 percent of households with annual incomes less than $25,000 were uninsured, as compared to 21.1 percent for those with incomes of $25,000–$49,999, 14.5 percent for those with incomes of $50,000–$74,999, and 7.8 percent for those with incomes greater than $75,000. Additionally, 32.1 percent of Hispanics and 19.5 percent of blacks, as compared to 10.4 percent of non-Hispanic whites, were uninsured in 2007.[85] Of note, two-thirds of the non-elderly uninsured U.S. population is employed.[86]

Obviously, this method of financing in the United States is a regressive one, with the poor paying relatively more for health care. Data suggest that the poorest one-fifth of Americans spend 18 percent of their income on health care, as compared to 3 percent for the richest one-fifth of Americans.[87] Additionally, low-income patients, even those with insurance, often defer seeking care, with recent data suggesting that nearly half of working-age adults with below-average incomes who were insured went without needed care.[88]

The organization and reimbursement of health care services in the United States are quite fragmented. Physicians may organize as solo practitioners or join a single- or multi-specialty group practice. Additionally, providers may be employees of a private or public hospital. The government provides little oversight concerning the proportionate balance of primary and specialty care. Currently, the ratio of specialist to generalist providers in the United States is approximately 65 percent to 35 percent.[89] Depending on the insurance plan, patients may or may not be required to be referred by a generalist to a specialist for evaluation and treatment. Managed care plans tend to emphasize this generalist role of "gate-keeper" in an effort to control costs. Unlike the coordination of care seen in the United Kingdom, there is little regional coordination of care at the hospital level in the United States. Conversely, hospitals tend to compete for patients, particularly in urban areas. This competitive model leads to redundancy of care and excessive administrative and marketing costs.

Considerable variability in provider reimbursement also characterizes the U.S. health system. Payment for outpatient services may occur on either a fee-for-service basis or capitation among both private insurance plans and state Medicaid programs. Increasingly, state Medicaid programs are enrolling individuals in managed care–type plans to control costs, with an emphasis on capitation and an increasing role of generalist providers.[90] Some physicians are salaried employees of a group practice or hospital. Regarding inpatient care, payment methods are more consistent. For inpatient services, the reimbursement method is one of capitation, with hospitals receiving fixed payments based on DRGs. DRGs are reviewed and set annually by Medicare, and most private insurers follow a similar reimbursement scheme for inpatient services. Because of this variability in payment schemes, cost-containment efforts are difficult to implement consistently across the health care system.

Recent survey data estimate that CAM use in the United States has a prevalence of 38.3 percent among adults and 11.8 percent among children, with the most common being use of nonvitamin/nonmineral natural products, deep breathing exercises, and chiropractic and osteopathic manipulation.[91] Even though there is limited coverage by some private health insurance plans for specific CAM therapies, including chiropractic, acupuncture, and massage therapy, overall coverage is limited. As a result, 2007 data suggest that adults in the United States paid an estimated $33.9 billion out of pocket for CAM therapies.[92] Although considered a type of CAM therapy elsewhere, osteopathy training in the United States is very similar to that of traditional Western medicine, and a doctor of osteopathic medicine (DO) has the same legal and professional rights and responsibilities as a doctor of medicine (MD). With the exception of chiropractic care, which is regulated by the American Chiropractic Association, most other forms of CAM are not regulated. Of particular note, the herbal product industry is not subject to the same safety and efficacy restrictions as the pharmaceutical industry. Herbal products may be purchased over-the-counter without the prescription of a licensed health care provider.

Comparing Expenditures and Outcomes Across National Health Care Systems

The health status of any population is determined by the interplay of many different factors. These determinants include, but are not limited to, population wealth, public health measures such as the provision of widespread access to clean water supplies and population-level health education, engineering interventions that ensure safe buildings and roadways, and the quality of and access to health care services.[93] As a result of this complexity, it is difficult to disentangle the specific contribution that health care delivery systems make toward the overall health of a population. Further, because global uniformity of data on population health measures is often lacking, it can be particularly challenging to make comparisons regarding the quality of health care delivery systems among countries.

Despite these challenges, the WHO created a model that allows for the measurement of national health care system performance and, thus, more formal comparisons among countries. Using the model, the WHO ranked the performance of the health care systems of 191 countries. The rankings were intended to assess how well investments in public health and medical care were meeting goals of improving population health, reducing health disparities, protecting households against health-related poverty traps, and providing responsive services that respect the dignity of patients.[94] According to these 2000 WHO rankings, the health care system of France was ranked first. The countries for which case studies were presented in this chapter ranked as follows: the United Kingdom—18, the United States—37, Cuba—39, the Republic of Korea—58, Rwanda—172, and South Africa—175.[95] Although the methodology of the WHO report has been criticized,[96] the WHO comparative model has served as a launching point for increasing emphasis on comparative analyses of national health care system performance.

Several key indicators exist that allow for comparisons to be made regarding the health of populations. Life expectancy at birth, healthy life expectancy at birth, and age-, cause-, and gender-specific mortality rates are a few examples of available measures. Again, even though it is difficult to disentangle the role of health care delivery systems from other economic, social, and lifestyle factors that shape population health, comparisons of countries of similar socioeconomic status allow for some interesting observations, particularly when framed against national health care investments. Additionally, disparities in health outcomes among countries of differing socioeconomic status highlight not only the need for enhancements in the health care systems of lower-income countries but also the need for improvements of the socioeconomic conditions in which populations in these countries live. In a similar vein, disparities of outcomes among wealthy and poor populations *within* high-income countries underscore the need to expand access to health care to low-income populations in developed countries and to address the socioeconomic disadvantages faced by these populations.

Comparative data presented in Table 10.1 are illustrative. According to gross national income per capita, Rwanda and South Africa are considerably poorer than the other countries, with significantly lower investments in health care expenditures per capita. Perhaps not surprisingly, population health outcomes for every reported measure are worse than those for the other four countries. Comparative data between these two countries are also interesting. South Africa has higher gross national income than Rwanda and spends significantly more on health care per capita than Rwanda. Yet, South Africa's performance on most health indicators is not dramatically higher than Rwanda's. In fact, life expectancy is somewhat

TABLE 10.1 Comparative Health Care Expenditures and Health Outcomes, Six Countries

Variable	Rwanda	Cuba	South Africa	Republic of Korea	United Kingdom	United States
Gross national income per capita (PPP int. $[a])	1,110	*	9,790	27,840	36,240	46,790
Total expenditure on health as a percentage of GDP[b]	10.4	11.9	8.3	6.6	9.0	16.0
Per capita total expenditure on health (PPP int. $[a])	107	1,132	826	1,820	3,230	7,536
Physician density (per 10,000 population)	<0.5[g]	64.0	7.7	17.1	21.4	26.7
Hospital beds (per 10,000 population)	17[g]	60	28	86	39	31
Life expectancy at birth (years)	58	77	53	80	80	78
Healthy life expectancy at birth (years)	43[g]	69	48	71	72	70
Neonatal mortality rate[c] (per 1,000 live births)	35	3	20	2	3	4
Infant mortality rate[d] (per 1,000 live births)	72	5	48	5	5	7
Under 5 mortality rate[e] (per 1,000 live births)	112	6	67	5	6	8
Maternal mortality ratio (per 100,000 live births)	540	53	410	18	12	24
Adult mortality rate[f]	303	102	520	76	78	107

[a]PPP int. $—purchasing-power-parity international dollar
[b]GDP—gross domestic product
[c]Neonatal mortality rate—number of deaths during the first 28 completed days of life per 1,000 live births
[d]Infant mortality rate—probability of dying between birth and age 1 per 1,000 live births
[e]Under 5 mortality rate—probability of dying under age 5 per 1,000 live births
[f]Adult mortality rate—probability of dying between 15 and 60 years per 1,000 population
[g]All data are from 2008 except for physician density (2002–2006), hospital beds (2000–2007), and healthy life expectancy at birth (2000–2007)
*WHO data not available but estimated to be an upper-middle-income economy ($3,924–$12,195)

Sources: World Health Organization, Global Health Observatory, available online at: http://www.who.int/gho/en/; The World Bank, Country and Lending Groups (2010), available online at: http://data.worldbank.org/about/country-classifications/country-and-lending-groups/.

higher in Rwanda than in South Africa, and the adult mortality rate is somewhat lower. The critical difference between the two countries appears to be that Rwanda has significantly lower health outcomes for maternal and child health conditions, perhaps not surprising given the higher levels of poverty in Rwanda.

However, increasing wealth and health care expenditures are not consistently associated with better health outcomes. For example, the United States annually spends greater than fourfold per capita more on health care than the Republic of Korea yet performs slightly worse on each health outcome variable. South Korea has better health outcomes despite having fewer physicians per population than does the United States. Similar trends are seen when comparing the United States with the United Kingdom, with the United Kingdom demonstrating slightly better health outcomes than the United States despite lesser per capita spending on health care and similar numbers of physicians and hospital beds per population. Even more strikingly, Cuba performs almost as well as the United States on most health

indicators despite spending significantly less on health per capita.

Inspection of data comparing national health care investments and utilization lends some insight into possible explanations for these similar population-level health outcomes despite marked differences in national health care expenditures. Organization for Economic Co-operation and Development (OECD) data on South Korea, the United Kingdom, and the United States, presented in Table 10.2, highlight some critical points. First, excess expenditures by the United States compared with the other countries cannot be explained by more frequent health care encounters; annual physician visits per capita and average length of stay for hospital admissions are greater in both of the other countries. However, some evidence exists that the United States provides more intensive care at the point of service encounters. For example, U.S. rates of birth by cesarean section are modestly higher than those in the United Kingdom. More dramatically, rates of costly coronary revascularization procedures such as bypass surgery are utilized at more than

TABLE 10.2 Comparative Health Investments and Utilization, Three Countries

Variable	Republic of Korea	United Kingdom	United States
Annual doctor visits per capita	10.6	5.3	3.9
Average length of hospital stay per admission (days)	10.6	6.6	5.6
Percentage of live births that are cesarean section	*	22	28
Rates of coronary revascularization procedures[a]	*	154	587
Number of MRI[b] scanners per 100,000 population	11	5	26.6
Average generalist compensation (in U.S. $1,000s)	*	118	161
Average subspecialist compensation (in U.S. $1,000s)	*	115	230
Pharmaceutical spending per capita (in U.S. dollars)	315	*	752
Health administrative and insurance costs[c]	40	57	465

[a]Rates per 100,000 population
[b]MRI—magnetic resonance imaging
[c]Amounts are adjusted using U.S. dollar purchasing-power parities
*Notes categories for which data are not recently available

Source: C.L. Peterson and R. Burton, Congressional Research Service 2007; based on Organization for Economic Cooperation and Development Health Data 2006: CRS-5–CRS-30.

twice the OECD average for countries where such data are available. Additionally, physician compensation and expenditures on pharmaceuticals are higher in the United States than in the other OECD nations. The fragmentation and resultant redundancy of services that exist in the U.S. health care system likely contribute significantly to the excess spending that occurs when compared with other countries. For example, the United States has significantly more resource-intensive technologies, such as magnetic resonance imaging (MRI) scanners, per population than other countries. Redundancy in the U.S. health care system also contributes to considerable health administrative and insurance costs.[97]

Critics of the use of health indicators such as mortality data and life expectancy at birth for comparing the quality of health care systems argue that these measures are more indicative of disparities in socioeconomic conditions and differences in lifestyles than of the quality of these systems. Although this criticism is partially accurate when comparing countries like the United States and South Africa, it is perhaps more difficult to accept when comparing systems of developed countries like the United States and the United Kingdom. It also fails to explain why a country like South Korea outperforms the United States on these indicators. Others argue that there are qualitative components of health care systems that these measures fail to capture, such as wait times for the receipt of health care services. Certainly, patients in the United Kingdom may wait on average several months longer for elective, nonemergent procedures and surgeries, such as knee replacement surgery, than patients in the United States. However, wait times in all countries were longer for low-income patients than high-income patients. Interestingly, these disparities in access for poor individuals were greater in the United States than in other countries.[98]

Further, data have shown that patients in the United States have more difficulty accessing same-day or after-hours care from a non–emergency room physician than individuals in the United Kingdom.[99] These data suggest that,

although wealthier individuals in the United States may have better access to high-quality care than their counterparts in other countries, the United States may fail to deliver the same high level of care more broadly at the population level. Reasons for such disparities in health outcomes in the context of high per capita health care expenditures are likely attributable in large part to the large number of individuals in the United States who lack health care insurance.

Conclusion

States necessarily play a critical role in efforts to promote global health. For better or worse, they remain the most powerful and influential actors in the international system. National governments influence population health through the adoption of policies that determine the nature of the national health system, the creation of public health infrastructure, the implementation of programs designed to address specific health challenges, monitoring and surveillance activities, and international development and health aid. Taken together, all these forms of health-related spending and policy action by states far outweigh spending and programming by international organizations and non-state actors. Thus, states play a role in global health promotion that must be taken into consideration in any analysis of global health.

This chapter has shown that the relationship among national wealth, health expenditures by states, and population health outcomes is a complicated one. On the one hand, it is clear that high-income countries tend to perform better on key health indicators than low-income countries. On the other hand, the positive correlation among wealth, health expenditures, and health outcomes is not absolute. Higher levels of national income and health care expenditures do not necessarily produce better health outcomes, as the comparative data in this chapter have shown. Rather, significant inequities in health outcomes *within* particular countries, whereby low-income populations rank much lower on key health indicators than wealthy populations, may bring down a country's aggregate performance on these indicators. Conversely, low-income countries that spend less on health care may perform as well as or better than high-income countries on health indices despite the fact that their overall national income or health expenditures are lower. This fact underscores the reality that national health systems—reflecting different policy priorities—matter in determining the quality of health experienced by populations in different countries.

In this regard, this chapter highlighted that states operate in a political, social, and economic context. The health systems that emerge in specific states reflect a unique set of historical circumstances, economic resources, political systems, social structures, and cultural influences. Because of these diverse social, economic, political, and cultural influences, each national government will face a different set of countervailing political pressures that determine the type of health system that emerges and the kinds of health policies that can be pursued. Even if we acknowledge that some types of health systems seem to produce better health outcomes than others, we cannot necessarily assume that different models are readily transferable from one country to another. Changing a national health system requires changing the political calculus in a specific country. Therefore, students and engaged citizens interested in changing health care systems must be committed to understanding the nature of political systems in particular countries.

Discussion Questions

1. How can states shape health outcomes both within their own borders and in other countries?

2. To what extent do states need to collaborate with other state and non-state actors in order to positively affect health outcomes?

3. Do you think states are motivated primarily by principled considerations or self-interest when they provide health aid to other countries? Do state motivations matter? Why or why not?

4. Review the alternative approaches for financing, reimbursing, delivering, and organizing health care in national health care systems. What are the advantages and disadvantages of these different models of health systems?

5. Discuss the relationship among national wealth, health care expenditures, and health outcomes. Is there a significant correlation among these variables?

6. How does a middle-income country like Cuba perform almost as well as a high-income country like the United States on key health indicators despite the fact that the United States has significantly higher health care expenditures per capita?

7. What are some of the unique challenges faced by the national health systems in low-income countries?

Web Resources

United Nations Development Programme: Human Development Reports: http://hdr.undp.org/en/

U.S. Centers for Disease Control and Prevention: http://www.cdc.gov/

World Health Organization: World Health Report 2000—Health Systems: Improving Performance: http://www.who.int/whr/2000/en/

World Health Organization: World Health Statistics: http://www.who.int/whosis/whostat/en/

CHAPTER 11

Promoting Global Health from the Bottom Up: Non-state Actors

Introduction

A wide variety of non-state actors are engaged in activities that fundamentally shape global health. This chapter provides a basic overview of various non-state actors, including non-governmental organizations (NGOs), corporations, transnational social movements (TSMs), and individuals, acting as citizens and consumers. In doing so, it examines the economic, social, and political dynamics involved in bottom-up efforts to promote public health. Additionally, it explores the ways in which non-state actors interact with state actors in global health promotion endeavors. The chapter closely examines the activities of a variety of NGOs that work on global health issues. In doing so, it discusses the ways in which NGOs, states, and international organizations compete as well as collaborate on global health initiatives. In examining the role of non-state actors, the chapter considers the economic, political, and legal obstacles that arise when seeking to promote global health in a bottom-up fashion.

Categories of Non-state Actors

Broadly speaking, non-state actors include every actor in the international system, with the exception of states and international organizations.[1] Conceptualized in this way, tens of thousands of non-state actors have the capacity to participate in global health promotion efforts. (If we count every individual as a separate non-state actor, then literally billions of non-state actors exist.) Thus, in order for this very broad category to have any analytical utility, it is necessary to further distinguish non-state actors by type. Non-state actors can be divided into at least four categories: (1) NGOs, (2) corporations, (3) TSMs, and (4) individuals. Each of these categories has unique attributes and differs according to size, purpose, degree and type of institutional organization, global reach, and scope of activity. Significant variations exist not only between categories but also within categories. This section describes the different categories of non-state actors and provides a brief overview of the ways in which they have the capacity to shape global health.

Non-governmental Organizations

Non-governmental organizations are nonprofit voluntary organizations that can be local, national, or transnational in nature. This category includes issue-specific advocacy organizations (such as human rights or environmental NGOs), identity-based organizations (including churches or ethnic associations), and charity or service organizations (for example, humanitarian organizations or philanthropic foundations).[2] As nonprofit entities, NGOs are motivated to a large extent by the core objectives of their mandates, whether those are primarily issue-specific, identity-based, or ideational in nature. Drawing attention to the distinction between for-profit and nonprofit governing structures does not, however, indicate that NGOs are not self-interested. NGOs also strive for power and organizational health and must compete with other NGOs for influence and limited resources. Thus, NGOs are constrained by economic and political realities.

NGOs vary widely in their size, structure, purpose, global reach, and relationships with state actors, other NGOs, and international organizations. There are very small NGOs operating locally as well as large NGOs with global reach. For example, Village Health Works is a small NGO that operates a health clinic in Burundi. In contrast, Oxfam International is an umbrella organization of fourteen organizations that work together, along with over 3,000 partner organizations, on poverty and human rights issues in countries across the globe. NGOs can be organized around single-issue campaigns, or they can be involved in broad-based advocacy work. Some organizations are organized for the explicit purpose of working on specific aspects of global health. For instance, Doctors Without Borders is primarily concerned with providing aid and medical care in zones of conflict or natural disaster or in a humanitarian crisis. Other organizations, such as Save the Children, do work on development and children's rights that has clear implications for the promotion of children's health. Similarly, some NGOs focus primarily on funding activities, as in the case of the Gates Foundation. Alternatively, other NGOs are highly involved with field work, as is the case with Doctors Without Borders. Yet other NGOs, such as Physicians for Human Rights, have mandates focused on advocacy. The mandates of some NGOs, such as Food for the Poor, are grounded in religion, whereas other NGOs, like the GAVI Alliance, are secular in nature.

The distinguishing features of particular NGOs result in unique sets of operating and political constraints, and any effort to evaluate the work of NGOs in the field of global health needs to be cognizant of these distinctions. NGO activities in the field of global health are explored in greater detail in a subsequent section of this chapter.

Corporations

Corporations are business entities that operate for profit and are given many legal rights separate from their owners or shareholders. Like NGOs, corporations can operate locally, nationally, or transnationally. Because they are larger and more likely to shape health outcomes on a global scale, **multinational corporations** (MNCs) are particularly relevant here. MNCs are for-profit organizations that operate in more than one country. MNCs are sometimes referred to as transnational corporations (TNCs) to emphasize that these corporate entities are not fundamentally grounded in the state-centric nature of the international system. They operate not just *within* two or more states but *across* state borders.

Because corporations are for-profit entities, their orientation to global politics differs significantly from that of nonprofit NGOs. In their operations, corporations will almost always be driven by a concern for bottom-line profits. MNCs, in particular, are among the most powerful non-state actors, and their activities and operations have significant and complicated effects, for better or worse, on human health. Industrial activity produces environmental costs that can have detrimental effects on human health. Conversely, MNCs can contribute to the kinds of economic growth that help produce and sustain public health infrastructure.

Major pharmaceutical companies are an important example of the complex ways in which corporations affect human health. On the one hand, the pharmaceutical industry produces drugs that play a critical role in providing health care to the world's population. However, as corporate entities interested in the bottom line, they are motivated primarily by concern with corporate profit rather than meeting the immediate health needs of the world's population. As a result, they have been criticized for practices that restrict the access of poor people to lifesaving drugs. Pharmaceutical companies may not market lifesaving drugs in countries where doing so does not generate adequate profits. For example, the drug eflornithine was developed as a potential treatment for cancer. Although it proved to be ineffective in treating cancer, it was shown to treat resistant forms of African sleeping sickness. Despite the fact that the drug for the treatment of this disease would have saved thousands of lives in sub-Saharan Africa, the company that developed it abandoned its production due to a projected lack of profitability.[3] (Subsequently, another drug company began to manufacture the drug for use against sleeping sickness.)

In a similar vein, the tension between corporate interest and the health needs of individuals is evident in the pharmaceutical industry's attempts to limit the development of generic versions of lifesaving drugs, a practice that has been especially controversial in relation to effective drugs for the treatment of HIV/AIDS. Pharmaceutical companies defend this practice as necessary for the protection of intellectual property rights, which are embodied in patent protections that give drug companies exclusive rights to market new drugs for extended periods of time. Drug companies further argue that the profit motive provides necessary incentives for them to spend significant funds on the research and development of new drugs. They contend that, in the absence of such incentives, lifesaving drugs simply would not be developed. Thus, they argue that the health-producing benefits of a system that protects intellectual property rights outweigh the costs in the long run. Critics charge that it is unethical to prevent poor countries from developing affordable generic versions of drugs that could save the lives of thousands of people who would otherwise die because they cannot afford brand-name versions of these drugs.[4]

Transnational Social Movements

Transnational social movements involve networks of activists and citizens organized around specific issues, ideas, or values in global politics.[5] Because they do not necessarily involve formal organizational structures, these social movements are distinct from NGOs. These loosely organized but broad-based movements shape international responses to important global issues. Unlike either MNCs or NGOs, TSMs are loose networks of individuals and groups and, as such, operate under different constraints. Nevertheless, they involve explicitly political actors that operate within the economic, social, and political dynamics of the international system.

Margaret E. Keck and Kathryn Sikkink explain how transnational advocacy networks, a term that is essentially synonymous with *transnational social movements*, can help define and shape the agendas of states and international organizations on important global issues. Keck and Sikkink define transnational advocacy networks as networks of activists organized around important ideas or values. These networks provide alternative channels of communication for non-state actors to make their concerns known, to share suppressed information, and to bring alternative policy visions and ideas into consideration. In doing so, transnational advocacy networks expand the number of "voices" that shape domestic and international policies. According to Keck and Sikkink, "These voices argue, persuade, strategize, document, lobby, pressure, and complain. The multiplication of voices is imperfect and selective—for every voice that is amplified, many others are ignored—but in a world where the voices of states have predominated, networks open channels for bringing alternative visions and information into the international debate."[6] Transnational advocacy networks are made up of a wide range of actors, including NGOs, consumer groups, engaged citizens, and networks of scientists, experts, and professionals in particular fields. When a range of actors coalesces around a specific global issue, this coalition can be seen as a transnational advocacy network or social movement that has the capacity to shape policy even in the absence of formalized institutions.

TSMs have influenced the way in which the international community has responded to global health issues. TSMs can shape the global health agenda in two fundamental ways: (1) by influencing *whether* states and international organizations treat global health as a priority and (2) by helping to determine *which* health issues rise to the top of the global health policy agenda.

First, TSMs can influence the extent to which global health, in general, is seen as a priority by states and international organizations. Indeed, a TSM led by biomedical scientists, public health officials, funding agencies like the Rockefeller Foundation, and NGOs involved in health advocacy played a critical role in the emergence of global health norms and institutions beginning in the period between World War I and World War II. Notably, the League of Nations played a significant role in generating momentum for the emergence of this global health regime, illustrating the ways in which non-state actors collaborate with states and international organizations in global health promotion efforts.[7] Subsequently, UN organs working on public health also collaborated with medical professionals, scientists, public health officials, and NGOs in further consolidating global health norms and institutions.

In this regard, major events or crises with serious health consequences can help health-related TSMs mobilize public support for global health. In the face of a serious global health challenge, non-state actors involved in global health advocacy can "capitalize" on new health threats by using highly visible events or issues to persuade the public that global health should be a priority, to lobby for specific global health policies, or simply to pressure for greater attention to global health in general. For instance, advocacy groups working on global health issues have emphasized the transnational nature of the HIV/AIDS crisis to generate public support and funding not only for this disease but also for other global health initiatives.[8] This strategy has been pursued not just by isolated NGOs but by a network of advocacy organizations, suggesting that this political response represents the ideas and political strategy of a TSM loosely organized around the issue of global health.

Second, TSMs help determine which global health issues are treated as priorities on the

---

KEY ACTORS IN GLOBAL HEALTH GOVERNANCE

Corporations: business entities that operate for profit and are given many legal rights separate from their owners or shareholders.

Multinational Corporations (MNCs): business entities that operate in more than one country for profit and are given many legal rights separate from their owners or shareholders.

Non-governmental Organizations (NGOs): nonprofit voluntary organizations that can be local, national, or transnational in nature.

Public-private Partnerships (PPPs): formal partnerships between governments and the private sector involving collaboration, normally involving government funding to private actors to implement specific programs or services, intended to provide public goods.

Transnational Social Movements (TSMs): networks of activists and citizens organized around specific issues, ideas, or values in global politics.

international agenda. The disproportionate global funding of initiatives directed at certain diseases in comparison with the relative neglect of other diseases by the international community provides a striking example of the potential influence of TSMs on the global health agenda. In the first years of the 21st century, HIV/AIDS was responsible for approximately 5 percent of morbidity and mortality in low- and middle-income countries. Yet, this disease received over one-third of major donor funding during the same time period. This discrepancy is notable because other diseases, including diarrheal illnesses and pneumonia, are responsible for a higher proportion of the burden of disease in these countries (as well as globally). Moreover, simple, low-cost, effective interventions exist to treat diarrheal illness, pneumonia, and other communicable illnesses, whereas the prevention and treatment of HIV/AIDS is more complicated and expensive. According to Jeremy Shiffman, the effectiveness of a TSM—in this case, a global health policy community—helps explain this disconnection in global health aid between the actual burden of disease and funding levels for different diseases.[9]

Interestingly, TSMs often cross boundaries between non-state actors, states, and international organizations and can involve extensive collaboration among these actors. Since the advent of the UN system, a strong institutional foundation for global health promotion has been in existence at the international level. A well-established network of NGOs focused on global health emerged during the 20th century. Along with agencies focused on health within states, these actors constitute the core of a global health policy community that plays a significant role in bringing some global health issues to the top of the international agenda while neglecting other global health challenges.[10]

Individuals

Individuals, as citizens and consumers, have the potential to alter the economic, social, and political dynamics that undergird the international system. As citizens, individuals can seek to shape national health policy in their own countries. Individual voters play a role in determining whether health care policies or issues are important electoral issues. For instance, in the 2008 presidential election in the United States, candidate positions on health care policy emerged as a major campaign issue. Widespread dissatisfaction with the state of the U.S. health care system among the American electorate helped ensure the prominence of health care as a campaign issue. Notably, President Obama signed health care reform legislation into law in March 2010.

As consumers, individuals have the capacity to pressure corporations to adopt policies with the potential for improving public health. For example, consumers may boycott products with negative health effects or boycott companies that they believe undermine public health. The international boycott of the Nestlé Corporation in the 1980s is a prominent case in point. The Nestlé Corporation came under fire due to its policy of aggressively marketing infant formula to new mothers in developing countries. Responding to this marketing campaign, many mothers opted for formula instead of breast-feeding. These mothers, many of whom were poor, mixed the formula with water from frequently unsafe sources. As a result, many babies became ill and died. In response, many consumers across the globe participated in a boycott of Nestlé, organized by the International Baby Food Action Network (IBFAN). Reacting to the boycott, Nestlé agreed to abide by a WHO code for marketing infant formula. Nevertheless, according to IBFAN, Nestlé continues to violate the WHO code. Thus, IBFAN continues to advocate for an ongoing consumer boycott of Nestlé.[11]

Individuals acting alone can also make important lifestyle changes that have personal as well as public health benefits. The slow food movement is a notable example of individuals altering their personal behavior in ways with potentially far-reaching public health benefits. The slow food movement is the label used to describe the network of individuals and organizations that advocates for sustainable, small-scale agriculture; the purchase of local food produced by small farmers; and the preparation of nonprocessed and organic food. As its label suggests, this movement is a direct reaction to fast food. Instead of embracing fast food, which critics view as not only having negative effects on individual health but also being detrimental to environmental and social health, participants in the slow food movement contend that a wide range of health benefits can be gained simply by slowing down and reducing in scale every aspect of our approach to food. Slow food proponents often tend their own gardens and try to produce as much of their own fresh food as possible. If they do not grow their own food, they often participate in community-supported agriculture, which involves directly supporting local farmers with financial investments and/or contributions of labor and then sharing part of the harvest. Even if individuals choose not to grow their own food or to participate in community-supported agriculture, they are still urged to buy fresh, local ingredients when possible, to prepare home-cooked meals rather than prepackaged or processed food, and to take time to enjoy meals.[12]

Critics of the slow food movement argue that it represents a lifestyle that only upper-middle-class people can afford, both in terms of time and money. Proponents of the slow food movement contend that it not only produces health benefits for individuals but also has broader public health benefits for society. For example, they argue that an expansion of the slow food lifestyle would help combat the diseases of globalization (heart disease, diabetes, and obesity) and the social and financial costs created by these diseases. They also argue that the small-scale methods involved in this approach to agriculture, food preparation, and

eating are more environmentally sustainable and, thus, produce environmental as well as personal health benefits.

Circumventing the State: Health Governance Without Government

Non-state actors contribute to systems of global governance even in the absence of formal governing institutions. In this context, "governance refers to activities backed by shared goals that may or may not derive from legally and formally prescribed responsibilities and that do not necessarily rely on police powers to overcome defiance and attain compliance."[13] Non-state actors are especially likely to play such a role in response to interdependencies that make states mutually vulnerable to transnational challenges and threats, such as environmental degradation, financial crises, and, most relevant for our purposes here, transnational health problems.[14] Non-state actors also may seek to fill policy gaps created by globalizing dynamics that limit states' ability to meet critical needs.[15] In the words of a prominent scholar of international relations, "Some of the functions of governance, in other words, are now being performed by activities that do not originate with governments."[16] In short, the dynamics of globalization and the conditions of interdependence have led non-state actors to play an increasingly important role in mobilizing global norms, resources, and policies intended to contribute to an emerging system of global health governance.

Non-state actors vary according to their relationship to states. In general, three basic dynamics shape interactions between states and non-state actors in international relations: circumvention, competition, and collaboration. First, non-state actors circumvent the state in numerous ways. Non-state actors sometimes seek to work around state regulations in the pursuit of specific objectives. For example, an MNC headquartered in a country with strong

UNDER THE MICROSCOPE

Providing Clean Water to the Poor in Developing Countries

Lack of access to clean water and adequate sanitation are major causes of morbidity and mortality worldwide. Diarrhea causes approximately 1.8 million deaths across the globe each year. Almost 40,000 people in the developing world die *each week* due to lack of access to clean water.[a] The great majority of these cases—88 percent—are caused by unsafe water, sanitation, or hygiene. Most of the fatalities are among children, and almost all of these cases occur in the developing world.[b]

The creation of public water systems, water treatment mechanisms, and public sewers has cut down on deadly waterborne illnesses and saved countless lives, and these public health interventions are among the most important of the 20th century. Indeed, public health experts have estimated that access to piped water, improved sanitation, and chlorination of water sources were responsible for approximately half of the reduction in overall mortality rates and almost three-quarters of the reduction of infant mortality rates during the first half of the 20th century.[c]

Unfortunately, much of the world's population does not have access to clean water or adequate sanitation. Globally, over 1 billion people—roughly 16 percent of the world's population—do not have access to improved water (which generally means access to a tap or a well). Almost 40 percent—2.6 billion people—do not have access to improved sanitation.[d] As the data suggest, closing this gap in access to improved water and sanitation would go a long way to improving population health in developing countries. Regrettably,

[a]Robert D. Morris, *The Blue Death: Disease, Disaster, and the Water We Drink* (New York: HarperCollins Publishers, 2007): 263–264.

[b]World Health Organization, *Global Health Risks: Mortality and Burden of Disease Attributable to Selected Major Risks* (December 2009): 23. Available online at: http://www.who.int/healthinfo/global_burden_disease/GlobalHealthRisks_report_full.pdf.

[c]Abhijit V. Banerjee and Esther Duflo, *Poor Economics: A Radical Rethinking of the Way to Fight Global Poverty* (New York: Public Affairs, 2011): 46.

[d]Morris: 264.

regulations providing worker protections or with high tax rates might relocate operations to a country without such regulations. NGOs might seek to circumvent states by providing public goods that states fail to provide. For instance, humanitarian and development NGOs frequently provide aid to poor populations in developing countries where governments are unwilling or unable to do so.

Second, non-state actors compete with states for control over the policy agenda in global politics, for access to and use of limited international resources, and for influence over significant global issues. MNCs frequently compete with states in this regard, and it can be difficult for states to maintain regulatory control over specific issue areas when MNCs have so much control over vast economic and most developing countries cannot afford to spend the estimated $20 monthly fee per household that it would cost to provide improved water and sanitation.

A success story involving the work of Gram Vikas, an NGO operating in Orissa, India, suggests that NGOs may be able to mobilize global norms and resources in order to fill this critical gap in health governance. Gram Vikas (a term that means "village development") has a mission focused on the provision of sustainable, socially inclusive, and gender-equitable improvements in the quality of life of poor and marginalized rural people and communities.[e] One of Gram Vikas's major initiatives has involved efforts to provide improved water and sanitation to the populations living in Orissa, an Indian state with high levels of poverty. Social inclusion is a critical element of the NGO's approach to increasing access to clean water and sanitation. The organization works with communities and requires that all households—including high-caste and low-caste homes—be connected to the same water mains before it will agree to work with the village. Because of the nature of the caste system in India, high-caste populations often are reluctant to share the same water system with low-caste populations, leading some villages to refuse to participate in the initiative. For those villages that agree to the terms, Gram Vikas helps fund and build water systems that provide a tap, toilet, and separate bathroom for each house in the village.[f]

Notably, the Gram Vikas water initiative has produced clear, measurable health improvements in the communities where it has been implemented. As part of the program, the organization collects monthly data on health visits by members of households in participating villages. Its data indicate a 50 percent reduction in cases of severe diarrhea and a 33 percent reduction in cases of malaria. The cost per household for the system is only $4 per month—compared to the estimate of $20 per month that development experts believe it would cost governments to provide access to improved water and sanitation. Gram Vikas asks participating villages to contribute enough funds to allow for the maintenance of the water system and expansion of the water system to any new households. Remaining program costs—including monthly per-household water and sanitation costs—are subsidized by donations collected by the organization.[g]

---

[e]Gram Vikas mission statement. Available online at: http://www.gramvikas.org/.

[f]Banerjee and Duflo: 45–48.

[g]*Ibid.*: 47–48.

financial resources and when their mobility enables them to escape state regulation. NGOs also compete with states in terms of shaping policy agendas, resource prioritization, and programming related to specific issue areas, such as human rights or humanitarian work.

Finally, non-state actors can collaborate with states. A prominent example of collaboration between states and non-state actors involves humanitarian agencies that work in conflict zones. The ability of humanitarian agencies to carry out relief work depends on the consent of states. Development NGOs also collaborate with states, both donor and recipient countries, in their implementation of poverty-reduction initiatives. In the area of global health, **public-private partnerships (PPPs)** play an increasingly important role in collaborative efforts to promote global health among states, non-state actors, and international organizations. The Global Alliance for Vaccines and Immunizations (GAVI), the Global Polio Eradication Initiative, and the Roll Back Malaria campaign are global health initiatives that involve critical partnerships between state and non-state actors.

All of these dynamics—circumvention, competition, and collaboration—characterize activity by non-state actors in the area of global health. Doctors Without Borders is a prominent example of an NGO whose work circumvents the state in some respects. Doctors Without Borders seeks to maintain strict neutrality and independence in its medical humanitarian efforts. To this end, almost 90 percent of its funding comes from private sources rather than governments. Despite its neutrality, it has been willing to criticize governments and to call for military action in response to violations of international human rights and humanitarian law, as it did in the case of the genocide in Rwanda. The Gates Foundation provides a striking example of the ways in which non-state actors can compete with states. Collaborative interactions between non-state and state actors are illustrated by the GAVI Alliance. Formerly known as the Global Alliance for Vaccines and Immunisation, the GAVI Alliance involves an elaborate PPP of NGOs, vaccine manufacturers, national governments, and international organizations that collaborate to save lives through increased access to immunization in poor countries. In this way, a PPP like the GAVI Alliance is not technically a non-state actor but a "hybrid" actor, representing states and international organizations as well as non-state actors.

These circumventing, competitive, and collaborative dynamics are not mutually exclusive, and non-state actors may simultaneously engage in all three behaviors in their interactions with states. Nevertheless, it is useful to highlight the diverse nature of strategies and approaches used by non-state actors in their efforts to influence international relations, in the area of global health as in other issue areas.

The subsequent analysis of specific NGOs involved in global health advocacy, aid, and program implementation illustrates the variety of ways in which non-state actors can circumvent, compete with, or collaborate with states in global health promotion efforts. It also highlights the potential benefits as well as the limitations of bottom-up efforts to promote global health.

Non-governmental Organizations and Global Health Advocacy

The quantity of NGOs involved in global health work number in the thousands.[17] These NGOs play an increasingly important role in mobilizing global norms, resources, and policies pertinent to global health. In terms of financial resources, NGOs generally are still overshadowed by state actors and international organizations. Nevertheless, the volume of their activities and the amount of their spending are on the rise, and they fundamentally shape the political landscape in the realm of global health.

The proportion of NGO spending on global humanitarian assistance—just one piece of the global health puzzle—is instructive. Estimates suggest that, in recent years, approximately 40 percent of funds for global humanitarian assistance has come from NGOs.[18] As shown in Figure 11.1, two NGOs—Doctors Without Borders and Caritas—were among the top ten donors of humanitarian assistance globally. Only the United States and the United Kingdom spent more on humanitarian assistance than Doctors Without Borders. Three additional NGOs—Oxfam International, World Vision, and the International Rescue Committee—were in the top twenty donors of humanitarian assistance worldwide.[19] It should be noted that NGOs are funded by national governments as well as voluntary contributions, so a rise in NGO spending on humanitarian assistance and global health does not necessarily signal that the role of states is

FIGURE 11.1 Humanitarian Assistance by Select Donor Countries and NGOs, 2006

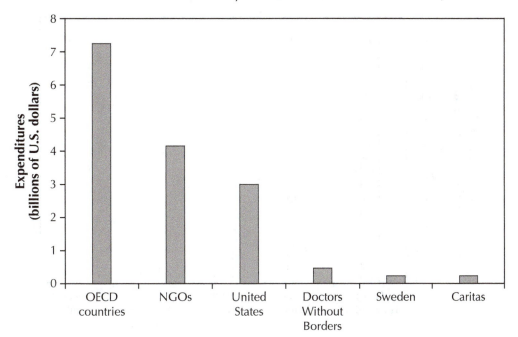

Source: Development Initiatives, *Public Support for Humanitarian Crises Through NGOs* (February 2009). Available online at: http://www.globalhumanitarianassistance.org/wp-content/uploads/2010/07/2009-Focus-report-Public-support-for-humanitarian-crises-through-NGOs.pdf.

diminishing. Nevertheless, the significant amount of humanitarian assistance channeled through NGOs is a sign of the increasingly important role they play in health-related global initiatives.

As outlined in the previous section, NGOs are formed around a range of organizing principles, including issue advocacy, ideology, or identity, or for the provision of service, aid, or charity. Sometimes NGOs are grounded in multiple principles simultaneously. NGOs from each of these categories are involved in global health promotion initiatives. This section provides a brief overview of several NGOs involved in global health promotion, including the Gates Foundation, Save the Children, Village Health Works, the GAVI Alliance, Partners in Health, and Doctors Without Borders. Each of these organizations has a different size and organizational structure, a unique mandate and purpose, a varying scope of activity, and a unique orientation toward

state actors and international organizations. As shown in Figure 11.2, the amount of expenditures on health-related programming by each organization varies dramatically. Although the discussion that follows is far from a comprehensive overview of NGO advocacy in the area of global health, the goal of these mini case studies is to compare and contrast different types of NGOs in an effort to identify some of the strengths and weaknesses of various bottom-up strategies for promoting human health.

The Gates Foundation

The Bill and Melinda Gates Foundation is one of the biggest funders of global health initiatives. Between 1994 and 2010, the Gates Foundation funded over $13 billion in global health grants and almost $3 billion in global development grants. The Gates Foundation works both in developing countries, where it focuses on poverty-reduction efforts and

FIGURE 11.2 Health-Related Program Expenditures by Select NGOs

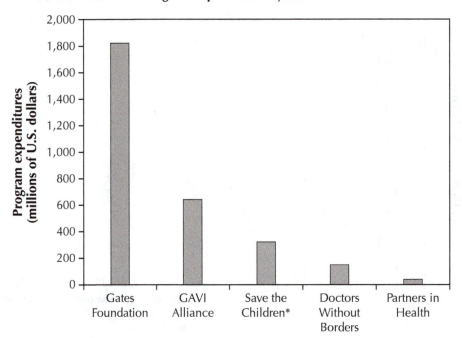

*Save the Children's overall program expenditures were $474 million in fiscal year 2010. Approximately 67 percent of these expenditures ($317 million) was for the organization's health-related programs, including health and nutrition, HIV/AIDS, child poverty, and emergency response initiatives.

Sources: Figures were gathered from the annual reports and financial statements available on the Web pages of selected organizations. Program expenditure information for Save the Children is from its 2010 annual report. For all other organizations, 2009 data were used. Data on Village Health Works were unavailable.

health-related initiatives, and in the United States, where its work is concentrated on providing equal opportunities for the poor, especially in education. Its work in developing countries involves giving grants in global development and global health in a variety of areas, including infectious diseases, family planning, maternal and child health, agricultural development, financial services, water, sanitation and hygiene, and urban poverty. According to its guiding principles, the foundation's purposes are focused primarily on funding and shaping the agenda in its areas of focus. It works closely with its partners in developing countries in overseeing and assessing the implementation of these grants. The Gates Foundation also engages in advocacy and lobbying for policy change.[20]

The Gates Foundation's health initiatives have global reach. The foundation funds grants in over 100 countries and in every state

in the United States. It takes a collaborative approach to global health promotion, working with states, international organizations, and other NGOs. Its grantees include prominent NGOs that work on global health, including the GAVI Alliance, Save the Children, and the PATH Malaria Vaccine Initiative. It also has made grants to international organizations, including the UN-affiliated World Food Programme. The foundation's global health work has a wide scope, and it funds a range of programs, including projects targeting childhood immunization, reductions in child mortality, support for farmers in developing countries, financial services for individuals living in extreme poverty, infectious diseases, family planning, maternal health, and educational programs. This range of funding activities, which covers preventive and curative medicine as well as programs that address the socioeconomic determinants of health, indicates that the foundation takes a holistic view of health. The foundation's global reach, its wide scope of activities, and its significant resources indicate that it has the potential to contribute to major improvements in global health.

But despite its great potential, the Gates Foundation faces important criticisms of its work. One serious criticism is that its extensive financial resources enable it to overshadow other actors. In particular, critics argue that the Gates Foundation, which is a private entity and not a representative body, has disproportionate influence over the global health agenda. Indeed, some critics argue that the Gates Foundation has greater influence over the global health agenda than many donor or recipient countries. Furthermore, the Gates Foundation is not a democratic institution, and it has enormous influence over global health issues without having any accountability.[21] Its guiding principles call for the foundation to "seek and heed the counsel of outside voices" (Guiding Principle #9) and to treat grantees as valuable partners and the intended beneficiaries of foundation funding with respect (Guiding Principle #10).[22] However, no mechanisms exist by which to ensure that the foundation lives up to these principles. Critics also charge that the foundation's work is insufficiently transparent and that a disproportionate amount of the foundation's funding goes to organizations in wealthy donor countries.[23]

Save the Children

Save the Children's mission is to promote "lasting, positive change in the lives of children in the U.S. and around the world."[24] Its priorities include the promotion of education, health, nutrition, and economic security for children everywhere. Its programs include training community health workers, helping to promote disaster preparedness in at-risk communities, promoting access to education in conflict zones, and providing food, shelter, and medical aid in humanitarian crises. Save the Children's global health programming specifically prioritizes newborn and child health, reproductive

health, HIV/AIDS, and school health and nutrition. It has a network of country offices and partners with local organizations, other NGOs, and government agencies in implementing its programs. The organization also sponsors research in key program areas and engages in advocacy on behalf of children.

As a large NGO with a broad mission, Save the Children has a number of potentially advantageous features as a mechanism for promoting health for children across the globe. The organization has broad reach. Save the Children funds programs in over fifty countries and claims to serve 64 million children. It collaborates with states, international organizations, and other NGOs on its health and development initiatives and, in doing so, has increased the potential impact of its programs. Save the Children's work, which addresses infectious diseases, poverty-related health challenges, and other socioeconomic determinants of health, takes a comprehensive view of human health. Another possible benefit of Save the Children's model, as an organization focused on children as a broad funding category, is that it enables the organization to disperse funds where they are most needed during a particular time period. This approach has potential advantages over fund-raising directed at particular crises or humanitarian emergencies, which may have distorting effects in that any excess earmarked funds cannot be directed toward places or issues with more pressing immediate needs once a crisis has passed.

Despite the fact that Save the Children is a highly rated charity,[25] critics charge that a significant portion of funds classified as programming funds is used to cover travel expenses, salaries, and benefits for field staff, along with other operational costs. In other words, critics claim that the proportion of funding spent directly on targeted populations is actually less than that reported by the organization. Another criticism of Save the Children, as well as other large NGOs with broad mandates, is that it is a bloated, inefficient bureaucracy that lacks transparency and accountability. Critics also contend that Save the Children does not have a coherent strategy for achieving its goals or adequate mechanisms for assessing the effectiveness of its programs. The most damning criticism is that large NGOs like Save the Children are merely self-perpetuating entities that raise enormous sums of money that disproportionately go toward maintaining the operational expenses and salaries of the organization's staff. One of the most egregious examples of such distorted spending priorities comes from a former country director of one of Save the Children's overseas operations, who claimed that the primary "benefit" that children in his program were receiving was Save the Children hats, t-shirts, and invitations to parties.[26]

Village Health Works

Village Health Works is a health clinic in Kigutu, Burundi, that is based on collaboration between members of the community and a group of Americans who donate money and time to the project. Citizens in the community came together to approve the plan for the clinic, raised funds in Burundi, and built the clinic themselves. This community-based initiative has resulted in a clinic with an inpatient and malnutrition ward. A staff of fifty local Burundians runs the clinic and has treated 28,000 patients in the two years the clinic has been open. A community committee, made up almost exclusively of women, helps coordinate volunteer contributions to the clinic. Volunteers helped construct a six-kilometer road to help facilitate transportation to the clinic in this undeveloped area. Village Health Works helped install a cistern in the community, providing a source of clean water. International contributions to this NGO primarily consist of fund-raising initiatives in the United States.

Village Health Works differs dramatically from large NGOs like Save the Children. Its activities are limited to a single community. International involvement is minimal. Its projects and programs depend on volunteer contributions of members of the community, and its staff is made up of Burundian citizens. Village Health Works is based on a holistic view of health that not only emphasizes the treatment of disease but also focuses on meeting basic needs, including nutrition and clean water, that are critical for human health. To this end, the NGO has contributed to the development of permanent infrastructure in the community through the provision of clean water and the building of a road to the clinic. In recognition of the socioeconomic determinants of health, the organization also defrays the costs of school uniforms and fees to encourage Kigutu children to attend school. In these ways, Village Health Works is building up the community as it addresses pressing health needs of residents.[27]

It is clear that Village Health Works has made significant contributions to public health in Kigutu. A small NGO like Village Health Works has the advantage of working closely with members of a community and building up infrastructure, resources, and skills within a targeted community rather than creating dependencies on international actors. However, questions remain about the utility of this approach as a template for bottom-up initiatives to promote global health. Its scope and reach are limited. There are countless communities and regions in the developing world that have similar needs, and it would require an immense effort to replicate this initiative in every community that would benefit from such a program.

The GAVI Alliance (formerly the Global Alliance for Vaccines and Immunisation)

The GAVI Alliance is a PPP of national governments, international organizations, corporations, and NGOs. As such, it is not purely a non-state actor. Rather, the GAVI Alliance represents a hybrid actor built on an institutionalized relationship among a variety of state and non-state actors. The GAVI Alliance brings together a wide range of partners, including governments from both aid donor and recipient countries, the Gates Foundation and other philanthropic foundations, vaccine manufacturers, the World Health Organization (WHO),

UNICEF, the World Bank, and a variety of NGOs involved in global health. The GAVI Alliance's mission is to increase access to immunization in poor countries in order to save children's lives and protect people's health.[28]

The GAVI Alliance is distinct from other non-state actors working on global health in a variety of ways. Its unique structure as a PPP is perhaps its most obvious distinguishing feature. Additionally, it differs from many other non-state actors involved in global health promotion in its large scale of operation focused on a relatively narrow global health issue. Unlike other large non-state actors involved with important global health initiatives, which often apply multitiered strategies for addressing broadly defined health objectives, GAVI focuses its efforts exclusively on vaccination initiatives, including programs focusing on the supply of vaccines and on vaccine delivery systems. Despite its narrow focus, it is a large organization with significant global reach. Over seventy countries, representing half the world's population, are eligible to apply for support from the GAVI Alliance. The organization claims that its vaccination initiatives save millions of lives worldwide, an estimate supported by the WHO.[29]

The GAVI Alliance's global vaccination initiative is a success story that has saved many lives. Because the Alliance focuses on a safe, simple, low-cost intervention, it is easier to evaluate the effectiveness of GAVI initiatives. However, the GAVI Alliance strategy can be criticized for failing to promote structural change in societies where poverty-related health problems are endemic. Dr. Paul Farmer, a well-known public health practitioner, has argued that such low-cost solutions are insufficiently attentive to the fundamental structural changes necessary to effectively promote human rights and health for the world's poor.[30] Dr. Farmer was not directly criticizing the work of the GAVI Alliance. Nonetheless, his critique highlights a limitation of such approaches to global health promotion. Focused campaigns, like the GAVI vaccination initiative, can produce results with immediate benefits but do not necessarily promote long-term sustainable health solutions in developing countries.

Partners in Health

Partners in Health (PIH), founded by renowned physician and public health advocate Paul Farmer and his colleagues Thomas White and Todd McCormack, defines its mission as both medical and moral. Its vision asserts that public health aid should be based on an attitude of solidarity with, rather than charity for, the poor. The organization, based in Haiti, was founded initially to address the pressing health needs of the destitute poor in the poorest region of Haiti. PIH health initiatives in Haiti have led to the creation of clinics, schools, a mobile medical unit to promote disease screening among Haitians in rural villages, and the training of health outreach workers. PIH now provides medical services and care to poor populations in numerous developing countries. It also engages in research, educational outreach, and advocacy and lobbying for health as a human right. PIH collaborates with the Harvard Medical School and the Francois-Xavier Bagnoud Center for Health and Human Rights at the Harvard School of Public Health.[31]

PIH represents a sort of middle ground between some of the large NGOs (for example, Save the Children and the Gates Foundation) and the small NGOs (for example, Village Health Works, with its highly targeted work) considered in this section. It works in eight countries. Like many of the organizations considered here, it has adopted a holistic, comprehensive vision of human health. Although it is involved in a wide range of health promotion activities, it is deeply engaged in its own field work, unlike some of the larger NGOs discussed here. It has constructed its own clinics and hospitals and conducts its own research in conjunction with its treatment of patients in these clinics. In all of its work, it has collaborated with local organizations, national and transnational NGOs, governmental agencies, and international organizations. Indeed, PIH stresses the importance of working with states in an effort to build up sustainable public infrastructure rather than creating parallel non-state health systems. All the while, PIH emphasizes the need to give voice to the perspectives of the people it is seeking to help. To this end, PIH involves members of the community at all levels of its work—design, implementation, assessment, and evaluation.

The middle ground represented by the PIH program appears to have many benefits. The scope of its work is wider, thereby increasing its capacity to improve global health on a larger scale than that of an organization like Village Health Works. It operates in eight countries: Haiti, Lesotho, Malawi, Peru, Russia, Rwanda, the United States, and Kazakhstan. It also works with organizations that have adopted the PIH model in other countries, including Mexico, Guatemala, Burundi, Mali, Nepal, and Liberia. (Village Health Works in Burundi is one of these partner organizations.) Although PIH has a broader scope of influence than single-country organizations, its relatively small size may make it less susceptible to charges of bureaucratic top-heaviness or inefficiencies than large organizations like Save the Children or the Gates Foundation. Its close collaboration with the people in the communities where it works also may make PIH less susceptible to charges of a lack of democracy or representativeness.

Despite these real advantages, the scope and reach of PIH are nonetheless limited. As in the case of Village Health Works, most of the world's poor do not have access to PIH programs. Scaling up the PIH model to reach the destitute poor everywhere would require an extraordinary commitment of political will and resources on the part of non-state and state actors alike. Even if sufficient political will and financial resources existed, questions remain about whether the PIH model could maintain its flexibility and community-based emphasis if applied on a larger, global scale.

Doctors Without Borders (Médecins Sans Frontières)

Doctors Without Borders, an NGO created in 1971 by a group of French physicians and journalists, has a mandate focused on providing aid to people suffering from violence, neglect, or catastrophe, particularly victims of armed conflict, natural disasters, epidemics, malnutrition, or exclusion from health care systems. Its primary mission is to provide medical and humanitarian aid. It operates according to the principles of impartiality, independence, and neutrality. In accordance with these principles, Doctors Without Borders does not take sides in armed conflicts and provides aid without regard to the ethnic/religious identities or political affiliations of people in need. The group's adherence to these principles is necessary, in part, because it must cooperate with states and non-state actors involved in armed conflict or humanitarian crises in order to gain access to the vulnerable populations it is seeking to help.

Despite its formal commitment to neutrality and impartiality, Doctors Without Borders "reserves the right to speak out to bring attention to neglected crises, to challenge inadequacies or abuse of the aid system, and to advocate for improved medical treatment and protocols." The organization has spoken out on numerous occasions when fundamental human rights were at stake. For example, Doctors Without Borders called for an international military intervention in response to the Rwandan genocide in 1994. In 2007, it condemned the targeting of civilians in the Democratic Republic of the Congo, Central African Republic, Chad, and Somalia. The organization has advocated on behalf of new protocols for the use of ready-to-use food to treat malnutrition and has criticized pharmaceutical companies' opposition to the development of generic drugs.[32]

In comparison with other NGOs considered in this section, Doctors Without Borders has a relatively focused mission. Unlike Save the Children or the Gates Foundation, which are involved in broad global health initiatives, Doctors Without Borders focuses primarily on the provision of emergency medical care and humanitarian aid. However, within the scope of its mission, the organization acts with a fairly broad perspective and provides not only emergency medical treatment but also routine medical care and is attentive to issues of malnutrition, mental health, and other health challenges in zones of conflict and humanitarian crises. In this way, the scope of its activities is broader than the vaccination campaign of the GAVI Alliance. The global reach of Doctors Without Borders is moderate in comparison with other NGOs examined here. The organization comprises associative organizations in nineteen countries: Australia, Austria, Belgium, Canada, Denmark, France, Germany, Greece, Holland, Hong Kong, Italy, Japan, Luxembourg, Norway, Spain, Sweden, Switzerland, the United Kingdom, and the United States. Notably, all of its associative organizations are in developed countries. Yet, Doctors Without Borders carries out most of its work in the developing world, in almost sixty countries each year.

Observers have praised Doctors Without Borders for its ability to respond quickly and efficiently to armed conflict, humanitarian crises, and natural disasters. Many observers also appreciate that Doctors Without Borders raises most of its funds from private sources—almost 90 percent—rather than from states or international organizations, a fact that helps ensure its political independence.[33] However, critics have raised concerns about the organization's strategy and activities. As previously noted, the mission of the organization embraces principles—neutrality and the willingness to speak out—that can create tension. Some critics contend that the organization's advocacy work brings it into conflict with states and non-state actors in areas where it operates and undermines its ability to effectively aid vulnerable populations in conflict zones. Indeed, Doctors Without Borders has been expelled from numerous countries where it has condemned governmental policies and actions.[34] Critics also have raised concerns about organizational policies that make distinctions between national staff, hired in countries where Doctors Without Borders is working, and expatriate staff, doing work outside their country of origin. Such policies come into tension with the organization's commitment to equity and nondiscrimination.[35]

Conclusion

This chapter highlighted strengths and weaknesses of bottom-up approaches to global health promotion. Non-state actors have the capacity to shape global health outcomes in important ways. NGOs shape global health in numerous ways: by directly providing health aid to vulnerable populations, by raising funds for important global health initiatives, by supporting or carrying out health research and promoting the use of best medical practices, and by advocating for important health policies and programs. Corporations are powerful non-state actors that shape global health outcomes, for better or worse. TSMs have played an important role in the emergence and consolidation of global health norms and institutions. Individuals, acting as citizens and consumers, can take actions that have consequences for their own personal health as well as implications for the health of the broader communities in which they live.

The non-state actors considered in this chapter have different sizes; organizational structures; mandates; scopes of activities; and relationships with states, international organizations, and other non-state actors. An important theme throughout this chapter is that non-state actors often collaborate with states and international organizations in their efforts to promote global health. Thus, this chapter suggested that it is incorrect to assume that top-down and bottom-up approaches to global health are mutually exclusive. Rather, these approaches often dovetail, and successful global health initiatives typically require collaborative contributions from international organizations and states as well as non-state actors.

This chapter also underscored the reality that non-state actors, just like states and international organizations, operate in a political, social, and economic context. Analysts of international relations almost universally acknowledge that states are self-interested actors. However, observers do not always recognize that non-state actors are also entities that are motivated by self-interest and that operate in the face of political, institutional, legal, and structural constraints. In this regard, it is important to note that non-state actors are not necessarily democratic, representative, transparent, or accountable. Just as in the case of international organizations, idealist scholars of international relations often assume that non-state actors, especially issue-oriented NGOs, transcend self-interested politics. In reality, non-state actors are shaped by a range of political, economic, and strategic interests, and students interested in improving global health outcomes will be well served by an understanding of the complicated dynamics that shape bottom-up efforts to promote global health.

Discussion Questions

1. What does the concept of health governance mean? Can non-state actors promote governance in the area of global health in the absence of formal law and governmental institutions? Why or why not?
2. Which general strategy for interacting with state actors—circumvention, competition, or collaboration—best enables non-state actors to promote global health? Explain your answer.
3. How do corporations, especially MNCs, shape global health outcomes? Are the effects of corporations on global health largely positive or largely negative? Why?
4. How do TSMs affect global health?
5. Do individuals have the potential to significantly change global health outcomes? Why or why not?
6. What features distinguish various NGOs that work on global health? How are they similar, and how do they differ from one another?
7. What are the relative advantages and disadvantages of different NGO models and strategies for promoting global health? Which type of NGO is most effective in promoting improvements in global health? Why?

8. What might you, as an individual consumer or citizen, do to improve global health?

Web Resources

The Bill and Melinda Gates Foundation: http://www.gatesfoundation.org/

CARE: http://www.care.org/

The Commission on Smart Global Health Policy (launched by the Center for Strategic and International Studies): http://smartglobal health.org/

Doctors Without Borders: http://www.doctors withoutborders.org/

Engender Health: http://www.engenderhealth.org/

Family Care International: http://www.family careintl.org/en/home/

Food for the Poor, Inc.: http://www.foodfor thepoor.org/

The GAVI Alliance (formerly Global Alliance for Vaccines and Immunisation): http://www.gavialliance.org/

Global Health Action: http://www.global healthaction.org/

International Medical Corps: http://www.imc worldwide.org/

Malaria No More: http://www.malarianomore.org/

MAP International: http://www.map.org/

ONE: http://www.one.org/

Oxfam International: http://www.oxfam.org/

Partners in Health: http://www.pih.org/

Physicians for Human Rights: http://www.physiciansforhumanrights.org/

The Population Council: http://www.popcouncil.org/

Population Services International: http://www.psi.org/

Rockefeller Foundation: http://www.rockfound.org/

Save the Children: http://www.savethechildren.org/

Slow Food International: http://www.slowfood.com/

Village Health Works: http://villagehealthworks.org/

Water for People: http://www.waterforpeople.org/

William J. Clinton Foundation: http://www.clintonfoundation.org/

Conclusion

In the field of international relations, scholars and policy makers have traditionally prioritized national security, war, and peace as the most critical global issues. Other global issues, such as human rights, the environment, and health, traditionally have been relegated to a lower place on the international agenda. However, in the 21st century, these global issues are rising to a place of priority on the agendas of states and international organizations. Increasingly, scholars and policy makers are recognizing that human rights, the environment, and global health are critical global issues because they are often at the root of violent conflicts between and within states. Environmental, human rights, and global health challenges displace human populations in ways that disrupt the territorial integrity of neighboring states and that can precipitate intrastate and interstate violence. In short, the distinctions between "high politics" and "low politics" are increasingly blurry, and it is crucial for students interested in global politics to understand the ways in which transnational threats affect the stability of the international system as well as the well-being of humans across the world.

Among the range of transnational threats, global health is one of the most critical global issues of the 21st century. Global health, perhaps more than any other global issue, has the potential to significantly affect the longevity and quality of human lives across the globe. At the same time, efforts to promote global health have proved to be successful. Millions of lives have been saved as a result of important global health initiatives, including vaccination programs, disease eradication efforts like the global campaign to eradicate smallpox, and the development of public water systems and other public sanitation measures that led to a significant reduction in deadly communicable illnesses. Notably, many of these global health promotion initiatives involve simple, safe, and low-cost interventions that could easily be replicated if sufficient political will to provide the necessary resources existed.

Take the example of preventable childhood deaths. As recently as 1990, an estimated 11.9 million children died each year from preventable causes, including communicable diseases that can be prevented through vaccination, diarrheal diseases that are readily treatable, and malnutrition or undernutrition. In 2010, an estimated 7.7 million children died from such preventable causes. Obviously, this number is enormous and tragic. Yet, it represents an incredible reduction from the 1990 figure of nearly 12 million preventable childhood deaths. Experts attribute this significant reduction to a range of public health interventions, including vaccination programs, vitamin supplements, oral rehydration therapy for the treatment of diarrhea, and insecticide-treated bed nets for the prevention of malaria.[1]

The example of preventable childhood deaths illustrates the tension between despair and hope in global health. The challenge is staggering. Millions of lives are at stake every single year. No other issue threatens as many lives across the globe. Yet, the challenges are not insurmountable. In this regard, global health challenges differ from other threats to human security. Interstate and intrastate conflicts often seem intractable. In most cases, easy answers to resolving issues of war and peace do not exist. In contrast, for many health challenges, effective global health interventions that can save millions of lives exist.

To acknowledge that workable solutions to global health challenges exist is not to say that promoting global health is an easy or straightforward endeavor. As the chapters in the last part of the book show, international organizations, states, and non-state actors face serious political, economic, and social constraints in their efforts to promote global health. The likelihood that global health initiatives will succeed depends on the political will, power, and resources of numerous actors involved in global health politics. These actors sometimes compete for influence and resources. Additionally, fundamental disagreements about the most appropriate responses to global health challenges characterize interactions among the international organizations, states, and non-state actors involved in global health promotion efforts.

Furthermore, a number of obstacles impede easy solutions to global health challenges. Potential trade-offs between competing goals in global health exist. There are no easy answers to the question of whether the international community should prioritize programs that would save lives in the short term or policies that promote structural changes with health-producing benefits in the long run. In an ideal world, trade-offs between short-term goals and long-term change would not exist. In reality, limited resources are available for global health promotion endeavors. Should these limited resources be directed at initiatives with proven success in saving lives in the here and now, such as vaccination campaigns? Or would it be better to use limited resources

to promote structural changes, such as policies to encourage democratization or development efforts designed to empower the poor and the vulnerable, intended to reduce the economic and social inequities that contribute to poverty-related health challenges?

Questions also remain about the extent to which successful global health initiatives depend on the cooperation of states. On the one hand, some critics see states as part of the problem. They see them as cumbersome, inefficient entities that are insufficiently responsive to the needs of their populations, especially their most vulnerable citizens and residents. State involvement in interstate and intrastate conflict also has significant detrimental effects on human health. Additionally, state violations of human rights produce grave threats to human health. On the other hand, the globalization of disease and wellness probably makes the contributions of states essential for successful global health initiatives. National governments are the key players in building effective national health care systems, an essential part of any effort to provide basic health care on a large scale. Moreover, the globalization of disease and wellness makes collaboration among states, international organizations, and non-state actors essential for the effective promotion of global health. In an era of globalization, the health of a population in one country is increasingly intertwined with the health of people in other countries. As a result, countries cannot effectively promote global health in isolation. Because states make up the membership of international organizations, their participation and consent are necessary for effective global health initiatives by international organizations. Similarly, the ongoing state-centric nature of the international system means that non-state actors cannot independently tackle transnational health challenges on a global scale.

As our conclusion indicates, we do not pretend that easy solutions to global health problems exist. Yet, it is clear that global health initiatives can save millions of lives. To this end, this book is a call for action on the part of engaged citizens everywhere. As a global issue with incredible human consequences as well as potentially effective solutions, global health challenges should be a policy priority for countries, international organizations, NGOs, and engaged citizens across the globe. Effective solutions will require critical study, advocacy, deliberation, lobbying, information sharing, and collaboration of the highest order. Such collaboration needs to cross not only territorial borders dividing states but also professional, ideological, and political borders that divide citizens.

In this regard, it is essential to remember that global health is not just the purview of medical professionals, health care experts, or policy makers. Effective global health interventions require input and insights from individuals with expertise in a wide range of fields—from doctors, to engineers, to economists, to educators, to social workers. For this reason, we hope the audience for this book goes beyond students who want to work in medicine, public health,

or international relations. Engaged citizens in every occupation at all levels of society—from the local to the global—have the ability to shape global health outcomes for better or worse. In order for engaged citizens to affect global health in mostly positive ways, we believe it is essential for them to have a fundamental understanding of the nature of global health challenges and the political, economic, and social dynamics that undergird global health politics. Individuals—in their professional lives, in their political actions as citizens, and in their behaviors as consumers—make choices that affect their own health as well as the health of other people across the globe. Our fundamental hope is that students who understand the ways in which they have the capacity to improve global health will become committed to finding solutions for transnational health challenges and to supporting public health initiatives in their own communities and countries and across the globe.

Notes

Chapter 1

1. Jeffrey P. Koplan, T. Christopher Bond, Michael H. Merson, K. Srinath Reddy, Mario Henry Rodriguez, Nelson K. Sewankambo, and Judith N. Wasserheit, for the Consortium of Universities for Global Health Executive Board, "Towards a Common Definition of Global Health," *Lancet* 373 (2009): 1993–1994. Available online at: http://www.hopkinsglobalhealth.org/resources/headlines/Definition%20of%20Global%20Health%20article.pdf.

2. *Ibid.*

3. *Ibid.*: 1995.

4. Charles-Edward Amory Winslow, "The Untilled Fields of Public Health," *Science* 51 (1920): 30.

5. Koplan et al.: 1993.

6. Preamble to the Constitution of the World Health Organization as adopted by the International Health Conference, New York, New York, June 19–July 22, 1946, by the representatives of 61 states (Official Records of the World Health Organization, no. 2, p. 100) and entered into force on April 7, 1948.

7. Koplan et al.: 1993.

8. Robert H. Blank and Viola Burau, *Comparative Health Policy*, 2d ed. (Houndmills, Basingstoke, Hampshire, England; New York: Palgrave Macmillan, 2007): 2.

9. Linda P. Fried, Margaret E. Bentley, Pierre Buekens, Donald S. Burke, Julio J. Frenk, Michael J. Klag, and Harrison C. Spencer, "Global Health Is Public Health," *Lancet* 375: 9714 (2010): 535–537.

10. Richard Skolnik, *Essentials of Global Health* (Sudbury, MA: Jones and Bartlett Publishers, 2008): xiii.

11. World Health Organization, *Reducing Mortality from Major Killers of Children*, Fact Sheet 178, available online at: http://www.who.int/inf-fs/en/fact178.html; Denise Grady, "Global Death Rates Drop for Children 5 or Younger," *New York Times*, May 23, 2010. Available online at: http://www.nytimes.com/2010/05/24/health/24child.html?emc=eta1/.

12. World Health Organization, United Nations Children's Fund, United Nations Population Fund, and the World Bank, *Maternal Mortality in 2005* (World Health Organization, 2007): 1. Available online at: http://www.who.int/whosis/mme_2005.pdf.

13. Garrett Hardin, "Lifeboat Ethics: The Case Against Helping the Poor," *Psychology Today* (September 1974): 800–812.

14. David Held and Anthony McGrew, "Globalization," in Joel Krieger, ed., *Oxford Companion to Politics of the World* (Oxford, England: Oxford University Press, 2001). Available online at: http://www.polity.co.uk/global/globalization-oxford.asp.

15. UNAIDS (Joint United Nations Programme on HIV/AIDS), *2008 Report*

on the Global AIDS Epidemic (July 2008). Available online at: http://data. unaids.org/pub/GlobalReport/2008/ JC1510_2008GlobalReport_en.zip.

16. Richard Dodson and Kelly Lee, "Global Health Governance: A Conceptual Review," in Rorden Wilkinson and Steve Hughes, eds., *Global Governance: Critical Perspectives* (London: Routledge, 2002): 93.

17. *Ibid.*: 94.

18. Andrew F. Cooper and John J. Kirton, eds., *Innovations in Global Health Governance* (Burlington, VT: Ashgate Publishers, 2009).

19. Adrian Kay and Owain Williams, "The International Political Economy of Global Health Governance," in Adrian Kay and Owain Williams, eds., *Global Health Governance: Crisis, Institutions, and Political Economy* (Basingstoke: Palgrave Macmillan, 2009): 13–14.

20. David P. Fidler, *SARS, Governance and the Globalization of Disease* (Basingstoke: Palgrave Macmillan, 2004).

21. Michael Reich, "Public-private Partnerships for Public Health," in Michael Reich, ed., *Public-private Partnerships for Public Health* (Cambridge, MA: Harvard Center for Population and Development Studies, 2002): 2–3.

22. *Ibid.*

Chapter 2

1. Sridhar Venkatapuram, "Global Justice and the Social Determinants of Health," *Ethics & International Affairs* 24: 2 (Summer 2010): 119–130.

2. World Health Organization, *World Health Statistics 2009* (2009). Available online at: http://www.who.int/whosis/whostat/2009/en/index.html.

3. Venkatapuram: 119.

4. P.W. Wilson, "Established Risk Factors and Coronary Artery Disease: The Framingham Study," *American Journal of Hypertension* 7: 2 (1994): 7S–12S.

5. A. Blum and N. Blum, "Coronary Artery Disease: Are Men and Women Created Equal?" *Gender Medicine* 6: 3 (2009): 410–418.

6. C.G. Victora, J. Bryce, J.O. Fontaine, and R. Monasch, "Reducing Deaths from Diarrhoea Through Oral Rehydration Therapy," *Bulletin of the World Health Organization* 78: 10 (2000): 1246–1255.

7. Wilson: 7S–12S.

8. *Ibid.*

9. LaTisha Marshall, Michael Schooley, Heather Ryan, Patrick Cox, Alyssa Easton, Cheryl Healton, Kat Jackson, Kevin C. Davis, and Ghada Homsi, "Youth Tobacco Surveillance—United States, 2001–2002," *Morbidity and Mortality Surveillance Summaries* 55: SS-3 (2006): 1–56.

10. D.J. Barker, "Fetal Origins of Cardiovascular Disease," *British Medical Journal* 311: 6998 (1995): 171–174.

11. Joint United Nations Programme on HIV/AIDS, *UNAIDS Report on the Global AIDS Epidemic 2010*: 20–21. Available online at: http://www.unaids.org/globalreport/Global_report.htm.

12. U.S. Centers for Disease Control and Prevention, *New Study in Low-income Heterosexuals in America's Inner Cities Reveals High HIV Rates* (July 19, 2010). Available online at: http://www.cdc.gov/nchhstp/newsroom/povertyand hivpressrelease.html.

13. E.H. Michelson, "Adam's Rib Awry? Women and Schistosomiasis," *Social Science & Medicine* 37: 4 (1993): 493–501; S.B. Kendie, "Survey of Water Use Behaviour in Rural North Ghana," *Natural Resources Forum* 16 (1992): 126–131.

14. V.N. Mishra, M. Malhotra, and S. Gupta, "Chronic Respiratory Disorders in Females of Delhi," *Journal of the Indian Medical Association* 88: 3 (1990): 77–80.

15. European Agency for Safety and Health at Work, *Gender Issues in Safety and Health at Work: Summary of an Agency Report* (2003): 2. Available online at: http://osha.europa.eu/en/publications/factsheets/42/.

16. S. Islam, A.M. Velilla, E.J. Doyle, and A.M. Ducatman, "Gender Differences in Work-related Injury/Illness: Analysis of Workers Compensation Claims," *American Journal of Industrial Medicine* 39: 1 (2001): 84–91.

17. World Health Organization, *Gender, Health, and Work* (2004): 3. Available online at: http://www.who.int/gender/other_health/Gender,HealthandWorklast.pdf.

18. M.G. Marmot, G.D. Smith, S. Stansfeld, C. Patel, F. North, J. Head, I. White, E. Brunner, and A. Feeney, "Health Inequalities Among British Civil Servants: The Whitehall II Study," *Lancet* 337: 8754 (1991): 1387–1393.

19. World Health Organization, *Healthy Environments for Children—Initiating an Alliance for Action* (2002): 11. Available online at: http://whqlibdoc.who.int/hq/2002/WHO_SDE_PHE_02.06.pdf.

20. S.H. Arshad, "Does Exposure to Indoor Allergens Contribute to the Development of Asthma and Allergy?" *Current Allergy and Asthma Reports* 10: 1 (2010): 49–55.

21. P.T. Nastos, A.G. Paliatsos, M.B. Anthracopoulos, E.S. Roma, and K.N. Priftis, "Outdoor Particulate Matter and Childhood Asthma Admissions in Athens, Greece: A Time-series Study," *Environmental Health* 9: 7 (2010): 45–53.

22. Alejandro Portes, "Social Capital: Its Origins and Applications in Modern Sociology," *Annual Review of Sociology* 24 (1998): 1–24.

23. Richard Rose, "How Much Does Social Capital Add to Individual Health? A Survey of Russians," *Social Science and Medicine* 51: 9 (2000): 1421–1435.

24. Richard G. Wilkinson, Ichiro Kawachi, and Bruce P. Kennedy, "Mortality, the Social Environment, Crime and Violence," *Sociology of Health & Illness* 20: 5 (1998): 578–597.

25. Ana V. Diez Roux and Christina Mair, "Neighborhoods and Health," *Annals of the New York Academy of Sciences* 1186 (February 2010): 125–145.

26. *Ibid.*

27. Leon Gordis, "Measuring the Occurrence of Disease," in *Epidemiology* (Philadelphia: W.B. Saunders Company, 1996): 32.

28. *Ibid.*: 31.

29. Marthe R. Gold, David Stevenson, and Dennis G. Fryback, "HALYs and QALYs and DALYs, Oh My: Similarities and Differences in Summary Measures of Population Health," *Annual Review of Public Health* 23 (May 2002): 115–134.

30. *Ibid.*

31. World Health Organization, "Part 4, Burden of Disease: DALYs," *The Global Burden of Disease 2004 Update* (2004). Available online at: http://www.who.int/healthinfo/global_burden_disease/GBD_report_2004update_part4.pdf.

32. Abdel R. Omran, "The Epidemiologic Transition: A Theory of the Epidemiology of Population Change," *Millbank Quarterly* 83: 4 (2005): 736–737.

33. *Ibid.*

34. U.S. Census Bureau, "International Population Reports WP/02," *Global Population Profile: 2002* (Washington, DC: U.S. Government Printing Office, 2004). Available online at: http://www.census.gov/prod/2004pubs/wp-02.pdf.

35. Ronald Lee, "The Demographic Transition: Three Centuries of Fundamental Change," *Journal of Economic Perspectives* 17: 4 (2003): 167–190.

36. *Ibid.*

37. *Ibid.*

Chapter 3

1. Kirk R. Smith, Carlos F. Corvalán, and Tord Kjellstrom, "How Much Global Ill Health Is Attributable to Environmental Factors?" *Epidemiology* 10: 5 (1999): 573.

2. *Ibid.*

3. World Health Organization, *Environmental Health.* Available online at: http://www.who.int/topics/environmental_health/en/.

4. Richard Skolnik, *Essentials of Global Health* (Sudbury, MA: Jones and Bartlett Publishers, 2008): 115.

5. Smith, Corvalán, and Kjellstrom: 573–584.

6. *Ibid.*: 575.

7. World Health Organization, *Global Health Risks: Mortality and Burden of Disease*

Attributable to Selected Major Risks (December 2009): 23–25. Available online at: http://www.who.int/healthinfo/global_burden_disease/GlobalHealthRisks_report_full.pdf.

8. Smith, Corvalán, and Kjellstrom: 580.

9. *Ibid.*: 579–580.

10. *Ibid.*: 582.

11. World Health Organization, *Global Health Risks*: 23.

12. Nigel Bruce, Rogelio Perez-Padilla, and Rachel Albalak, "Indoor Air Pollution in Developing Countries: A Major Environmental and Public Health Challenge," *Bulletin of the World Health Organization* 78: 9 (2000): 1078–1092.

13. *Ibid.*: 1087.

14. Skolnik: 34.

15. Michael Begon, Colin R. Townsend, and John L. Harper, *Ecology: From Individuals to Ecosystems*, 4th ed. (Malden, MA: Wiley-Blackwell, 2006): xi.

16. Dennis C. Pirages, "Nature, Disease, and Globalization: An Evolutionary Perspective," *International Studies Review* 9 (2007): 616–628; Andrew T. Price-Smith, *The Health of Nations: Infectious Disease, Environmental Change, and Their Effects on National Security and Development* (Cambridge, MA: MIT Press, 2002): 141–170.

17. Pirages.

18. *Ibid.*: 621–622.

19. *Ibid.*: 621.

20. David Quammen, "Deadly Contact: How Animals and Humans Exchange Disease," *National Geographic* (October 2007): 77–105.

21. Pirages: 625.

22. *Ibid.*: 622.

23. Adam Jones, *Genocide: A Comprehensive Introduction* (New York: Routledge, 2006): 67–77.

24. Cited in Quammen: 87.

25. Quammen: 88–89.

26. Laurie Garrett, *Betrayal of Trust: The Collapse of Global Public Health* (New York: Hyperion, 2000): 62, 99.

27. *Ibid.*: 100–101.

28. Quammen: 92–93.

29. Garrett, *Betrayal of Trust*: 104–121.

30. Quammen: 87–92.

31. Garrett, *Betrayal of Trust*: 116–117.

32. Robert D. Morris, *The Blue Death: Disease, Disaster, and the Water We Drink* (New York: HarperCollins Publishers, 2007): 264.

33. *Ibid.*: 1, 263–264.

34. World Health Organization, *Global Health Risks*: 23.

35. Skolnik: 121–122.

36. Garrett, *Betrayal of Trust*: 203–205.

37. Laurie Garrett, *The Coming Plague: Newly Emerging Diseases in a World out of Balance* (New York: Penguin Books, 1994): 203–205.

38. Morris: 265–268.

39. Larry Wheeler and Grant Smith, "Aging Sewers Release Sewage into Rivers, Streams," *USA Today*, May 8, 2008.

40. Morris: 282–284.

41. Elizabeth Economy, *The River Runs Black: The Environmental Challenge to China's Future* (Ithaca, NY: Cornell University Press, 2005).

42. Donald R. Mattison, "Environmental Exposures and Development," *Current Opinion in Pediatrics* 22: 2 (2010): 208–218.

43. Morris: 292.

44. Anthony Costello, Mustafa Abbas, Adriana Allen, Sarah Ball, Sarah Bell, Richard Bellamy, Sharon Friel, Nora Groce, Anne Johnson, Maria Kett, Maria Lee, Caren Levy, Mark Maslin, David McCoy, Bill McGuire, Hugh Montgomery, David Napier, Christina Pagel, Jinesh Patel, Jose Antonio Puppim de Oliveira, Nanneke Redclift, Hannah Rees, Daniel Rogger, Joanne Scott, Judith Stephenson, John Twigg, Jonathan Wolf, and Craig Patterson, "Managing the Health Effects of Climate Change," *Lancet* 373: 9676 (2009): 1639–1733.

45. World Health Organization, *Global Health Risks*: 23–25.

46. *Ibid.*

47. *Ibid.*: 24.

48. Elisabeth Rosenthal, "As Earth Warms Up, Tropical Virus Moves to Italy," *New York Times*, December 23, 2007.

49. Michael Finkel, "Bedlam in the Blood: Malaria," *National Geographic* (July 2007): 41.

50. F. Tanser and B. Sharp, "Global Climate Change and Malaria," *Lancet* 5: 5 (2005): 256–258.

51. R.J. Borroto, "Global Warming, Rising Sea Level, and Growing Risk of Cholera Incidence: A Review of the Literature and Evidence," *GeoJournal* 44: 2 (1998): 111–120.

52. Robin McKie, "Climate Change: Melting Ice Will Trigger Wave of Natural Disasters," *Observer*, September 6, 2009. Available online at: http://www.guardian. co.uk/environment/2009/sep/06/global-warming-natural-disasters-conference/.

53. Pirages: 622–623.

Chapter 4

1. John C. Sherris, "Overview," in John C. Sherris, ed., *Medical Microbiology: An Introduction to Infectious Diseases*, 2d ed. (New York: Elsevier, 1990): 1–10.

2. *Ibid.*

3. *Ibid.*: 4.

4. *Ibid.*

5. L. Corey, "Epidemiology of Infectious Diseases," in John C. Sherris, ed., *Medical Microbiology: An Introduction to Infectious Diseases*, 2d ed. (New York: Elsevier, 1990): 181–195.

6. Ciarán P. Kelly and J. Thomas LaMont, "*Clostridium difficile*—More Difficult than Ever," *New England Journal of Medicine* 18 (2008): 1932–1940.

7. World Health Organization, *World Health Organization Steps Up Action Against Substandard and Counterfeit Medicines* (2003). Available online at: http://www.who. int/mediacentre/news/releases/2003/pr85/en.

8. *Ibid.*

9. World Health Organization, *Smallpox—Historical Significance*. Available online at: http://www.who.int/mediacentre/factsheets/ smallpox/en/index.html.

10. World Health Organization, *Poliomyelitis*, Fact Sheet. Available online at: http://www. who.int/mediacentre/factsheets/fs114/en/ index.html.

11. World Health Organization, Department of Immunization, Vaccines, and Biologicals, and UNICEF Programme Division, Health Section, *GIVS—Global Immunization Vision and Strategy, 2006–2015* (2005). Available online at: http://www.who. int/vaccines-documents/DocsPDF05/ GIVS_Final_EN.pdf.

12. World Health Organization, Department of Immunization, Vaccines, and Biologicals, *Intellectual Property Rights and Vaccines in Developing Countries* (2004). Available online at: http://whqlibdoc.who.int/ hq/2004/WHO_IVB_04.21_(302KB).pdf.

13. World Health Organization, *The Global Burden of Disease: 2004 Update* (2008). Available online at: http://www.who.int/ healthinfo/global_burden_disease/GBD_ report_2004update_full.pdf.

14. *Ibid.*

15. World Health Organization, *WHO Global Strategy for Containment of Antimicrobial Resistance*: 1. Available online at: http:// www.who.int/csr/resources/publications/ drugresist/WHO_CDS_CSR_DRS_2001_ 2_EN/en/.

16. A.J. Alanis, "Resistance to Antibiotics: Are We in the Post-antibiotic Era?" *Archives of Medical Research* 36: 6 (2005): 697–705.

17. L.P. Ormerod, "Multidrug-resistant Tuberculosis (MDR-TB): Epidemiology, Prevention, and Treatment," *British Medical Bulletin* 73–74: 1 (2005): 17–24.

18. S.K. Fridkin, J.C. Hageman, M. Morrison, L.T. Sanza, K. Como-Sabetti, J.A. Jernigan, K. Harriman, L.H. Harrison, R. Lynfield, and M.M. Farley, for the Active Bacterial Core Surveillance Program of the Emerging Infections Program Network, "Methicillin-resistant *Staphylococcus aureus* Disease in Three Communities," *New England Journal of Medicine* 352: 14 (2005): 1436–1444.

19. D.L. Stevens, Y. Ma, D.B. Salmi, E. McIndoo, R.J. Wallace, and A.E. Bryant, "Impact of Antibiotics on Expression of Virulence-associated Exotoxin Genes in

Methicillin-sensitive and Methicillin-resistant *Staphylococcus aureus*," *Journal of Infectious Diseases* 195: 2 (2007): 202–211.

20. P.F. Harrison and J. Lederberg, *Antimicrobial Resistance Issues and Options* (Washington, DC: National Academy Press, 1998).

21. Alanis: 701; R.H. Schwartz, B.J. Freij, M. Ziai, and M.J. Sheridan, "Antimicrobial Prescribing for Acute Purulent Rhinitis in Children: A Survey of Pediatricians and Family Practicioners," *Pediatric Infectious Disease Journal* 16: 2 (1997): 185–190.

22. J.D. Cleary, "Impact of Pharmaceutical Sales Representatives on Physician Antibiotic Prescribing," *Journal of Pharmacy Technology* 8: 1 (1992): 27–29.

23. F. Marra, D.L. Monnet, D.M. Patrick, M. Chong, C.T. Brandt, M. Winters, M.S. Kaltoft, G.J. Tyrrell, M. Lovgren, and W.R. Bowie, "A Comparison of Antibiotic Use in Children Between Canada and Denmark," *Annual of Pharmacotherapy* 41: 4 (2007): 659–666; H. Goossens, M. Ferech, S. Coenen, and P. Stephens, European Surveillance of Antimicrobial Consumption Project Group, "Comparison of Outpatient Systemic Antibacterial Use in 2004 in the United States and 27 European Countries," *Clinical Infectious Diseases* 44: 8 (2007): 1091–1095.

24. Goossens et al.: 1091–1095.

25. B.L. Braun and J.B. Fowles, "Characteristics and Experiences of Parents and Adults Who Want Antibiotics for Cold Symptoms," *Archives of Family Medicine* 9: 7 (2000): 589–595.

26. A. Coco, L. Vernacchio, M. Horst, and A. Anderson, "Management of Acute Otitis Media After Publication of the 2004 AAP and AAFP Clinical Practice Guideline," *Pediatrics* 125: 2 (2010): 214–220; T. Wrigley, A. Tinto, and A. Majeed, "Age and Sex Specific Antibiotic Prescribing Patterns in General Practice in England and Wales, 1994 to 1998," *Health Statistics Quarterly* 14 (2002): 14–20.

27. P. Davey, E. Brown, L. Fenelon, R. Finch, I. Gould, A. Holmes, C. Ramsay, E. Taylor, P. Wiffen, and M. Wilcox, "Systematic Review of Antimicrobial Drug Prescribing Practices in Hospitals," *Cochrane Database of Systematic Reviews* 19: 4 (2005): CD003543.

28. M.E. Hulscher, J.W. van der Meer, and R.P. Grol, "Antibiotic Use: How to Improve It?" *International Journal of Medical Microbiology* 300: 6 (2010): 351–356.

29. E.A. Scicluna, M.A. Borg, D. Gür, O. Rassian, I. Taher, S.B. Redjeb, Z. Elnassar, D.P. Bagatzouni, and Z. Daoud, "Self-medication with Antibiotics in the Ambulatory Care Setting Within the Euro-Mediterranean Region; Results from the ARMed Project," *Journal of Infectious Public Health* 2: 4 (2009): 189–197.

30. *Ibid.*; R. Raz, H. Edelstein, L. Grigoryan, and F.M. Haaijer-Ruskamp, "Self-medication with Antibiotics by a Population in Northern Israel," *Israeli Medical Association Journal* 7: 11 (2005): 722–725; A. Awad, I. Eltayeb, L. Matowe, and L. Thalib, "Self-medication with Antibiotics and Antimalarials in the Community of Khartoum State, Sudan," *Journal of Pharmaceutical Sciences* 8: 2 (2005): 326–331.

31. E.K. Silbergeld, J. Graham, and L.B. Price, "Industrial Food Animal Production, Antimicrobial Resistance, and Human Health," *Annual Review of Public Health* 29 (2008): 151–169.

32. M. Mellon, C. Benbrook, and K.L. Benbrook, *Hogging It! Estimates of Antimicrobial Abuse in Livestock* (Cambridge, MA: Union of Concerned Scientists, 2001).

33. P.F. Harrison and J. Lederberg, *Antimicrobial Resistance: Issues and Options* (Washington, DC: National Academy Press, 1998).

34. J.P. Graham, J.J. Boland, and E. Silbergeld, "Growth Promoting Antibiotics in Food Animal Production: An Economic Analysis," *Public Health Reports* 122: 1 (2007): 79–87.

35. Silbergeld et al.: 153.

36. D.L. Smith, A.D. Harris, J.A. Johnson, E.K. Silbergeld, and J.G. Morris Jr., "Animal Antibiotic Use Has an Early but Important Impact on the Emergence

of Antibiotic Resistance in Human Commensal Bacteria," *Proceeds of the National Academy of Science* 99: 9 (2002): 6434–6439; World Health Organization, *The Medical Impact of Antimicrobial Use in Food Animals* (Report of a WHO meeting in Berlin, Germany, October 13–17, 1997). Available online at: http://whqlibdoc.who.int/hq/1997/WHO_EMC_ZOO_97.4.pdf.

37. F.M. Aarestrup, A.M. Seyfarth, H.D. Emborg, K. Pedersen, R.S. Hendriksen, and F. Bager, "Effect of Abolishment of the Use of Antimicrobial Agents for Growth Promotion on Occurrence of Antimicrobial Resistance in Fecal Enterococci from Food Animals in Denmark," *Antimicrobial Agents and Chemotherapy* 45 (2001): 2054–2059.

38. Andrew Pollack, "Antibiotic Research Subsidies Weighed by U.S.," *New York Times*, November 6, 2001: B1.

39. J.L. Jones, D.L. Hanson, M.S. Dworkin, D.L. Alderton, P.L. Fleming, J.E. Kaplan, and J. Ward, "Surveillance for AIDS-defining Opportunistic Illnesses, 1992–1997," *Morbidity and Morality Weekly Report* 48: 2 (1999): 1–22.

40. T.C. Quinn, "Global Burden of the HIV Pandemic," *Lancet* 348: 9020 (1996): 99–106.

41. World Health Organization, *Health, Economic Growth, and Poverty Reduction*, Report of the Working Group 1 of the Commission on Macroeconomics and Health (2002): 78. Available online at: http://whqlibdoc.who.int/publications/9241590092.pdf.

42. Joint United Nations Programme on HIV/AIDS (UNAIDS) and World Health Organization, *AIDS Epidemic Update* (2009). Available online at: http://data.unaids.org/pub/Report/2009/JC1700_Epi_Update_2009_en.pdf.

43. U.S. Centers for Disease Control and Prevention, *New Study in Low-income Heterosexuals in America's Inner Cities Reveals High HIV Rates* (July 19, 2010). Available online at: http://www.cdc.gov/nchhstp/newsroom/povertyand hivpressrelease.html.

44. Joint United Nations Programme on HIV/AIDS (UNAIDS) and World Health Organization, *AIDS Epidemic Update*: 33.

45. Joint United Nations Programme on HIV/AIDS (UNAIDS), *Injecting Drug Use: Focused HIV Prevention Works* (2007). Available online at: http://www.unaids.org/en/KnowledgeCentre/Resources/FeatureStories/archive/2007/20070511_BP_High_coverage_sites.asp.

46. R. Bunnell, A. Opio, J. Musinguzi, W. Kirungi, P. Ekwaru, V. Mishra, W. Hladik, J. Kafuko, E. Madraa, and J. Mermin, "HIV Transmission Risk Behavior Among HIV-infected Adults in Uganda: Results of a Nationally Representative Survey," *AIDS* 22: 5 (2008): 617–624.

47. *Kenya AIDS Indicator Survey* (KAIS) 2007 Data Sheet: 7. Available online at: http://www.prb.org/pdf09/kaiskenyadatasheet.pdf.

48. Joint United Nations Programme on HIV/AIDS (UNAIDS) and World Health Organization, *AIDS Epidemic Update*: 29.

49. N. Andersson, A. Ho-Foster, S. Mitchell, E. Scheepers, and S. Goldstein, "Risk Factors for Domestic Physical Violence: National Cross-sectional Household Surveys in Eight Southern African Countries," *BMC Women's Health* 7 (2007): 11.

50. R.C. Bailey, S. Moses, C.B. Parker, K. Agot, I. Maclean, J.N. Krieger, C.F. Williams, R.T. Campbell, and J.O. Ndinya-Achola, "Male Circumcision for HIV Prevention in Young Men in Kisumu, Kenya: A Randomised Controlled Trial," *Lancet* 369: 9562 (2007): 643–656.

51. Joint United Nations Programme on HIV/AIDS (UNAIDS), *Injecting Drug Use: Focused HIV Prevention Works*: 1.

52. Joint United Nations Programme on HIV/AIDS (UNAIDS) and World Health Organization, *AIDS Epidemic Update*: 26.

53. Joint United Nations Programme on HIV/AIDS (UNAIDS), *High Coverage Sites: HIV Prevention Among Injecting Drug Users in Transitional and Developing Countries* (2006). Available online at: http://data.unaids.org/Publications/IRC-pub07/JC1254-HighCoverageIDU_en.pdf.

54. Joint United Nations Programme on HIV/ AIDS (UNAIDS) and World Health Organization, *AIDS Epidemic Update*: 9.

55. *Ibid.*: 16.

56. *Ibid.*: 25.

57. R. Bonnel, *Economic Analysis of HIV/ AIDS. Background Paper for the African Development Forum, September 2000* (Washington, DC: The World Bank, 2000).

58. World Health Organization, *Health, Economic Growth, and Poverty Reduction*: 83.

59. P. Piot, M. Bartos, P.D. Ghys, N. Walker, and B. Schwartländer, "The Global Impact of HIV/AIDS," *Nature* 410: 6831 (2001): 968–973.

60. World Health Organization, *Anti-tuberculosis Drug Resistance in the World—Fourth Global Report* (2008). Available online at: http:// www.who.int/tb/publications/2008/drs_ report4_26feb08.pdf.

61. E. Nathanson, P. Nunn, M. Uplekar, K. Floyd, E. Jaramillo, K. Lönnroth, D. Wiel, and M. Raviglione, "MDR Tuberculosis—Critical Steps for Prevention and Control," *New England Journal of Medicine* 363: 11 (2010): 1050–1058.

62. J.C. Sherris and J.J. Plorde, "Mycobacteria," in J.C. Sherris, ed., *Medical Microbiology: An Introduction to Infectious Diseases*, 2d ed. (New York: Elsevier, 1990): 443–461.

63. World Health Organization, *Tuberculosis*, Fact Sheet (2008). Available online at: http://www.who.int/mediacentre/factsheets/ fs104/en/.

64. World Health Organization, *Improving TB Drug Management—Accelerating DOTS Expansion* (2002): 9. Available online at: http://www.stoptb.org/assets/documents/ gdf/whatis/DrugManagementPaper.pdf.

65. World Health Organization, *Global Tuberculosis Control—A Short Update to the 2009 Report* (2009): 9. Available online at: http://whqlibdoc.who.int/ publications/2009/9789241598866_ eng.pdf.

66. *Ibid.*: 20.

67. U.S. Centers for Disease Control and Prevention, "Trends in Tuberculosis—United States, 2007," *Morbidity and Mortality Weekly Report* 57: 11 (2008): 281–285.

68. K. Schwartzman, O. Oxlade, R.G. Barr, F. Grimard, I. Acosta, J. Baez, E. Ferreira, R.E. Melgan, W. Morose, A.C. Salgado, V. Jacquet, S. Maloney, K. Laseson, A. Pablos Mendez, and D. Menzies, "Domestic Returns from Investment in the Control of Tuberculosis in Other Countries," *New England Journal of Medicine* 353: 10 (2005): 1008–1020.

69. C.G. Ray, "Respiratory Viruses," in J.C. Sherris, ed., *Medical Microbiology: An Introduction to Infectious Diseases*, 2d ed. (New York: Elsevier, 1990): 499–516.

70. *Ibid.*: 501–502.

71. World Health Organization, *Influenza (seasonal)*, Fact Sheet (2010). Available online at: http://www.who.int/mediacentre/ factsheets/fs211/en/index.html.

72. U.S. Centers for Disease Control and Prevention, "Estimates of Deaths Associated with Seasonal Influenza—United States, 1976–2007," *Morbidity and Mortality Weekly Report* 59: 33 (2010): 1057–1062.

73. J.K. Taubenberger and D.M. Morens, "1918 Influenza: The Mother of All Pandemics," *Emerging Infectious Diseases* 12: 1 (2006): 15–22.

74. World Health Organization, *World Now at the Start of 2009 Influenza Pandemic* (2009). Available online at: http://www.who.int/mediacentre/news/ statements/2009/h1n1_pandemic_ phase6_20090611/en/index.html.

75. K. Khan, J. Arino, J.W. Hu, P. Raposo, J. Sears, F. Calderon, C. Heidebrecht, M. Macdonald, J. Liauw, A. Chan, and M. Gardam, "Spread of a Novel Influenza A (H1N1) Virus via Global Airline Transportation," *New England Journal of Medicine* 361: 2 (2009): 212–214.

76. World Health Organization, *Pandemic (H1N1) 2009—Update 111* (2010). Available online at: http://www.who.int/csr/ don/2010_07_30/en/.

77. World Health Organization, *Cumulative Number of Confirmed Cases of Avian*

Influenza A/(H5N1) Reported to WHO (2009). Available online at: http://www. who.int/influenza/human_animal_interface/ H5N1_cumulative_table_archives/en/index. html.

78. U.S. Centers for Disease Control and Prevention, *Updated Interim Recommendations for the Use of Antiviral Medications in the Treatment and Prevention of Influenza for the 2009–2010 Season* (2009). Available online at: http://www.cdc.gov/ H1N1flu/recommendations.htm.

79. U.S. Centers for Disease Control and Prevention, "2009–2010 Influenza Season Week 20 Ending May 22, 2010," *Fluview—A Weekly Influenza Surveillance Report by the Influenza Division* (2010). Available online at: http://www.cdc.gov/flu/ weekly/.

80. E.A. Belongia, B.A. Kieke, J.G. Donahue, R.T. Greenlee, A. Balish, A. Foust, S. Lindstrom, and D.K. Shay, "Effectiveness of Inactivated Influenza Vaccines Varied Substantially with Antigenic Match from the 2004–2005 Season to the 2006–2007 Season," *Journal of Infectious Diseases* 199: 2 (2009): 159–167.

81. World Health Organization, *Influenza: Surveillance and Monitoring.*. Available online at: http://www.who.int/influenza/ surveillance_monitoring/en/.

Chapter 5

1. World Health Organization, *The Global Burden of Disease: 2004 Update* (2008). Available online at: http://www.who.int/ healthinfo/global_burden_disease/GBD_ report_2004update_full.pdf.

2. *Ibid.*: 44.

3. World Health Organization, *Cardiovascular Diseases*, Fact Sheet (2009). Available online at: http://www.who.int/mediacentre/ factsheets/fs317/en/index.html.

4. Thomas A. Gaziano, Asaf Bitton, Shuchi Anand, Shafika Abrahams-Gessel, and Adrianna Murphy, "Growing Epidemic of Coronary Heart Disease in Low- and Middle-income Countries," *Current Problems in Cardiology* 35: 2 (2010): 72–115.

5. Luis G. Escobedo, Wayne H. Giles, and Robert F. Anda, "Socioeconomic Status, Race, and Death from Coronary Heart Disease," *American Journal of Preventive Medicine* 13: 2 (1997): 123–130; Centers for Disease Control and Prevention, "Trends in Ischemic Heart Disease Death Rates for Blacks and Whites—United States, 1981–1995," *Morbidity and Mortality Weekly Report* 47: 44 (1998): 945–949.

6. Mayo Clinic, *Heart Disease in Women: Understand Symptoms and Risk Factors.* Available online at: http://www.mayoclinic. com/health/heart-disease/HB00040/.

7. Peter W. Wilson, "Established Risk Factors and Coronary Artery Disease: The Framingham Study," *American Journal of Hypertension* 7: 7 Pt. 2 (1994): 7S–12S.

8. Arnon Blum and Nava Blum, "Coronary Artery Disease: Are Men and Women Created Equal?" *Gender Medicine* 6: 3 (2009): 410–418.

9. David J.P. Barker, "Fetal Origins of Cardiovascular Disease," *British Medical Journal* 311: 6998 (1995): 171–174.

10. Centers for Disease Control and Prevention, "Cigarette Smoking Among Adults and Trends in Smoking Cessation—United States, 2008," *Morbidity and Mortality Weekly Report* 58: 44 (2009): 1227–1232.

11. LaTisha Marshall, Michael Schooley, Heather Ryan, Patrick Cox, Alyssa Easton, Cheryl Healton, Kat Jackson, Kevin C. Davis, and Ghada Homsi, "Youth Tobacco Surveillance—United States, 2001–2002," *Morbidity and Mortality Surveillance Summaries* 55: SS-3 (2006): 1–56.

12. Adam Drewnowski, "Obesity, Diets, and Social Inequalities," *Nutrition Reviews* 67: Suppl. 1 (2009): S36–S39.

13. Ana V. Diez Roux and Christina Mair, "Neighborhoods and Health," *Annals of the New York Academy of Sciences* 1186: 1 (2010): 125–145.

14. Michael G. Marmot, George D. Smith, Stephen Stansfeld, Chandra Patel, Fiona North, Jenny Head, Ian White, Eric Brunner, and Amanda Feeney, "Health Inequalities Among British Civil Servants: The Whitehall II Study," *Lancet* 337: 8754 (1991): 1387–1393.

15. World Health Organization, *Report on the Global Tobacco Epidemic, 2008* (2008). Available online at: http://www.who. int/tobacco/mpower/mpower_report_ full_2008.pdf.

16. Sarah Wild, Gojka Roglic, Anders Green, Richard Sicree, and Hilary King, "Global Prevalence of Diabetes: Estimates for the Year 2000 and Projections for 2030," *Diabetes Care* 27: 5 (2004): 1047–1053.

17. Gaziano et al.: 101; David W. Haslam, W. Philip, and T. James, "Obesity," *Lancet* 266: 9492 (2005): 1197–1209.

18. Paolo Zaninotto, Jenny Mindell, and Vasant Hirani, "Prevalence of Cardiovascular Risk Factors Among Ethnic Groups: Results from the Health Surveys for England," *Atherosclerosis* 195: 1 (2007): e48–e57.

19. Barry M. Popkin and Penny Gordon-Larsen, "The Nutrition Transition: Worldwide Obesity Dynamics and Their Determinants," *International Journal of Obesity* 28: Suppl. 3 (2004): S2–S9.

20. David R. Whiting, Louise Hayes, and Nigel C. Unwin, "Diabetes in Africa: Challenges to Health Care for Diabetes in Africa," *Journal of Cardiovascular Risk* 10: 2 (2003): 103–110.

21. Gaziano et al.: 84, 89, 91.

22. World Health Organization, *The Atlas of Heart Disease and Stroke* (2004). Available online at: http://www.who.int/ cardiovascular_diseases/resources/atlas/en/.

23. George A. Mensah, "Eliminating Disparities in Cardiovascular Health: Six Strategic Imperatives and a Framework for Action," *Circulation* 111: 10 (2005): 1332–1336; Alaide Chieffo, Angela Hoye, Fina Mauri, Ghada W. Mikhail, Michelle Ammerer, Cindy Grines, Liliana Grinfeld, Mira Mada, Patrizia Presbitero, Kimberly A. Skelding, Bonnie H. Weiner, and Roxana Mehran, "Gender-based Issues in Interventional Cardiology: A Consensus Statement from the Women in Innovations (WIN) Initiative," *Catheterization and Cardiovascular Interventions* 75: 2 (2010): 145–152.

24. U.S. Centers for Disease Control and Prevention, *U.S. Obesity Trends, Trends by State 1985–2009* (2009). Available online at: http://www.cdc.gov/obesity/data/trends. html#State.

25. Tanika Kelly, Wenjie Yang, C-S Chen, Kristi Reynolds, and Jiang He, "Global Burden of Obesity in 2005 and Projections to 2030," *International Journal of Obesity* 32: 9 (2008): 1431–1437.

26. Cynthia L. Ogden, Katherine M. Flegal, Margaret D. Carroll, and Clifford L. Johnson, "Prevalence and Trends in Overweight Among US Children and Adolescents, 1999–2000," *Journal of the American Medical Association* 288: 14 (2002): 1728–1732; Cynthia L. Ogden, Margaret D. Carroll, Lester R. Curtin, Molly M. Lamb, and Katherine M. Flegal, "Prevalence of High Body Mass Index in US Children and Adolescents, 2007–2008," *Journal of the American Medical Association* 303: 3 (2010): 242–249.

27. Blanca M. Herrera and Cecilia M. Lindgren, "The Genetics of Obesity," *Current Diabetes Reports* 10: 6 (2010): 498–505.

28. Manu V. Chakravarthy and Frank W. Booth, "Eating, Exercise, and 'Thrifty' Genotypes: Connecting the Dots Toward an Evolutionary Understanding of Modern Chronic Diseases," *Journal of Applied Physiology* 96: 1 (2004): 3–10; Jonathan C.K. Wells, "Ethnic Variability in Adiposity and Cardiovascular Risk: The Variable Disease Selection Hypothesis," *International Journal of Epidemiology* 38: 1 (2009): 63–71.

29. David J. Barker, "The Fetal and Infant Origins of Adults Disease," *British Medical Journal* 301: 6761 (1990): 111; Angharad R. Morgan, John Thompson, Rinki

Murphy, Peter N. Black, Wen-Juin Lam, Lynnette R. Ferguson, and Ed A. Mitchell, "Obesity and Diabetes Genes Are Associated with Being Born Small for Gestational Age: Results from the Auckland Birthweight Collaborative Study," *BMC Medical Genetics* 11 (2010): 125–134.

30. Gary G. Bennett, Lorna H. McNeill, Kathleen Y. Wolin, Dustin T. Duncan, Elaine Puleo, and Karen M. Emmons, "Safe to Walk? Neighborhood Safety and Physical Activity Among Public Housing Residents," *PLoS Medicine* 4: 10 (2007): 1599–1606; Gregory J. Norman, Sandra K. Nutter, Sherry Ryan, James F. Sallis, Karen J. Calfas, and Kevin Patrick, "Community Design and Access to Recreational Facilities as Correlates of Adolescent Physical Activity and Body-mass Index," *Journal of Physical Activity and Health* 3: Suppl. 1 (2006): S118–S128.

31. Sarah E. Anderson and Robert C. Whitaker, "Household Routines and Obesity in US Preschool-aged Children," *Pediatrics* 125: 3 (2010): 420–428; Rebecca E. Lee, Katie M. Heinrich, Ashley V. Medina, Gail R. Regan, Jacqueline Y. Reese-Smith, Yuka Jokura, and Jay E. Maddock, "A Picture of the Healthful Food Environment in Two Diverse Urban Cities," *Environmental Health Insights* 4 (2010): 49–60.

32. Ronette R. Briefel, Mary K. Crepinsek, Charlotte Cabili, Ander Wilson, and Philip M. Gleason, "School Food Environments and Practices Affect Dietary Behaviors of US Public School Children," *Journal of the American Dietetic Association* 109: Suppl. 2 (2009): S91–S107.

33. Naomi S. Levitt, "Diabetes in Africa: Epidemiology, Management, and Healthcare Challenges," *Heart* 94: 11 (2008): 1376–1382.

34. World Health Organization, *Health, Economic Growth, and Poverty Reduction* (2002). Available online at: http://whqlibdoc.who.int/publications/9241590092.pdf.

35. Eric A. Finkelstein, Justin G. Trogdon, Joel W. Cohen, and William Dietz, "Annual Medical Spending Attributable to Obesity: Payer- and Service-specific Estimates," *Health Affairs* 28: 5 (2009): w822–w831; Thomas von Lengerke, Jürgen John, and Andreas Mielck, "Excess Direct Medical Costs of Severe Obesity by Socioeconomic Status in German Adults," *Psychosocial Medicine* 7: Doc01 (2010); Stefan Kuhle, Sara Kirk, Arto Ohinmaa, Yutaka Yasui, Alexander C. Allen, and Paul J. Veugelers, "Use and Cost of Health Services Among Overweight and Obese Canadian Children," *International Journal of Pediatric Obesity* Early online (September 27, 2010): 1–7.

36. Helena W. Rodbard, Kathleen M. Fox, and Susan Grandy, "Impact of Obesity on Work Productivity and Role Disability in Individuals with and at Risk for Diabetes Mellitus," *American Journal of Health Promotion* 23: 5 (2009): 353–360; Judith A. Ricci and Elsbeth Chee, "Lost Productive Time Associated with Excess Weight in the U.S. Workforce," *Journal of Occupational and Environmental Medicine* 47: 12 (2005): 1227–1234.

37. A. Avenell, J. Broom, T.J. Brown, A. Poobalan, L. Aucott, S.C. Stearns, W.C.S. Smith, R.T. Jung, M.K. Campbell, and A.M. Grant, "Systematic Review of the Long-term Effects and Economic Consequences of Treatments for Obesity and Implications for Health Improvement," *Health Technology Assessments* 8: 21 (2004): iii–iv, 1–182; Sanjib Saha, Ulf-G Gerdtham, and Pia Johansson, "Economic Evaluation of Lifestyle Interventions for Preventing Diabetes and Cardiovascular Diseases," *International Journal of Environmental Research and Public Health* 7 (2010): 3150–3195.

38. World Health Organization, *Global Strategy on Diet, Physical Activity, and Health* (2004). Available online at: http://www.who.int/dietphysicalactivity/strategy/eb11344/strategy_english_web.pdf.

39. Geoffrey Cannon, "Why the Bush Administration and the Global Sugar Industry Are Determined to Demolish

the 2004 WHO Global Strategy on Diet, Physical Activity and Health," *Public Health Nutrition* 7: 3 (2004): 369–380; Douglas Kamerow, "The Case of the Sugar Sweetened Beverage Tax," *British Medical Journal* 341 (2010): c3719.

40. Katariina Kallio, Eero Jokinen, Olli T. Raitakari, Mauri Hamalainen, Marja Siltala, Iina Volanen, Tuuli Kaitosaari, Jorma Viikari, Tapani Rönnemaa, and Olli Simell, "Tobacco Smoke Exposure Is Associated with Attenuated Endothelial Function in 11-year-old Healthy Children," *Circulation* 115: 25 (2007): 3205–3212.

41. Dwight T. Janerich, W. Douglas Thompson, Luis R. Varela, Peter Greenwald, Sherry Chorost, Cathy Tucci, Muhammad B. Zaman, Myron R. Melamed, Maureen Kiely, and Martin F. McKneally, "Lung Cancer and Exposure to Tobacco Smoke in the Household," *New England Journal of Medicine* 323: 10 (1990): 623–626.

42. Sarah E. Hill, Tony Blakely, Ichiro Kawachi, and Alistair Woodward, "Mortality Among Lifelong Nonsmokers Exposed to Secondhand Smoke at Home: Cohort Data and Sensitivity Analyses," *American Journal of Epidemiology* 165: 5 (2007): 530–540.

43. World Health Organization, *Tobacco*, Fact Sheet (2010). Available online at: http://www.who.int/mediacentre/factsheets/fs339/en/index.html.

44. Martin Bobak, Prabhat Jha, Son Nguyen, and Martin Jarvis, "Poverty and Smoking," in Prabhat Jha and Frank Chaloupka, eds., *Tobacco Control in Developing Countries* (Oxford, England: Oxford University Press for the World Bank and World Health Organization, 2000): 41–61.

45. Marshall et al.: 19.

46. James D. Sargent and Madeline Dalton, "Does Parental Disapproval of Smoking Prevent Adolescents from Becoming Established Smokers?" *Pediatrics* 108: 6 (2001): 1256–1262.

47. Melanie Wakefield, Brian Flay, Mark Nichter, and Gary Giovino, "Role of the Media in Influencing Trajectories of Youth Smoking," *Addiction* 98: Suppl. 1 (2003): 79–103;

Joseph R. DiFranza, Robert J. Wellman, James D. Sargent, Michael Weitzman, Bethany J. Hipple, and Jonathan P. Winickoff, "Tobacco Promotion and the Initiation of Tobacco Use: Assessing the Evidence for Causality," *Pediatrics* 117: 6 (2006): e1237–e1248; K. Viswanath, Leland K. Ackerson, Glorian Sorensen, and Prakash C. Gupta, "Movies and TV Influence Tobacco Use in India: Findings from a National Survey," *PLoS One* 5: 6 (2010): e11365.

48. John P. Pierce, Janet M. Distefan, Christine Jackson, Martha M. White, and Elizabeth A. Gilpin, "Does Tobacco Marketing Undermine the Influence of Recommended Parenting in Discouraging Adolescents from Smoking?" *American Journal of Preventive Medicine* 23: 2 (2002): 73–81.

49. World Health Organization, *WHO Report on the Global Tobacco Epidemic, 2008: The MPOWER Package* (2008). Available online at: http://whqlibdoc.who.int/publications/2008/9789241596282_eng.pdf.

50. C.M. Best, K. Sun, S. de Pee, M. Sari, M.W. Bloem, and R.D. Semba, "Parental Smoking and Increased Risk of Child Malnutrition Among Families in Rural Indonesia," *Tobacco Control* 17: 1 (2008): 38–45; C.M. Best, K. Sun, S. de Pee, M. Sari, M.W. Bloem, and R.D. Semba, "Parental Smoking and Increased Risk of Child Malnutrition Among Families in Rural Bangladesh," *Nutrition* 23: 10 (2007): 731–738.

51. U.S. Department of Health and Human Services, *The 2004 Surgeon General's Report: The Health Consequences of Smoking* (2004). Available online at: http://www.thriveri.org/documents/4g_health_consequences_smoking.pdf.

52. H.Y. Sung, L. Wang, S. Jin, T.W. Hu, and Y. Jiang, "Economic Burden of Smoking in China, 2000," *Tobacco Control* 15: Suppl. 1 (2006): i5–i11; R.M. John, H.Y. Sung, and W.B. Max, "Economic Cost of Tobacco Use in India, 2004," *Tobacco Control* 18: 2 (2009): 138–143.

53. Donna M. Vallone, Jane A. Allen, and Haijun Xiao, "Is Socioeconomic Status

Associated with Awareness and Receptivity to the Truth® Campaign?" *Drug and Alcohol Dependence* 104: Suppl. 1 (2009): S115–S120.

54. Heather Wipfli and Jonathan M. Samet, "Global Economic and Health Benefits of Tobacco Control: Part 2," *Clinical Pharmacology & Therapeutics* 86: 3 (2009): 272–280.

55. Melanie S. Dove, Douglas W. Dockery, and Gregory N. Connolly, "Smoke-free Air Laws and Secondhand Smoke Exposure Among Nonsmoking Youth," *Pediatrics* 126: 1 (2010): 80–87; M. Scollo, A. Lal, A. Hyland, and S. Glantz, "Review of the Quality of Studies on the Economic Effects of Smoke-free Policies on the Hospitality Industry," *Tobacco Control* 12: 1 (2003): 13–20.

56. World Health Organization, *WHO Framework Convention on Tobacco Control* (2003). Available online at: http://www. who.int/fctc/text_download/en/index.html.

57. World Bank, *The Economics of Tobacco Use & Tobacco Control in the Developing World* (2003). Available online at: http:// ec.europa.eu/health/ph_determinants/ life_style/Tobacco/Documents/ world_bank_en.pdf.

58. Sarah Wild, Gojka Roglic, Anders Green, Richard Sicree, and Hilary King, "Global Prevalence of Diabetes: Estimates for the Year 2000 and Projections for 2030," *Diabetes Care* 27: 5 (2004): 1047–1053; U.S. Centers for Disease Control and Prevention, "Press Release—Number of Americans with Diabetes Projected to Double or Triple by 2050" (2010). Available online at: http://www.cdc.gov/media/ pressrel/2010/r101022.html.

59. U.S. Renal Data System, *2010 Atlas of CKD & ESRD* (2010). Available online at: http://www.usrds.org/atlas.htm.

Chapter 6

1. Richard Skolnik, *Essentials of Global Health* (Sudbury, MA: Jones and Bartlett Publishers, 2008): xiii.

2. Ruth Levine, *Case Studies in Global Health: Millions Saved* (Sudbury, MA: Jones and Bartlett Publishers, 2007).

3. Andrew T. Price-Smith, *The Health of Nations: Infectious Disease, Environmental Change, and Their Effects on National Security and Development* (Cambridge, MA: MIT Press, 2002): 174.

4. Price-Smith: 77–116.

5. J. Gallup and J. Sachs, "The Economic Burden of Malaria," *American Journal of Tropical Medicine and Hygiene* 64: 1,2S (2001): 85–96.

6. World Health Organization, *Health, Economic Growth, and Poverty Reduction* (2002): 40. Available online at: http://whqlibdoc.who.int/ publications/9241590092.pdf.

7. United Nations Development Programme, *International Human Development Indicators*. Available online at: http://hdrstats.undp. org/en/indicators/default.html#G.

8. *Ibid.*

9. *Ibid.*

10. United Nations Development Programme, "Statistics of the Human Development Report," *Human Development Reports*. Available online at: http://hdr.undp.org/en/ statistics/. The online versions of the *Human Development Reports* provide access to its statistics in a variety of forms: by country, indicator, and tables. Users can also create their own tables, incorporating specific countries and indicators that interest them. To access these features, use the link listed in this citation and click on "Getting and Using Data."

11. *Ibid.*

12. United Nations Development Programme, "The Human Development Concept," *Human Development Reports*. Available online at: http://hdr.undp.org/en/ humandev/.

13. Population Reference Bureau, *2008 World Population Data Sheet*. Available online at: http://www.prb.org/Publications/ Datasheets/2008/2008wpds.aspx.

14. World Bank, *Poverty and Inequality Statistics*. Available online at: http://web.worldbank.

org/WBSITE/EXTERNAL/TOPICS/EXT
POVERTY/0,,contentMDK:22927860
~pagePK:148956~piPK:216618~theSit
ePK:336992,00.html.

15. Obijiofor Aginam, "Global Village, Divided
World: A South-North Gap and Global
Health Challenges at Century's Dawn,"
Indiana Journal of Global Legal Studies 7: 2
(2000): 603–628.

16. World Bank, *Poverty and Inequality Analysis.*
Available online at: http://web.worldbank.
org/WBSITE/EXTERNAL/TOPICS/EXTP
OVERTY/0,,contentMDK:22569747~page
PK:148956~piPK:216618~theSite
PK:336992,00.html.

17. *Ibid.*

18. United Nations Children's Fund, *Progress for
Children: A World Fit for Children Statistical
Review* No. 6 (December 2007): 23.
Available online at: http://www.unicef.org/
publications/files/Progress_for_Children_
No_6_revised.pdf.

19. Obijiofor: 608–623.

20. Amartya Sen, *Development as Freedom* (New
York: Anchor Press, 1999).

21. Scholars of international relations continue
to debate the criteria by which countries
should be classified as developed or
developing, and no consensus exists on a
comprehensive scheme of categorization.
The old practice of categorizing countries
as belonging to the First World (advanced
industrialized countries), Second World
(a term traditionally used to describe
the Soviet Union and the countries in
its sphere of influence), or Third World
(developing countries) has gone out of
fashion. Economists sometimes simply
refer to high-income, middle-income, and
low-income countries, with additional
variations acknowledged within these
categories (e.g., high-middle income,
low-middle income). Each approach to
categorizing countries according to levels
of economic and social development
has its own strengths and weaknesses.
A categorization based on a North-
South territorial divide makes broad
generalizations that do not capture
important differences across, between,
and within countries. Grouping countries
into several income categories captures
more of the differences between countries
but misses a larger systemic pattern that
reveals inequities rooted in the historical
legacy of colonialism. For our purposes,
the concept of a North-South gap
captures important realities about broad,
contemporary divisions between developed
and developing countries that are rooted
in historical social, economic, and political
processes even as it obscures important
differences across, between, and within
countries.

22. World Health Organization, Western
Pacific Regional Office, *Women, Girls,
HIV, & AIDS* (2004). Available online
at: http://www.wpro.who.int/NR/
rdonlyres/F1F88521-518C-4EAC-AF7E-
1F07A4E9FF0B/0/WAD2004_Women_
Girls_HIV_AIDS.pdf.

23. United Nations Children's Fund and World
Health Organization, *Diarhoea: Why Children
Are Still Dying and What Can Be Done*
(2009). Available online at: http://whqlibdoc.
who.int/publications/2009/9789241598415_
eng.pdf.

24. *Ibid.*: 23.

25. J.A. Schellenberg, C.G. Victora, A. Mushi,
D. de Savigny, D. Schellenberg,
H. Mshinda, and J. Bryce, "Inequities
Among the Very Poor: Health Care for
Children in Rural Southern Tanzania,"
Lancet 361: 9357 (2003): 561–566.

26. C.T. Sreeramareddy, R.P. Shankar,
B.V. Sreekuraman, S.H. Subba, H.S. Joshi,
and U. Ramachandran, "Care-seeking
Behavior for Childhood Illness—A
Questionnaire Survey in Western Nepal,"
*BMC International Health and Human
Rights* 6 (2006): 7–16.

27. J. Akin and P. Hutchinson, "Health Care
Facility Choice and the Phenomenon of
Bypassing," *Health Policy and Planning*
14: 2 (1999): 135–151; D. Chernichovsky
and O.A. Meesook, "Utilization of Health

Services in Indonesia," *Social Science & Medicine* 23: 6 (1986): 611–620.

28. D. Thomas, V. Lavy, and D. Strauss, "Public Policy and Anthropometric Outcomes in the Côte d'Ivoire," *Journal of Public Economics* 61: 2 (1996): 155–192.

29. F. Castro-Leal, J. Dayton, L. Demery, and K. Mehra, "Public Social Spending in Africa: Do the Poor Benefit?" *World Bank Research Observer* 14: 1 (1999): 66–74.

30. World Health Organization, *Health, Economic Growth, and Poverty Reduction* (2002): 37. Available online at: http://whqlibdoc.who.int/publications/9241590092.pdf.

31. J. Sachs and P. Malaney, "The Economic and Social Burden of Malaria," *Nature* 415 (2002): 680–685.

32. Jeffrey Long and Rick Kittles, "Human Genetic Diversity and the Nonexistence of Biological Races," *Human Biology* 75: 4 (2003): 449–471.

33. Kenneth D. Kochanek, Jiaquan Xu, Sherry L. Murphy, Arialdi M. Miniño, and Hsiang-Ching Kung, "Deaths: Preliminary Data for 2009," *National Vital Statistics Report* 59: 4 (2011): 1–51.

34. *Ibid.*

35. Glenn Flores and the Committee on Pediatrics Research, "Racial and Ethnic Disparities in the Health and Health Care of Children," *Pediatrics* 125: 4 (2010): e979–e1020.

36. Janet Smylie, Deshayne Fell, and Arne Ohlsson, "A Review of Aboriginal Infant Mortality Rates in Canada: Striking and Persistent Aboriginal/Non-Aboriginal Inequities," *Canadian Journal of Public Health* 101: 2 (2010): 143–148; Charles H. Wood, José A. Magno de Carvalho, and Cláudia J. Guimarães Horta, "The Color of Child Mortality in Brazil, 1950–2000: Social Progress and Persistent Racial Inequality," *Latin American Research Review* 45: 2 (2010): 114–139.

37. U.S. Centers for Disease Control and Prevention, "CDC Health Disparities and Inequalities Report—United States, 2011," *Morbidity and Mortality Weekly Report* 60: Suppl. (2011): 1–114.

38. Stacey Jolly, Eric Vittinghoff, Arpita Chattopadhyay, and Kirsten Bibbens-Domingo, "Higher Cardiovascular Disease Prevalence and Mortality Among Younger Blacks Compared to Whites," *American Journal of Medicine* 123: 9 (2010): 811–818; Tanisha D. Hill, LeRoy M. Graham, and Varada Divgi, "Racial Disparities in Pediatric Asthma: A Review of the Literature," *Current Allergy & Asthma Report* 11: 1 (2011): 85–90; Ganna Chornokur, Kyle Dalton, Meghan E. Borysova, and Nagi B. Kumar, "Disparities at Presentation, Diagnosis, Treatment, and Survival in African American Men Affected by Prostate Cancer," *Prostate* 71: 9 (2011): 985–997.

39. Holly Mead, Lara Cartwright-Smith, Karen Jones, Christal Ramos, and Bruce Siegel, "Racial and Ethnic Disparities in U.S. Health Care: A Chartbook," *The Commonwealth Fund* (2008). Available online at: http://www.commonwealthfund.org/Publications/Chartbooks/2008/Mar/Racial-and-Ethnic-Disparities-in-U-S—Health-Care—A-Chartbook.aspx.

40. Antonio A. Lopes, "End-stage Renal Disease Due to Diabetes in Racial/Ethnic Minorities and Disadvantaged Populations," *Ethnicity & Disease* 19: Suppl. 1 (2009): 47–51.

41. Morton N. Beiser and Feng Hou, "Ethnic Identity, Resentment Stress and Depressive Affect Among Southeast Asian Refugees in Canada," *Social Science & Medicine* 63: 1 (2006): 137–150; M. Kelaher, Sheila Paul, Helen Lambert, Waqar Ahmad, Yin Paradies, and George Davey Smith, "Discrimination and Health in an English Study," *Social Science & Medicine* 66: 7 (2008): 1627–1636; Margarita Alegria, Melissa Vallas, and Andres J. Pumariega, "Racial and Ethnic Disparities in Pediatric Mental Health," *Child and Adolescent Psychiatric Clinics of North America* 19: 4 (2010): 759–774.

42. Martin Brockerhoff and Paul Hewett, "Inequality of Child Mortality Among

Ethnic Groups in sub-Saharan Africa," *Bulletin of the World Health Organization* 78: 1 (2000): 30–41; Mats Målqvist, Nguyen T. Nga, Leif Eriksson, Lars Wallin, Dinh P. Hoa, and Lars Å. Persson, "Ethnic Inequity in Neonatal Survival: A Case-referent Study in Northern Vietnam," *Acta Paediatrica* 100: 3 (2011): 340–346.

43. David Mayer-Foulkes and Carlos Larrea, "Racial and Ethnic Inequities: Bolivia, Brazil, Guatemala, Peru," in Antonio Giuffrida, ed., *Racial and Ethnic Disparities in Health in Latin America and the Caribbean* (Washington, DC: Inter-American Development Bank, 2007): 131–137. Available online at: http://idbdocs.iadb.org/wsdocs/getdocument.aspx?docnum=1148586.

44. M. Hashibe, B. Siwakoti, M. Wei, B.K. Thakur, C.B. Pun, B.M. Shrestha, Z. Burningham, Y.C. Lee, and A. Sapkota, "Socioeconomic Status and Lung Cancer Risk in Nepal," *Asian Pacific Journal of Cancer Prevention* 12: 4 (2011): 1083–1088.

45. Brandon A. Kohrt, Rebacca A. Speckman, Richard D. Kunz, Jennifer L. Baldwin, Nawaraj Upadhaya, Nanda R. Acharya, Vidya D. Sharma, Mahendra K. Nepal, and Carol M. Worthman, "Culture in Psychiatric Epidemiology: Using Ethnography and Multiple Mediator Models to Assess the Relationship of Caste with Depression and Anxiety in Nepal," *Annals of Human Biology* 36: 3 (2009): 261–280.

46. Robert A. Hummer, Maureen R. Benjamins, and Richard G. Rogers, "Racial and Ethnic Disparities in Health and Mortality Among the U.S. Elderly Population," in Norman B. Anderson, Rodolfo A. Bulatao, and Barney Cohen, eds., *Critical Perspectives on Racial and Ethnic Differences in Health in Late Life* (Washington, DC: The National Academies Press, 2004): 53–94; Peter Franks, Peter Muennig, Erica Lubetkin, and Haomiao Jia, "The Burden of Disease Associated with Being African-American in the United States and the Contribution of Socio-economic Status," *Social Science & Medicine* 62: 10 (2006): 2469–2478.

47. Ana V. Diez-Roux and Christina Mair, "Neighborhoods and Health," *Annals of the New York Academy of Sciences* 1186: 1 (2010): 125–145.

48. Jennifer Northridge, Olivia F. Ramirez, Jeanette A. Stingone, and Luz Claudio, "The Role of Housing Type and Housing Quality in Urban Children with Asthma," *Journal of Urban Health* 87: 2 (2010): 211–224.

49. Julie L. Crouch, Rachelle F. Hanson, Benjamin E. Saunders, Dean G. Kilpatrick, and Heidi S. Resnick, "Income, Race/Ethnicity, and Exposure to Violence in Youth: Results from the National Survey of Adolescents," *Journal of Community Psychology* 26: 6 (2000): 625–641.

50. World Health Organization, *World Report on Child Injury Prevention* (World Health Organization, 2008): 1–211. Available online at: http://whqlibdoc.who.int/publications/2008/9789241563574_eng.pdf.

51. Kathy Sanders-Phillips, Beverlyn Settles-Reaves, Doren Walker, and Janeese Brownlow, "Social Inequality and Racial Discrimination: Risk Factors for Health Disparities in Children of Color," *Pediatrics* 124: Suppl. 3 (2009): S176–S186.

52. Mead et al.: 44.

53. Natalie D. Crawford, Camara P. Jones, and Lisa C. Richardson, "Understanding Racial and Ethnic Disparities in Colorectal Cancer Screening: Behavioral Risk Factor Surveillance System, 2002 and 2004," *Ethnicity & Disease* 20: 4 (2010): 359–365; William R. Carpenter, Paul A. Godley, Jack A. Clark, James A. Talcott, Timothy Finnegan, Merle Mishel, Jeannette Bensen, Walter Rayford, L. Joseph Su, Elizabeth T. Fontham, and James L. Mohler, "Racial Differences in Trust and Regular Source of Patient Care and the Implications for Prostate Cancer Screening Use," *Cancer* 115: 21 (2009): 5048–5059.

54. Yuanyuan Wang, Julie A. Simpson, Anita E. Wluka, Donna M. Urquhart, Dallas R. English, Graham G. Giles, Stephen Graves, and Flavia M. Cicuttini, "Reduced Rates of Primary Joint Replacement for Osteoarthritis in Italian and Greek Migrants

to Australia: The Melbourne Collaborative Study," *Arthritis Research & Therapy* 11: 3 (2009): R86.

55. Ezequiel Bellorin-Font, Nidia Pernalete, Josefina Meza, Carmen L. Milanes, and Raul G. Carlini, "Access to and Coverage of Renal Replacement Therapy in Minorities and Ethnic Groups in Venezuela," *Kidney International* Suppl. 97 (2005): S18–S22.

56. Sarah Burgard, "Race and Pregnancy-related Care in Brazil and South Africa," *Social Science & Medicine* 59 (2004): 1127–1146.

57. Zeida R. Kon and Nuha Lackan, "Ethnic Disparities in Access to Care in Post-apartheid South Africa," *American Journal of Public Health* 98: 12 (2008): 2272–2277.

58. Glenn Flores and Sandra C. Tomany-Korman, "Racial and Ethnic Disparities in Medical and Dental Health, Access to Care and Use of Services in US Children," *Pediatrics* 121: 2 (2008): e286–e296.

59. Ian M. Bennett, Jing Chen, Jaleh S. Soroui, and Sheida White, "The Contribution of Health Literacy to Disparities in Self-rated and Preventive Health Behaviors in Older Patients," *Annals of Family Medicine* 7: 3 (2009): 204–211.

60. Bussarawan Teerawichitchainan and James F. Phillips, "Ethnic Differentials in Parental Health Seeking for Childhood Illness in Vietnam," *Social Science & Medicine* 66: 5 (2008): 1118–1130; Målqvist et al.: 340.

61. Karen S. Collins, Allyson Hall, and Charlotte Neuhaus, "U.S. Minority Health: A Chartbook," *The Commonwealth Fund* (1999). Available online at: http://www. common wealthfund.org/Publications/ Chartbooks/1999/May/U-S—Minority-Health—A-Chartbook.aspx.

62. Darrell J. Gaskin, Christine Spencer, and Patrick Richard, "Do Hospitals Provide Lower-quality Care to Minorities than to Whites?" *Health Affairs* 27: 2 (2008): 518–527.

63. *Ibid.*

64. Duncan Thomas, Victor Lavy, and John Strauss, "Public Policy and Anthropometric Outcomes in the Côte d'Ivoire," *Journal of Public Economics* 61: 2 (1996): 155–192.

65. U.S. Office for Civil Rights, *Guidance to Federal Financial Assistance Recipients Regarding Title VI and the Prohibition Against National Origin Discrimination Affecting Limited English Proficient Persons—Summary* (Washington, DC: U.S. Department of Health and Human Services, 2000). Available online at: http:// www.hhs.gov/ocr/civilrights/resources/laws/ summaryguidance.html.

66. Robert Wood Johnson Foundation, "Language Barriers Contribute to Health Care Disparities for Latinos in the United States of America," *Pan American Journal of Public Health* 11: 1 (2002): 56–58.

67. Mee L. Wong, Kee S. Chia, Sharon Wee, Sin E. Chia, Jeannette Lee, Woon P. Koh, Han M. Shen, Julian Thumboo, and Dickey Sofjan, "Concerns over Participation in Genetic Research Among Malay-Muslims, Chinese and Indians in Singapore: A Focus Group Study," *Community Genetics* 7: 1 (2004): 44–54.

68. Carpenter et al.: 5048.

69. Michelle van Ryn and Jane Burke, "The Effect of Patient Race and Socio-economic Status on Physicians' Perceptions of Patients," *Social Science & Medicine* 50: 6 (2000): 813–828.

70. Louis Sullivan and Ilana S. Mittman, "The State of Diversity in the Health Professions a Century After Flexner," *Academic Medicine* 85: 2 (2010): 246–253.

71. World Health Organization, *Closing the Gap in a Generation: Health Equity Through Action on the Social Determinants of Health* (2008). Available online at: http:// whqlibdoc.who.int/hq/2008/WHO_IER_ CSDH_08.1_eng.pdf.

72. Institute of Medicine of the National Academies, *Unequal Treatment: What Health Care System Administrators Need to Know About Racial and Ethnic Disparities in Healthcare* (Institute of Medicine of the National Academies, 2002). Available online at: http://www.nap.edu/openbook. php?record_id=10260&page=1.

73. Mayra Buvinic, André Médici, Elisa Fernández, and Ana Cristina Torres, "Gender Differentials in Health," in Dean T. Jamison,

Joel G. Breman, Anthony R. Measham, George Alleyne, Maria Claeson, David P. Evans, Prabhat Jha, Anne Mills, and Phillip Musgrove, eds., *Disease Control Priorities in Developing Countries*, 2d ed. (New York: Oxford University Press; Washington, DC: The World Bank, 2006): 197.

74. World Health Organization, *World Health Statistics 2009* (2009): 44. Available online at: http://www.who.int/whosis/whostat/EN_WHS09_Full.pdf.

75. Data on life expectancy from both the UNDP and the WHO confirm women's advantage in life expectancy in all regions. World Health Organization, *World Health Statistics 2009*: 44; United Nations Development Programme, "Statistics of the Human Development Report," *Human Development Report* 2009. Available online at: http://hdr.undp.org/en/statistics/.

76. *Ibid.*

77. *Ibid.*

78. World Health Organization, *World Health Statistics 2009*: 44.

79. *Ibid.*: 36–43.

80. Colin D. Mathers, Christopher J.L. Murray, and Joshua A. Salomon, "Methods for Measuring Healthy Life Expectancy," in Christopher J.L. Murray and David B. Evans, eds., *Health Systems Performance Assessment: Debates, Methods, and Empiricism* (Geneva: World Health Organization, 2003): 439.

81. World Health Organization, *World Health Statistics 2009*: 44.

82. Morbidity simply refers to illness "or any departure, subjective or objective, from a psychological or physiological state of well-being." Skolnik: 22.

83. World Health Organization, *The Global Burden of Disease: 2004 Update*: 46.

84. Buvinic et al.: 199.

85. *Ibid.*

86. *Ibid.*: 196.

87. *Ibid.*: note 2 at 209.

88. World Health Organization, "Disease Incidence, Prevalence, and Disability," in *The Global Burden of Disease: 2004 Update* (2008): 36.

89. World Health Organization, *The Global Burden of Disease: 2004 Update*: 10.

90. "Gendercide: The Worldwide War on Baby Girls," *The Economist*, March 4, 2010. Available online at: http://www.economist.com/node/15636231/.

91. Buvinic et al.: 197.

92. "Mars vs. Venus: The Gender Gap in Health," *Harvard Men's Health Watch* (January 2010). Available online at: http://www.health.harvard.edu/newsletters/Harvard_Mens_Health_Watch/2010/January/mars-vs-venus-the-gender-gap-in-health/.

93. In fact, the role of female hormones in reducing the risk of cardiovascular disease was sufficiently well established by the 1990s that doctors recommended hormone replacement therapy (HRT) for peri/postmenopausal women not solely for relief from the symptoms of menopause but also to decrease the incidence of coronary disease. However, in the early years of the 21st century, a large randomized controlled trial (the Women's Health Initiative) demonstrated just the opposite effect—an increased risk of stroke and heart attack in the first two years of HRT. Thus, the pendulum swung, and the medical profession quit routinely using HRT for symptomatic control of hot flashes, except in cases of severe menopausal symptoms not responsive to nonhormonal treatments, out of fear of this increased cardiovascular risk. Writing Group for the Women's Health Initiative Investigators, "Risks and Benefits of Estrogen Plus Progestin in Healthy Postmenopausal Women: Principal Results from the Women's Health Initiative Randomized Control Trial," *Journal of the American Medical Association* 288 (2002): 321–333.

94. United Nations Development Programme, "Millennium Development Goals: A Compact Among Nations to End Human Poverty," *Human Development Report 2003*: 9. Available online at: http://hdr.undp.org/en/reports/global/hdr2003/.

95. Buvinic et al.: 197.

96. *Ibid.*: 198.

97. Jelke Boesten and Nana K. Poku, *Gender and HIV/AIDS: Critical Perspectives from the Developing World* (Burlington, VT: Ashgate Publishers, 2009).

98. I would like to thank Dr. John Murray, a consultant on child and maternal mortality with the World Health Organization, for discussions that contributed to this insight.

99. Charli Carpenter, "'Women and Children First': Gender Norms and Humanitarian Evacuation in the Balkans: 1991–1995," *International Organization* 57: 4 (2003): 661–694.

100. Adam Jones, "Gendercide and Genocide," *Journal of Genocide Research* 2: 2 (2000): 185–211.

101. Joshua Goldstein, *War and Gender: How Gender Shapes the War System and Vice Versa* (Cambridge, UK: Cambridge University Press, 2001): 128–182.

102. Will Courtenay, "A Global Perspective on the Field of Men's Health: An Editorial," *International Journal of Men's Health* 1: 1 (2002): 4.

Chapter 7

1. William R. Slomanson, *Fundamental Perspectives on International Law*, 5th ed. (Belmont, CA: Thomson Wadsworth, 2007): 66–67.

2. David P. Fidler, "Public Health and National Security in the Global Age: Infectious Diseases, Bioterrorism, and Realpolitik," *George Washington International Law Review* 35: 4 (2003): 787–856.

3. *Ibid.*: 848–849.

4. *Ibid.*: 793.

5. *Ibid.*: 793–794.

6. *Ibid.*: 794.

7. Andrew T. Price-Smith, *Contagion and Chaos: Disease, Ecology, and National Security in an Era of Globalization* (Cambridge, MA: MIT Press, 2009): 16–17.

8. *Ibid.*: 33–56.

9. Fidler, "Public Health and National Security": 848–849.

10. Stefan Elbe, "HIV/AIDS and the Changing Landscape of War in Africa," *International Security* 27: 2 (2002): 159–177; Lindy Heinecken, "Living in Terror: The Looming Security Threat to Southern Africa," *African Security Review* 10: 4 (2001): 7–17.

11. Robert L. Ostergard, "Politics in the Hot Zone: AIDS and National Security in Africa," *Third World Quarterly* 23: 2 (2002): 333–350.

12. Price-Smith: 89–116.

13. *Ibid.*: 179.

14. Mark Wheelis, "A Short History of Biological Warfare and Weapons," in Marie Isabelle Chevrier, Krzysztof Chomiczewski, Henri Garrigue, Gyorgy Granasztói, Malcolm R. Dando, and Graham S. Pearson, eds., *The Implementation of Legally Binding Measures to Strengthen the Biological and Toxin Weapons Convention* (The Netherlands/Norwell, MA: Kluwer Academic Publishers, 2004): 15–31; Adrienne Mayor, *Greek Fire, Poison Arrows, and Scorpion Bombs: Biological and Chemical Warfare in the Ancient World* (Woodstock, NY: Overlook Press, 2003).

15. Although many of the deaths among indigenous people resulted from their exposure to diseases like measles and influenza, to which they had no immunity, the British, in some cases, exposed indigenous people to the smallpox virus, often by infecting blankets that they gave to people as part of trade deals, with the *intent* of killing. In short, European powers intentionally exposed the indigenous population to deadly illness as part of their strategy of "conquering" the Continent. American Medical Association, "Smallpox as a Biological Weapon," *Journal of the American Medical Association* 281: 22 (1999): 2128–2130.

16. Elizabeth A. Fenn, "Biological Warfare in Eighteenth-Century North America: Beyond Jeffrey Amherst," *Journal of American History* 86: 4 (2000): 1553–1554.

17. Robert Gould and Nancy D. Connell, "The Public Health Effects of Biological Weapons," in Barry S. Levy and Victor W. Sidel, eds., *War and Public Health* (Washington, DC: American Public Health Association, 2000): 100.

18. Fidler, "Public Health and National Security": 815–817.

19. Daniel Barenblatt, *A Plague Upon Humanity: The Secret Genocide of Axis Japan's Germ Warfare Operation* (New York: Harper Collins Publishers, 2004).

20. Barenblatt: xii.

21. Gould and Connell: 101.

22. *Ibid.*: 101–102, 110–111.

23. *Ibid.*: 101–107.

24. *Ibid.*: 100.

25. Joshua Goldstein, *International Relations*, Brief Edition (New York: Longman, 2002): 170–173.

26. Gary A. Ackerman and Kevin S. Moran, "Bioterrorism and Threat Assessment," *Report Prepared for the Weapons of Mass Destruction Commission*: 2. Available online at: http://www.wmdcommission.org/files/No22.pdf.

27. *Ibid.*: 15.

28. *Ibid.*: 6–12.

29. Wheelis: 15.

30. Richard M. Garfield and Alfred I. Neugut, "The Human Consequences of War," in Barry S. Levy and Victor W. Sidel, eds., *War and Public Health* (Washington, DC: American Public Health Association, 2000): 29.

31. Ziad Obermeyer, Christopher J.L. Murray, and Emmanuela Gakidou, "Fifty Years of Violent War Deaths from Vietnam to Bosnia: Analysis of Data from World Health Survey Programme," *British Medical Journal* 336 (June 2008): 1482–1486.

32. Human Security Report Project, *Human Security Report 2009/2010: The Causes of Peace and the Shrinking Costs of War* (New York and Oxford: Oxford University Press, 2011). Available online at: http://www.hsrgroup.org/human-security-reports/20092010/text.aspx.

33. M. Marsh, S. Purdin, and S. Navani, "Addressing Sexual Violence in Humanitarian Emergencies," *Global Public Health: An International Journal for Research, Policy and Practice* 1: 2 (2006): 133–146; Debra L. DeLaet, "Gender, Sexual Violence, and Justice in War-torn Societies," *Global Change, Peace & Security* 20: 3 (2008): 323–338.

34. Richard Skolnik, *Essentials of Global Health* (Sudbury, MA: Jones and Bartlett Publishers, 2008): 252.

35. United Nations High Commissioner for Refugees, "The Rwandan Genocide and Its Aftermath," *State of the World's Refugees 2000: Fifty Years of Humanitarian Action* (January 2000): 253. Available online at: http://www.unhcr.org/4a4c754a9.html.

36. Skolnik: 252.

37. Human Security Report Project, *Human Security Report 2009/2010*: 10.

38. United Nations Inter-Agency Standing Committee, *Civil-Military Guidelines & Reference for Complex Emergencies* (2008): 8. Available online at: http://www.unhcr.org/refworld/docid/47da82a72.html.

39. Richard J. Brennan and Robin Nandy, "Complex Humanitarian Emergencies: A Major Global Health Challenge," *Emergency Medicine* 13: 2 (2001): 149.

40. Skolnik: 253.

41. Human Security Report Project, *Human Security Report 2009/2010*: 17.

42. *Ibid.*: 17.

43. *Ibid.*: 10.

44. *Ibid.*: 12–13.

45. Human Security Report Project, *Human Security Explained*. Available online at: http://www.hsrgroup.org/index.php?option=content&task=view&id=344&Itemid=69.

46. United Nations Development Programme, *Human Development Report 1994*: 22. Available online at http://hdr.undp.org/en/media/hdr_1994_en_chap2.pdf.

47. Fidler, "Public Health and National Security": 807.

48. United Nations Development Programme: 27–28.

49. Ole Waever, "Securitization and Desecuritization," in R.D. Lipschutz, ed., *On Security* (New York: Columbia University Press, 1995): 46–86.

50. David Fidler, "A Pathology of Public Health Securitism: Approaching Pandemics as Security Threats," in Andrew F. Cooper, John J. Kirton, and Ted Schrecker, eds., *Governing Global Health* (Burlington, VT: Ashgate Publishers, 2007): 41–66.

51. Stefan Elbe, "Should HIV/AIDS Be Securitized? The Ethical Dilemmas of Linking HIV/AIDS and Security," *International Studies Quarterly* 50 (2006): 120.

52. Fidler, "Public Health and National Security": 841.

53. Elbe: 120.

54. Ostergard: 337.

Chapter 8

1. The Constitution of the World Health Organization. Available online at: http://www.searo.who.int/LinkFiles/About_SEARO_const.pdf.

2. The legal status of preambles to international treaties is somewhat ambiguous. If substantive language in the main body of a treaty creates concrete obligations that are intended to implement ideals set out in the preamble, then the substantive articles lend legal validity to any norms specified in the preamble. However, in the absence of concrete obligations in the body of the treaty, any norms set forth in a preamble are not binding. See Hans Kelsen, *The Law of the United Nations: A Critical Analysis of Its Fundamental Problems* (New York: Praeger, 1950): 9–10. Because the WHO Constitution does not specify a right to health in its substantive articles and does not set out concrete obligations on the part of state parties directed toward the fulfillment of a human right to health, it cannot be said to have codified a binding right to health under international law.

3. Under international law, declarations adopted by the UN General Assembly, which are passed by a one-state, one-vote decision-making process, are not binding on states. However, because votes on substantive matters in the UN General Assembly must be passed by a two-thirds majority, such declarations signal significant global support for measures passed by the General Assembly. As a result, some scholars of international law believe that General Assembly resolutions provide evidence of customary law (norms that have not been formally written down and ratified by states but reflect near-universal consensus by states), and customary law represents a binding form of international law. However, positivism, the dominant paradigm of international law, downplays the importance of custom and instead suggests that states give explicit consent in order for customary norms to be considered binding.

4. According to a positivist approach to international law, states must give explicit consent for a global norm to be considered binding. The primary mechanism for generating binding international law is through treaties. Under the UN system, treaties are first submitted for signature by states. Subsequently, they must be ratified by states under specific procedures required under each state's domestic legal system. Every treaty will require a specified number of ratifications for it to enter into force. A treaty is not considered binding until it has received the specified number of ratifications and has been entered into force.

5. Denise Grady, "Global Death Rates Drop for Children 5 or Younger," *New York Times,* May 23, 2010. Available online at: http://www.nytimes.com/2010/05/24/health/24child.html?emc=eta1.

6. Debra L. DeLaet, *The Global Struggle for Human Rights* (Belmont, CA: Thomson Wadsworth, 2006): 109.

7. *Ibid.*: 140.

8. *Ibid.*: 139–141.

9. *Ibid.*: 34.

10. Declaration of Geneva (1948, 1968, 1983, 1994, 2005) excerpted in Stephen P. Marks, *Health and Human Rights: Basic International Documents*, 2d ed. (Cambridge, MA: Harvard University Press, 2006): 27.

11. Daniel Barenblatt, *A Plague upon Humanity: The Secret Genocide of Axis Japan's Germ Warfare Operation* (New York: Harper Collins Publishers, 2004); Robert Gould and Nancy D. Connell, "The Public Health Effects of Biological Weapons," in Barry S. Levy and Victor W. Sidel, eds., *War and Public Health* (Washington, DC: American Public Health Association, 2000).

12. Association of American Medical Colleges Curriculum Directory 1998–1999, 27th ed. (Washington, DC: Association of American Medical Colleges, 1998); General Medical Council, *Tomorrow's Doctors* (London: General Medical Council, 1993): 14, 26.

13. K. Rameshkumar, "Ethics in Curriculum: Ethics by the Teachers for Student and Society," *Indian Journal of Urology* 25: 3 (2009): 332–339.

14. A.S. Brogen, B. Rajkumari, J. Laishram, and A. Joy, "Knowledge and Attitudes of Doctors on Medical Ethics in a Teaching Hospital, Manipur," *Indian Journal of Medical Ethics* 6: 4 (2009): 194–197.

15. David T. Stern and Maxine Papadakis, "The Developing Physician—Becoming a Professional," *New England Journal of Medicine* 355: 17 (2006): 1794–1799.

16. Statement available online at: http://www.ama-assn.org/ama/pub/physician-resources/medical-ethics/code-medical-ethics.html.

17. "Medical Professionalism in the New Millennium: A Physician Charter," *Annals of Internal Medicine* 136: 3 (2002): 243–246.

18. Medical Council of India statement available online at: http://www.mciindia.org/rules-and-regulation/Code%20of%20Medical%20Ethics%20Regulations.pdf.

19. *Nurses and Human Rights (1998)* excerpted in Stephen P. Marks, *Health and Human Rights: Basic International Documents*, 2d ed. (Cambridge, MA: Harvard University Press, 2006): 28–29.

20. Madrid Declaration on Ethical Standards for Psychiatric Practice (1996, 2002) excerpted in Stephen P. Marks, *Health and Human Rights: Basic International Documents*, 2d ed. (Cambridge, MA: Harvard University Press, 2006): 29–34.

21. Jean Heller, "Syphilis Victims in U.S. Study Went Untreated for 40 Years; Syphilis Victims Got No Therapy," *New York Times*, July 26, 1972.

22. Declaration of Helsinki: Ethical Principles for Medical Research Involving Human Subjects (1964, 1975, 1983, 1989, 1996, 2000, 2002) excerpted in Stephen P. Marks, *Health and Human Rights: Basic International Documents*, 2d ed. (Cambridge, MA: Harvard University Press, 2006): 36–39.

23. International Ethical Guidelines for Biomedical Research Involving Human Subjects (2002) excerpted in Stephen P. Marks, *Health and Human Rights: Basic International Documents*, 2d ed. (Cambridge, MA: Harvard University Press, 2006): 39–47.

24. M. Gregg Bloche and Jonathan H. Marks, "Doctors and Interrogators at Guantanamo Bay," *New England Journal of Medicine* 353: 1 (2005): 6–8.

25. J.W. Boyd, D.U. Himmelstein, K. Lasser, D. McCormick, D.H. Bor, S.L. Cutrona, and S. Woolhandler, "U.S. Medical Students' Knowledge About the Military Draft, the Geneva Conventions, and Military Medical Ethics," *International Journal of Health Services* 37: 4 (2007): 643–650.

26. Nina Hjelde, Clara Libbrecht, and Sophie Bennett, "Violation of Human Rights by Doctors Today," *Lancet* 374: 9696 (2009): 1147–1148.

27. DeLaet: 12–13.

28. Mala Sen, *Death by Fire: Sati, Dowry Death, and Female Infanticide in Modern India* (New Brunswick, NJ: Rutgers University Press, 2001): 79–85.

29. Richard Skolnik, *Essentials of Global Health* (Sudbury, MA: Jones and Bartlett Publishers, 2008): 63.

30. Celia W. Dugger, "TB Patients Chafe Under Lockdown in South Africa," *New York Times*, March 25, 2008.

31. Skolnik: 63–64.

32. D.T. Ridley, "Jehovah's Witnesses' Refusal of Blood: Obedience to Scripture and Religious Conscience," *Journal of Medical Ethics* 25: 6 (1999): 469–472.

33. Dirk Johnson, "Trials for Parents Who Chose Faith over Medicine," *New York Times*, January 20, 2009.

34. DeLaet: 54–55.

35. Abhijit V. Banerjee and Esther Duflo, *Poor Economics: A Radical Rethinking of the Way to Fight Global Poverty* (New York: Public Affairs, 2011): 58–64.

36. Matthew Steinglass, "It Takes a Village Healer: Anthropologists Believe Traditional Medicine Can Remedy Africa's AIDS Crisis. Are They Right?" *Lingua Franca* 11: 3 (2001): 1–2.

37. Jonathan M. Mann, Sofia Gruskin, Michael A. Grodin, and George J. Annas, "Introduction," in Jonathan M. Mann, Sofia Gruskin, Michael A. Grodin, and George J. Annas, eds., *Health and Human Rights: A Reader* (New York and London: Routledge, 1999): 3.

38. Jonathan M. Mann, Lawrence Gostin, Sofia Gruskin, Troyen Brennan, Zita Lazzarini, and Harvey Fineberg, "Health and Human Rights," in Jonathan M. Mann, Sofia Gruskin, Michael A. Grodin, and George J. Annas, eds., *Health and Human Rights: A Reader* (New York and London: Routledge, 1999): 7.

Chapter 9

1. A confederal system of government is one in which the powers of any "central government" are derived exclusively from the constituent member states of that system. In this regard, it is a weak form of government with only minimal authority over its member states. Confederalism, in this way, contrasts with federalism, a system of government in which governmental authority is constitutionally divided between a central government and its constituent member states. One of the most well-known examples of a confederal system of government is the United States under the Articles of Confederation, the first constitution of the United States that was in effect from 1781 to 1788. The U.S. Constitution adopted in 1787 and implemented in 1788 created a federal system of government that remains in effect today. The United Nations system can be characterized as a loose confederation of states. The European Union provides greater powers to its common institutions of governance and, thus, has some features of federalism. Yet, its member states retain sovereignty over many matters. Therefore, it can still be classified as a confederation, albeit a stronger one than the United Nations.

2. The WHO, an independent international entity, has a relationship with the United Nations under Article 57 of the UN Charter. According to Article 57, "The various specialized agencies, established by intergovernmental agreement and having wide international responsibilities, as defined in their basic instruments, in economic, social, cultural, educational, health, and related fields, shall be brought into relationship with the United Nations in accordance with the provisions of Article 63." Article 57 specifies that these agencies will be referred to as specialized agencies. Under Article 63 of the UN Charter, the Economic and Social Council (ECOSOC) defines the terms on which specialized agencies are brought into a relationship with the United Nations, subject to the approval of the General Assembly. ECOSOC may coordinate the activities of, consult with, and make recommendations to these specialized agencies, either directly or through recommendations to the General Assembly and UN member states.

3. Richard Skolnik, *The Essentials of Global Health* (Sudbury, MA: Jones and Bartlett Publishers, 2008): 251–256.

4. Catherine Caufield, *Masters of Illusion: The World Bank and the Poverty of Nations* (New York: Henry Holt and Co., 1997); Michael Goldman, *Imperial Nature: The World Bank and Struggles for Social Justice in the Age of Globalization* (New Haven, CT: Yale University Press, 2005).

5. In the case of the Americas, the Pan-American Health Organization doubles as the regional WHO office.

6. Approximately 195 states are in the international system today. Due to the contested status of some entities (which are recognized as states by some but not all other states), it is impossible to settle on a precise number of states. The membership of the WHO is virtually identical to that of the UN, with one exception. The Cook Islands is a member of the WHO but not the UN.

7. Preamble to the Constitution of the World Health Organization as adopted by the International Health Conference, New York, New York, June 19–July 22, 1946, by the representatives of 61 states (Official Records of the World Health Organization, no. 2, p. 100) and entered into force on April 7, 1948.

8. World Health Organization, "Governance," home page of the World Health Organization. Available online at: http://www.who.int/governance/en/index.html.

9. Articles 61–65 of the Constitution of the World Health Organization.

10. Simon Rushton, "Global Governance Capacities in Health: WHO and Infectious Disease," in Adrian Kay and Owain Williams, eds., *Global Health Governance: Crisis, Institutions, and Political Economy* (Basingstoke: Palgrave Macmillan, 2009): 60–80.

11. I am indebted to Dr. John Murray, an independent consultant with the WHO, for his insights on the strengths and weaknesses of the WHO. Dr. Murray has done extensive work on child health programs for the WHO in various countries in Africa and Asia, and I have drawn on my conversations with him in writing this section of the chapter.

12. Conversation with Dr. Murray, April 21, 2008.

13. The variola virus that causes smallpox was typically transmitted from person to person through the air. It caused fever, rash, ulcerating lesions, and flulike symptoms. The virus killed roughly one-third of the people it infected, scarred most of its survivors with deeply pitted marks, and often led to blindness among other survivors. Ruth Levine, *Case Studies in Global Health: Millions Saved* (Sudbury, MA: Jones and Bartlett Publishers, 2007): 2.

14. Levine: 1.

15. *Ibid.*: 3.

16. *Ibid.*: 2–3.

17. S. Bhattacharya, "The World Health Organization and Global Smallpox Eradication," *Journal of Epidemiology and Community Health* 62 (2008): 909–912.

18. *Ibid.*: 909.

19. The name of this institution was subsequently changed to the U.S. Centers for Disease Control and Prevention (CDC).

20. Levine: 3–4.

21. *Ibid.*: 4–5.

22. Bhattacharya: 911–912.

23. The bifurcated needle is inexpensive, can be reused many times (after boiling or flaming), requires less vaccine, and is easy to use. Levine: 4.

24. *Ibid.*: 2.

25. *Ibid.*: 5.

26. *Ibid.*: 1, 5.

27. *Ibid.*: 6.

28. United Nations General Assembly Resolution 55/2 (September 18, 2000). Available online at: http://www.un.org/millennium/declaration/ares552e.pdf.

29. Paragraph 11 of the UN Millennium Declaration.

30. Paragraph 19 of the UN Millennium Declaration.

31. United Nations Development Programme, "What Are the Millennium Development Goals?" *Millennium Development Goals* page. Available online at: http://www.undp.org/mdg/basics.shtml#.

32. Colin I. Bradford Jr., "Reaching the Millennium Development Goals," in Andrew F. Cooper, John J. Kirton, and Ted Schrecker, eds., *Governing Global Health* (Burlington, VT: Ashgate Publishers, 2007): 79–86.

33. United Nations Department of Economic and Social Affairs, Statistics Division, *Millennium Development Goals: 2009 Progress Chart*. Available online at: http://unstats.un.org/unsd/mdg/Resources/Static/Products/Progress2009/MDG_Report_2009_Progress_Chart_En.pdf.

34. *Ibid.*

35. Adam Wagstaff, Mariam Claeson, Robert M. Hecht, Pablo Gottret, and Qui Fang, "Millennium Development Goals for Health: What Will It Take to Accelerate Progress?" in Dean T. Jamison, Joel G. Breman, Anthony R. Measham, George Alleyne, Mariam Claeson, David B. Evans, Prabhat Jha, Anne Mills, and Philip Musgrove, eds., *Disease Control Priorities in Developing Countries*, 2d ed. (New York: Oxford University Press; Washington, DC: The World Bank, 2006): 182.

36. *Ibid.*

37. United Nations Department of Economic and Social Affairs, Statistics Division, *Millennium Development Goals: 2009 Progress Chart*.

38. *Ibid.*

39. Wagstaff et al.: 190.

40. *Ibid.*: 193.

41. *Ibid.*: 184.

42. Levine: 1–8.

43. *Ibid.*: xxvi–xxvii.

44. *Ibid.*: 17–24.

45. *Ibid.*: 57–64.

46. Laurie Garrett, *The Coming Plague: Newly Emerging Diseases in a World out of Balance* (New York: Penguin Books, 1994): 456.

47. *Ibid.*: 449.

48. *Ibid.*: 453–456.

49. Joint United Nations Programme on HIV/AIDS, *2008–2009 Unified Budget and Workplan*: 5. Available online at: http://data.unaids.org/pub/BaseDocument/2007/2008_2009_ubw_en.pdf.

50. UNAIDS/The Henry J. Kaiser Foundation, *Financing the Response to AIDS in Low and Middle Income Countries: International Assistance from the G8, European Commission and Other Donor Governments in 2008* (July 2009). Available online at: http://www.kff.org/hivaids/7347.cfm.

51. Laurie Garrett, "The Challenge of Global Health," *Foreign Affairs* (January/February 2007).

52. Michael Greig and Paul F. Diehl, "The Peacekeeping-Peacemaking Dilemma," *International Studies Quarterly* 49 (2005): 621–645.

Chapter 10

1. World Health Organization, "Health Systems: Improving Performance," *World Health Report 2000* (2000). Available online at: http://www.who.int/whr/2000/en/whr00_en.pdf.

2. *Ibid.*

3. Ruth Levine, "Eliminating Measles in Southern Africa," in *Case Studies in Global Health: Millions Saved* (Sudbury, MA: Jones and Bartlett Publishers, 2007): 127–133.

4. U.S. Centers for Disease Control and Prevention, *CDC Responds to Cholera Outbreak in Haiti* (November 15, 2010). Available online at: http://www.cdc.gov/haiticholera/update/.

5. Peter J. Hotez, "Parasites in Paradise," *New York Times*, May 14, 2010.

6. The White House, Office of the Press Secretary, *Statement by the President on Global Health Initiative*, May 5, 2009.

7. Philip Musgrove, Riadh Zeramdini, and Guy Carrin, "Basic Patterns in National Health Expenditure," *Bulletin of the World Health Organization* 80: 2 (2002): 134–142.

8. Thomas S. Bodenheimer and Kevin Grumbach, *Understanding Health Policy: A Clinical Approach*, 2d ed. (Stamford, CT: Appleton & Lange, 1998): 7–20.

9. World Health Organization, *Traditional Medicine*, Fact Sheet (2008). Available online at: http://www.who.int/mediacentre/factsheets/fs134/en/index.html.

10. *Ibid.*

11. Ezekiel J. Emmanuel, "Cost Savings at the End of Life: What Do the Data Show?" *Journal of the American Medical Association* 275: 24 (1996): 1907–1914; Johan J. Polder, Jan J. Barendregt, and Hans van Oers, "Health Care Costs in the Last Year of Life— The Dutch Experience," *Social Science & Medicine* 63: 7 (2006): 1720–1731; Friedrich Breyer and Stefan Felder, "Life Expectancy and Health Care Expenditures: A New Calculation for Germany Using the Costs of Dying," *Health Policy* 75: 2 (2006): 178–186.

12. J. William Thomas, Erika C. Ziller, and Deborah A. Thayer, "Low Costs of Defensive Medicine, Small Savings from Tort Reform," *Health Affairs* 29: 9 (2010): 1578–1584.

13. Based on 2010 World Bank classifications of countries by income status. Available online at: http://data.worldbank.org/country/.

14. Dorothy E. Logie, Michael Rowson, and Felix Ndagije, "Innovations in Rwanda's Health System: Looking to the Future," *Lancet* 372 (2008): 256.

15. *Ibid.*: 258–259.

16. *Ibid.*: 256.

17. *Ibid.*: 257.

18. *Ibid.*

19. *Ibid.*: 260.

20. "Sharing the Burden of Sickness: Mutual Health Insurance in Rwanda," *Bulletin of the World Health Organization* 86: 11 (2008): 824.

21. Donald G. McNeil Jr., "A Poor Nation, With a Health Plan," *New York Times*, June 14, 2010.

22. Logie, Rowson, and Ndagije: 256.

23. McNeil.

24. Logie, Rowson, and Ndagije: 257.

25. McNeil.

26. Based on 2010 World Bank classifications of countries by income status. Available online at: http://data.worldbank.org/country/.

27. Hoosen Coovadia, Rachel Jewkes, Peter Barron, David Sanders, and Diane McIntyre, "The Health and Health System of South Africa: Historical Roots of Current Public Health Challenges," *Lancet* 374: 9692 (2009): 817–834.

28. Claire Botha and Michael Hendricks, "Financing South Africa's National Health System Through National Health Insurance: Possibilities and Challenges," in *Human Sciences Research Council Press* (Cape Town, South Africa: HSRC Press, 2008): i–xiv, 1–48. Available online at: http://www.hsrc.ac.za/Document-2623.phtml.

29. *Ibid.*: 30.

30. Coovadia et al.: 826–827.

31. *Ibid.*: 820.

32. Parliamentary Monitoring Group, *Public Inquiry: Access to Health Care Services* (2009). Available online at: http://www.pmg.org.za/files/docs/090315healthpublicenquiry.pdf.

33. Mickey Chopra, Joy E. Lawn, David Sanders, Peter Barron, Salim S. Abdool Karim, Debbie Bradshaw, Rachel Jewkes, Quarraisha Abdool Karim, Alan J. Fischer, Bongani M. Mayosi, Stephen M. Tallman, Gavin J. Churchyard, and Hoosen Coovadia, "Achieving the Health Millennium Development Goals for South Africa: Challenges and Priorities," *Lancet* 374: 994 (2009): 1023–1031.

34. Di McIntyre, Jane Doherty, and Lucy Gilson, "A Tale of Two Visions: The Changing Fortunes of Social Health Insurance in South Africa," *Health Policy and Planning* 18: 1 (2003): 47–58.

35. David Harrion, "An Overview of Health and Health Care in South Africa 1994–2010: Priorities, Progress and Progress for New Gains," A Discussion Document Commissioned by the Henry J. Kaiser Family Foundation to Help Inform the National Health Leaders' Retreat (Muldersdrift, January 24–26, 2010). Available online at: http://www.doh.gov.za/docs/reports/2010/overview1994-2010.pdf.

36. Parliamentary Monitoring Group: 41.
37. Karl Peltzer, "Traditional Health Practicioners in South Africa," *Lancet* 374: 9694 (2009): 956–957.
38. Based on 2010 World Bank classifications of countries by income status. Available online at: http://data.worldbank.org/country/.
39. Felipe Eduardo Sixto, "An Evaluation of Four Decades of Cuban Healthcare," Unpublished paper: 328. Available online at: http://www.centerforurbanstudies.com/.
40. Pan American Health Organization, *Cuba: Profile of the Health Services System* (Washington, DC: United Nations Publications, 1999); Sixto: 325–326.
41. Chelsea Merz, "The Cuban Paradox," *Harvard Public Health Review* (Summer 2002). Available online at: http://www.hsph.harvard.edu/review/review_summer_02/txt677cuba.html.
42. *Ibid.*
43. Theodore H. MacDonald, *A Developmental Analysis of Cuba's Health Care System Since 1959* (Queenston, England: Edward Mellen Press, 1999).
44. Sixto: 334–342.
45. *Ibid.*
46. A.F. Kirkpatrick, "Role of the USA in Shortage of Food and Medicine in Cuba," *Lancet* 348: 9040 (1996): 1489–1491.
47. Merz.
48. Kathleen Hirschfeld, "Re-examining the Cuban Health Care System: Towards a Qualitative Critique," *Cuban Affairs* 2: 3 (2007): 6–8.
49. Miguel A. Faria Jr., "Socialized Medicine in Cuba Part II: 'Doctor Diplomacy', Sex Tourism, and Medical Apartheid in Cuba," *Surgical Neurology* 62: 3 (2004): 275–277.
50. Hirschfeld: 10–12.
51. Merz.
52. Based on 2010 World Bank classifications of countries by income status. Available online at: http://data.worldbank.org/country/.
53. Soonman Kwon, "Thirty Years of National Health Insurance in South Korea: Lessons for Achieving Universal Health Care Coverage," *Health Policy and Planning* 24: 1 (2009): 63–71.
54. Randall S. Jones, "Health-care Reform in Korea," *OECD Economics Department Working Papers, No. 797* (OECD Publishing, 2010). Available online at: http://www.oecd-ilibrary.org/economics/health-care-reform-in-korea_5kmbhk53x7nt-en/.
55. Kwon, "Thirty Years of National Health Insurance": 64–65.
56. Jones: 6–7.
57. Kwon, "Thirty Years of National Health Insurance": 67.
58. *Ibid.*: 66.
59. Jones: 8.
60. *Ibid.*: 6–8.
61. Soonman Kwon, "Payment System Reform for Health Care Providers in Korea," *Health Policy and Planning* 18: 1 (2003): 84–92.
62. Kwon, "Thirty Years of National Health Insurance": 66.
63. Jones: 9.
64. Kwon, "Thirty Years of National Health Insurance": 66.
65. Jones: 11.
66. Wung-Seok Cha, Jun-Ho Oh, Hi-Joon Park, Sang-Woo Ahn, Se-Yeong Hong, and Nam-Il Kim, "Historical Difference Between Traditional Korean Medicine and Traditional Chinese Medicine," *Neurological Research* 29: Suppl. 1 (2007): S5–S9.
67. Based on 2010 World Bank classifications of countries by income status. Available online at: http://data.worldbank.org/country/.
68. World Health Organization, *World Health Statistics 2007* (2007). Available online at: http://www.who.int/whosis/whostat2007.pdf.
69. The United Kingdom Department of Health, *Departmental Report 2006* (2006). Available online at: http://www.dh.gov.uk/en/Publicationsandstatistics/Publications/AnnualReports/DH_4134613/.
70. Her Majesty's Revenue & Customs, The United Kingdom, *National Insurance—The Basics* (2010). Available online at: http://www.hmrc.gov.uk/ni/intro/basics.htm.
71. World Health Organization, *Highlights on Health in the United Kingdom 2004* (2006). Available online at: http://www.euro.who.int/__data/assets/pdf_file/0018/103617/E88530.pdf.

72. *Ibid.*: 33.
73. Martin Roland, "Linking Physicians' Pay to the Quality of Care—A Major Experiment in the United Kingdom," *New England Journal of Medicine* 351: 14 (2004): 1448–1454.
74. World Health Organization, *Highlights on Health in the United Kingdom 2004*: 33.
75. *Ibid.*
76. E. Ernst and A.R. White, "The BBC Survey of Complementary Medicine Use in the UK," *Complementary Therapies in Medicine* 8: 1 (2000): 32–36.
77. United Kingdom National Health Service, *Complementary and Alternative Medicine (CAM)* (2010). Available online at: http://www.nhscareers.nhs.uk/details/Default.aspx?Id=910.
78. *Ibid.*
79. Based on 2010 World Bank classifications of countries by income status. Available online at: http://data.worldbank.org/country/.
80. World Health Organization, *World Health Statistics 2007*: 72.
81. Umut Sarpel, Bruce C. Vladeck, Celia M. Divino, and Paul E. Klotman, "Fact and Fiction: Debunking Myths in the US Healthcare System," *Annals of Surgery* 247: 4 (2008): 563–569.
82. U.S. Department of Health and Human Services, Centers for Medicare and Medicaid Services, *Medicare*. Available online at: http://www.cms.gov/home/medicare.asp.
83. U.S. Department of Health and Human Services, Centers for Medicare and Medicaid Services, *Medicaid*. Available online at: http://www.cms.gov/home/medicaid.asp.
84. U.S. Department of Health and Human Services, Centers for Medicare and Medicaid Services, *Children's Health Insurance Program*. Available online at: http://www.cms.gov/home/chip.asp.
85. Carmen DeNavas Walt, Bernadette D. Proctor, and Jessica C. Smith, U.S. Census Bureau, *Income, Poverty, and Health Insurance Coverage in the United States: 2007* (2008). Available online at: http://www.census.gov/prod/2008pubs/p60-235.pdf.

86. The Henry J. Kaiser Family Foundation, *Who Are the Uninsured? A Consistent Profile Across National Surveys* (Menlo Park, CA: The Henry J. Kaiser Family Foundation, 2006). Available online at: http://www.kff.org/uninsured/upload/7553.pdf.
87. Cathy A. Cowan, Patricia A. McDonnell, Katharine R. Levit, and Mark A. Zezza, "Burden of Health Care Costs: Businesses, Households, and Governments, 1987–2000," *Health Care Financing Review* 23: 3 (2002): 131–159.
88. Cathy Schoen, Robin Osborne, David Squires, Michelle Doty, Roz Pierson, and Sandra Applebaum, *How Health Insurance Design Affects Access to Care and Costs, By Income, in Eleven Countries* (2010). The Commonwealth Fund. Available online at: http://www.commonwealthfund.org/~/media/Files/Publications/In the Literature/2010/Nov/Int Survey/1457_Schoen_how_hlt_ins_design_2010_intl_survey_HA_WebFirst_11182010_ITL_v2.pdf.
89. Harry A. Sultz and Kristina M. Young, "Medical Education and Changing Practice of Medicine," in Harry A. Sultz and Kristina M. Young, eds., *Health Care USA: Understanding Its Organization and Delivery*, 7th ed. (Sudbury, MA: Jones and Bartlett Learning, 2010): 151–183.
90. The Henry J. Kaiser Family Foundation, *Medicaid and Managed Care: Key Data, Trends, and Issues* (Menlo Park, CA: The Henry J. Kaiser Family Foundation, 2010). Available online at: http://www.kff.org/medicaid/upload/8046.pdf.
91. P.M. Barnes, B. Bloom, and R. Hanhin, "Complementary and Alternative Medicine Use Among Adults and Children: United States, 2007," *CDC National Health Statistics Report #12* (2008). Available online at: http://www.cdc.gov/nchs/data/nhsr/nhsr012.pdf.
92. National Center for Complementary and Alternative Medicine, *Paying for CAM Treatment* (2010). Available online at: http://nccam.nih.gov/health/financial/.

93. James A. Johnson and Carleen H. Stoskopf, *Comparative Health Systems: Global Perspectives for the 21st Century* (Boston: Jones and Bartlett Publishers, 2009).

94. Christopher J.L. Murray and Julio Frenk, "Ranking 37th—Measuring the Performance of the U.S. Health Care System," *New England Journal of Medicine* 362: 2 (2010): 98–99.

95. World Health Organization, "Health Systems: Improving Performance": 152–155.

96. Philip Musgrove, "Health Care System Rankings," *New England Journal of Medicine* 362: 16 (2010): 1546.

97. Chris L. Peterson and Rachel Burton, "U.S. Health Care Spending: Comparison with Other OECD Countries," *Congressional Research Service Report for Congress* (2007). Available online at: http://digital commons.ilr.cornell.edu/cgi/viewcontent. cgi?article=1316&context=key_workplace.

98. Robert J. Blendon, Cathy Schoen, Catherine M. DesRoches, Robin Osborn, Kimberly L. Scoles, and Kinga Zapert, "Inequities in Health Care: A Five-Country Survey," *Health Affairs* 21: 3 (2002): 182–191.

99. Cathy Schoen, Robin Osborn, Phuong Trang Huynh, Michele Doty, Karen Davis, Kinga Zapert, and Jordan Peugh, "Primary Care and Adult Health System Performance: Adults' Experiences in Five Countries," *Health Affairs*, Web Exclusive (October 28, 2004): W4-487-W4-503. Available online at: http://content.healthaffairs.org/cgi/reprint/hlthaff.w4.487v1.pdf.

Chapter 11

1. International organizations are not typically considered non-state actors, because states make up the membership of these organizations. In this regard, it might be more accurate to refer to international organizations as "interstate" organizations.

2. NGOs represent a broad category of non-state actors, and it is important to note that the lines between different types of NGOs (for instance, advocacy versus identity-based organizations) can be blurry, as many NGOs are organized around multiple principles.

3. Rhona MacDonald and Gavin Yamey, "The Cost to Global Health of Drug Company Profits," *Western Journal of Medicine* 174: 5 (2001): 302–303.

4. *Ibid.*

5. Margaret E. Keck and Kathryn Sikkink, *Activists Beyond Borders: Advocacy Networks in International Politics* (Ithaca, NY: Cornell University Press, 1998): 41.

6. *Ibid.*

7. Charles Chatfield, "Intergovernmental and Nongovernmental Associations to 1945," in Jackie Smith, Charles Chatfield, and Ron Pagnucco, eds., *Transnational Social Movements and Global Politics: Solidarity Beyond the State* (Syracuse, NY: Syracuse University Press, 1997): 38–40.

8. Dongbau Yu, Yves Souteyrand, Mazuwa A. Banda, Joan Kaufman, and Joseph H. Perriens, "Investment in HIV/AIDS Programs: Does It Help Strengthen Health Systems in Developing Countries?" *Global Health* 4: 8 (2008). Available online at: http://www.ncbi.nlm.nih.gov/pmc/articles/PMC2556650/.

9. Jeremy Shiffman, "A Social Explanation for the Rise and Fall of Global Health Issues," *Bulletin of the World Health Organization* 87 (2009): 608–613.

10. *Ibid.*: 610.

11. International Baby Food Action Network, *History of the Campaign*. Available online at: http://www.babymilkaction.org/pages/history.html.

12. Michael Pollan is one of the most prominent proponents of the slow food movement, and his books provide a good overview of the movement. Michael Pollan, *The Omnivore's Dilemma: A Natural History of Four Meals* (New York: Penguin Press, 2006); Michael Pollan, *In Defense of Food: An Eater's Manifesto* (New York: Penguin Press, 2008).

13. James N. Rosenau, "Governance, Order, and Change in World Politics," in James N. Rosenau and Ernst-Otto Czempiel, eds., *Governance Without Government: Order and Change in World Politics* (Cambridge, UK: Cambridge University Press, 1992): 4.

14. *Ibid.*: 3.

15. Andrew F. Cooper and John J. Kirton, eds., *Innovations in Global Health Governance* (Burlington, VT: Ashgate Publishers, 2009).

16. Rosenau: 3.

17. Richard Skolnik, *Essentials of Global Health* (Sudbury, MA: Jones and Bartlett Publishers, 2008): 15.

18. Development Initiatives, *Public Support for Humanitarian Crises Through NGOs* (February 2009): 1. Available online at: http://www.globalhumanitarianassistance. org/wp-content/uploads/2010/07/2009-Focus-report-Public-support-for-humanitarian-crises-through-NGOs.pdf.

19. *Ibid.*: 9–10.

20. The Bill and Melinda Gates Foundation, home page, http://www.gatesfoundation. org/.

21. Editorial, "What Has the Gates Foundation Done for Global Health?" *Lancet* 373: 9675 (2009): 1577.

22. The Bill & Melinda Gates Foundation, "Guiding Principles." Available online at: http://www.gatesfoundation.org/.

23. Devi Sridhar and Rajaie Batniji, "Misfinancing Global Health: A Case for Transparency in Disbursements and Decision-Making," *Lancet* 372: 9644 (2008): 1185–1191.

24. Save the Children, home page, http://www. savethechildren.org/.

25. Save the Children is rated as a four-star charity, the highest available rating, by Charity Navigator. Charity Navigator's ratings are available online at: http://www. charitynavigator.org/.

26. Michael Maren, *The Ravaging Effects of Foreign Aid and International Charity* (New York: Free Press, 1997): 136–160.

27. Village Health Works, home page, http:// villagehealthworks.org/.

28. GAVI Alliance, home page, http://www. gavialliance.org/.

29. *Ibid.*

30. Paul Farmer, "Global Health Equity," *Virtual Mentor: American Medical Association Journal of Ethics* 6: 4 (2004). Available online at: http://virtualmentor. ama-assn.org/2004/04/oped1-0404.html.

31. Partners in Health, home page, http://www. pih.org/.

32. Doctors Without Borders, home page, http://www.doctorswithoutborders.org/.

33. Dan Bortolotti, *Hope in Hell: Inside the World of Doctors Without Borders* (Buffalo, NY: Firefly Books, 2004): 14.

34. Renée Fox, "Medical Humanitarianism and Human Rights: Reflections on Doctors Without Borders and Doctors of the World," *Social Science and Medicine* 41: 12 (1995): 1607–1616.

35. Olga Shevchenko and Renée C. Fox, "'Nationals' and 'Expatriates': Challenges of Fulfilling 'Sans Frontieres' ('Without Borders') Ideals in International Humanitarian Action," *Health and Human Rights* 10: 1 (2008): 109–122.

Conclusion

1. Denise Grady, "Global Death Rates Drop for Children 5 or Younger," *New York Times*, May 23, 2010. Available online at: http://www.nytimes.com/2010/05/24/ health/24child.html?emc=eta1/.

Index

Note: Page numbers followed by f *or* t *refer to figures or tables, respectively.*

About the Authors

Debra L. DeLaet is professor and chair of politics and international relations at Drake University in Des Moines, Iowa. She teaches courses on human rights, global health, the United Nations, international law, and gender and world politics. She is the author of *U.S. Immigration Policy in an Age of Rights* and *The Global Struggle for Human Rights*. She has also published several articles and book chapters in her areas of research interest, which include human rights, gender issues in world politics, and global health.

David E. DeLaet is assistant professor of internal medicine and pediatrics at Mount Sinai School of Medicine. He received his MD from the University of Cincinnati College of Medicine in 1995 and completed dual residency training in internal medicine and pediatrics at Cincinnati Children's Hospital Medical Center and the University of Cincinnati in 1999. In 2001, he received an MPH in epidemiology at the Columbia University Mailman School of Public Health.